DATE DUE

DEMCO 38-297

Sino-American Relations

Sino-American Relations

Mutual Paranoia

Radha Sinha

Emeritus Professor
Glasgow University

First published 2003 by
PALGRAVE MACMILLAN
Houndmills, Basingstoke, Hampshire RG21 6XS and
175 Fifth Avenue, New York, N.Y. 10010
Companies and representatives throughout the world

PALGRAVE MACMILLAN is the global academic imprint of the Palgrave
Macmillan division of St. Martin's Press, LLC and of Palgrave Macmillan Ltd.
Macmillan® is a registered trademark in the United States, United Kingdom
and other countries. Palgrave is a registered trademark in the European
Union and other countries.

ISBN 0–333–75114–0

This book is printed on paper suitable for recycling and made from fully
managed and sustained forest sources.

A catalogue record for this book is available from the British Library.

A catalogue record for this book is available from the Library of Congress.

10   9   8   7   6   5   4   3   2   1
12   11   10   09   08   07   06   05   04   03

Printed and bound in Great Britain by
Antony Rowe Ltd, Chippenham and Eastbourne

For the past twenty years the government and people of the United States have been acting on the belief that communism is on the march for the conquest of the world and that it is the manifest destiny of the United States to save the world from suffering this fate....Americans have believed that America has practically the whole human race on her side in her anti-Communist stand....this picture is not founded on facts...

...The revolt of the 'native' majority of mankind against the domination of the Western minority – this, and not the defense of freedom against communism by the leading Western country, the United States, is the real major issue in the world today....Is the United States St. George fighting against the dragon? Or is the [sic] Goliath fighting David? The question is important, because St. George is a winner but Goliath is not. The [US] President manifestly believes that he is speaking with Churchill's voice – the Churchill of 1940 – but to the ears of people who have suffered Western domination in the past, his voice sounds like the Kaiser's and Hitler's.

...The American picture of aggressive ecumenical communism is a mirage, but the reality which America is up against today is something much more formidable. She is up against the determination of the non-Western majority of mankind to complete its self-liberation from Western domination.

A. Toynbee (*Vancouver Times*, 11 May 1965)

Contents

Preface

One day a close family friend of ours in Britain asked me why I lived in Britain if I was so critical of the country. I explained to her that I was critical of Prime Minister Thatcher's policies, which was not the same as being critical of Britain. In my view, Mrs Thatcher was undermining some of the basic British values that I loved. Born and raised during the heyday of India's struggle for independence, I had come to admire and cherish democratic values and the tenets of social justice incarnated in the British Welfare State and President Franklin Roosevelt's Atlantic Charter. As a student going through school and university and through Gandhian camps of training for non-violence and democratic dissent (known in those days as passive resistance), I was proud that we in India were aiming to achieve democracy, social justice, and secularism through our struggle. It was somewhat difficult for my friend to see that in a free society 'dissent is not revolution,' as President George W. Bush pointed out to the students of Xinhua University in Beijing.

Something similar happened as I was writing this book. When I passed on the first draft of my book just the day before September 11, for comments to some American friends, one or two of them refused to read beyond the first few pages because they found it to be 'anti-American.' Insensitive, perhaps; offensive, possibly; but anti-American, certainly not. As George Monbiot, a respected columnist at the *Guardian* points out, '...the charge of "anti-Americanism" is itself profoundly anti-American. If the US does not stand for freedom of thought and speech, for diversity and dissent, then we have been deceived as to the nature of the national project. Were the founding fathers to congregate today to discuss the principles enshrined in their declaration of independence, they would be denounced as "anti-American" and investigated as potential terrorists. Anti-American means today precisely what un-American meant in the 1950s. It is an instrument of dismissal, a means of excluding your critics from rational discourse' (George Monbiot, 'Gagging the sceptics' in the *Guardian*, 16 October 2001).

Democratic dissent is so much embedded in the American ethos that the Supreme Court under Chief Justice Earl Warren reaffirmed the right of even the most unpopular viewpoints to First Amendment protection. Democratic dissent is what made America great. As Eric Foner, the author of *The Story of American Freedom* (New York: W.W. Norton & Company, 1998) reminds us, '...our civil rights and civil liberties – freedom of expression, the right to criticize the government, equality before the law, restraints on the exercise of police powers – are not gifts from the state that can be rescinded when it desires. They are the inheritance of a long history of struggles: by abolitionists for the ability to hold meetings and publish their views in the face of mob violence; by labor leaders for the power to organize unions, picket, and distribute literature without fear of arrest; by feminists for the right to disseminate birth-control information without being charged with violating the obscenity laws; and by all those who braved jail and worse to challenge entrenched systems of racial inequality' (Eric Foner, 'The Most Patriotic Act' in the *Nation*, 8 October 2001).

In a globalized world, dissent is globalized. If American foreign policy or, for that matter, domestic policies, have consequences to be borne by people living outside the confines of America, those people have the right to criticize such acts and America has the moral imperative to listen to them. Whether such acts involve the profligate use of scarce natural resources which might deprive others of enjoyment, or the invasion of Iraq with all its economic, social, and political consequences for the world and particularly the people in the Middle East.

This book, based on my 50 years of teaching in various countries and interacting with my internationally diverse group of students, has been written in a spirit of democratic dissent; if it can convey the widespread sense of frustration and anger generated by the mismatch between America's professed values and their betrayal in practice, I would consider it successful.

*   *   *

I am deeply indebted to my friends who took the time to read my drafts and provide me with insights on various issues involved. I am particularly thankful to Professors Brian Bridges, Jim Bruce, Mark Elvin, Sheila Gidwani, Y. Y. Kueh, John Money, Ramon Myres, and Andrew Watson for their painstaking and incisive comments on the previous drafts. I am also thankful to Cliff Barnes, Mark McCarthy, and Dick Nanto for their help in keeping me on the right track and helping me to make the book less 'insensitive' than it would otherwise have been. I am also thankful to Elizabeth and Walter Fife, and Kurt and Sheila Lewenhak for their valuable comments and encouragement at various stages of the book.

I owe a great sense of gratitude to Kelly Beachell Gasner, a budding linguist, who took great pains to assist me with research and editing and also for her constant reminders that I watch my condescending and self-righteous tone. The manuscript would not have been ready in time without the unquestioning support of Aparna Majumder in the final stages of its preparation.

Last, but not least, I am thankful to my own family members who provided me with the support that kept me going. I am particularly thankful to Evelina Francis, Chanchal Narain, Saroj Parasuraman, Raja Parasuraman, Saket Priyadarshi, Steffen Schearer, Pranav Sinha, Rashmi Sinha, Rhona Sinha, Suarabh Sinha, and Andrea Williamson for commenting on various drafts. My special thanks also to my two American granddaughters, Rachna and Shanta Parsuraman, who allowed me to use their computers, even at the cost of foregoing chat rooms and electronic games. They were also my barometer for checking my 'insensitivity.' I also acknowledge with thanks their help in finding a title for this book.

Smriti, my wife, has always complained that I have never thanked her for her deprivations while I was writing my previous books. Perhaps, in the long-held Indian tradition, I was taking her for granted. Therefore, this time I must express my great sense of gratitude to her for her constant complaints regarding my deep snoring, which kept me out of her room and gave me a lot of time to think about and write this book during the quiet of the Scottish and American nights.

It goes without saying that I, alone, am responsible for the errors and omissions in the book.

Radha Sinha
Bethesda, Maryland and Glasgow, Scotland

List of Tables

List of Abbreviations

ABM treaty	Antiballistic Missile Treaty
AFP	Agence France Presse
AG	Australia Group
AI	Amnesty International
APC	Advance Production Cooperatives
APEC	Asia-Pacific Economic Cooperation
ARF	ASEAN Regional Forum
ASEAN	Association of South-East Asian Nations
ASG	Abu Sayyaf Group
ATC	Agreement on Textile and Clothing
BIS	Bank for International Settlements
BMD	Ballistic Missile Defense
BW	Biological Weapons
BWC	Biological Warfare Convention
CASS	Chinese Academy of Social Sciences
CBO	Congressional Budget Office
CCP	Chinese Communist Party
CD	Conference on Disarmament
CNP	Comprehensive National Power
CNPC	China National Petroleum Corporation
COINTELPRO	Counter Intelligence Program
COMECON	Council for Mutual Economic Assistance
CRS	Congressional Research Service
CTBT	Comprehensive Test Ban Treaty
CW	Chemical Weapons
CWC	Chemical Weapon's Convention
DCI	Director of Central Intelligence
DNC	Democratic National Committee
DOC	Department of Correction
DOE	Department of Energy
EAAU	East Asia Analytical Unit
ECA	Economic Cooperation Administration
EEZ	Exclusive Economic Zone
ERS	European Remote Sensing
EU	European Union
FAIR	Fairness and Accuracy in Reporting
FBI	Federal Bureau of Intelligence
FEC	Federal Election Commission
FDA	Federal Drug Administration

FDI	Foreign Direct Investment
FISA	Foreign Intelligence Surveillance Act
FLSA	Fair Labor Standards Act
FOIA	Freedom of Information Act
GAO	General Accounting Office
GATT	General Agreement for Trade and Tariffs
GDP	Gross Domestic Product
GPCR	Great Proletarian Cultural Revolution
HRW	Human Rights Watch
IAEA	International Atomic Energy Agency
IBM	International Ballistic Missile Treaty
ICBM	Intercontinental Ballistic Missiles
ICCPR	International Covenant on Civil and Political Rights
IDA	International Development Association
IIRIRA	Illegal Immigration Reform and Immigrant Responsibility Act
ILO	International Labor Organization
IMF	International Monetary Fund
IMO	International Maritime Organization
IPR	Intellectual Property Rights
ITC	International Trade Centre?
IW	Information warfare
JCS	Joint Chiefs of Staff
LACM	Land-Attack Cruise Missiles
LOS	Law of the Sea Convention
LTBT	Limited Test Ban Treaty
MFN	Most Favored Nation
MOFTEC	Minister of Foreign Trade and Economic Cooperation
MPLA	Popular Movement for the Liberation of Angola
MRBM	Medium-Range Ballistic Missile
MTCR	Missile Technology Control Regime
MTOPS	Millions of theoretical operations
NEI	Netherlands East Indies
NEC	National Economic Council
NATO	North Atlantic Treaty Organization
NGO	Non-Governmental Organizations
NMD	National Missile Defense
NNWS	Non-Nuclear Weapon States
NPC	National People's Congress
NPT	Non-proliferation Treaty (Treaty on the Non-Proliferation of Nuclear Weapons)
NSC	National Security Council
NSG	Nuclear Suppliers Group
NTB	Non-Tariff Barrier
NYPD	New York Police Department

OECD	Organization for Economic Cooperation and Development
OPC	Office of Policy Coordination
OPEC	Organization of Petroleum Exporting Countries
OSIA	On-Site Inspection Agency
PGM	Precision-Guided Munition
PLA	People's Liberation Army
PLAAF	PLA Air Force
PLANAF	PLA Naval Air Force
PNTR	Permanent Normal Trade Relations
PPP	Purchasing Power Parity
PRC	Peoples Republic Of China
PSB	Public Security Bureau
RRU	Rapid Reaction Unit
SAM	Surface to Air Missile
SAR	Synthetic Aperture Radar
SAR	Special Administrative Region
SAVAK	Iranian Security and Intelligence Service
SDI	Strategic Defense Initiative
SEANWFZ	Southeast Asian Nuclear Weapons Free Zone
SIPRI	Stockholm International Peace Research Institute
SOE	State-Owned Enterprise
SRBM	Short-Range Ballistic Missile
STE	State Trading Enterprise
TCHRD	Tibet Centre for Human Rights and Democracy
TIPS	Terrorism Information and Prevention System
TRQ	Tariff-Rate Quota
TTBT	Threshold Test Ban Treaty
UCS	Union of Concerned Scientists
UFCO	United Fruit Company
UN	United Nations
UNISCOM	United Nations Special Commission
UNDP	United Nations Development Programme
USTR	United States Trade Representative
VAP	Voting Age Population
WMD	Weapons of Mass Destruction
WTO	World Trade Organization

1
Why Does America Need Enemies?

> A society guided by survival of the fittest is torn apart internally unless there is something that keeps it together. . . . And what keeps it together best is a threat from the outside. This was provided by the Cold War, where the US could be the leader of the free world. They are hankering after that situation, so they are casting around for enemies, looking high and low, and I think by doing it they're going to find them high and low.
>
> (George Soros[1])

Introduction

September 11, 2001 became a day of infamy when nearly 3000 innocent people were brutally massacred by highjackers who slammed civilian airplanes into the twin towers of the World Trade Center in New York, the citadel of capitalism, and the Pentagon complex in Washington, the nerve center of the mightiest army on Earth. The loss of life on American soil alone reached a magnitude unparalleled in its history since the Civil War. The mere symbolism of the attack and the choice of the date 9/11 – the telephone number to call the police in the United States in case of emergency – were infuriating. Naturally, this was seen as an 'attack on America' and President George W. Bush declared a 'War against Terrorism' – a war not particularly of the president's choosing but one that was God-sent for a president whose legitimacy was in doubt.[2] Numb with a tragedy the people had so vividly experienced through the television, the country solidly supported the president. The country has a tradition of supporting the president in times of war and President Bush's popularity immediately soared to an unprecedented height. The 'War on Terrorism' that began with the invasion of Afghanistan has already moved to Pakistan and the Philippines, and with the passage of time new theatres of war might be added. We are told the war against this elusive enemy will continue for a long time, possibly as long as the Cold War. At last, America had found the enemy it was looking for.

No sooner had the Cold War ended than the search for the next enemy was on. To Samuel Huntington, a senior scholar at Harvard and an influential voice within the international relations fraternity, the 'dangerous clashes of the future are likely to arise from the interaction of Western arrogance, Islamic intolerance and Sinic assertiveness.'[3] In his view, 'the power and assertiveness of both in relation to the West ... are multiplying and becoming more intense.' He also foresees a 'Confucian–Islamic connection' against the West.[4] Huntington claims that his book, *The Clash of Civilizations and the Remaking of World Order*, attempts to interpret 'the evolution of global politics after the Cold War.' It aspires to present a framework, a paradigm, for viewing global politics that will be meaningful to scholars and useful to policymakers.[5] The obvious question is whether a paradigm based on false premises and a distortion of facts, intended or unintended, can be of any use to scholars? Such a framework may well be all too dangerous for policymakers, as has already been shown by experiences during the Cold War years. After all, the stalemate in Korea that led to the estrangement of China and America, the defeat of the United States in the Vietnam War, and the immense sufferings of the people in Southeast Asia and elsewhere were the direct results of the false premises and blatant disregard for the facts on which the Cold War paradigm was based.

The Soviet Union at the time of George Kennan's 'long telegram' in 1946 was in no condition to challenge the might of the United States. At that time there was still a possibility of moderating the Soviet Union's future direction. As Kennan, with a self-effacing frankness, pointed out in his address to the Council of Foreign Relations on his ninetieth birthday:

> even if the militarists had been responsible for Moscow's final capitulation – and they hadn't – their victory was awfully slow in coming. Billions of dollars had been wasted; millions of lives had been lost in Korea, Vietnam, and other flashpoints along the superpower front; and Eastern Europe – the cause of the whole thing – had been consigned to forty years of terror, oppression, and poverty. If American leaders had been willing to negotiate with Moscow after World War II, instead of insisting on what amounted to the Kremlin's unconditional surrender ... these tragic consequences might have been averted.[6]

Apart from the human and financial costs of the ever-voracious appetite of the war machine created in the United States and in its response in the Soviet Union, the greatest casualties of such a response were American values: democracy, human dignity, self-determination, and freedom of thought and speech. While claiming to save democracy abroad, the United States went on a world rampage: smothering nascent democracies, supporting totalitarian regimes, ignoring or underwriting human rights violations, and disregarding international law with impunity. At home, it let loose intelligence agencies virtually independent of democratic control, silenced dissent, and organized a witch-hunt of 'communist sympathizers.' Much of this was initiated not by the lunatic fringe led by Senator Joseph McCarthy, but by American administrations under presidents Truman and Eisenhower, and their successors. Given the messy outcome of the Cold War strategy, one would have expected a serious scholar like Huntington to be more circumspect in churning out new paradigms for managing the planet, based more on fertile imagination rather than on reality.

Chinese assertiveness

Of the three basic premises that are thought likely to lead to a 'clash of civilizations' (Western arrogance, Islamic intolerance, and Sinic assertiveness), the last, Sinic assertiveness toward the West, falls directly within the purview of this book. It examines various aspects of China's relations with the United States more extensively in the chapters that follow. At present, it might suffice to suggest that China is neither economically nor militarily in a position to present a real threat to American interests in Asia. With nearly five times the population of the United States, China has only one-tenth of the American gross domestic product (GDP). Even in terms of purchasing power parity (PPP) calculations, which account for the price differentials between the two countries, the Chinese GDP is a little more than half the US GDP. There is no denying that with a more rapid rate of economic growth than that of the United States, China's share of the world income will grow, enabling it to invest more in economic and military development. However, in terms of military expenditure, China is currently dwarfed by the United States. With roughly the same land area, sharing common boundaries with many more countries (some of them potentially hostile), China spends only one-eighth of the United States' military expenditure. Even American military assessments indicate that China does not possess the military capability to take over Taiwan, let alone threaten wider US interests in Asia.

In the economic sphere, as shown during the World Trade Organization (WTO) accession negotiations, China has become more accommodating than assertive. In fact, soon after its victory over the Nationalists in the Chinese Civil War, the leadership of the Chinese Communist Party sought some form of reconciliation with the United States. Unfortunately, such attempts were thwarted by successive American administrations, partly from ignorance of Asian realities but much more so for fear of a conservative backlash at home. The Chinese leadership, even under Chairman Mao, and increasingly more so after the demise of the Soviet Union, felt that visible improvements in the standard of living were essential for peace and stability within China. More recently, the very credibility of the Communist Party is seen as dependent on continuing improvements in living standards. As a result, the leadership has assigned a much greater priority to economic development than to the modernization of the armed forces. The leadership also realizes that much of the modernization of the Chinese economy, and of the military, depends on the import of advanced technology, capital goods, and military hardware – resources that must be obtained through foreign trade. In both the contexts of trade and of technology transfer, the Chinese leadership appreciates the importance of its relations with the United States, Japan, and the Western European countries. For military technology and hardware, it must look to Russia, partly because some of its aging technology and hardware originated in the old Soviet Union. Another reason for turning to Russia, of course, is that the West may not always be accommodating in doing business with China when it comes to arms. Besides, depending too much on any one source leads to strategic vulnerability.

Islamic intolerance

If China is not becoming increasingly assertive, the Islamic world is becoming even less so. Perhaps the Organization of Petroleum Exporting Countries' (OPEC's) success in pushing up oil prices beyond the expectations of the West, the Khomeini takeover in Iran, and the occasional terrorist assault on Western interests, including high-profile highjacking of planes, and particularly the carnage of September 11, are what really lie behind the anti-Islamic frenzy in the Western media. However, of late, the bargaining power of OPEC has waned. The worst of the Iranian revolution has passed; a reformist government in Iran is taking halting steps toward normalization of its relations with the West. Ignoring the main causes of the Islamic discontent that is deeply rooted in the American foreign policy of bolstering undemocratic regimes in those Islamic (and other) countries which have done little to reduce the burden of poverty and inequity in their own societies, and condoning Israeli excesses at the cost of the Arabs – much of the American media presents Islam as a threat to the West and, with few exceptions, associates Muslims the world over with terrorism, violence, and fundamentalism.

For the American media, as Said points out, 'fundamentalism equals Islam equals everything-we-must-now-fight-against, as we did with communism during the Cold War; in fact . . . the battle is graver, more profound, and dangerous with Islam.'[7] To begin with, despite the universal umbrella of the religion, Islam has never been monolithic. There is a long tradition, going back to the seventh century, of contending views both on Islamic theology (*kalam*) and Islamic philosophy (*falsafah*). Considerable tolerance for minority religions was a general rule rather than an aberration in Muslim countries.

The identification of Islamic fundamentalism with violence is another irony. 'Islamic fundamentalist,' a term borrowed from Protestantism in America, or 'Islamic integrists,' a term derived by Catholic Europe (particularly France), refers to the Islamic socio-religious movements which believe that modernist views and practices have led the faithful astray and call for a return to older, purer, more correct views and practices.[8] In this sense, Islamic fundamentalists are no different from the Jewish, Hindu, Buddhist, or Christian fundamentalists. As Wallerstein stresses, 'they all seem to share certain common features – the rejection of "modernist", secularist tendencies within the group; the insistence on a puritanical version of religious practice; a celebration of the integrity of the religious tradition, and its eternal, unchangeable validity. But they share a second feature, even in their Christian versions: an opposition to the dominant power structures of the modern world-system. It is this combination – a reformist demand of a return to "fundamentals" within the religious group, and an anti-systemic rhetoric that goes beyond merely religious issues – that is both their defining feature and the key to an analysis of their significance in the evolving history of the modern world-system.'[9]

It is, therefore, highly erroneous to use the term 'Islamic fundamentalism' as though it were a unique and monolithic menace. In reality, there is a considerable diversity of thought and practice ranging from the arch-conservatism of Saudi Arabia to the populism of the socialist state of Libya. In terms of political alignments, too, diversity is the rule. While Libya and Iran are patently anti-America, Pakistan and Saudi Arabia have been loyal allies of the United States. So was Iraq until its invasion of Kuwait. The *Taliban*, now the archenemy, received unflinching support from America, China, and Pakistan in its resistance against the Soviet occupation of Afghanistan. Osama Bin Ladin, the man most wanted by the United States, was once a protégé of the CIA much praised for his valor.

Admittedly, the tradition of active dissent or rebellion against an impious authority has been persistent in Islam, going as far back as the third caliphate; but it was never a dominant feature. The *Khawarij*, literally meaning 'seceders,' not only believed in active dissent but also in the vindication of truth by the sword. The *Khawarij* gradually mutated into fanatics, intolerant of any established political authority, and incessantly resorted to rebellion. They were almost wiped out during the first two centuries of Islam.[10] More recent versions of Islamic groups that believed in violence did not fare much better. In Iran, when the 'Devotees of Islam' under the leadership of Navvab Safavi were implicated in the assassinations of a prime minister and leading secular intellectuals, they were suppressed and Navvab himself was executed.[11] In Egypt, the 'Society of the Muslim Brethren' founded by Hasan al-Banna was ruthlessly suppressed by Gamal Abdel Nasser. As has Hosni Mubarak, ruthlessly suppressed militant groups. The government of Jordan has also regularly arrested or expelled the leaders of militant groups. The current military government in Algeria continues to put down such groups. The arbitrary measures to suppress militant Islamic groups in Egypt, Algeria, or Jordan often violate human rights norms.

The Confucian–Islamic connection

Huntington's vision of an emerging 'Confucian–Islamic connection' is, if not unreal, at present grossly premature. China sells advanced weapons and technology to Iran, Iraq, Libya, Pakistan, and Saudi Arabia (all of them Muslim countries), primarily to earn foreign exchange. America makes similar sales to its own Islamic client states; the sales are of significantly higher value than China's and no less sophisticated. The Chinese sales of arms may possibly undermine US non-proliferation objectives, but the US selling advanced weapons to Saudi Arabia and Israel compels rival regimes in the region to stock up with similar arms.

Understandably, with a growing dependence on imported oil, it is prudent for China to have friendly relations with oil producing countries in the Middle East and Central Asia; China has common borders with several of them. Religious identification in a communist country being difficult, estimates vary. If one goes by Muslim sources, China with nearly 140 million Muslims, will compare favorably with India. China has a long history of trade and cultural relations with Islamic countries. The present efforts toward strengthening its ties with them have little to do with undermining American interests. In fact, China of late has attempted to mend its fences with all its neighboring countries, including India, Russia, and Vietnam.

American arrogance

Of Huntington's three main causes of the impending 'clash of civilizations,' two – Sinic assertiveness and Islamic intolerance – are certainly out of all proportion. But what about the third element, 'Western [more accurately, American] arrogance?' Some American arrogance is understandable in view of its success translating democratic ideals into reality, in achieving a high level of economic prosperity, and in developing an unprecedented level of military prowess – a combination of the three attributes that the world has rarely experienced before. There is a continuing love–hate relationship between the world-at-large and America. People the world over, barring a small minority of obscurantists, admire American values but despise the discordance between American principles and practice that has led to an unending saga of misery – even allowing for American acts of charity and compassion – for people within America and outside.

Being born in the era of the European Enlightenment, it was natural for the founders of the new republic of the United States to incorporate some of the best elements of the Enlightenment – 'the best in the Western liberal traditions' – into the American Constitution. As McClelland points out:

> Enlightenment believed in institutionalism and in civil liberties; in the abolition of slavery; in gradualism and moderation; in the reform of manners, morals and politics; in peace and internationalism; in social

and economic progress with due respect for national and local tradition; in justice and the rule of law; in freedom of opinion and association; in the balancing of the powers of government and the division of political authority between different agencies of government as a weapon against despotic rule by individuals, groups or majority; in social equality but not to the extent that it threatened liberty, and above all Enlightenment believed in liberty under an enlightened system of law so that liberty would not disturb the orderly processes of government.[12]

It was under the inspiration of the Enlightenment thinkers that the American Constitution, the Bill of Rights, and the successive judicial interpretations guarantee freedom of speech, press, religion, and the right to peaceful assembly and protest. They also provide protection against unreasonable searches, seizures of property and arrest, and entitle a person the right to trial under a due process of law in all criminal cases; to a fair and speedy trial by jury, and to protection against cruel and unusual punishment.

Essentially, the American values of 'a belief in the essential dignity of all human beings and their inalienable right to democracy, liberty and equal opportunity,' as Eric Foner points out, have been 'both a reality and a mythic idea.' For most white males such rights were a reality but, for non-whites, women, labor, and slaves they were a 'cruel mockery.'[13] In a society based on slavery, notions of the essential dignity of human beings, together with the inalienable rights of democracy, liberty and equality, were little but a mockery. The American Constitution, framed by a 'colonial elite,' was essentially oligarchic and 'the subsequent constitutional history,' as McClelland points out, has been 'a running battle to democratise' the Constitution.[14] Yet for the under-privileged of America, the 'mythic idea' has been a rallying point and a goal to achieve. Freedom, in the words of the philosopher Samuel DueBois Cook, 'is the fruit of struggle, tragic failures, tears, sacrifices, and sorrow.'[15] The struggle for freedom in the new republic began even before the Bill of Rights was ratified by the states. It was as early as 1781 that Quork Walker, a black slave, won his freedom by arguing that the state constitution said that, 'all men are born free and equal.'[16] It was this 'mythic idea' that made Abigail Adams, wife of John Adams, one of the founding fathers, question the inconsistency of slavery and the denial of voting rights to women with liberty.[17] It was the same 'mythic idea' that made Benjamin Rush, a Pennsylvanian patriot, call slavery a 'national crime' and John Allen, a Massachusetts clergyman denounce the American passion for liberty a 'mockery' in view of the 'trampling on the sacred natural rights an privileges of the *Africans*.'[18] When Martin Luther King, Jr chastised the American establishment for not fulfilling the promises of the Emancipation Proclamation even after a century had passed, he was inspired by the very same 'mythic idea.'

The world's humanity, longing for their freedom from imperial bondage, looked up to this 'mythic idea' for inspiration:

> Leaders as diverse as Louis Kossuth and Mohandas Gandhi, Louis Thiers and Sukarno cited it [the American lesson]. Thomas Masaryk's declaration of Czech independence in October 1918 followed the American model. Ho Chi Minh's declaration of Vietnamese independence in September 1945 began with a paraphrase of the Jeffersonian preamble of 1776, then proceeded to list colonial grievances as the American document had done. Even Lenin, bitter enemy of the capitalist republican system supported by America, declared in 1918 that the United States had 'set the world an example of a revolutionary war against feudal subjection.'[19]

Much of the continuing world-wide criticism – often branded as 'anti-American' – relates to America's failures to live up to its promises. The most common grievance emanates from the mismatch between principles advocating the essential dignity of all human beings – democracy, liberty and equality, and the 'rule of law' – and their actual practice particularly in respect of foreign policies that causes dehumanization, humiliation, and suffering to populations in foreign countries (Iraqis and Palestinians being the prime contemporary examples) that have no influence on decision-making in America. In its misplaced evangelism for bringing its version of enlightenment to the world, America, rather than setting an example, such as Winthrop's shinning 'city upon a hill,' that would have been attractive enough for the world to follow, tends instead to use economic and military strangulation of recalcitrant countries, whether or not the 'American model' is relevant for a particular country at a particular period of time. Thus, American leaders fail to recognize that in forcing their own version of enlightenment on others, they undermine one of the basic tenets of the right of self-determination, which Americans have prized most for themselves.[20]

This mismatch between principles and practice is largely the outcome of America's own perception of itself as the 'chosen people' and the belief in exceptionalism. Added to that is the growing influence of big business in politics which generates and sustains a military–industrial–political nexus. This alliance of self-serving groups needs enemies and 'winnable' wars for its self-aggrandizement. These tendencies are exacerbated by the failures of the safeguarding mechanisms, such as the media. It is this mismatch between principles and practice reflected in the American foreign policy, that is most resented by those who are on the receiving end, China not excluded.

The 'chosen' people

American 'exceptionalism' is rooted in the belief that it 'is not only different in kind from other countries but superior in its morality and institutions.'[21] This exceptionalism, from the birth of the republic to the present, is seen in the American somewhat naïve belief that 'the salvation of the world depended on them.'[22] Also, that salvation can come only if 'the other regions of the world look more like America – if not always the imperfect America of the present, then the ideal America of their dreams.'[23] To some, called exemplarists by Brands, this conversion of other countries into the American image can come about by the sheer setting of example – by perfecting America from within so as to make it attractive for others to emulate. Yet there are others – Brand's vindicators or 'realists' in the international relations jargon – who would not hesitate to use American military might to convert others to the American image. American foreign policy, largely rooted in this brand of exceptionalism, that has proved disastrous for much of the world might, to a considerable extent, answer the question, 'why do they hate us so much,' raised so often in America in the aftermath of September 11.

To summarize, the vindicators' view of exceptionalism – to which most conservative thinkers and politicians in America would subscribe – is based on four rather questionable premises: first, that America is superior to other countries morally and in terms of its institutions; secondly, that America is 'indispensable' for world progress in terms of prosperity and peace; thirdly, other countries must in their own interest, emulate America and conform to American policies; and fourthly, if they do not, America is morally entitled to take punitive measures either in terms of economic sanctions or launch military attacks – *à la* George W. Bush's new doctrine of pre-emptive strikes – against it.[24]

A corollary to this brand of exceptionalism is that the American elite knows all there is to know about world problems, better than those directly concerned, and therefore advice by friendly countries or allies is irrelevant; yet friends and allies are expected to fall in line. This kind of American unilateralism is certainly not a new phenomenon. George Ball, commenting on the Nixon Doctrine, lamented that 'the objective [of unilateralism] was to increase America's reach, not by consolidating our strength with that of other like-minded nations but by increasing our freedom of action through the stripping off of irksome obligations to consult and act collectively.'[25] He described the strategy as 'Ptolemaic, pre-Copernican; it perceived the United States as the center of the cosmos with other nations in orbit around it. Rejecting the fiction of equality that would require us to factor the views of our allies into common decisions, we would expect our allies to follow our lead without grumbling while we measured their value to us by the degree to which they uncritically supported our actions.'[26]

As former German chancellor Helmut Schmidt underlines, 'United States policies concerning the rest of the world are marked by idealism, romanticism, and faith in America's own power and greatness. If the rest of the world does not live up to the Americans' ideals and their methods to turn them into reality, so much the worse for the rest of the world!'[27] This genre of unilateralism in world affairs is not a monopoly of one or the other political party; 'no matter who occupies the presidency, Washington tends to unilateralism.'[28] If there is a difference, it is more of degree than of kind. For instance, President Clinton was less of a unilateralist than George W. Bush, whose father believed much more in coalition building than his son. On the other hand, when it came to the 'War on Terror' George W. Bush did not hesitate to build a coalition *albeit*, as the *New York Times* editorial pointed out, by embracing countries and groups that were flouting American values of democracy and human rights with impunity.[29]

American unilateralism and international obligations

American belief in its exceptionalism and its own infallibility often leads to a cavalier attitude to its international obligations. This attitude is currently reflected in the Bush administration's decisions to opt out of several international treaties and protocols including the International Ballistic Missile Treaty (IBM) and the International Crime Court. One can trace such an attitude to the very beginning of the republic, particularly to its treaty obligations to the Native Americans. They were dispossessed of their land, driven away from their territories under very cruel circumstances, and in some instances even exterminated in spite of their treaty rights. Sometimes such treaty rights were established in the United States courts but the decisions of the courts were never implemented. This fact of broken promises by the federal government is candidly conceded by the State Department in its *Initial Report to the United Nations Committee on the Elimination of Racial Discrimination*. It points out: 'From 1778 until 1871, the United States entered into numerous treaties with Indian tribes, which recognized tribal self-government, reserved tribal lands as "permanent homes" for Indian tribes, and pledged Federal protection for the tribes. Yet the United States engaged in a series of Indian wars in the 19th century, which resulted in significant loss of life and lands among Indian tribes.'[30]

Throughout its history, the United States government failed to respect the territorial integrity and sovereignty of its neighbors and militarily intervened in their affairs. According to a Congressional Research Service (CRS) study, between 1798 and 1993 the United States intervened militarily in foreign countries 234 times to promote US interests[31] Interventions continued in the 1990s and thereafter. In addition, the United States government launched peacetime covert actions to overthrow legitimate governments or to assassinate foreign political leaders, including Chinese Premier Zhou Enlai.[32]

Among the more recent examples are the interventions in Nicaragua, Grenada, and Panama. In all three cases, America violated international law. In the case of mining Nicaraguan harbors, before Nicaragua filed a case the United States government gave a notice to the International Court, effective immediately (contrary to its 1946 commitment to give six months' notice), that America would not consider the Court's jurisdiction compulsory.[33] The

Court found the United States in violation of international law. The United States withdrew from the jurisdiction of the Court initially for two years, afterwards permanently.[34] In one of the covert operations engineered to overthrow President Sukarno of Indonesia, nearly half a million Indonesians were killed in an anti-communist frenzy. It was reportedly the American Embassy in Jakarta that provided the names of as many as 5000 communists to be liquidated in this pogrom. All this was done in utter disregard of international law by a country built on the very foundation of the rule of law.

America's widespread violation of international law in its conduct of wars, has been the topic of much commentary. As has been pointed out by Peter Dale Scott, right from the founding of the republic, the American 'military tradition explicitly defended the selective use of terror, whether in suppressing Indian resistance on the frontiers in the 19th Century or in quelling the rebellion against U.S. interests abroad in the 20th Century.'[35] In 1864, General Sherman used terror to destroy the South's will to fight. His devastation 'left plantations in flames and brought widespread Confederate complaints of rape and murder of civilians.'[36] Similar terror tactics used by Colonel Chivington and the Third Colorado Cavalry included scalping and knocking out brains, ripping open women with knives, clubbing children and knocking their heads with guns, and other gruesome atrocities. In the Philippines, US commander General Bell used similar tactics against the Filipinos in the Philippine–American War (1899–1902). The anti-imperialist group in Congress denounced his practices, but military strategists acclaimed Bell's terror tactics as 'pacification in its most perfected form.'[37] The carpet bombing of Dresden and Hamburg, the fire bombing of Tokyo, the use of nuclear bombs on Hiroshima and Nagasaki during the Second World War, and the Phoenix Program in Vietnam all fit disturbingly but neatly into the pattern of terror tactics used by United States forces to destroy the enemy's will to fight. Commenting on the carpet-bombing of Darmstadt and Dresden – cities with little strategic importance and not many industries supporting war efforts – leading German historian Golo Mann said:

We know from past experience that war makes people stupid. They see only one goal, victory, and nothing else . . . .

The attitude of the Allies matched that of the German tyrant. The worst that can be said of them is that, during the last years of the war, they sometimes descended to his level, that in their rage, their just horror and their impatience, they too sometimes did things, which Hitler had been the first to do . . . .

Allied air strategy aimed at spreading terror and wearing down enemy morale. The conviction was widespread that against Nazi Germany any means was justified and that the will of the Germans must be broken somehow.[38]

The contraventions of international law by American forces were also prolific in the Vietnam War. The hearings of the International War Crime Tribunal established by British philosopher Bertrand Russell revealed that the US armed forces bombarded civilian targets (dwellings, villages, dams, dikes, medical establishments, leper colonies, schools, churches, pagodas, historical and cultural monuments), and repeatedly violated the sovereignty, neutrality, and territorial integrity of Cambodia.[39]

The bombing of civilian targets leading to a large number of deaths of innocent civilians was widely reported during the Persian Gulf War, the war in Yugoslavia, and the ongoing war in Afghanistan. In Iraq, facilities essential to civilian life such as residential buildings, electricity generating plants, water treatment, pumping and distribution systems, reservoirs, food processing, storage and distribution facilities, infant milk formula and beverage plants, animal vaccination facilities and irrigation sites, and transport facilities were indiscriminately bombed, killing at least 125,000 men, women, and children.[40] Subsequently, many more children died from malnutrition and a shortage of medicines and medical care. Napalm, cluster, and anti-personnel fragmentation bombs were used against civilian targets in densely populated cities; many of these weapons are illegal under international law. Similarly, in Yugoslavia, North Atlantic Treaty Organization (NATO) bombing was aimed at 'depriving Serbia of electricity, and disrupting its water supplies, communication, and civilian transport' in order to bring 'economic life nearly to a standstill.'[41] The use of cluster bombs, in explicit contravention of the Ottawa Convention, killed as many civilians as soldiers, children being no exception.[42] Although the Pentagon is keeping a tight lid on the progress of the Afghanistan War, it is widely known that high altitude bombing is killing large numbers of innocents. Maltreatment of war prisoners, both in Cuba at Guantanamo Bay Naval Base and in Afghanistan, has been widely commented upon by public interest groups in America and abroad.[43] Such actions are in direct violation of The Hague and Geneva Conventions, the Nuremberg Charter, and the Charter of the United Nations. Even a cursory glance at American military interventions abroad underlines the justification of Helmut Schmidt's statement that 'America's foreign policy can be just as ruthless as the foreign policy of the European nations was for hundreds of years.'[44]

Another major problem is that the Americans have an 'idealistic tendency to see everything in black and white terms' and to divide all other nations into two categories: 'good' ones consisting of those who are loyal to America, and 'bad' ones who are not.[45] President Eisenhower's secretary of state, John Foster Dulles's description of non-alignment as immoral, President Reagan's 'evil empire' rhetoric, and President George W. Bush's 'civilization versus terrorist' slogan, all reflect a cultural arrogance, as Alan Bloom, in commenting on Reagan's 'evil empire' rhetoric pointed out:

What was offensive to contemporary ears in President Reagan's use of the word 'evil' was its cultural arrogance, the presumption that he, and America, know what is good; its closedness to the dignity of other ways of life; its implicit contempt for those who do not share our ways. The political corollary is that he is not open to negotiation. The opposition between good and evil is not negotiable and is a cause of war. Those who are interested in 'conflict resolution' find it much easier to reduce the tension between values than the tension between good and evil.'[46]

Once it is established that the fight is against evil, any means, however illegitimate and inimical to the American values, are legitimized. '"Combatants," an historian wrote long ago, "exchange qualities." Hitler had adopted nothing from the Anglo-Saxons but the Anglo-Saxons had adopted characteristics of Hitler's.'[47] In its war against terrorism, George W. Bush's America risks adopting the characteristics of 'terrorists.'

Questionable moral high ground

There is no doubt that Americans, individually, are highly moralistic and generous. As Helmut Schmidt stresses, 'when anyone appeals to their help-fulness, Americans are the world's most generous nation.'[48] This is reflected in millions of dollars from individual charities for domestic and overseas causes, thousands of young men and women working in remote corners of the world as members of the Peace Corps, and numerous adoptions of children from developing countries by American couples. On the other hand, many of the very same people advocate, support, or ignore illegitimate state actions, bordering on what American left-wing intellectuals, such as Noam Chomsky, call 'state terrorism.'[49]

This anomaly can partly be explained in terms of, first, the American belief in exceptionalism and the infallibility of America; secondly, of people's disenchantment with the political system over which they do not seem to have much control and, finally, of widespread American ignorance of conditions in the world outside, resulting from the failure of the media to present objective interpretations of world issues, or to reflect genuinely the international opinion on such issues. Particularly in times of war, there is a widespread tendency among the media to support the American govern-ment irrespective of the objectives and the morality of a specific war. At such junctures dissent – a vital prerequisite of a functioning democracy – is labelled unpatriotic. This gives, as is happening in the aftermath of September 11, a *carte blanche* to the government and its security apparatus to undermine freedoms, the very essence of liberty. In a recent *Cato* Institute paper, Timothy Lynch questions the wisdom of the Bush admin-istration's anti-terrorism policy of 'secretive subpoenas, secretive arrests, secretive trials, and secretive deportation that clearly violate America's vital constitutional principles.'[50] To all the extra-constitutional policies of the administration, one might add arbitrary labelling of American citizens as 'enemy combatant,' denying a trial under the due process of law guaranteed by the Bill of Rights, racial profiling, fingerprinting of visitors from selected countries, and the Terrorism Information and Prevention System (TIPS) which might use neighbors and utility workers to snoop on unsuspecting householders. Lynch warns that if the present enhancement of state power is continued, it is possible that in the next twenty years, 'America will drift toward national identification cards, a national police force and more extensive military involvement in domestic affairs . . . those are the telltale signs of societies that are unfree.'[51]

Democracy undermined by inequities

American economic prosperity has certainly been the envy of the world, yet one is aghast – as was veteran American writer John Gunther in 1946 – that amidst the phenomenal prosperity of America, considerable hunger and homelessness persisted. Gunther was appalled by the fact that 'the United States produced the most titanic harvest in its history – and could not feed its own people. It performed magnificent and inordinate miracles of production during the war – and cannot build homes for its own citizens.'[52] He was talking about the immediate post-World War II America, but as late as 1999, after a decade of continued economic prosperity, nearly 32 million people, one out of every eight citizens (but one out of four Native Americans, Hispanics and African Americans) were poor. Among the 21 most affluent countries the United States had the highest incidence of child poverty with 17 per cent of all children poor. In 2000, as many as 11 million households were food insecure, in the sense that they could not secure the minimum nutrition for a time within the year for lack of money. A third of such households had one or more members hungry for a time; remaining two thirds of the households could avoid hunger as a result of federal assistance programs or charitable soup kitchens.[53] Between two and seven million Americans are homeless.[54] Forty million Americans have no health insurance.[55] Almost as many Americans are functionally illiterate. On one of the most telling social indicators, the expectation of life at birth, which can encapsulate to a considerable extent the average standard of living of a country, the United States is almost the lowest of all the most industrialized countries of the West. On this score, Cuba, with a much lower per capita income, is not far behind the United States. Again the relatively high infant mortality rate in America is comparable only to the poorest Western European countries and to Cuba. The infant mortality rate among the African American population is almost twice as high as amongst whites. Among all advanced industrialized countries, the rate of violent crimes is the highest in the United States. Approximately 13 million people (roughly 5 per cent of the population) are victims of crime in America every year.[56] Annually, 13,000 deaths are caused by the illegal use of firearms in murder or non-negligent manslaughter. The number of violent crimes totals 440,000 each year.[57] These are numbers far in excess of those killed on September 11, but thanks to the Gun Lobby, a president who has declared 'War on Terrorism' seems to have little to offer.

The United States has, from its very inception, shown an uncanny tolerance of highly skewed distribution of income and wealth. It now has one of the most unequal distributions of income in the world; with the lowest quintile (20 per cent) of households earning less than 4 per cent of the total household income, while the highest quintile earns as much as half. The share of the top 5 per cent amounts to 22 per cent. The distribution of wealth in America is far more unequal than the distribution of income. In 1995, the richest 1 per cent owned 47 per cent of the country's wealth. Gross inequality of income and wealth, uninhibited by state intervention, leads to unequal access to opportunity and to political power. In a country where access to education for children depends upon the income and wealth of their parents, equality of opportunity – the very basis of democracy – becomes largely mythical. Apart from the expensive private schools to which children from rich families invariably go, gross disparities exist even in the public school system. Suburban schools have 'clean buildings, modern sports and science facilities, and well-stocked libraries, and inner-city schools with broken windows, deteriorating buildings and empty bookshelves.'[58] Notwithstanding scholarships for poor deserving students at most universities, access to the top private institutions of higher studies often depends on family income and alumni connections. For instance, nearly 'one fifth of Harvard's students have been legacies [children from families which have given substantial gifts to the university], or children of alumni' even if they are significantly less qualified than other students.[59] As Lind cogently concludes, 'the effect of legacy preference is to retard social mobility and to turn the new American oligarchy into a semihereditary aristocracy.'[60]

Influence of big business in politics

Inequalities of income and wealth, as well as the nature of the political system, have led to the growing influence of big business in politics. It is usually the rich who have the resources to contest elections for the presidency and for the federal and state legislatures. According to the Center for Responsive Politics, the average winning House campaign during the elections of the year 2000 cost an average $686,000, and Senate campaigns $5.6 million. The total cost of the 2000 Congressional and presidential elections was at least $3 billion.[61] Such high costs have meant that only those people that are wealthy themselves or are supported by big business or by labor unions can take part; contributions from the former are almost 12 times that of the latter.[62] In the Senate for the years 1998–2000, 39 out of the 100 senators were millionaires, 16 of them multi-millionaires.[63] Other candidates have to depend largely on corporations and labor unions for financial support.

One of the other features of the American constitution is that the presidential elections take place every four years, the House elections are held every two years, a third of the Senate members retire every two years and vacancies are filled by new elections. There is no restriction on the outgoing member seeking reelection. As a result, the political parties and the incumbent president have to fight elections every two years. This means that the political parties are in constant need for money, and corporations are ready to oblige. The direct *quid pro quo* is never easy to establish, but politicians hoping to continue receiving the business largesse have to safeguard the interests of the benefactors during their tenure of office.

The tradition of business influencing policy-making through buying the favors of politicians in America goes back to the US Civil War (1861–65). As early as the 1870s, President Rutherford Hayes complained that 'this is a government of the people, by the people and for the people no longer. It is a government of corporations, by corporations, and for corporations.'[64] In his book *Wealth Against Commonwealth*, Henry Demarest Lloyd described how the Standard Oil Company manipulated the market to drive out competition and bribed legislators to undermine the political process. Lloyd concluded that liberty and monopoly could not live together.[65] President Theodore Roosevelt proposed banning corporate contributions to any candidate for federal office and advocated the public funding of federal election campaigns.[66] A ban on contributions from corporations and banks for federal election campaigns was enacted in 1907, and from labor unions in 1947.[67] Subsequent attempts to regulate the funding of elections by corporations and other interest groups have often been frustrated and laws concerning political contributions largely circumvented. The most recent campaign finance bill to restrict 'soft money' was reluctantly signed by President George W. Bush in March 2002; but soon thereafter Republican Senator Mitch McConnell and the National Rifle Association, later joined by the Republican National Committee, went to court to challenge the constitutionality of the law.[68]

It is common knowledge that whenever the interests of business come into conflict with social interests, those lawmakers who receive money from corporations tend to protect the interests of big business. Two examples may suffice. According to the Center for Responsive Politics, the tobacco industry contributed nearly $8.4 million dollars to the 2000 election campaigns; a total of $45 million between 1990 and 2002, with three-quarters going to the Republicans.[69] The 42 senators who voted to kill Senator McCain's tobacco legislation for the regulation of the industry by the Federal Drug Administration (FDA) received four times as much as those senators who supported the bill.[70] Similarly, the gun rights groups contributed as much as $4 million during the 2000 election cycle, and a total of $15 million between 1990 and 2000, two-thirds going to the Republicans. For the entire period, groups advocating gun control contributed only $1.4 million, mostly to the Democrats.[71] Gun control has remained elusive in spite of the high incidence of gun related crimes.

As a result of another quirk of the political system, corporations can directly influence policymaking when corporate executives join the government. Under the American Constitution, many of the senior administrators appointed by the outgoing president leave office with him. The incoming president fills these vacancies. Both Democratic and Republican presidents have depended heavily on big business to fill the cabinet positions. George W. Bush's cabinet appointees – Vice President Dick Cheney, the Secretary of State Colin Powell, Defense Secretary Donald Rumsfeld, Attorney General John Ashcroft, Treasury Secretary Paul O'Neill, Director of the Office of Budget Management Mitch Daniels, Jr, and several others – have close corporate connections.[72] As Dumhoff suggests, 'the highest levels of the executive branch . . . are interlocked constantly with the corporate community . . . there is enough continuity for the relationship to be described as one of "revolving interlocks."'[73]

The deepening ties between the corporate world and the world of politics and government – competing public interest groups only having marginal influence – has resulted in disenchantment with the political process. This is reflected in the declining number of voters participating in elections. The voter turnout in 2000 was only 51 per cent, against nearly 63 per cent in 1960. In Hawaii, it was as low as 41 per cent; in Arizona 42 per cent; and in Texas, 43 per cent.[74] In the mid-term Congressional elections in 1998, the turnout of voting age population (VAP) for the country as a whole was as low as 36.4 per cent; it was the lowest turnout since 1942. In some states (Mississippi, Tennessee, Texas, and West Virginia) only one in four eligible voters turned out to vote.[75] In some districts, members of the House of Representatives were elected by only 20 per cent of the electorate.[76] Voter participation in America is the lowest among the Western democracies. In most of the Western European countries, the turnout is over 70 per cent; in the cases of Scandinavian countries, it is over 80 per cent.[77] Primarily the American working class and the lower middle class have withdrawn from the electoral process, while the participation of the white-collar workers has increased.[78] Thus, the outcome of elections is increasingly being determined by the affluent, and therefore the priorities of the affluent are increasingly becoming the priorities of the government

Of late, the plethora of corporate scandals in the aftermath of the Enron and WorldCom collapses has further intensified people's disenchantment. While there is continued support for President George W. Bush's handling of the 'War on Terror,' there is considerable scepticism regarding his ability to reform the corporate sector. People seem to have lingering feelings that the president and the vice-president are not telling the whole truth regarding their behavior when they were corporate executives.

Military–corporate–political nexus

Corporations can be helped in various ways. Currently, several industrial sector industries are hoping that President Bush will relax environmental regulations; energy sectors are hoping that the president will allow prospecting on the Florida coast or in Alaska. Loggers are hoping that restrictions on logging in national forests will be less rigorous. Much more important to big business, particularly to the high-tech industries such as aerospace, electronics, and communications, are the opening of foreign markets *á la* WTO or the North American Free Trade Area and the defense expenditures at home and abroad. A large defense program also promotes science and technology. Defense research centered on core technologies such as electronics, computers, and aerospace, has numerous applications for commercial spin-offs. An increase in military expenditure gives another advantage: since weapons and other military equipment are often purchased on non-market prices and are generally over-priced, military purchases act as subsidies for civilian products, as the military contractors and civilian suppliers are often the same firms. The legislative surveillance of defense expenditure by Congress and the Armed Services Committee has, by now, turned out to be largely ceremonial, because those lawmakers who sit on these committees have close common interests with the military.[79] 'Congress is extremely friendly to the military, at least in part because the military has become such a powerful force in the districts of most congressmen. Military bases are an important source of jobs for many Americans.'[80] The need to keep their constituents satisfied, coupled with the ever-increasing need for campaign finance, forces legislators to woo the military and defense industries into their constituencies.

As Galbraith points out, 'the result has been in substantial military control of the legislative process.' The military establishment not only 'largely determines the military mission that it pursues and the manpower and weaponry that support it' but also effectively 'controls the support or funding – the effective demand – for that mission, manpower and weaponry.'[81]

Nevertheless, the existence of such a large military establishment and a military expenditure of even the pre-September 11 scale – as in 1999, nearly 30 per cent more than the total for all the major Western European allies and Japan[82] – has to be justified. After the debacle in Vietnam, a major war cannot be easily contemplated, the increased tax burden and the risk of piling up 'body bags' being the main deterrent. It is here that 'small military exercises of no enduring pain or importance' come in handy. As Galbraith points out, *'such military activities [as in Grenada, Panama, and Nicaragua], however remote from any rationally established need, served in an important way the broad purpose of the military establishment. They were visible justification of its eminence and power; small, safe and spectacular, they were a reminder that military force was of continuing relevance.'*[83] [Italics mine.]

Similarly, the intervention in Iraq was primarily aimed at justifying 'the development of advanced communications and other electronic aircraft and military technology.'[84] The Persian Gulf War also provided an opportunity for American troops to be stationed indefinitely in Saudi Arabia. This might ensure the survival of the Saudi Arabian regime, which is one of the largest buyers of US armaments and whose money provides huge profits for American banks such as Chase Manhattan.[85] The US military presence in the region is also a major deterrent against any future oil embargos against the West.

Not unlike the Iraq–Kuwait dispute, in the case of Kosovo the US government preferred a military solution to a diplomatic one.[86] The actual purpose, of course, was to provide a justification for NATO, which lost its *raison d'être* after the collapse of the Soviet Union. The bombing was to establish the credibility of NATO: 'to walk away now would destroy NATO' credibility as British Prime Minister Tony Blair conceded.[87] The question of credibility had become all the more important, as a European diplomat inadvertently declared, 'at this time as we approach the NATO summit in celebration of its fiftieth anniversary.'[88] Without NATO, the stationing of American troops in Europe may not be easily justifiable.

The fourth estate: a corporate poodle

The influence of big business on the American political process has been considerably strengthened as a result of corporate takeovers of media and the increasing concentration and cross-ownership of the media conglomerates. It has also undermined the freedom of the press guaranteed by the First Amendment. Only nine giant firms – Time Warner, Disney, Bertelsmann, Viacom, News Corporation, TCI, General Electric, Sony, and Seagram – now dominate the global commercial media landscape. These global conglomerates have interests in film production, book publishing, music, TV channels and networks, retail stores, amusement parks, magazines, newspapers, and the like.[89] The natural consequence of corporate control of the media has been an emphasis on earnings, creating a conflict of interest between shareholders and society as a whole.

To the extent that the media must increasingly depend on advertising revenue, media managers aggressively court the affluent who are the target group for the advertisers.[90] The corporate media managers make no secret of the fact that they are in business to serve their advertisers; or that this is their *raison dêtre*.[91] In search of profit, corporate managers fail to reinvest profits in staff training, investigative reporting, salaries, plants, and equipment. Increasing unemployment and plummeting salaries, (except for the elite press corps), have led to a collapse of the morale of US journalists.

According to Tom Rosenstiel, the director of the Project for Excellence in Journalism financed by the Pew Charitable Trust, and Washington correspondent for the *Los Angeles Times*, 'what is going on in the so-called serious press is a crisis of conviction, a philosophical collapse in the belief in the purpose of journalism and the meaning of news.'[92]

The corporate masters of the media do not have much interest in journalism or public affairs; for them, covering items such as sports, light entertainment, and action movies favored by the upper-middle and upper classes is the preferred option.[93]

Short of resources – newsgathering is an expensive proposition – the media depend greatly on official and corporate sources of information. 'The White House, the Pentagon, and the State Department, in Washington, DC are central nodes of such news activity. On a local basis, city hall and the police department are the subject of regular news "beats" for reporters. Business corporations and trade groups are also regular and credible purveyors of stories deemed newsworthy. These bureaucracies turn out a large volume of material that meets the demands of news organizations for reliable, scheduled flows.'[94] Thus, there develops a symbiotic relationship between the mass media and the government and business bureaucracies. The media find it difficult to refuse to carry stories, even dubious ones, supplied by the government or business. On foreign policy issues, even the prominent US newspapers, as Senator William Fulbright observed in Senate Hearings on Government and the Media in 1966, 'have become almost agents or adjuncts of the government, that they do not contest or even raise questions about government policy.'[95] Commenting on such tendencies, Hodding Carter sarcastically wrote in the *Wall Street Journal* some time ago that the media 'have an overwhelming tendency to jump up and down and bark in concert whenever the White House – any White House – snaps its fingers.'[96]

The media does question government policy, reflecting the differences of opinion among the elite, but as Noam Chomsky points out, 'they do so almost exclusively within the framework determined by the essentially shared interests of state-corporate power.'[97] A major survey of journalists by the Pew Research Center for the People and the Press and the *Columbia Journalism Review* reported that as many as a quarter of journalists acknowledged self-censorship, and as many as 41 per cent admitted to reshaping or toning down stories.[98] As many as half of local journalists and nearly one-third of national journalists conceded that corporate owners exert a fair amount of influence on decisions about what to publish.[99] On the question of whether the media do a good job of informing the public, only around one-third of the journalists polled gave the media high marks; nearly two-thirds of both local and national journalists felt the media do only a fair job.[100]

As suggested earlier, on foreign policy in particular, the media with few exceptions supports the official line. One of the most glaring cases of media default relates to the Gulf War. The Bush (Sr) administration imposed a draconian censorship on war reporting, repeating what the Pentagon had done in Panama and Grenada: namely, created a pool of journalists and sent it to Grenada too late, and in Panama virtually imprisoned the pool on an army base. 'In both cases, reporters missed the fighting entirely, and the American public was treated to antiseptic military victories minus any scenes of killing, destruction, or incompetence.'[101] During the Gulf War 1200 American journalists, located largely in Saudi Arabia, were simply not allowed by the US military to see 'anything of real significance.'[102] Some of the most respected journalists simply repeated the Pentagon version of the 'astonishing precision' of the Patriot and other missiles.[103] According to the information released by the US Air Force, some 82,000 tons of bombs dropped were traditional unguided bombs; only 7000 were guided bombs. Artillery shells from battleships and rocket launchers discharged anywhere between 20,000 and 30,000 tons of explosives.[104] In view of the use of fire bombs, napalm, cluster, and antipersonnel bombs, and the sheer amount of explosives dropped, it is incredible that experienced reporters could not see through the Pentagon's claim of 'surgical strikes.'

The only exception was the CBS broadcasting network, which had withdrawn from the official pool and reported independently. The team, which went into Iraq, was later arrested by Iraqi troops and incarcerated for forty days. A CNN crew and one reporter from *El Mundo*, a Spanish newspaper, also stayed in Baghdad. So did a reporter from *USA Today*, an American photographer, and some British journalists (including those from the BBC and the *Independent*). Altogether, 33 news reporters stayed, but none of those reporters were from the four most important American newspapers; their managements withdrew them.[105] When the *St. Petersburg Times*, basing its information on Soviet commercial satellite pictures, challenged the official version of the number of Iraqi troops in Kuwait, no major newspaper took it seriously; main news services did not report it.[106] When some of the smaller news organizations challenged in a court action the censorship in the name of the First Amendment, major newspapers declined to join in the challenge.[107] Macarthur, in his interview with the media elite and bureaucrats, did not find many who were seriously concerned about the loss of freedom resulting from the censorship.[108] The one major exception was Dan Rather of CBS. He candidly conceded that the media did not learn from their experience in Grenada and had failed to objectively report on the Gulf War. He further added:

> I can't make this case too strong, but it is not the role of the press to be an attack dog in my view, but it's damn well not being a lapdog. These days the lapdog is in. These days if you want to 'make it,' the belief runs strong that you can make it faster by convincing the audience that you're really on good terms with the mayor, or the sheriff, or fill in the blank.[109]

The major media channels also totally ignored the hearings of Ramsey Clark's Commission of Inquiry for the International War Crime Tribunal on Iraq. Obviously, the proceedings had no legal validity. Those indicted could not be brought to justice, but the inquiry was an effort by a person, who was at one time the attorney general of the United States, to set the record right. He, with the help of world jurists, was trying to expose an administration that had not only misled Congress but also allowed the American armed forces to indulge in activities that were contrary to the Geneva Convention, Nuremberg Charter, and the Charter of the United Nations. Nearly 1500 observers from different countries had assembled in New York to hear the verdict of the tribunal, but the major media of the United States remained unconcerned. The news was widely covered by the world media. Among the American media that covered the story were the listener-sponsored radio stations, African American weekly newspapers, much of the Spanish language media, and a number of progressive weeklies.[110]

Pentagon control of news of the war in Afghanistan has been almost absolute. With few exceptions, the media reproduces what the Pentagon reports. In view of the likely adverse reaction of the American people on the conduct of war, the media has, by and large, avoided reporting the numbers of innocents killed by aerial bombardment in Afghanistan. As Norman Solomon, a veteran media critic, points out, 'media scrutiny of atrocities committed by the U.S. government is rare.'[111] In their immediate reaction to September 11, media heavyweights were reminiscent of the late nineteenth and early twentieth century lynch mobs of the American South. *Time Magazine*'s Lance Morrow exhorted the country to relearn the lost virtues of 'self-confident relentlessness' and 'hatred;' the article called for 'a policy of focused brutality.'[112] Similarly, on the Fox News Channel Bill O'Reilly advised the US government to 'bomb the Afghan infrastructure to rubble – the airport, the power plants, their water facilities and the roads' if the Taliban delayed handing over Osama bin Laden. *New York Post* columnist Steve Dunleavy would not hesitate to bomb the cities or countries hosting the 'worms' [terrorists] 'into basketball courts.' Rich Lowry, the editor of *National Review*, recommended flattening Damascus or Tehran or whatever it took.[113] These journalists, in their rage for vengeance, were asking their own government to descend to level of the terrorists. They were also totally oblivious to the fact that they were asking their country to commit crimes against humanity. With friends like these, America does not need enemies.

This tendency of toeing the official line, coupled with the disproportionate influence of the conservative journalists of the main media, has often undermined objective reporting on China as well. One of the manifestations of this trend is the glowing reporting on economic achievements of post-reform China (the period after 1978) because the changes seem to conform to American views of a market economy; pre-reform China almost always receives bleak appraisal.

Partisan judiciary

Americans had a much greater trust in the judiciary as a defender of the Constitution – in spite of the partisan nature of the appointment of the judges – but in the wake of the Supreme Court decision with regard to the 2000 presidential election in Florida, there has been growing disillusionment with the Supreme Court judges. Thousands of letters sent by Americans to the Court in response to the decision were highly critical, some sarcastic, and some menacing. Some letters contained voter registration cards, suggesting that voting at the election was a waste of effort. One had an illustration of a skull and cross bones.[114] The decision has also come under serious criticism from the legal profession. In early January 2001, 554 law professors from 120 law schools of various political and ideological persuasions signed a full-page *New York Times* advertisement protesting the 9 December 2000 halting of a Florida vote recount that might have reversed Bush's tiny lead. The advertisement said that 'by stopping the vote count in Florida, the U.S. Supreme Court used its power to act as political partisans, not judges of a court of law ... By taking power from the voters, the Supreme Court has tarnished its own legitimacy. As teachers whose lives have been dedicated to the rule of law, we protest.'[115] Basically, the lawyers were reiterating what one of the four dissenting judges, Justice John Paul Stevens, lamented in his written opinion: ' ... although we may never know with complete certainty the identity of the winner of this year's presidential election, the identity of the loser is perfectly clear. It is the nation's confidence in the judge as an impartial guardian of the rule of law.'[116] There are some indications that the judiciary is questioning the current administration's actions with regards to American citizens alleged to have been involved in terrorist activities. Only time will tell whether the judiciary takes a stand in defending personal liberties being seriously threatened by the current administration in the name of fighting terrorism.

Pluto-democracy

All in all, the picture of American democracy in practice is not at all a flattering one. A president and a Congress beholden to big business tailoring policies to suit big-business interests, a big-business-owned and subservient media, a partisan judiciary, and a disenchanted citizenry increasingly withdrawing from political participation, do not present a healthy picture of a working democracy. It is no surprise that analysts have come to call the American political system an oligarchy of a 'white overclass.'[117] Commenting on the presidential election, the veteran American novelist Gore Vidal wrote, 'American politics is essentially a family affair, as are most oligarchies.'[118]

Some informed foreign observers go even further. William Keegan, a well-known British journalist, commented on the presidential election:

> The whole business has, of course, cast a cloud over the legitimacy not only of the US democratic process itself, but of the presumption – which has operated since the second world war – that the US has the right to persuade other countries to approximate as closely as possible to its form of 'democratic capitalism.' . . . The US is a Pluto-democracy – a democracy in which the rich and powerful compete for office, and the 'transition' to office, not to say office itself, sees a lot of campaign debts being honoured.[119]

Notwithstanding the weaknesses of the American political system that undermine the very essence of democracy, certain democratic freedoms in America, such as the freedom of speech or expression, have been a reality. Hundreds of individuals and public interest groups, even in the current testing time, are actively fighting for essential American values. Whether they have much influence on the power elite is a matter of controversy, yet there are successes. As Chomsky stresses, 'the right to freedom of speech in the United States was not established by the First Amendment to the Constitution, but only through dedicated efforts over a long period by the labor movement, the civil rights and anti-war movements of the 1960s, and other popular forces. James Madison pointed out that a "parchment barrier" will never suffice to prevent tyranny. Rights are not established by words, but won and sustained by struggle.'[120] In parenthesis one may note, as Chomsky points out, that the 1969 Supreme Court decision reinforcing freedom of speech was given in defense of the Ku Klux Klan.[121] More recently, the Supreme Court endorsed the big business contention that spending money was a form of speech deserving First Amendment protection.[122]

Similar protection is not readily available to left-leaning dissident groups in spite of the fact that the Supreme Court under Chief Justice Earl Warren had 'reaffirmed the right of even the most unpopular viewpoints to First Amendment protection . . . and ruled that even advocacy of violence could not be prohibited unless the danger of inciting lawless acts was imminent.'[123] While the Court was reaffirming freedom of expression to all Americans, the FBI was engaged in a domestic covert operation named COINTELPRO, which stood for counter intelligence program. It used infiltration, psychological warfare, and harassment through the legal system, as well as extralegal force and violence including break-ins, vandalism, assaults, and beatings. The object was to frighten dissidents and disrupt their movements. This program was directed not only against militant groups such as the Black Panthers and Brown Berets, but also against 'other activists who wanted to end US intervention abroad or institute racial, gender, and class justice at home.'[124] The surveillance covered César Chávez, Reverend Jesse Jackson, David Dellinger, the National Council of Churches, and other leading pacifists. Reverend Martin Luther King, Jr was also being investigated by the FBI and was marked to be discredited and neutralized, so as to prevent him from emerging as a 'messiah' who could 'unify, and electrify' the Black movement.[125] The Senate Intelligence Committee investigated the operation. Some of the top FBI agents were indicted for their illegal activities, two were convicted, several were retired or resigned, and the operation was shut down. Yet the Federal Bureau of Investigation (FBI) activities against movements concerning African Americans, Latin Americans, Puerto Ricans, women, lesbians, and gays continued into the 1980s; almost two hundred organizations were labelled 'terrorist fronts;' these included the Southern Leadership Conference of Rev. Martin Luther King, Jr. and various church and student organizations.[126] It is strange that even given the dubious histories of the security agencies in America, the George W. Bush administration, in the aftermath of September 11, is giving what amounts to a *carte blanche* to the very same agencies. This does not bode well for personal freedoms in America. Clearly, the American credibility for pressuring China to extend personal freedoms will be seriously questioned if such freedoms are eroded within America.

Conclusion

If one adds the economic and social ills – the poverty, the hunger, homelessness, and gnawing inequality of income and wealth – to the political malaise, a disconcerting picture of American democracy emerges. It illustrates the self-delusion of many Americans who consider America to be a 'righteous state,' worth emulating.[127] America has been able to fulfil the promises of the American Creed – a belief in the essential dignity of all human beings and their inalienable right to democracy, liberty, and equal opportunity – or of the Atlantic Charter – freedom of speech, freedom of worship, freedom from want, and freedom from fear – neither at home nor abroad.

Yet, the American insistence that China and India – for that matter most developing countries – follow the 'American-model' is largely based on false pretences. America is a rich country with well-meaning citizenry but social justice remains far from being fulfilled. If, with all its riches, it cannot guarantee the basic needs – food, health, shelter, and education – of all its citizens, the 'model' is of little use to poor countries such as China and India, which face rapidly rising populations, poverty, unemployment, and landlessness. China, in its rush for economic reform, already realises that growing inequality and unemployment are divisive forces that destroy social cohesion, and that the pace of change must slow down if it wishes to avoid instability and disintegration.

China's search for political stability with economic growth needs sympathetic world attention. Yet the repeated portrayal of China as a strategic threat and the emerging American military strategy to counteract it has been extremely worrying for the Chinese leadership. Neither the economic nor the military strength of China seem to present a threat to American interests in Asia or elsewhere, yet the American paranoia – in large part aided and abetted by conservative thinkers and think-tanks close to the American defense establishment – persists. Though ill founded, this American paranoia generates an equally intense – possibly justifiable – Chinese paranoia.

This book discusses the failings of America's China policy as rooted in American exceptionalism and in its socio-political structure and culture. Emphasis is placed on explorations of the increasing dependence of politicians on big business for ever-increasing campaign finance for never-ending electioneering, a growing political–industrial–military nexus, and the emergence of an autonomous military machine incessantly looking for enemies and winnable wars for self-justification. The three historical chapters following the introduction begin with a review of the discovery of America that led to European and American prosperity through the globalization of world trade, but misery for others in terms of dispossession of the Native Americans, slave trade, and traffic in opium. The review also describes how America, as a free rider within the politico-economic regime established by the British, shared unscrupulously all the imperialistic privileges enjoyed by the Europeans. It also tries to show the reason American policy-makers ignored the Japanese transgression of China's sovereignty and integrity during the first half of the twentieth century. This is followed by an analysis of the post-World War II period when American ignorance of China's relationship with the Soviet Union and the broader Asian realities alienated China. It also shows how American credibility as a champion of anti-colonialism, democracy, and the rule of law was tarnished by its support for the French in Vietnam and its covert operations in Indonesia and elsewhere to overthrow democratically elected governments; and how its transgressions of international law and human rights in the Vietnam War destroyed its remaining credentials as a country committed to the rule of law. The review then proceeds with the examination of the twists and turns of the American China policy under various presidents. It finally looks briefly into the China policy of the newly elected president, George W. Bush, and the departures it portends from the previous administration.

Chapter 5 examines the possibility of China posing an economic threat to American interests, particularly with regard to food grains and energy. Chapter 6 compares human rights transgressions in China with those in America and shows that the progress on this front is going to be slow. Unless special effort is made to combat such tendencies, the transgressions continue even in democracies, as happened in the American South during the nineteenth and early twentieth centuries, where democratically elected executives and legislators aided and abetted gross human rights violations against the Afro-Americans. The human rights transgressions in India can be taken as contemporary examples.

Chapter 7 examines China's military modernization as a potential security threat to American interests and the American reaction to it. The final chapter concludes that China poses neither economic nor military threat to American interests in Asia. It also argues that those who see China as a potential threat may be making the same mistakes that US policymakers did with respect to the Soviet Union immediately after the Second World War, leading to an arms race between the two, and to proxy wars in the different regions of the world, leading to major human disasters all over the world. Exaggerating the China threat may be welcome to the Pentagon, the Chinese defense establishment, and the world armament industry, but the arms race that it might unleash is of no use to world humanity nor to the deprived within America. From its own post-World War II experience, America has two alternative policy choices; one that it followed in Western Europe and Japan and the other that it imposed on the developing countries world over. In the first set of policies, America poured massive resources into rehabilitating the war-torn economies and nurtured the development of democratic institutions in Germany and Japan, gradually giving these countries a genuine role in common decision-making. This created a sense of partnership rather than subservience. Both Europeans and Japanese, even those critical of American policies, have a lot of respect for America. One does not fully understand why a policy which had proved its success was given up and replaced by nineteenth century imperialistic policies of military interventions to undermine democratically elected governments in developing countries, and of sustaining or supplanting regimes that tormented their own people by American trained military machines, financed and armed by America. The continuation of interventions covert or overt – as planned as a part of the 'War on Terror' – may buy America a little extra time; but violence begets violence. In a globalized world, violence has come to be globalized, giving respite to no one; nowhere is beyond the reach of globalized violence. Ultimately, America has to think seriously about using what Joseph Nye, Jr. calls 'soft power'[128] – an idea very close to the views of Brand's 'exemplarists' – and co-opting people in a consensual world order internationally by creating a more humane society at home. Not many Chinese want confrontation; what they are seeking is a sense of participation in a consensual world order. A British journalist recently wrote, 'to lead, you have to be loved.'[129] American values can be admired; American politico-economic culture in practice, has been disconcerting. To be loved, America needs to resurrect the values upon which it was founded.

2
America's Discovery: the Globalization of Trade and Misery

The American self-image in the nineteenth century heightened this myopia, for the Americans set themselves apart from all the Old World, claiming and proclaiming a new vision of man and society, and inveighing against all empires, at the very same time that they found it necessary and desirable to accept the treaty system with all its imperial privileges, so similar to the privileges enjoyed by European imperialists in their own colonies. This was an accident of history: that we Americans could enjoy the East Asian treaty privileges, the fruits of European aggression, without the moral burden of ourselves committing aggression. It gave us a holier-than-thou attitude, a righteous self-esteem, an undeserved moral grandeur in our own eyes that was built on self-deception and has lasted into our own day until somewhat dissipated by our recent record in Vietnam.

(John K. Fairbank[1])

Introduction

The discovery of the Americas, which heralded a new age of immense progress in wealth, standards of living, science, and technology in Europe and America, owed as much to the lure of profits as to the intellectual transformation taking place in Europe at the beginning of the fifteenth century. For centuries Europe traded with Asia; and for centuries it remained a one-way trade. An insatiable European demand for luxuries – silk, cotton textiles, and spices – was met by payment in gold and silver, for the Asians did not need much that was produced in contemporary Europe. The lion's share of the profits invariably went to the Muslim traders who controlled the routes to the East; therefore, 'to eliminate the exorbitant profits of these oriental middlemen by the establishment of some direct means of contact with the east became an inevitable object of economic desire.'[2]

Though the lure of profit motivated the discoveries begun in the 15th century, the role of the intellectual transformation in Europe that paved the way for these discoveries cannot be denied. From the twelfth century onwards, Islamic learning had an important influence on Europe; in fact, the Arabs transmitted the ancient Greek, Persian, and Indian sciences to Europe.[3] 'Ptolemy's astronomical theories reached the West by this route and were found a satisfactory basis for cosmology and navigation until the sixteenth century. The astrolabe had been a Greek invention, but its use was spread in the West by Arab writings.'[4]

The Europeans initially learned about the medical works of Aristotle, Galen, and Hippocrates through Arabic translations. The Arabs also passed on their knowledge of therapeutics, anatomy, and pharmacology. Overall, the Islamic influence had much to do with the emergence of modern science in Europe.[5] Much later, particularly during the seventeenth and eighteenth centuries, Chinese science and technology was transferred into Europe and some of the European science and technology brought to China through the Jesuit missionaries, until then Europe was more influenced by China than the other way around.[6]

Armed with the knowledge of Ptolemy's astronomical theories and Arabic cosmology and navigational ideas, the Europeans began to look for an alternative route to the East. The rivalry of the two major city-states of Venice and Genoa also played a part. Venice, through its friendship with Egyptian rulers and the Mamelukes, monopolized the distribution of the eastern commodities arriving via the Red Sea. Genoa, ever desirous of undermining the monopoly of Venice, was at the forefront of the new discoveries. Ugolino di Vivaldo, a Genoese, first attempted to sail around Africa on the route to India in 1291, but he was lost at sea. From the Genoese the Portuguese learned to build and sail ocean-going ships.[7] In 1434 the Portuguese reached Cape Bojador on the West African coast. Ten years later, they reached Cape Verde, and soon after arrived in Senegal. In 1487 they had already reached the Cape of Good Hope, and in 1498 Vasco da Gama reached India. By this time, Christopher Columbus, a Genoese, had arrived in the West Indies. The new continent came to be known later as 'America' after the Italian navigator Amerigo Vespucci, who, by sailing to the southern tip of South America, proved the existence of a vast continent between Europe and Asia.[8]

The discoveries, particularly those of the Americas, provided the Europeans with vast amounts of gold and silver that led to a rise in prices and profitability in Europe. The resulting improvements in agricultural and industrial technology ultimately culminated in what came to be known as the Industrial Revolution. The newly developing industries, particularly the cotton textiles that thrived under high tariff barriers imposed by the mercantilist states of Europe, needed raw materials (such as cotton) which the vast tracts of land in the new world could produce. Thus, the symbiotic relationship that developed between Europe and the Americas brought about their economic transformation, contributing to ever-increasing levels of income and standards of living.

The European success also brought with it an arrogance and contempt for other cultures and civilizations. The trail of disaster that followed the march of Western civilization into non-Western lands – in Africa, in the Americas, and in Asia – continues to linger. The plunder of Africa and Latin America began as a quest for riches. The dispossession and in many cases virtual extermination of the native populations in the Americas – perhaps the Argentinean campaign against the native populations were the worst – by the land-hungry populations of Europe continued well into the nineteenth century. African countries continued to be ravaged for the benefit of the slave trading industry for decades.[9] Slavery provided captive labor for the mines and plantation agriculture that developed in the Americas to meet the ever-expanding demand for cotton and sugar in Europe, and much needed gold and silver to finance the East Asian trade.

Silver, sugar, and slavery

While the Portuguese expanded their influence in Asia and (from 1500 onwards in Brazil), the Spanish colonized the lands west of 'a line of longitude running 370 leagues west of Cape Verde' given to Spain by the treaty of Tordesillas in 1494. All the land east of the line went to Portugal.[10] The Spanish had come to the Americas in search of land and gold, and, above all, to spread the gospel. In 1496 they founded Santo Domingo on Hispaniola. This was the first European city in this hemisphere with a cathedral (built in 1523) and a university (built in 1538). The Spanish colonized Cuba in 1511; Mexico's turn came soon after.[11] 'By 1600 the Spanish ruled, in name at least, much of what is now the south-western United States, almost all of Mexico, Central America, the islands of the Caribbean and what is now Venezuela, Colombia, Ecuador, Peru, Chile and the coasts of Argentina and Uruguay. To create this huge structure, the *conquistadores* overthrew the Aztec and Inca empires, two complex social and governmental systems with great resources behind them.'[12]

An indirect consequence of the Spanish conquest of the Americas was a drastic decline in local labor. Many died in the wars with the *conquistadores*; many more died because of the ruthless exploitation of indigenous labor by the Spanish employers. Those who remained died of European diseases to which they had little resistance. Some became victims of indiscriminate killing by their colonizers. Contemporary historical accounts describe how the Spanish colonists (*hidalgos*) hanged 'Tainos [Indians of Hispaniola] en masse, roasting them on spits or burning them at the stake (often a dozen or more at a time), hacking their children into pieces to be used as dog food and so forth, all of it to instill in the natives a "proper attitude of respect" toward their Spanish "superiors."'[13]

To meet the shortage of labor for the mines and plantations, the Spanish began importing slaves into the colonies. The earliest account of the export of slaves from Spain to its American colonies was in 1505 when the King of Spain sent seventeen black slaves from Seville. Another, bigger group of slaves was sold in the West Indies in 1510 and the first batch of slave-grown Caribbean sugar landed in Spain in 1515. The demand for African slaves continued to grow, but during the sixteenth century the King of Spain kept the numbers relatively low – around 4250 per year – not necessarily for his piety but because by this time, slave revolts were proving to be expensive for the planters.[14] However, the Portuguese sent many more slaves to the Brazilian sugar plantations. Demand for slaves continued to grow as the English, French, Dutch, and other European settlers established colonies in North America and founded large cotton and sugar plantations. By the early eighteenth century, particularly as a result of the War of Spanish Succession, England won the monopoly of supplying slaves to the Spanish American empire and replaced the Netherlands as the greatest slave-trading nation.[15]

Nearly twelve million slaves reached the Americas alive; possibly two million died.[16] The dehumanization and the suffering of the slaves until their emancipation and the continuing distress of their progeny constitute a sad commentary on the Europeans who have repeatedly claimed to be the repository of all moral virtues of humanity. As Hill points out, 'the consequences of the slave trade in brutalizing English opinion, and in fostering the Puritan tendency to hypocrisy, should not be underestimated.'[17]

The price revolution

Between 1540 and 1650 as much as 16,000 tons of silver and 180 tons of gold objects came to Europe.[18] American gold dwindled to comparative insignificance in the second half of the sixteenth century.[19] Silver received by Spain, either through legal trade or by smuggling, circulated among most European countries and led to a great price revolution. The extravagance of the European courts and the Spanish Wars were also to blame for the rise in prices. Jean Bodin, who developed the Quantity Theory of Money, in his *Response* to the *Paradoxes sur le faict des Monnoyes* published in 1566, suggested that American silver was the most important cause of the price revolution.[20] During the period of prolonged inflation, wage earners and those with fixed incomes suffered while the capitalist farmers and landlords gained much. The inflationary profits of the rich and of those who had directly or indirectly gained from the slave trade and the plantations in the Americas spurred the demand for quality foods such as fish and milk, consumer goods (glass, cutlery, domestic pots and pans, sugar, salt, beer, soap, and particularly cotton textiles), conspicuous housing, and shipbuilding.[21] Industries such as cloth, leather, metallurgy, gunpowder, paper, and brewing were all stimulated by state and army contracts.[22] The prosperity of the English iron industry during the first half of the eighteenth century owed much to the demands of the English army stationed in America. America and the East and West Indies became increasingly important as their share of English exports increased from a mere 13 per cent in 1700–01 to as much as 46 per cent by 1772–73.[23] The Navigation Act of 1651 (modified in 1660), which excluded foreign ships from the trade between England and its colonies, stimulated the shipbuilding industry. The slave trade and the trade monopoly of the East India Company further added to the industry's growth.[24]

In spite of the massive in-flow of silver and gold, the trade balance with the East did not improve much. The import of treasure had, in fact, created a greater demand for Eastern luxuries. 'The Mediterranean as a whole operated as a machine for accumulating precious metals, of which, be it said, it could never have enough. It hoarded them only to lose them all to India, China and the East Indies. The great discoveries may have revolutionized routes and prices, but they did not alter this fundamental situation, no doubt because it was still a major advantage to westerners to have access to the precious merchandise of the East . . . '.[25]

First globalization of trade

Historians have often written about the 'triangular trade' after 1650, involving exports of European textiles, rum, guns, and sundries to West Africa, which supplied human cargo for the Americas. From the Americas came the sugar, the cotton, and above all the silver. Focusing only on the Atlantic trade gives an incomplete picture of international commerce of the time. To complete the picture one has to take account of the silver and gold gained from the slave trade being directed to China, India, and the Spice Islands to buy silk, calicos, and spices, which were sold at enormous profits in Europe. This was the first globalization of trade fuelled by human cargo, sugar, cotton, and silver. The acquisition of India by the East India Company that began in 1757 with obtaining the right of revenue collection in Bengal, provided immense sources of income both in terms of money and commodities. Commenting on the looting of India by the East India Company employees in the early years of company rule, Hill wrote, 'there had been nothing like it in history since the Spanish *conquistadores* looted the Aztec and the Inca civilizations of America in the early sixteenth century.'[26] Subsequently, opium produced by the East India Company and pushed into China by British and American traders alike was used to balance the East Asia trade.

Anglo-Saxon America declares independence

While the British consolidated their hold on India, the American colony was slipping away from their clutches. Most English colonies in North America in the early seventeenth century began as trading posts owned by merchants for settling their employees.[27] By 1763, the colonies numbered thirteen with a population of 1.5 million people, one-third of them being African slaves.[28] The Americans in 1763 'were not only content but proud to be part of the British imperium. But they did feel very strongly that they were entitled to all constitutional rights that Englishmen possessed in England.'[29] When the breach came, it centered on the question of whether the British Parliament had the right to impose taxes on the colonies without their consent. On matters of taxation, the government in England was prepared to compromise and had repealed the Stamp duty and the Townshend taxes, but a three-pence duty on tea was not repealed. The import duty on tea entering Britain had already been repealed, and the East India Company was allowed to export tea directly to the American colonies. This should have undercut prices charged by smugglers and made tea cheaper for the Americans. Nevertheless, when the tea arrived in Boston, radicals known as the 'Sons of Liberty,' disguised as Mohawk Indians and blacks, dumped 342 big chests of tea into the sea. In reaction, the British Parliament passed the 'Coercive or Intolerable Acts.' The scene was set for a showdown. When efforts at conciliation repeatedly failed, the colonists adopted principles of independence on the fateful evening of 4 July 1776.[30] 'The new republic, however, was hailed with enthusiasm by all liberal elements of England and Europe ... The French intelligentsia hailed the triumph of liberty and reason over tradition and autocracy; they looked forward to doing the same thing for their own country, and had not long to wait. European liberals everywhere, filled with an unsatisfied longing for liberty, equality, and the rule of reason, felt that the triumph of the American Republic portended a new order for old Europe.'[31] Yet for the non-European populations, the new republic did not turn out to be much different from the imperial powers of Europe. The American promise of a new political force wedded to human freedom and an international morality different from naked imperialism remained an ever-receding goal.

Early expansionism

The first and most direct impact of American expansionism on the continent was felt by the Native Americans, whose lands were often expropriated by ignoring their treaty rights. The Mexicans were the next to feel the impact of the American drive for land. They lost their lands in rebellions or in wars that were often stage-managed by the Americans. The expansion of American possessions on the continent during the first half of the nineteenth century – from 838,000 to 3.5 million square miles – underlines 'the role of power rather than, as many [American] citizens liked to think, that of virtue or moral principle.'[32]

Thomas Jefferson looked at the Native Americans a little more favorably than the blacks (now African Americans), but for him, 'the ultimate point of rest and happiness for them is to let our settlements and theirs meet and blend together, to intermix, and become one people.'[33] Yet, what he and many others in power meant was virtual extinction of the tribes.

Many Native Americans died from diseases, such as smallpox, brought by the immigrants. However, there is some evidence that both the colonial government and its successors deliberately spread smallpox by distributing contaminated blankets.[34] The practice of exterminating the Native Americans by one means or another seems to have been quite widespread. As the *Daily Alta California* wrote, people 'are . . . ready to knife them, shoot them, or inoculate them with smallpox – *all of which have been done*.'[35]

The dispossession of the Native Americans took place with the active support or connivance of the colonial authorities and, later, of the new democratic government of the United States of America, which entered into treaties with the Indians for the transfer of land but, as already mentioned before, rarely respected those treaties. The United States Congress clearly stated that 'the United States are fixed in their determination, that justice and public faith shall be the basis of all their transactions with the Indians.'[36] However, soon after a new frontier was set up in accordance with the three treaties between Indian superintendents and the Iroquois, the Cherokee, and the Creek nations, George Washington wrote to William Crawford that 'I can never, never look on that proclamation in any other light (but this I say between ourselves) than as a temporary expedient to quiet the minds of the Indians and must fall of course in a few years . . . Any person therefore who neglects the present opportunity of hunting out good lands and in some measure marking . . . them for their own (in order to keep others from settling them) will never regain it.'[37] In 1803 President Jefferson wrote to Andrew Jackson requesting him to ask the Indians to become farmers or suffer removal to the west.[38] As soon as Andrew Jackson became president, an Indian Removal Bill was enacted. The Act had not authorized a forced removal, yet force was used.[39] The beneficiary states of Georgia, Alabama, and Mississippi outlawed tribal governments and placed the Indians under the jurisdiction of state laws. Clearly, such actions went against the treaties and assurances given to the Native Americans by Congress. The Jackson administration simply refused to comply with the treaty obligations and enforced new treaties for the removal of the Native Americans beyond the Mississippi.[40] The removal continued for many years. The Cherokee Indians even went to court to defend their treaty rights and won their case in the United States Supreme Court. Chief Justice John Marshall declared that the actions of the state of Georgia had violated the 'solemn treaty rights.' Yet President Jackson refused to enforce the court decision and forced a new treaty on the Cherokee for a westward removal. The forced removal that ensued cost the lives of a quarter of the Cherokee population.[41]

The government subjugated one tribe after the next. Some fought very bravely, but against far superior weapons, it was difficult to survive. There were many settlers who felt sympathy and goodwill toward the Indians. There were many more who favored their extermination, the American army not excluded. Some officers hated such acts but 'in general the forces combined for the great extermination program went to their work with enthusiasm, and the peak year of 1864 recorded hundreds of armed encounters.'[42] Overall, in 1900 only 237,000 Indians were left.[43] Conjectural estimates suggest that around A.D 1500, the number of Indians living in territories now incorporated into Canada and the United States ranged between 900,000 and 1.5 million.[44] While the Native American population was decimated, the European population continued to increase, putting unceasing pressure on Indian lands. In 1820, the total population of the United States was only 9.2 million. In 1860, it had gone up to 31.5 million and by 1930, 131.7 million.[45]

Of course, there were occasional bursts of good will on the part of federal government to ameliorate the conditions of the Indians. Much of the effort focused on transforming the Native Americans into farmers and assimilating them into the Anglo-Saxon race. Reservations were broken into allotments and given to the Native Americans for farming. With few resources and little training to farm, they tended to lease or sell the allotments almost as soon as they got them.[46] More recently, Native Americans have been given compensation for mistreatment and forced removals. Their population has also increased. Yet most continue to be 'very poor, their health is poor, and the general level of education is poor.'[47]

American expansionism abroad

Contrary to what is commonly believed, the United States 'has never been truly isolationist.'[48] True, President George Washington advocated 'neutralism' as a state policy 'to gain time to our country to settle and mature its yet recent institutions and to progress without interruption to that degree of strength and constancy which is necessary to give it command of its own fortunes.'[49] However, James Madison, one of the Founding Fathers, firmly believed that 'expansion was the key to preventing factions – themselves primarily the result of economic conflicts – from disrupting the fabric of society. Institutional checks and balances could help, and were therefore necessary, but they were not enough in and of themselves. Expansion was essential to mitigate economic clashes by providing an empire for exploitation and development . . . '.[50]

The Monroe Doctrine unveiled before the United States Congress in 1823 reflected the quintessence of American expansionism. The Doctrine unilaterally declared that any act of intervention by European powers in the affairs of the newly independent Latin American countries would be treated as an unfriendly act by the United States government. Positioned as a highly principled act – a newly independent country guaranteeing the freedom of other newly independent neighbors must be seen as noble – the Doctrine opened the way for the United States' annexation of foreign territories in North America. In the absence of European support, Mexico gradually lost Texas,

Utah, Nevada, California, and most of Arizona. By violating the Clayton–Bulmer Treaty of 1850 with Britain, the United States acquired exclusive right of transit in Nicaragua.[51] In 1898, the Americans went to war with Spain to 'liberate' Cuba. The basic policy toward Cuba was formulated as early as 1823, when then-Secretary of State John Quincy Adams stated that 'the annexation of Cuba to our federal republic will be indispensable to the continuance and integrity of the Union itself.'[52] Even President Thomas Jefferson regarded Cuba as appropriate for American expansion. Similarly, President Millard Fillmore's secretary of state, Edward Everett, claimed that Cuba was 'almost essential to our safety.'[53] After the American victory in the war against Spain in 1898, Cuba assumed independence, but American troops were stationed there between 1898 and 1902. In 1901, by introducing the Platt Amendment to the Cuban Constitution, the United States obtained the right to intervene in Cuban affairs and established military bases and a naval base at Guantanamo Bay. The American troops occupied Cuba between 1906 and 1909, again in 1912, and from 1917 to 1923.[54] Spain also ceded Puerto Rico and Guam to America after the war. In order to build the Panama Canal, America stage-managed and financed an independence movement and the subsequent independence of Panama from Columbia. The US obtained the right to maintain public order in Panama and sent US troops in 1908, 1912, and 1918.[55] When José Santos Zelaya, the leader of the Liberal government in Nicaragua, attempted to negotiate loans with British and Japanese syndicates to finance the construction of a canal through its own territory, the United States government backed an insurrection, which led to the overthrow of the government.[56]

The US annexed Hawaii in 1898. By this time, American policymakers had begun viewing US expansion in the Far East as equally important to that in Latin America.[57] The Philippines were occupied in 1898 and shortly thereafter, annexed as a colony. The Filipinos, desirous of independence, attempted to negotiate a settlement with the American occupiers, but President William McKinley decided to annex the Philippines. In the ensuing war, nearly 200,000 civilians died from famine and various other causes, including atrocities committed by both sides.[58] The racist attitude of the American soldiers also exacerbated the situation. Many American soldiers 'saw nothing wrong with shooting prisoners, enemy wounded, and native women and children.'[59] Writing about one of the campaigns a soldier wrote, 'this shooting human beings is a "hot game," and beats rabbit hunting all to pieces. We charged them and such a slaughter you never saw. We killed them like rabbits; hundreds, yes thousands of them. Every one was crazy.'[60] On the ruthless suppression of the Filipinos, Mark Twain, in disgust, suggested that the American flag ought to be redesigned with 'the white stripes painted black and the stars replaced by the skull and crossbones.'[61]

However, the American government, like any other imperialistic power, did not feel a sense of guilt. President McKinley 'stressed the altruistic rather than the economic causes.'[62] In a speech given in Boston on 16 February 1899, he claimed:

> The Philippines, like Cuba and Porto Rico, were entrusted to our hands by the war, and to that great trust, under the providence of God and in the name of human progress and civilization, we are committed . . .
>
> We could not discharge the responsibilities upon us until these colonies became ours, either by conquest or treaty. Our concern was not for conquest or trade or empire, but for the people whose interests and destiny, without our willing it, had been put in our hands.[63]

The truth, of course was that McKinley had already decided that he 'could not turn them over to France or Germany – our commercial rivals in the Orient – that would be bad business and discreditable.'[64] His acting secretary of state, William R. Day and Massachusetts Republican Senator Cabot Lodge also felt that America needed foreign markets, particularly in the Orient, to absorb the increasing industrial surplus.[65] America had not yet recovered from the effects of the Great Depression of 1873–96, when it experienced massive bankruptcy of financiers and failures of manufacturing industries.[66] During the same period, however, American industrial capacity had expanded considerably. It was therefore natural that economic and political thinking supported expansion abroad. 'Not a single major historical work written in this period about contemporary diplomatic affairs took an outright antiimperialist line.'[67] The advocates of expansionism argued that in order to avoid business depressions, the United States had to have colonies, protectorates, or commercial treaties.[68] Alfred Thayer Mahan, a great advocate of naval power who influenced President Theodore Roosevelt's thinking, supported the establishment of naval bases in the Caribbean, the Isthmus of Panama, Hawaii, and the Philippines.[69] In Roosevelt's view, the entire history of the United States had been one of expansion.[70] In a similar vein, Henry Cabot Lodge said that 'if the arguments which have been offered against our taking the Philippine Islands because we have not the consent of the inhabitants be just, then our whole past record of expansion is a crime.'[71] Most analysts of American diplomacy writing around the turn of the century conceded 'that imperialism was indeed in line with America's past expansionist diplomacy.'[72] Most of them advocated further expansion into Asia.

The advocacy of colonial expansion to absorb the surplus of manufactures and capital had a long pedigree going back to Adam Smith. Even Smith felt that colonies might provide opportunities to widen the market and vent-for-surplus.[73] Smith also supported 'a British commonwealth, with an imperial parliament, of quasi-independent countries, modeled upon the empire of ancient Athens.'[74] Edward Gibbon Wakefield later developed Smith's idea. The Wakefield School argued that 'colonies would become the sites for the investment of England's overflowing capital, and would provide the markets for Britain's surplus manufactures. Indeed, such empire-building, they believed, could provide an answer – *the answer* – to virtually all the most pessimistic prophecies of the practitioners of the dismal science.' (Italics added.)[75] What the Wakefield School preached in the mid-nineteenth century, American proponents of expansionism advocated at the end of the century.

Free trade imperialism and China

China attracted American attention long before 'free trade imperialism' was actively promoted by the American elite. James Logan of Philadelphia was the first American to come into contact with Confucian thought. In 1733, he imported a copy of the first European printing of Confucius' philosophy.[76] Benjamin Franklin was also interested in China and Confucian ideas. He maintained a lifelong interest in China and thought highly of 'the industry of its people, their high standard of living, their skill in agriculture, and their great population.'[77] Thomas Paine was also impressed with China and its people. Paine felt that the 'Chinese are a people who have all the appearance of far greater antiquity than the Jews, and in point of permanency there is no comparison. They are also a people of mild manners and of good morals, except where they have been corrupted by European commerce.'[78] Thomas Jefferson spoke approvingly of the Chinese restrictions on foreign trade and advocated a similar policy for the United States.[79] The intellectual interest in China seemingly continued amongst the American elite and 'a considerable body of respectable and influential writing' was produced. However, until the first quarter of the nineteenth century the Americans had much less knowledge about China than the French, English, or the Germans.[80]

Yet the lure of trade with China captivated the American mind as much as the European. As early as 1784 *Empress of China* left New York for China. The expedition was a modest affair; on its outward journey ginseng was the main cargo. The *Empress* made a profit of 25 per cent – not considered an impressive return. A smaller vessel, the *Experiment*, which sailed from New York in December 1785, did much better with a profit of 100 per cent within one and a half years. By 1795–96, the annual number of American ships at Canton had reached 10, and by 1812–19, 47. In 1818–19 the American trade with China exceeded the English East India Company's trade with China.[81] However, the American traders also faced the perennial problem of having little to offer that the Chinese were willing to buy. Ultimately, like the English, the American traders found their salvation in opium.

Much of the opium brought into China was produced in India and auctioned by the East India Company in Calcutta.[82] American traders brought some of their opium from Turkey. Among the British traders the Scottish firm of Jardine, Matheson & Company dominated, and among the Americans

Russell and Company of Boston and Providence of Rhode Island were fore-most.[83] In the first decade of the nineteenth century, as much as 600,000 pounds of opium was imported into China by British traders. By 1839 this volume had reached four million pounds.[84] As Fairbank suggests, opium 'became the marijuana/heroin of the time.'[85] 'Basically,' as Barbara Tuckman points out, 'the issue was not simply opium but the fact that the Chinese wanted to restrict, and the West to expand, their intercourse. The West pre-vailed.'[86] The war that ensued was denounced by Tory opposition in the British Parliament. W. E. Gladstone, a prominent Tory member, denounced the war as 'unjust and iniquitous.'[87] Another scathing criticism came from The *Spectator*, which found the war '*unjust, unnecessary and dishonourable.*'[88]

On the request of the American traders in China, a frigate and a small vessel were sent from America, but they did not take part in the war. However, Lawrence Kearney, the frigate commander, negotiated an indemnity for past injuries done to Americans.[89] Subsequently, in 1844 the Treaty of Wangxia secured the same privileges in trade and extra-territoriality for the United States that the British gained with the Opium War.[90] 'Throughout the process of the opening of China,' as Barbara Tuckman pointed out, 'the United States followed through portals cut by the British, avoiding the aggression and inheri-ting the advantages.'[91] This was a typical 'free-ride' by the United States, an accusation that it makes frequently these days against Japan and other allies. To Fairbank, the Opium War of 1839–42, was a case of 'classic iniquity:'

> Opium sales to China were necessary to balance the triangular trade that moved Canton teas to London, and London goods and investments to India. The leading British opium merchants on the China coast, headed by Dr. William Jardine of Jardine Matheson & Company, helped Palmerston work out the aims and strategy of the war. They leased vessels to the British fleet, along with pilots and translators, and from their con-tinued sales of opium accumulated the silver that the British expedition bought and used for its expenditures in China. It was indeed an opium-colored war, even though the basic issue was whether Peking would accept relations with Britain as between equal states. By refusing to give up his ancestral claim to superiority, Tao-kuang found himself loaded with the unequal treaties.'[92]

Thus, the forced opening of China (and later of Japan) in the name of *high principles* – 'the equality of nations,' 'freedom of trade,' and 'freedom of the seas' – was only a disguise for promoting commercial interests. 'If free trade had been the overriding principle of the British policy makers,' argues Wong, 'then one of the very first things they would have done was open the opium industry of Bengal to free enterprise. But they did not.'[93]

The Opium War (1849–52)[94] could be seen as a rerun of the crusades, which were, essentially, conceived as religious wars. The take-over of lucrative trade routes to Asia worked as an important incentive for Venice and Genoa, which provided assistance with men and money.[95] Commenting on the first four crusades, Roberts writes:

> Its religious impulse could still move men, but the first four crusades had clearly shown the unpleasant face of greed and cupidity. They were the first examples of European overseas imperialism, both in their character-istic mixture of noble and ignoble aims and in their abortive colonialism. In Syria and Palestine, Europeans were not simply pushing forward their frontier in a movement of settlement as in Spain or on the pagan marches of Germany. *They were attempting to transplant western institutions to a remote and exotic setting, to seize lands and goods no longer easily avail-able in the West, and they could do all this with clear consciences because their opponents were infidels* . . . (Italics added.)[96]

The Chinese case was not so different. The Anglo-Chinese settlement at Nanking was 'remarkably similar' to what the Chinese authorities had already conceded to Kokand, a Central Asian principality.[97] Perhaps, a rea-sonable negotiated settlement between China and the European powers was possible even without a war, but as Fairbank underlines, 'Britain, the United States, and France were expansive maritime powers from another world, addicted to sea power, violence, law and treaty rights, and for them the first treaty settlement of 1842–44 was only a beginning of encroachment. Imperialism supervened.'[98]

In short, a defeat at the hands of the 'foreign barbarians' destroyed what-ever legitimacy was left of China's imperial system. Rising inefficiency and corruption within the government, an increasing burden of taxation on the peasants, and a complete collapse of law and order resulted in mass discon-tent. In the wake of the discontent came a great popular uprising known as the Taiping Rebellion that lasted for 15 years and took a toll of 29 million lives. The Taiping rulers established their capital at Nanjing and it seemed as if they would prevail and push aside Ch'ing rule. But the foreign govern-ments intervened. They had a vested interest in the survival of the imperial regime; without its survival they might lose the privileges they had gained in the Opium Wars and through subsequent treaties. The pattern that was established, of foreign powers keeping a corrupt and inefficient regime alive in order to retain the privileges gained, continues to the present day.

Those progressive Chinese who, drawing inspiration from the Meiji 'mod-ernizers,' attempted to remodel China along western lines were circum-vented by the reactionary mandrinate around Empress Dowager Tzu Hsi. China lost territories to the British and the French in 1885 and to the Japanese in 1895 during the 'rampant' age of imperialism. America, how-ever, 'caught between hunger [for wealth and power] and principle' as Tuchman remarks:

had joined in the exploitation of China without compromising her scruples against taking territory. In 1898 this combination of profit and principle was elevated to a doctrine of foreign policy by John Hay. Called the Open Door (though not by him), it managed to sound generous, high-minded and somehow protective of China while meaning, if anything at all, that the door for penetration should be opened equally to everybody.

American infiltration of China by this time was a two-pronged affair of business and the gospel. Agents of Standard Oil purveying kerosene for every household lamp in China may have found more receptive customers, but the missionaries were to leave a greater mark on relations between the two countries.[99]

The Boxer Rebellion of 1899–1900, virtually the last gasp of an anti-imperialistic struggle that degenerated into an anti-Christian crusade, was much less organized than the Taiping Rebellion and was led by the fanatics of secret societies in China. Riding on a wave of xenophobia, they murdered missionaries, their families, and Chinese 'collaborators.' However, the reprisal, when it came, was no less despicable. The American Minister wrote that in Peking, all cadres of foreign soldiers and civilians, members of the diplomatic corps, and the churches had 'stolen, sacked, pillaged, and generally disgraced themselves.'[100] But in the eyes of the victors China alone had committed crimes 'against civilization' and was required to pay a huge indemnity. Her customs revenues were held as security.[101]

In the face of increasing public discontent with the Ch'ing rule and the realization that without modernization China could not regain her dignity or catch up with the West, a reform movement ultimately culminated in the establishment of a republic in 1911. Nevertheless, in the best of times, the central government's power remained curtailed both by the warlords, who controlled the countryside, and by the fact that the 'treaty ports' remained under foreign powers. Life in republican China was no better than that in a 'semi-colonial' country; 'foreigners did not control the polity, though their privileges impaired its sovereignty . . . '.[102]

Inter-war diplomacy and China

With the coming of World War I, Japan was quick to expand its influence in China at the expense of the Germans, going far beyond the British request for 'protection of the sea trade.'[103] Anticipating Japanese incursions into Chinese territory, Yuan Shih-k'ai, president of the republic at the time, approached the United States to take over German interests in China temporarily. The United States replied that 'it would be quixotic in the extreme to allow the question of China's territorial integrity to entangle the United States in international difficulties.'[104] Some groups within the Japanese government opposed blatant interventionism in China, yet it did not prevent

Foreign Minister Kato from setting a long list of demands, known as the 'Twenty-one Demands,' before China. If accepted, they constituted virtual Chinese consent to become a Japanese protectorate. Contrary to the Japanese caution to keep these demands secret, Yuan leaked them, hoping that some foreign intervention might save the integrity of China. No assistance came.[105]

Britain even advised compliance. President Wilson found the Japanese demands 'deeply offensive,' but 'caught between his idealistic notion of the integrity of China and his real desire not to harm the Allied cause, [he] was stymied.'[106] However, President Wilson's secretary of state, Robert Lansing, defined the 'American interest in the Far East as commercial rather than political,' and was sympathetic 'with the Japanese aspirations for colonization in Manchuria.'[107] Lansing felt that not allowing Japan a sphere of influence would undercut the American stand on the Monroe Doctrine. Lansing even thought of buying off Japan by turning the Philippines over to it. This idea was not acceptable to the president.[108] Lansing, in his efforts to appease Japan, subsequently reached the Lansing-Ishii Agreement of November 1917. The United States, while not giving up the Open Door Policy, conceded that Japan had 'special interests in China.'[109]

During the period when the Allied powers were engaged in the war against Germany, Japan continued to increase its influence by providing 'industrial' loans, the proceeds of which were commonly used to corrupt politicians and military officials.[110] Japan also persuaded the Tuan Ch'i-jui government to sign a Sino-Japanese military alliance that enabled the arrival of some 16,000 Japanese troops on the pretext of meeting the military needs of Siberia.[111] In an effort to undermine Japanese influence, the United States secretary of state proposed the creation of an international consortium to administer all types of loans to China. America also proposed an arms embargo until the Chinese overlords had reached a peace settlement. The Japanese government reluctantly accepted both proposals. Yet, despite the treaties, Japanese arms and money continued to flow into China. American attempts to maintain the embargo were undermined by arms imports from several countries.[112] The embargo ended in 1929 on the request of the Kuomintang government.[113] By this time, the Kuomintang army had succeeded in subduing the warlords and unifying the country.

Soon thereafter, in March 1932, the Japanese army in Manchuria set up a puppet government called Manchukuo.[114] The United States refused to recognize it. The League of Nations declared the Japanese action illegal, and the Japanese angrily stormed out of the League. The League had earlier sounded out Henry Stimson, the American secretary of state, regarding the possibility of an embargo against Japan for its aggression against China, but the League was simply rebuffed.[115] President Hoover, rejecting Secretary of War Patrick Hurley's recommendation to be tough with Japan, categorically stated that 'he would fight for [the] Continental United States as far as anybody, but he would not fight for Asia.'[116] Other countries were not prepared to fight Japan either. The British, always sympathetic to Japan, viewed the Anglo-Japanese Treaty as a safeguard against Soviet expansionism in the East. France was publicly supportive of the League of Nations, but privately let Japan know that the French appreciated Japan's problems in China.[117] The Soviet Union would have joined in a collective action by other states, but it was not willing to act alone. The League did not have any enforcement machinery other than the military power of the major states, and in this instance no major power was willing to take up the Chinese case.

The American government did not show much concern even over the 'Nanking Massacre' of innocent civilians by the Japanese armed forces in December 1937. Between 250,000 and 350,000 Chinese were killed; an estimated 20,000 to 80,000 women were raped.[118] In fact, the bombing of the *Panay*, a US gunboat, by the Japanese Air Force 'caused more of an uproar in the United States than all the wholesale rape and slaughter in Nanking combined.'[119]

The lack of substantial business interests in China was, perhaps, one of the main reasons that America did not take definitive action against Japan over the Amau Doctrine,[120] Manchuria, or over Japan's continued march into Southern China. In 1937, China was taking only 10 per cent of United States exports to the Far East; Japan's share was as high as 53 per cent. Therefore, American businessmen opposed sanctions against Japan for its invasion of China.[121] One commentator went so far as to suggest that the Japanese takeover of China might mean greater prosperity for American businesses.[122]

As late as mid-1937, the *Wall Street Journal* was saying that ' . . . our relations with China are less important to us than our relations with Japan.'[123] American business interests were also wholeheartedly supporting both the Fascists in Italy and Nazis in Germany. Many US multinationals made cash contributions to the German S. S. (the Sonder Konto S.) until 1944.[124] Newly declassified United States intelligence records confirm that the United States and Allied corporations had extensive dealings with Axis enterprises through 'shadow agreements' with companies located in neutral countries such as Spain, Sweden, and several Latin American countries.[125]

The American government, in political terms, saw Fascism and Nazism as bulwarks against Bolshevism, while in economic terms, the expansion of American business and investment remained uppermost in its mind. Secretary of the Treasury Andrew Mellon, himself a businessman, was a keen supporter of Mussolini.[126] President Coolidge, who took over as president in August 1923, ' . . . like the vast majority of Americans, saw no serious problem in the rise of fascist governments in Italy and Spain.'[127] Even President Roosevelt held positive views about Mussolini and in May 1933 'sought to use Mussolini as an arbitrator in the Far East [Manchurian crisis].'[128] However, as soon as Roosevelt heard of the Italian invasion of Ethiopia, he invoked the recently passed Neutrality Act, and prohibited the export of American arms to Italy, but refused to join in any collective action under the auspices of the League of Nations. When the British asked the administration to join in sanctions, Secretary Hull categorically stated that the United States would not go along with any such action by the League.[129] Roosevelt felt betrayed by Mussolini's Ethiopian invasion but did not change his mind about Mussolini; as late as December 1938, Roosevelt wrote to Mussolini to set aside part of Ethiopia for European Jewish refugees.[130] Roosevelt also attempted economic appeasement of Germany. The State Department thought that 'economic appeasement should prove to be the surest route to world peace.'[131] Only in 1941, after the Japanese march into Southeast Asia and the consequent loss of access to raw materials, did American business begin to see Japan as a threat to US interests in the Pacific.

If trade with China was not important for the United States, its capital investment in China was even less so. According to Remer, in 1931, the total foreign investment in China amounted only to $3.2 billion (at 1932 dollar parity), of which nearly 37 per cent was Great Britain's share, 35 per cent that of Japan, and only 6 per cent for the United States.[132] Nearly one-third of total United States investments were in import and export. Among public utilities, the Americans had controlling interests in the Shanghai Power Company and the Shanghai Telephone Company, but the British, Chinese, and Japanese nationals also subscribed shares. American investments in manufacturing were largely limited to manufacturing of Chinese carpets in Tientsin and Peking. Some American manufacturing plants were involved in importing, assembling, and operating cars, manufacturing electrical equipment, shipping containers, and producing cigarettes.[133] The total US manufacturing investment represented around 6 per cent of the total foreign investment in manufacturing in China, whereas the Japanese share was 44 per cent.[134] Clearly, the American stake in China was neither important in trade nor in investment.

American China policy plagued by ignorance

The stage for Japan's march into Asia was set in the 1860s and 1870s, as is reflected in the *Seikan Ron* ('Conquer Korea Argument'), and in 1890, when Prime Minister Yamagata Aritomo made a distinction between Japan's 'line of sovereignty' and 'line of interest or advantage;' the first, arguably, could not be maintained without the second.[135] Whether a tougher attitude by the United States would have halted Japanese adventurism in Asia is debatable, yet American inaction must have encouraged Japanese aggression, as there was no threat of reprisal.

American inaction was rooted in various causes: firstly, the Americans really felt that Japan's status as a world power – proven by Japan's victory over China and Russia – justified its need for a sphere of influence, in much the same way as the British, French, or the Americans themselves had their own spheres. Secondly, subjugating weaker countries was not seen as immoral. Thirdly, many Americans and Europeans felt that China was too 'backward' and divided to govern itself. Fourthly, America did not have much economic interest in China. Finally, the American policymakers were only barely informed about China's political situation.

This lack of knowledge about China was clearly reflected in the failure of the United States to build up a strong anti-Japanese offensive in China. According to Fairbank:

> The epitaph for America's China policy in the 1940s should begin by noting the Americans' profound ignorance of the Chinese situation. They were preoccupied with their official contacts with the Nationalists and their own logistic war effort in China. They sensed the Nationalist deterioration but had little detailed knowledge of it. The CCP [Chinese Communist Party] side of the picture was meanwhile almost entirely blank to the Americans. The few observers who got to Yenan responded to the upbeat optimism and determination of the CCP, but there were no American observers in North China except for a very few journalists, who however had very limited observations. The result was that the CCP power was completely underestimated. In 1948 the American estimate was that the Nationalists could not defeat the CCP, but neither could the CCP defeat the Nationalists. This view showed a total incomprehension of the reality of China.[136]

On the basis of such ignorance, the Americans chose to back the Nationalists and not only lost the war in China, but also lost the opportunity to moderate the CCP in its early days. The American mind failed to comprehend that much of the use of terms such as 'Communism' and 'Socialism' in developing countries was synonymous with 'nationalism' and 'anti-colonialism.'

Grave errors of judgment in understanding the Chinese Communists not only delayed the emancipation of China from Japanese aggression, but also embittered the Communists towards the United States, with serious implications for the world. In Tuchman's view, 'their [the Communist's] future alignment in international affairs was not, in 1944, necessarily fixed. What course Chinese Communism might have taken if an American connection had been brought to bear is a question that lost opportunities have made forever unanswerable. The only certainty is that it could not have been worse.'[137]

Arguably, it was more the ideology than the lack of knowledge that compelled American policymakers to support Chiang Kai-shek.[138] The military weaknesses of the Nationalist regime were known; yet conservatives within the United States Congress, popularly known as the 'China Bloc,' would not easily have allowed President Truman to give up Chiang in support of Communism.[139]

For their part, the Communists continued to provide sufficient, albeit confused signals regarding their willingness to make some kind of deal with America if it agreed to discontinue its diplomatic relations with the Chiang. Mao Zedong had never liked Joseph Stalin and was particularly upset about the 'unequal treaties' that the Soviets had imposed on China with the Sino-Soviet Treaty of February 1950 and a related secret protocol in which Stalin had forced China to concede that no citizen of a third country would be allowed to settle or to carry any industrial, financial, trade, or related activities in Manchuria and Xinjiang. The Soviet Union would reciprocate by preventing nationals of third countries from engaging in similar activities in the Soviet Far East and the Central Asian republics.[140] The protocol included provisions which required China to sell a certain proportion of the minerals produced in these areas exclusively to the Soviet Union while at the same time requiring China not to sell any to a third party without the prior consent of the Soviet Union. The secret protocol also stipulated extra-territoriality; any Soviet citizen committing a crime in China could not be tried in a Chinese court.[141]

If the Americans had been forthcoming, Mao might have avoided committing exclusively to the Soviet camp. Shortly after the liberation of northeast China, the Communists continued to have friendly relations with Angus Ward, the American consul general in Shenyang (Mukden). They met Ward several times and expressed their willingness to cooperate and strengthen ties, which Ward also reciprocated.[142] The CCP Central Committee had instructed the local authorities to treat foreign diplomats with discretion. They were asked not to undertake body searches of the diplomats while going in and out of the consulates. The Chinese local authorities were also advised to consult the Soviet diplomats because the Chinese felt that they did not fully understand the diplomatic niceties. But at the same time, the officials were warned that the Soviet advice ought to be 'treated as no more than suggestions, and any matter related to policy should be reported to the Central Committee for instructions before action.'[143] The Soviet representative, I. V. Kovalev, was reportedly uneasy about the Chinese leniency toward foreign consulates, and had reported to Stalin that 'the Chinese were too delicate in dealing with the Americans.'[144] In the meantime, on the advice of Kovalev, the American Consulate was blockaded by the People's Liberation Army (PLA) and Ward was charged with spying and put under house arrest when he refused to hand over the consulate transmitter. However, Mao disregarded the Soviet advice of entering the consulate to seize the transmitter.[145] Mao also criticized the Shenyang Military Control Commission for not obtaining instructions from party leadership before setting a 36 hour deadline for handing over the transmitters. Zhou Enlai was also critical of the actions of the Communist Party in relation to the treatment of foreigners.[146] Much to the discomfiture of Kovalev, the CCP leadership did not ask the American Navy to leave

Qingdao, which was in Chinese territorial waters.[147] Furthermore, when the Communist forces took over the Nationalist capital in Nanjing, Mao and Zhou invited United States Ambassador John Stuart to visit them but instructions from Washington prevented such a meeting. Nevertheless, Stuart stayed in Nanjing for a time and the channels of communication between him and the Communists remained open. Mao made it clear to Stuart that China's policy of 'leaning to one side' did not stand in the way of normalizing economic and diplomatic relations with the United States.[148] The Communists had always made it clear that they would pursue trade relations with the West. As early as 1946, Zhou told George Marshall that China would certainly 'lean to one side. However, the extent [of our leaning to the Soviet side] depends on your policy toward us.'[149] On the other hand, Mao had also approved of the decision to isolate the American consulate by cutting it off from outside contacts.[150] The mistreatment of the consular officials continued until they left China under deportation orders on 10 December 1949; this inevitably irked America and made it more difficult to contemplate early recognition of the Communist regime.

Mao's dilemma was acute. He was certainly in favor of rapprochement with the United States but at the same time was not prepared to strain China's relations with the Soviet Union. So long as the United States government continued to recognize the Nationalist government as the lawful regime representing the whole of China and to provide economic assistance to it, Mao had to depend on Soviet support.

Under normal circumstances, the Truman administration might have recognized the Communist government in China. It was certainly aware that most of the American allies, including the British, were ready to recognize the new regime.[151] The American government was also conscious of the potential of the Chinese market and did not wish to lose it altogether to its competitors. Above all, there were geopolitical reasons for disallowing China's total absorption into the Soviet bloc. For these reasons, the US National Security Council supported the continuance of 'ordinary economic relations between China on the one hand and Japan and the Western world on the other.'[152] In spite of the harassment of the consular officials, the American oil companies were allowed to continue supplying kerosene and motor gasoline to the Communist areas until late 1950. In a statement on 5 January 1950, President Truman declared that America had no designs on Formosa or any other Chinese territory and that the United States government did not intend to provide military aid or send military advisers to Formosa. However, the aid already authorized under the Economic Cooperation Administration (ECA) was to continue. By this time 24 governments had already recognized the Communist regime, yet recognition by the United States was not in sight.

The problem, of course, was that the Republicans in Congress were making matters difficult for Truman concerning his China policy. American paranoia regarding Communism started soon after the Russian Revolution of 1917, and following a short interlude during the Second World War when the Soviets were allies fighting against the Germans, the paranoia returned. Some right wing conservatives in both political parties, Republican and Democratic, even saw a close connection between Roosevelt's New Deal and Communism.

Walter Judd, one of Chiang's ardent supporters, had begun to allege that the State Department harbored Communists. A similar allegation had been made earlier by General Patrick Hurley, the president's special envoy to China, who claimed that his efforts were undermined by subversives in the State Department.[153] Another Chiang supporter, Styles Bridges, engineered the removal of Carter Vincent, one of the State Department officials responsible for China policy, from his assignment by alleging that Vincent had leftist tendencies.[154] John Taber, chairman of the House Appropriations Committee, also insisted that the State Department was full of Communists. Joseph Martin, the speaker of the House of Representatives in the Eighteenth Congress, also asserted that there was no room 'in the government of the United States for any who prefer the Communist system' or anyone who did not believe 'in the way of life which had made this [the United States] the greatest country of all time.' Congressmen Mundt and Dirksen advocated the removal of Communists from the federal payroll.[155]

In August 1948, Whittaker Chambers, a self-confessed Soviet agent and an editor of *Time* magazine, accused Alger Hiss, the president of the Carnegie Endowment for International Peace, of giving him secret government documents in the 1930s.[156] The case against Hiss could not be proved, but in 1950 he was convicted of perjury. In early 1950, even the moderate Republicans had begun to denounce the policies of the Truman administration and directed their ire toward Secretary of State Acheson.[157] By this time, a combination of arch-isolationists, anti-New-Dealers, and those belonging to the 'China Bloc' had begun to make intemperate personal criticisms of Acheson; the Senate Republican leader, Kenneth Wherry, even called for his dismissal. Truman stood by his secretary of state.

In the meantime, the Soviet Union exploded its own nuclear device, challenging the American monopoly on the weapon. Soon thereafter, the news came that a top nuclear scientist, Klaus Fuchs, had been arrested in London in February 1950 for passing atomic secrets to the Soviet Union. His two colleagues were later arrested in New York. Within a week, Senator Joseph McCarthy made headlines by suggesting that he possessed a list of 205 Communists still working in the State Department. He never made his list public, nor did his numbers remain consistent, but his statements led to a witch-hunt involving prominent members of American society, including Owen Lattimore, a Johns Hopkins University professor and well-known expert on China. 'McCarthy remained a force through the spring of 1950 because the Republican Right supported him viscerally. Republican moderates were loath to denounce him squarely ... At least half the Republicans in the Senate actively cheered McCarthy on, including the titular leader Wherry and de facto leader Taft.'[158] In those days of anti-Communist frenzy and what leading American historian Richard Hofstadter called 'the paranoid style in American politics,'[159] it would have been political suicide for any administration to recognize China or to support Communist China's admission to the United Nations. Yet the delay in diplomatic recognition and US efforts toward preventing Communist China's entry into the United Nations increasingly soured Sino-American relations and, unfortunately, brought China closer to the Soviet Union.

Conclusion

By the time the United States came into contact with Asia, in spite of its professed idealism, its expansionist tendencies were well matured. Its main aim was to obtain privileges for the United States that had been acquired by Britain and the other European powers. Whether the United States had 'scruples against taking territory' in China, to use Barbara Tuchman's phrase, is highly questionable in view of the ease with which it justified the annexation of Native American and Mexican territories, Hawaii, and the Philippines. Expansionism remained the very basic tenet of American foreign policy. Arguably, it was more a matter of convenience, not of principles, that the United States did not attempt to carve up its own zone of influence in China. The 'Open Door' had ensured that trade and diplomatic benefits were accessible to the United States without antagonizing any of the major powers. It is a strange irony that even President Wilson's much vaunted internationalism failed to arouse the American conscience or to motivate the other major powers to take a coordinated action against Japan in its blatant aggression against China.

China stood betrayed. Another betrayal came when, either out of sheer ignorance, or out of its prejudice against Communism, or out of the American administration's lack of ability to confront the conservatives at home, the United States failed to recognize Chinese Communist leadership, making a mockery of international law. American credentials of adherence to the 'rule of law' were left in tatters. The corollary of non-recognition meant that the United States actively prevented Communist China from taking over its legitimate seat in the Security Council – a clear undermining of the United Nations Charter. Whether any US accommodation with Communist China would have prevented China entering into the Korean War is anybody's guess, but the fact remains that, devoid of US support, Communist China had to depend exclusively on the goodwill of the Soviet Union, a prospect that Mao never favored.

3
Enemies Become Strategic Partners

Like most Americans, I saw Communism as monolithic. I believed the Soviets and Chinese were cooperating in trying to extend their hegemony. In hindsight, of course, it is clear that they had no unified strategy after the late 1950s . . .

. . . we – certainly I – badly misread China's objectives and mistook its bellicose rhetoric to imply a drive for regional hegemony. We also totally underestimated the nationalist aspect of Ho Chi Minh's movement. We saw him first as a Communist and only second as a Vietnamese nationalist.

(Robert S. McNamara[1])

Introduction

From the very inception of the People's Republic of China in 1949, both China and the United States wanted to improve their relationship, but ideological differences, mutual suspicions, and the lack of adequate knowledge about each other prevented a rapprochement. The dominance of the conservatives in the US Senate and their commitment to Nationalist China and their domestic anti-Communist *jihad* were the other complicating factors. The machinations of the Soviet Union, ever desirous of inserting a wedge between China and the United States, also thwarted China's efforts to normalize relations with the United States. The outbreak of the Korean War hardened attitudes on both sides. At the end of World War II, Korea, though independent of the Japanese occupation, found itself divided at the 38th parallel. The Soviet forces had reached Korea first and had crossed the 38th parallel, but on the arrival of the American forces several weeks later had retreated north of the parallel.[2]

This division of the zones of influence coincided with the division agreed upon between the Japanese and the Russians under the Yamagata-Lobanov protocol of 28 May 1896.[3] As early as March 1943 the United States had suggested a multi-lateral trusteeship for Korea, after the Japanese defeat, designed to lead to an eventual independence. The Soviet Union had accepted the

US proposal. The joint Soviet–American commission, provided by the Foreign Ministers' Conference in Moscow held in December 1945, met to thrash out the differences between the two powers. Unfortunately they often disagreed on the issues of free consultations and the inclusion of Korean political groups in the establishment of the national government. Ultimately, in 1947 the US-sponsored initiative in the UN General Assembly for Korean unification failed because of Soviet opposition. Yet a UN-supervised election was held in South Korea the following year, and on 15 August 1948, the Republic of Korea, headed by newly elected President Syngman Rhee, was established. In the North, a Communist government – the Democratic People's Republic of Korea – was founded on 8 September 1948 under Kim Il Sung.

Rhee held the election under US pressure, but his party was routed, with only 48 against 120 seats from other parties, mostly from the left. The new Assembly was overwhelmingly in favor of unification, even on North Korea's terms. Perhaps these results encouraged the North to invade the South. With new material available from Chinese and Soviet archives, it can now be inferred that both the Soviet and the Chinese leaderships knew, by the end of 1949, that Kim Il Sung planned to attack the South; only the timing was unknown.[4] Recently released documents from Russian archives also show that both Stalin and Mao were reluctant to enter into direct confrontation with the United States. Had the Truman administration assured the Soviet Union and China that it had no intention to attack Mainland China or the Soviet Far East, both governments might have decided to let Kim Il Sung's regime go under and agree to a Korean settlement proposed by the U.N. It was largely General MacArthur's repeated threats, particularly against the PRC, that pushed the Chinese to enter the Korean war almost against their will.[5]

Soviet Union too weak to challenge American might

Stalin was worried about American intervention in Korea as he was in no mood to enter into a war against America. The proceedings of a Soviet Polit Buro meeting on 5 October 1950 reveal the general mood. In the context of Kim's reverses in the Korean War, all the members felt that a direct confrontation with the United States had to be avoided. Upon hearing that Kim's defeat would mean that the Americans would come as far as Soviet borders, Stalin's reply was, 'So what? Let the United States be our neighbors in the Far East. They will come there, but we shall not fight them now. We are not ready to fight.'[6]

Stalin's reluctance to enter into direct conflict with the United States stemmed from the Soviet Union's fundamental economic and strategic weaknesses. The country had lost as many as 7.5 million people in the armed forces and between 6 to 8 million civilians as a result of the German invasion. Adding the indirect loss of population as a result of reduced food intake, forced labor and increased hours of work, the total loss might add to

20 to 25 million people.[7] One estimate puts it as high as 30 million, equivalent to fifteen percent of the 1940 population of the country.[8] By the end of the war, the total output of the country was only eighty per cent of what it was just before the war. Nearly a third of the capital stock had disappeared.[9] A significant proportion of railway tracks, bridges and rolling stock had been destroyed. As were urban and rural living spaces almost 1.2 million houses in urban areas and 3.5 million in the rural areas.[10]

Evidently, rhetoric apart, in the immediate post-war years the Soviet Union was in no shape to challenge the military might of the United States. As early as 1946 an aide to Secretary of the Navy James Forrestal wrote:

> The Red Fleet is incapable of any important offensive or amphibious operations . . . a strategic air force is practically non-existent either in material or concept . . . economically, the Soviet Union is exhausted. The people are undernourished, industry and transport are in an advanced state of deterioration, enormous areas have been devastated . . . .The USSR is not expected to take any action during the next five years which might develop into hostilities with Anglo-Americans.[11]

In much the same vain, Walter Bedell Smith, the ambassador to the Soviet Union, told C. L. Sualzberger, then-foreign service chief of the *New York Times*, that he was 'convinced there will be no war with Russia. The Russians are too weak. They have no air force. It will take them much more than twenty years to build a good fleet, no matter how hard they try.'[12] Even George Kennan, who was otherwise pessimistic about the future of the US–Soviet relations, explicitly mentioned in his long-telegram sent from Moscow on 22 February 1946, that 'Gauged against Western World as a whole, Soviets are still by far the weaker force.'[13]

Neither the Truman administration nor the Western European governments believed that a full-scale war with the Soviet Union was a real possibility. The economic and military power of the United States far outweighed that of the Soviet Union. At the time of the North Korean invasion of the South, the Soviet nuclear capability was comparable to America's in 1947, while the US had stockpiled as many as five hundred atomic bombs and two hundred and sixty-four aircrafts capable of delivering them.[14] Any major war with America would have brought utter destruction to the Soviet Union.

The Truman administration was not keen on a war with the Soviet Union either. Even when the United States authorities knew that Soviet pilots were providing air cover to the Chinese troops in Korea, Washington did not officially acknowledge their participation. Acknowledging them would have meant a declaration of war against the Soviet Union, and the US administration was not prepared for such an eventuality. When Stalin gave his consent to Kim's invasion of the South, perhaps he thought more of the involvement of the Chinese armed forces than that of the Soviets. He had made it clear to Kim that if 'you should get kicked in the teeth, I shall not lift a finger. You have to ask Mao for all the help.'[15]

Chinese reluctant to get involved in Korea

For the Chinese leadership, a war in Korea was even more difficult to swallow. Its priority was to liberate Taiwan. Besides, the Chinese Communist Party (CCP) had been in power for less than a year; apart from establishing peace and order, it needed to organize economic and social life in such a way that people might see discernible improvements in their living conditions. On the question of armed intervention in Korea against the United States, Zhou Enlai and Lin Biao were totally opposed to the idea. Until 1 October 1950 even Mao conveyed to Stalin the Chinese reluctance to enter the war on Kim's behalf.

What Mao least wanted was a war against the United States. China had the advantage of having a large army, but couldn't match America's sophisticated weapons. China also lacked the industrial capacity to produce and sustain the supply of weapons in the event of a protracted war. Mao felt that this deficiency could possibly be ameliorated if the Soviet Union provided advanced weapons and air cover.[16] On the other hand, a war against America would certainly eliminate the possibility of a rapprochement with the United States for a long time making China increasingly dependent on Stalin – a prospect that Mao disliked immensely.

At the time, the Chinese Communist leadership did not intend to export revolution abroad, nor had any plans to take over Southeast Asia, as the Washington elite invariably believed. This is evident from the remarks of Ralph McGehee, a Central Intelligence Agency (CIA) officer who had come across a 40-page-long internal Chinese document intended for Chinese diplomats detailing China's intentions towards other countries. In McGehee's view, 'China planned to act in a responsible way and that its goals to a large extent paralleled our own.' In spite of his best efforts, China desk had no interest in disseminating the document because the report 'might stimulate some government leaders to question the CIA's insistence that China deserved to be on the top of its operational target list.'[17]

Mao expressed misgivings regarding Kim's proposal of invading the South to unify the country by force and he tried to persuade Kim to reconsider; but Kim had made up his mind. Kim had an exaggerated sense of his military strength and his revolutionary appeal to the South. He did not even anticipate the need for the deployment of Chinese soldiers in Korea, because he was confident that the Soviet Union would provide adequate assistance. To the chagrin of the Chinese leadership, neither the North Koreans nor the Soviet Union informed China about their military preparations. Soviet arms were sent to North Korea by sea, not by trains which would have passed through Chinese territory and alerted China's leaders.[18]

Truman orders US forces to repel Kim's forces

The North Korean attack on the South came on 25 June 1950, launching a three-pronged strategy. The land invasion was aided by tanks, and North Korean troops marched towards the 38th parallel and crossed it within a few hours. Military vessels sailing down the east coast landed troops behind the South Korean lines, while airplanes began to bombard the airfield at Seoul. Within a few hours, the North Korean troops controlled all the territory north of the Imjin River.[19] The very next day Truman ordered American air and naval forces to proceed to South Korea to repel the North Korean invasion. The US Seventh Fleet was dispatched to the Taiwan Strait to defend Formosa as the US announced military aid to the Philippines and to the French in Indo-China.

Already in April, Truman had approved NSC 68, which was intended to rearm the United States for the unilateral defense of the free world against Communist aggression. As Ambrose has pointed out, NSC 68 was a natural extension of the Truman Doctrine, which as early as March 1947 declared that 'it must be the policy of the United States to support free peoples who are resisting attempted subjugation by armed minorities or by outside pressures.'[20] The Truman administration saw the North Koreans invasion as a threat to US security interests in Asia. As a corollary, meeting the Communist threat in Indo-China also became imperative.

Truman, as many others in Washington, felt that Chinese and Vietnamese Communism were simply extensions of Soviet Communism and a part of the Soviet conspiracy to take over the world.[21] The administration was totally oblivious to the historical Chinese distrust of the Russians (later the Soviet Union) and the Vietnamese distrust of the Chinese. Truman and his advisers also underestimated the intensity of nationalism in these countries.[22] As early as 1936 Mao had told Edgar Snow that the Communists were not fighting for the emancipation of China simply to 'turn the country over to Moscow.'[23] The Americans also ignored the fact that the Soviet Union supported the Nationalists during the greater part of the Chinese Civil War and was ready to recognize the Chiang Kai-shek regime as 'the central government of China.'[24] The administration also failed to realise how affronted the Chinese Communist leadership was to know that Stalin was party to a decision made at the Yalta Conference that provided for the return of 'former rights of Russia violated by the treacherous attack of Japan in 1904,' as well as the extraterritorial rights in China.[25]

US involvement in Vietnam not an afterthought of Korean War

The decision to come to France's rescue in Indo-China on 26 June was not made as precipitately as it seemed at the time. It is important to note that:

this decision was made prior to rather than as a result of the Korean War, although the Korean invasion had the effect of increasing to some extent the scope and amount of assistance being given to Indochina. Here, too, it is sometimes taken for granted that the decision to intervene in Indochina was a result of overt aggression by the Communists in Korea. Quite the contrary is true. Indeed, it was assumed [in Washington] in the spring of 1950 that Indochina was the key area of Asia threatened by the Communists and the one in which US interests were paramount. The Korean War did not change that calculation; if anything, Indochina became relatively more important.[26]

The actual involvement of the US government in the Indo-Chinese war began on 24 April 1950, when, on the recommendation of the National Security Council (NSC), Truman approved NSC 64, aimed at the prevention of Communist expansion in Southeast Asia. The document acknowledged that without US assistance, the native Indo-Chinese and French troops could not withstand an assault by Ho Chi Minh's forces if the latter was supported by armed forces or massive arms supplies from China.[27] A State Department working group had already asserted in February that 'the choice confronting the United States is to support the French in Indo-China or face the extension of Communism over the remainder of the continental area of Southeast Asia and, possibly, further westward.'[28] Thus, one must look to Truman's NSC 64 as the inception of the 'domino-theory' – though the term itself was not used as such – and not until its later enunciation by President Eisenhower.

Truman ignores the UN and orders troops to cross the 38th parallel

US aircrafts and ships had already began to attack the invading North Korean forces on 26 June.[29] The very next day, the United Nations Security Council recommended that all the members of the UN 'furnish such assistance to the Republic of Korea as may be necessary to meet the armed attack.'[30] The Soviet Union did not have a chance to veto the UN resolution, as it had refused to take part in the UN proceedings as a protest against US insistence on the continuation of Chiang's representation in the United Nations.[31]

Even before the tide of the war had turned in favor of the UN troops, questions were raised regarding the ultimate objectives of the defending army. Should the UN forces simply push the invading forces north of the parallel or should they advance beyond the parallel and try to unify the country? President Rhee argued that the North Korean invasion had obliterated the 38th parallel and unification of the country was the only means of securing permanent peace and stability.[32] Opinions in Washington remained divided. George Kennan opposed the crossing of the parallel. The majority in the State Department, however, supported the idea of crossing the parallel. To the Pentagon it did not make military sense to stop. MacArthur favored pursuing the North Korean forces beyond the parallel and destroying them.

On 17 July, Truman asked the NSC to make a recommendation on appropriate actions following the retreat of the North Koreans north of the parallel. In the meantime, both the British and the Indian governments put forward plans for a peaceful settlement of the Korean problem acceptable to China and the Soviet Union. However, these plans were not acceptable to the US government.[33] On the recommendations of the NSC, Truman approved NSC 81/1 on September 11, authorizing MacArthur to cross the parallel and take military control of North Korea with the proviso that if the Chinese or the Soviet troops intervened, only the South Korean and not the US troops were to cross the parallel.[34] MacArthur did not obey these instructions and in the name of military necessity sent the US troops north of the parallel even after the Chinese intervened. On the decision to cross the parallel the UN was not consulted, the decision was, in fact, contrary to the assurances given by the United States to the UN Security Council – and implicitly to the Soviets and the Chinese – that the military action was intended to restore the 38th parallel as the dividing line, and was not an attempted rollback.[35] However, Warren Austin, the American delegate to the UN, simply stated on 10 August and again on 17 August that the aim of the military action was to unify Korea.[36] Secretary of Defense George Marshall informed MacArthur, 'Evident desire is not to be confronted with necessity of a vote on passage of 38th parallel, rather to find you have found it militarily necessary to do so.'[37] This was giving MacArthur a great deal of latitude, an idea that did not find favor with Kennan. 'By permitting General MacArthur,' Kennan wrote to Secretary of State Dean Acheson, 'to retain the wide and relatively uncontrolled latitude he has enjoyed in determining our policy in the north Asian and western Pacific areas, we are tolerating a state of affairs in which we do not really have full control over the statements that are being made – and the actions taken – in our name.'[38] This leniency toward MacArthur came back to haunt Truman, who later disingenuously denied his involvement with the decision to cross the 38th parallel.

Chinese 'volunteers' enter the Korean War

A massive involvement of American troops in Korea and Truman's willingness to allow MacArthur to cross the 38th parallel, the Seventh Fleet in the Taiwan Strait along with US support for the French in Vietnam naturally seemed ominous to the Chinese. Another less publicized fact was that the CIA carried out a number of raids into Communist China's territory with the help of Nationalist troops that had escaped to northern Burma.[39] The Chinese, through K. M. Pannikar, the Indian ambassador in Beijing, made it known to the US that China would enter the conflict if the UN forces continued their advance beyond the parallel.[40] Senior State Department officials did not take the Chinese warnings seriously. Strangely, in his meeting with Truman on Wake Island, MacArthur too ruled out the possibility of a Chinese involvement. By that time, a high-ranking Nationalist Chinese officer turned spy, who was air-dropped on the Chinese mainland by the CIA in late 1950, had already warned that the crossing of the Yalu River by Chinese troops was imminent. MacArthur later denied having seen such a report, but Truman contradicted MacArthur and said that he had read a report on the concentration of Chinese troops along the Yalu River.[41]

Truman spurns negotiated settlement

Miscalculations regarding Chinese non-involvement had created a sense of near euphoria in Washington, and throughout the first half of October, State Department officials prepared contingency plans for the military occupation of the North and the post-war reconstruction of Korea. General MacArthur and his supporters in Congress had begun to advocate strategic bombing of the Chinese mainland and in a press interview Truman stated that the use of the atomic bomb as a military weapon had always been in active consideration.

The British were so alarmed by the prospect of another major conflagration in the Far East that they came forward with a new plan of negotiated peace, including a proposal to change America's stand on China's entry into the United Nations. Prime Minister Attlee came to Washington in December 1950 to plead with Truman to opt for a negotiated settlement. Truman did not agree, as he was too worried about domestic opposition.[42] As Ambrose points out:

> A negotiated settlement with the Chinese would bring the wrath of the Republicans on their heads, and congressional elections were only a few days away. If peace came, there would be no N.S.C. 68 and American foreign policy would be back where it was before the Korean War – much bluster and little muscle.[43]

The Chinese Communist Party, which had not yet fully consolidated its control in China, would certainly have liked to give a peaceful solution a chance. Liberating Taiwan to unify the country was certainly their main priority. Hence, on invitation, they came to the United Nations. They arrived on 24 November to be greeted with the news that MacArthur, in his characteristic hyperbole, had promised to bring 'the boys "home by Christmas" after they had all been to the Yalu.'[44] The Chinese delegation immediately returned home. European allies of the United States were furious; the French government openly charged that MacArthur had 'launched his offensive at this time to wreck the negotiations.'[45]

Within two weeks the Chinese 'volunteers' reversed the fortunes of war, routing the UN forces out of North Korea. As Mansourov, on the basis of newly released documents from the archives of the Russian federation, concludes:

> there was little political will and much less hope in Moscow, Beijing, and even Pyongyang to defend North Korea to the last man when the military situation collapsed in mid-October 1950. Therefore, had the United

States been less ambivalent, more consistent, and more persuasive on the diplomatic front in stating to Moscow and Beijing the goals of its Korean campaign – e.g., that it had no desire to attack Mainland China or threaten the territory of the Soviet Far East – the Soviet and Chinese governments could well have decided to let Kim IL Sung's acquiesced to a UN-proposed Korean settlement. However, Gen. MacArthur's repeated unconditional surrender demands, coupled with barely veiled direct threats against the PRC and the USSR, coming out of Tokyo headquarters, literally pushed the insecure Chinese to the brink, compelling them almost against their will to intervene in Korea . . . '[46]

Yet again, the chance of a negotiated, mutually acceptable peace between the United States and China was thrown to the wind.

Unparalleled militarization of America begins

In the meantime, to appease his Republican critics in Congress, Truman initiated an unparalleled military build-up in America. He obtained emergency powers to expedite war mobilization and reintroduced selective service, increasing the army to 3.5 million soldiers. He also doubled the air groups to total ninety-five and expanded the military presence in Europe to six divisions.

On the diplomatic front, he obtained bases in Morocco, Libya, and Saudi Arabia, and initiated the process to extend membership in NATO to Greece and Turkey and to provide aid to Fascist Spain in exchange for military bases.[47] Subsequently, with the signing of the peace treaty with Japan in September 1951 and the US–Japan Security Treaty soon thereafter, the US obtained military bases in Japan.[48]

In retrospect, if the Cold War armament race between America and the Soviet Union was one of the main causes of the economic collapse of the latter, the credit ought to go to Harry Truman rather than Ronald Reagan, for it was Truman who initiated the arms race. Reagan only followed in his footsteps in the dying days of Soviet Communism, a system mortally wounded by its inherent contradictions. Truman, in his later life, lamented 'that the Korean War, which he had much supported, began the militarization of American foreign policy.' Senator Moynihan does not fully agree with Truman, but concedes that 'in Korea, as in Vietnam, we . . . confused the national interest with an ideological preference.'[49]

The non-recognition of Communist China as the legitimate government was clearly a mockery of international law. The US policy of preventing Communist China from assuming its legitimate seat in the United Nations was also indefensible.[50] Yet, in the aftermath of the Korean War and in the anti-Communist frenzy created by McCarthy, Acheson's moderate policies toward China gave way to the more militant Communist-bashing policies of Dean Rusk and John Foster Dulles. The increasing wave of conservatism within America and the colonial and authoritarian bias in foreign relations created a sense of disenchantment with America's democratic credentials among the developing countries. Whatever doubt remained in their minds regarding America's goodness vanished with America's involvement in Indo-China in defense of European colonialism, the subsequent overthrow of the democratically-elected governments, and successful or failed assassination attempts at the leaders of several Third World countries. These included Mohammad Mossagegh in Iran, Jacobo Arbenz Guzman in Guatemala, Patrice Lumumba in Congo, Achmed Sukarno of Indonesia, Fidel Castro in Cuba, Salvador Allende in Chile, Zhou Enlai, the Chinse premier and Prime Minister Jawaharlal Nehru of India. In each of these episodes, the CIA or its counterparts in other Western European countries were involved.[51] Franklin Roosevelt was 'a sincere opponent of old-style colonialism and wanted the British out of India, the Dutch out of the N.E.I. [Netherlands East Indies], the Americans out of the Philippines, and the French out of Indo-china.'[52] One hoped that Truman would follow in his footsteps. However, at the peak of anti-Communism, anti – Communist sentiments took precedence over all other American ideals. As Freeland suggests:

> In fact, in 1947–48 Truman and his advisers employed all the political and programmatic techniques that in later years were to become associated with the broad phenomenon of McCarthyism. It was the Truman administration that developed the association of dissent with disloyalty and communism, which became a central element of McCarthyism. It was the Truman administration that adopted the peacetime loyalty program, which provided a model for state and local governments and a wide variety of private institutions. It was the Truman administration, in the criteria for loyalty used in its loyalty program, that legitimized the concept of guilt by association, a favorite tactic of McCarthy . . .
>   But in 1947–8, in order to mobilize the country behind his foreign policies, Truman himself employed and permitted his subordinates to employ many of the same means of restricting democratic freedoms that he would later condemn. He legitimized or tried to legitimize for use in peacetime restrictions on traditional freedoms that had previously been limited in application to wartime emergencies. The practices of McCarthyism were Truman's practices in cruder hands, just as the language of McCarthyism was Truman's language, in less well-meaning voices.[53]

Eisenhower carries on a cautious crusade

In 1952 President Dwight D. Eisenhower, with his World War II reputation and anti-Communist rhetoric, was elected by a landslide. With him came John Foster Dulles, the Cold War warrior, who was 'absolutely certain of his

own and his nation's goodness, Dulles's unshakable beliefs were based on
general American ideas. They hardly differed at all from those of Truman,
Acheson, Main Street in Iowa City, or Madison Avenue in New York City. All
the world wanted to be like America; the common people everywhere
looked to America for leadership; Communism was unmitigated evil
imposed by a conspiracy on helpless people, whether it came from the outside as in East Europe or from within as in Asia; there could be no permanent reconciliation with Communism because "this is an irreconcilable
conflict."'[54] By the time Eisenhower was elected, the war in Korea had come
to a stalemate. In his election campaign the new president made a pledge to
end the Korean war and to visit Korea personally 'in the cause of peace.'[55]
Once elected he did go to Korea and, judging the situation at the front,
decided in favor of a peace effort. Stalemate was expensive both in financial
and human terms; a new offensive had little chance to succeed.

Stalin's death brings the armistice nearer

On 26 June 1951, Jacob Malik, the Chief Soviet delegate to the United
Nations, proposed a cease-fire, initiating a series of substantive talks between
General Nam Il of the Korean army and Admiral Joy of the US Navy.[56] On
November 28 the truce was signed and the two armies separated along the
38th parallel, the agreed upon truce line. For the next two years the situation remained at a stalemate, with occasional open confrontation between
the belligerent forces. UN warplanes continued heavy bombardment of
Pyongyang and oil installations as late as September 1952. The last Chinese
assault, ostensibly to gain some last minute advantage before the signing of
the armistice, came on 15 June 1953. In order to put psychological pressures
on the Chinese, Eisenhower claimed that he 'discreetly' let the Chinese
know that:

> in the absence of satisfactory progress, we intended to move decisively
> without inhibition in our use of weapons, and would no longer be
> responsible for confining hostilities to the Korean Peninsula. We would
> not be limited by any world-wide gentleman's agreement. In India and in
> the Formosa Straits area, and at the truce negotiations at Panmunjom, we
> dropped the word, discreetly, of our intention. We felt quite sure it would
> reach Soviet and Chinese Communist ears.
>   Soon the prospects for armistice negotiations seemed to improve.[57]

At a meeting in Bermuda, Dulles also told the British and the French that
nuclear warheads and nuclear-capable aircraft had been moved nearer Korea
(to the US base in Okinawa) and the threat of the intensification of war had
brought the Chinese back to the armistice talks. Thus, both Eisenhower and
Dulles claimed that the threat of the use of atomic weapons and the

extension of the war to the mainland of China brought the armistice nearer. McGeorge Bundy doubts this. He argues that:

> One major difficulty is with dates. It seems probable that the most important Chinese decisions came before the most important American signals. The first indication of a new Chinese seriousness came at the end of March, when the Communist negotiators accepted a six-week-old proposal from General Mark Clark, the UN commander, for an exchange of sick and wounded prisoners . . . . Then on March 30 Zhou Enlai, returning from Stalin's funeral in Moscow, announced a major Chinese concession on the largest single point of disagreement in the truce negotiations. With North Korean concurrence he reversed the previous Communist insistence that all Chinese and North Korean prisoners in UN hands must be repatriated, by force if necessary.[58]

According to Bundy, the Chinese would not have known of the nuclear-capable force's movement before softening their attitude because these movements took place some time in the spring; the Indian warning did not come until Dulles's visit to India in May. No warning could have been given in Panmunjom, because no meeting had taken place. On the basis of information from reliable Chinese sources, Bundy comes to the conclusion that it was largely Stalin's death that brought the armistice nearer.[59] The armistice was signed on 27 July 1953.

Eisenhower sees Asian Communism as a Soviet conspiracy

Eisenhower, like Truman, Acheson, and many others in Washington, saw the spread of Communism as a Soviet conspiracy to take over the world.[60] Hence, Eisenhower argued that the spread of Communism in Vietnam would eventually lead to the conversion of all the Southeast Asian countries one after another into Communism like a row of dominos gradually extending the Soviet sphere of influence and undermining the vital interests of the United States. As McNamara later pointed out, many of the American preconceptions were based on ignorance regarding the strength of the nationalist movements in these countries. It was something bizarre to expect that the countries that had fought and suffered deprivation in their long struggle for independence from European colonizers would so easily surrender their freedom to the Soviet Union, another European country.

Within the United States, the Soviet threat was often played up for the benefit of the domestic audience. As mentioned earlier, an American president has to face the electorate every four years. Elections for a third of the Senate seats take place every two years; and the House of Representatives is elected every two years. As a result, for an American president electioneering is rarely a distant phenomenon. With a large number of immigrants from Russia,

Poland, and other Eastern European countries in the voting population, anti-Soviet rhetoric paid a large political dividend during the Cold War.[61] The anti-Soviet rhetoric worked even better with the Republican Right and the Southern Democrats who wielded considerable influence in Congress. Conscious of their influence and the difficulties they had created for Truman, Eisenhower placated them by accepting their party platform, an extreme right-wing document.[62] The Republican election platform denounced the Truman-Acheson policy of containment as essentially 'negative, futile, and immoral' and promised to rollback the iron curtain to liberate the enslaved world over. Eisenhower appointed several of the favorites of the Right to 'nominally important posts.'[63] All this pleased the Republican Right and the wider electorate, sensitized by the anti-Communist frenzy of the McCarthy days. However, in his inaugural speech, Eisenhower had hardly any firebrand rhetoric to please the Right. While assuring the Americans that he would 'neither compromise, nor tire, nor ever cease' to seek an honorable peace, he stressed that in a nuclear age there was an urgent need for peace, because science had provided mankind the capacity to annihilate itself.[64] Right through his presidency, Eisenhower remained opposed to the use of nuclear weapons.[65] On five occasions in 1954 alone, the NSC, the Joint Chiefs of Staff (JCS), and the State Department advised the president to use atomic bombs against China, but he resisted the temptation.[66]

Eisenhower's covert actions protect big-business

Eisenhower passionately favored covert operations to subvert the spread of Communism, and the CIA was given unprecedented latitude during his administration. Between 1949 and 1952, the number of personnel in the Office of Policy Coordination (OPC), the branch of the Agency responsible for covert operations, rose from 302 to 2812, with an additional 3142 persons overseas under contract with the Agency. During the same period, OPC's budget skyrocketed from a mere $4.7 million to $82 million.[67] In 1949 Congress had already exempted the CIA from all federal laws which would have required it to disclose the details of the terms of appointment of its operatives and had given *carte blanche* regarding the funding of its operations.[68] Two of the CIA's covert operations launched by Eisenhower – one in Iran to overthrow Mossadegh and the other in Guatemala to displace Arbenz – had, in fact, removed two duly elected leaders with little to do with Communism; but both were in favor of policies that might have undermined Western business interests. Mossadegh had attempted to nationaize the British-owned Anglo-Iranian Oil Company; and Arbenz attempted to take over some land owned by the United Fruit Company (UFCO), a US agri-business concern.

After the overthrow of Mossadegh, the Shah of Iran became a loyal ally of the United States, providing facilities for electronic eavesdropping and radar installations, and for launching surveillance flights over the Soviet Union.[69]

In exchange, the CIA trained Shah's torture machine, the Iranian Security and Intelligence Service, the SAVAK, continued to terrorize Iranian dissenters around the globe until the Shah was overthrown by the Ayatollah Khomeini revolution. Inadvertently, the CIA had prepared the groundwork for the overthrow of the Shah. While the continuing SAVAK attrocities added recruits for the Khomeini revolution from among the disenchanted Iranians, supposedly to buy the silence of the fundamentalists, the Agency strengthened the financial base of the Iranian religious hierarchy by paying regularly huge sums until 1977, when President Carter stopped the practice.

Eisenhower also initiated the covert operation in Guatemala. The newly elected president, Jacobo Arbenz Guzman, was no Communist. His main crime was that in the course of implementing his land reform policy (with a highly skewed land ownership in Latin America, land reform was almost a precondition for reducing poverty) he attempted to take over some unused land owned by the United Fruit Company (UFCO), a US agri-business concern. The Guatemalan government was ready to pay $627,572 in compensation based on the tax valuation of the land declared by the UFCO to the Guatemalan tax authorities. The State Department under Dulles pressed for 25 times as much. The fact was that both John Foster Dulles and his brother, CIA director Allen Dulles, had previously worked for a New York law firm with close ties with the UFCO. Similarly, several other members of the Eisenhower administration, Walter Bedell Smith, Eisenhower's aide and undersecretary of state, Anne Whitman, Eisenhower's personal secretary, John M. Cabot, the assistant secretary of state for Inter-American Affairs, all had close associations with the UFCO.[70] The overthrow of Arbenz was followed by a 40-year reign of terror perpetrated by successive military dictatorships under the direct patronage and support of the US government.

Other major covert operations initiated by the Eisenhower administration either failed or were passed on to succeeding administrations. The administration's effort to support the Sumatran and Sulawesi (Indonesia) dissidents with financial and military aid in order to fragment the country in 1957–58 failed dismally.[71] However, the CIA continued to cultivate the Indonesian armed forces. By the time the second opportunity came in 1965, nearly a third of the Indonesian general staff and almost half of the officer corps had been trained in United States.[72] Supported by the CIA and with the active involvement of the American Embassy in Jakarta, the army faction under General Suharto committed massacres of Communist leaders and sympathizers by employing death squads. The death totals remain debatable but at least half a million Indonesians are estimated to have been killed.[73] The *New York Times* called the massacre 'one of the most savage mass slaughters of modern political history.'[74] As Kathy Kadane of States News Service has pointed out, this 'mass murder' was conducted with the direct involvement of United States officials, with the approval of Marshall Green, the American ambassador in Jakarta.[75] The Johnson administration was duly informed about the cruelties. In the words of Howard Federspiel, the Indonesia expert at the State Department's Bureau of Intelligence and Research, 'No one cared, as long as they were Communists, that they were being butchered.'[76]

In this case too, protecting American big business was one of the main reasons for the slaughter.[77] Sukarno had taken over the Good Year Tire and Rubber Company, one of the biggest American operations in Indonesia, and had forced the oil companies to enter into new contracts requiring them to pay 60 per cent of the profits to the Indonesian government.[78]

Perhaps the most famous of the CIA's covert operations related to the overthrow of Castro in Cuba, which ended up in the Bay of Pigs fiasco during the Kennedy administration.[79] Early in 1960 Eisenhower authorized an invasion of Cuba by an army of exiled Cubans armed, trained, and directed by the CIA. John Kennedy, the new president, gave a go-ahead, albeit reluctantly. The Cuban forces mopped up the landing force of fourteen or fifteen hundred exiled Cubans within three days. Interestingly, until early 1959, neither Dulles nor Nixon thought Castro was a Communist.[80] Right through 1959, the Eisenhower administration assured Castro of financial assistance, but Castro's stance on non-alignment irked the administration. So did his attempts to nationalize the sugar industry, which affected American business interests.

The CIA also mounted a covert hit-and-run operation in China with the help of Nationalist China's soldiers who had escaped into Burma. The largest raid came as early as April 1951. In this raid a few thousand Nationalist soldiers, aided by CIA advisers and supported by air drops of arms and ammunitions by American planes, moved into Yunnan province. They were driven back by the PRC forces with heavy casualties, including several CIA personnel. These hit-and-run operations continued intermittently until January 1961.[81]

Another CIA venture against China involved its alliance with the Tibetan rebels. This covert operation, directed from New Delhi and subsequently from Kathmandu, transported Tibetan rebels from India to Taiwan, Guam, Saipan, Okinawa and, for a time, to Colorado for training, after which they were airdropped into Tibet. Tibetian discontent with the Chinese for undermining Buddhism and Tibet's traditional customs and manners, the colonization of Tibet by the Han, and the harsh treatment of Tibetans at the hands of the People's Liberation Army (PLA) were increasing the numbers of rebels. By 1957, as many as 80,000 Tibetans and another 10,000 bandits and local tribesmen were estimated to be fighting the Chinese.[82]

Hit-and-run raids aimed at destroying roads and ambushing the Chinese soldiers continued. The viability of the project became much more questionable after the capture of Gary Powers, one of the CIA pilots flying U2 spy planes over the Soviet Union. Until then, the United States government had denied that such flights were taking place, and that Powers was not authorized to fly over the Soviet Union.[83] Out of sheer embarrassment, Eisenhower ordered the cessation of all flights into Communist air space. This came as the death knell to CIA operations into Tibet, because supplying the Tibetan rebels by land was inordinately difficult. Subsequently, John Kenneth Galbraith, appointed by John F. Kennedy as the ambassador to India, convinced him of the utter futility of the project. The CIA was forced to relocate the direction of the operation to Nepal. There it continued until 1973, when, under pressure from Beijing, the king of Nepal moved against the Tibetan rebels operating from Nepal. A few leaders escaped; the others were arrested and imprisoned.

China begins shelling Quemoy and Matsu islands

A major confrontation between the Chinese and the Eisenhower administration came in September 1954 when the Communist government began to shell Quemoy and Matsu, two tiny islands near the mainland occupied by the Nationalists and used for hit-and-run raids into China, and to disrupt coastal shipping. Eisenhower's Joint Chiefs of Staff recommended the direct involvement of American forces and the bombing of the mainland, which Eisenhower rejected outright. However, he did obtain the authority from Congress 'to employ the armed forces of this nation [the United States] promptly and effectively for the purposes indicated if in his judgment it became necessary.'[84] He also allowed Dulles to let it be publicly known that the United States, in the eventuality of a war in the Formosan Straits, might use some small tactical weapons. On 16 March 1955, Eisenhower, in response to a question from Charles von Fremd, a CBS journalist, explicitly stated that 'they would be used.'[85] Beijing took the threat seriously and on 23 April at the Bandung conference, Zhou stated that the Chinese Communists did not want a war with the United States and were prepared to negotiate. He further stated that Beijing was not prepared to give up striving 'for the liberation of Formosa by peaceful means as far as this is possible.'[86] By mid-May shelling of the two islands had ceased.

In the first half of 1962 a new crisis situation arose, this time created by Chiang. The mainland was suffering from a serious famine as a result of the excesses of the Great Leap and the rapid organization of unmanageably large communes in rural areas. Naturally, this fomented a period of major discontent on the mainland. Communist China and the Soviet Union were also engaged in a bitter ideological struggle, so much so that the Soviet Union had withdrawn its experts from China; many of them had left with blueprints of unfinished construction projects. It was no surprise that Chiang wanted to take advantage of the situation. In response, the Communist government began to concentrate ground troops and the air force in Fujian Province. President John F. Kennedy was as committed to the defense of Formosa as his predecessors. However, chastened by his Bay of Pigs misadventure, he made it clear that the American commitment was defensive in nature and that he would not support Chiang in any offensive against Communist China. He also let a similar message be conveyed to the Chinese through ambassadorial talks in Warsaw. This had a sobering effect on both sides and further confrontation was averted.[87]

Kennedy and Johnson expand US commitment in Vietnam

Kennedy also believed in the 'domino theory' and felt that the fall of South Vietnam would lead to the loss of Southeast Asia. In September 1963, Kennedy told Chet Huntley on NBC television categorically that if South Vietnam went, other Southeast Asian countries might follow.[88]

All of his policymaking team, including Dean Rusk, Kennedy's choice for secretary of state, held similar views; the only exceptions were Chester Bowles, then undersecretary of state, who subsequently became the ambassador to India, and his successor, George Ball. There remained strong support in Congress for containment and defense of Vietnam and Southeast Asia. Therefore, Kennedy readily approved a major expansion of the US commitment in Vietnam within a few days of taking over the presidency.[89] At the time of Kennedy's inauguration there were no more than 750 American military advisors; at the time of his assassination, there were as many as 20,000, many of them actively engaged in combat.[90]

Like his predecessors, Kennedy remained wedded to the ideas of nonrecognition of the PRC and opposition to Chinese entry into the United Nations. On the other hand, he sensed that there was something unreal about America's China policy. He stated that the United States was 'not wedded to a policy of hostility to Red China.'[91]

He also showed much greater understanding about the 'non-alignment' of the Third World and, contrary to Eisenhower's impatience with Sukarno, developed a friendly relationship with him. He agreed to supply arms to India at the time of the Chinese invasion of India without insisting on India entering into a security arrangement with the United States

McNamara tells us that as early as 2 October 1963, Kennedy had also decided to withdraw American troops from Vietnam. The withdrawal of one thousand troops had to be completed by the end of 1963, and a complete withdrawal of all American troops by the end of 1965.[92] However, William Bundy suggests that Kennedy was opposed to withdrawal except in the case of 'most dire extremes.'[93] Robert Kennedy, in an oral history interview with John Bartlow Martin of the John F. Kennedy Library, also categorically stated that there was no consideration given to withdrawal. On the other hand, McNamara quotes from a tape kept in the John F. Kennedy Library and made accessible to him by the Kennedy family. From what we know of John Kennedy's pragmatism and his capacity to learn from past mistakes, McNamara's revelations may not be surprising, yet Robert Kennedy's lack of knowledge of the above fact is somewhat surprising. In any case, the withdrawal did not take place because President Johnson, who succeeded Kennedy, wanted to 'win the war,' and in his search for an elusive victory escalated the war so much so that by the end of 1966 nearly half a million American soldiers were fighting in Vietnam. In 1964 and 1965, he ordered the bombing of North Vietnam, which increased China's concern for its own security. The Chinese had given Hanoi advice and assistance in their fight against the French, but the Chinese effort intensified after the American bombing of North Vietnam.[94]

Nixon disregards international law

President Nixon's Vietnam policy was virtually 'the extension and exaggeration of the Johnson policy. It aimed at achieving the same results but used military power more brutally and recklessly.'[95] This included the massive bombing of Cambodia and Laos (both neutral countries) and the covert pacification or neutralization program.[96] Richard Falk, the Milbank Professor of International Law at Princeton University, points out that the Phoenix Program, aerial and naval bombardment of undefended villages, destruction of crops and forests, 'search-and-destroy missions,' 'harassment and interdiction' fire, forcible removal of civilian populations, and the reliance on a variety of weapons prohibited by treaty followed on a massive scale and those responsible for the policies ought to be prosecuted as war criminals.[97] However, none of the American actions succeeded in breaking the morale of the North Vietnamese leadership, which launched a major conventional offensive in 1972. In response, the Nixon administration further intensified the bombing of the North, including Hanoi, and mined Haiphong harbor. The administration claimed that this intensified bombing brought the North Vietnamese leaders to Paris to negotiate a 'peace with honor,' to use Nixon's phrase, and a peace accord was signed on 27 January 1973. This, as Sulzberger wrote, 'theoretically put a formal end to the Vietnam War, but in fact all it accomplished was a means of swiftly withdrawing US troops, abandoning to its own considerable resources a bewildered South Vietnamese government.'[98] In a queer twist of fate, America ultimately lost South Vietnam to Communism in Paris in 1973, which it could possibly have saved if it had not undermined the Geneva Accord of 1954.

Nixon seeks China's help for ending the Vietnam War

The Chinese, were at the Geneva Conference of 1954. John Foster Dulles had refused even to shake hands with Zhou Enlai. Yet when the time came to extricate America from the Vietnam War, President Nixon – a former McCarthyite congressman – embarked on a 'self-invited' state visit to China. Admittedly, Vietnam alone did not inspire Nixon go to China; he had already conceded in a 1967 *Foreign Affairs* article that 'any American policy toward Asia must come urgently to grips with the reality of China.'[99] The same year, during a visit to India, he told Chester Bowles, the American ambassador to India, that in his view, 'good relationships with China were more important than good relations with the Soviet Union.'[100] In 1968 the Chinese leadership had also begun to put out feelers toward reconciliation. Even before assuming office, Nixon sent a message to China through the French President, General De Gaulle, that he was in favor of 'normalization of relations.' He also 'foresaw the admission of Peking to the United Nations.'

President Nixon's visit certainly opened the way for normalization of the Sino-American relationship. Sino-American contacts, established in the mid-1950s, continued either 'by proxy through third world countries' or bilateral talks even at ambassadorial levels in third countries or at international conferences.[101] As Barnett stresses, 'From 1959 on it was Washington rather than Peking that pressed for agreement on secondary issues, such as the exchange of newsmen and an increase of other nonofficial contacts. On these issues, its positions became increasingly flexible.'[102]

Kennedy talked of not only broadening non-official contacts but also of the possibility of providing food to China [in the famine years in the wake of the Great Leap] and the need to include China in disarmament talks. 'But Kennedy, fearful of the domestic political costs of dealing with the controversial China issue, deferred consideration of substantial changes in China policy.'[103]

A Senate Foreign Relations Committee hearing on China policy in 1966 found considerable public support for a new China policy, and in response President Johnson came out in favor of a reconciliation; however, too engrossed with Vietnam, he did very little.[104] Hubert Humphrey, the Democratic nominee for the presidency, called for 'the building of bridges to the people of mainland China' and a partial removal of the trade embargo. Nelson Rockefeller, Nixon's rival for the Republican nomination, had also advocated opening the channels of communications with China.[105] Several prominent Democrats – including Senator Edward Kennedy – favored a change in the United States policies; several expressed their desire to visit China.[106] Nixon trumped the Democrats and ensured his chances of being re-elected by being the first American dignitary to visit China. In fact, Nixon had, through Pakistan and Henry Kissinger, asked the Chinese not to grant visas to Democrats before his own visit.[107]

In this context, Nixon's idea to normalize relations with China was not original. Nevertheless, he succeeded in changing the policies because of his credentials as a one-time McCarthyite Communist-hater. He was also favored by circumstances. By this time there was an enormous opposition to the Vietnam War in America because increasing numbers of young American men were returning home in coffins.[108] The country wanted America out of Vietnam and Nixon, during his election campaign, promised to end America's involvement in the war. George Ball credits the Nixon administration for three major diplomatic moves:

First, it sought to correct two aberrations of existing American policy – our involvement in Vietnam and our lack of communications
with China.

Second, it took advantage of the Soviet Union's tactical decision to
adopt a less bellicose attitude toward the West by encouraging a mutual
improvement in manners ambiguously called *détente*, which led to
understandings in limited areas of direct bilateral relations.

Third, it undertook diplomatic efforts to buy time in the Middle East.[109]

The first two of the administration's diplomatic achievements are directly
relevant to our subject matter. Nixon hoped that by normalizing relations
with China, the Chinese might help the administration extricate America
from the Vietnam War. However, the process of normalization with China
itself was a major achievement.

To put things into proper perspective, both Kennedy and Johnson would
have liked to normalize relations with China, but Kennedy was elected by a
very slim majority and was worried about the influence of the Republican
Right. He left the question of the recognition of the People's Republic to be
tackled during his second term. He also felt that the war in Vietnam should
be fought by the South Vietnamese themselves and was in favor of withdrawing American troops from Vietnam by the end of 1965. Thus, it was
Kennedy who originated the idea of 'Vietnamization' of the war, a policy
later implemented by Nixon.

Kennedy's belief in coexistence is self-evident from his speech at the
American University in 1963. He said: 'World peace . . . does not require
that each man love his neighbor . . . only that they live together in
mutual tolerance, submitting their disputes to a just and peaceful settlement.'[110] During every crisis involving the Soviet Union – in Berlin,
Southeast Asia, and Cuba – he kept in touch with Khrushchev, persuading
him 'to return to the path of accommodation, to prevent violence and
distrust from reproducing themselves.'[111] Johnson continued Kennedy's
policy of *détente*. As he himself told Ludwig Erhard, the German chancellor, America was going down the road to peace and *détente* with the Soviet
Union 'with or without others.'[112] Johnson did not have to labor the
point because the thinking on *détente* had gone ahead for some time in
West Germany.

The 'replacement of the Cold War with a new view of how to deal with
the Soviet Union was becoming the philosophical basis for the entire policy
of *détente* as it was practiced by West Germany from the mid-1960s until the
late 1970s.'[113] By the 1960s, the new liberalism, supported by the academic
intelligentsia and its students, was replacing old-style conservatism in West
Germany.[114] Its ideas of *détente* and *Ostpolitik* (Eastern policy) flourished
under Willy Brandt and Helmut Schmidt. The exaggerated American concern that Brandt's policy of *détente* with the Soviet Union might increase the

influence of the Russians in West Germany and lead to the 'finlandization' of West Germany pushed Nixon and Kissinger to move ahead with *détente* with the Soviet Union.[115] De Gaulle advocated *détente* even earlier. He wrote in his memoirs:

> My aim, then, was to disengage France, not from the Atlantic alliance, which I intended to maintain by way of ultimate precaution, but from the integration realized by NATO under American command; to establish relations with each of the States of the Eastern bloc, first and foremost Russia, with the object of bringing about a *détente* followed by understanding and co-operation; to do likewise, when the time was ripe, with China; and finally, to provide France with a nuclear capability such that no one could attack us without running the risk of frightful injury.[116]

While admitting that there was not much in Nixon's China or Vietnam policies that could be considered strictly original, he was still prepared to grasp the nettle in the hour of need, taking advantage of the growing split between the two Communist giants. In so doing, he 'unquestionably left its imprint on American foreign policy.'[117] There is certainly some truth in Kissinger's claim that much of the American major foreign policies practiced 'today were designed originally during the Nixon presidency.'[118]

Whether the initiation of talks with China needed the secrecy or the melodrama is still questionable, yet the normalization of relations with China was long overdue. Arguably, secrecy was intended to minimize opposition from the Republican Right. However, Kissinger needed secrecy for his own reasons. He disliked Secretary of State William Rogers and wanted to undercut him. Kissinger even intended to downplay Nixon's role, telling an Italian journalist, Oriana Fallaci, that he [Kissinger] 'always acted alone.'[119] Melodrama played up the events to guarantee Nixon's reelection.

Nixon plays the China card

The time was ripe for some agreement; both China and America felt they needed each other and were prepared to make concessions. The Americans accepted that there was only one China and that Taiwan was a province of China. The Chinese, on their part, accepted that they would try to reincorporate Taiwan by peaceful means, but never gave up the military option. The Mao–Nixon meeting opened the way to normalization of the US relations with China.[120] By this time, the Sino-Soviet discord that began brewing in the late fifties had boiled into an open confrontation in March 1969. The provocation quite possibly came from China, which claimed Damansky Island (Zhengbao in Chinese) on the Usury River to be Chinese territory, while the Soviet Union was ready to defend its own claim. Naturally the Nixon administration took advantage of this open confrontation; it perfectly fitted Nixon's plan to normalize relations with China. It was hoped, though repeatedly denied, that the 'China card' would be useful to obtain concessions from the Soviet Union in forthcoming arms reduction negotiations. For their part, the Chinese leaders were increasingly suspicious of Soviet designs on China and were worried about the risk of the Soviet Union attempting to launch a preemptive strike on China's nascent nuclear weapon producing facilities. China saw America as a counterbalancing force.

However, the Chinese were not prepared to accept at face value Kissinger's repeated attempts to convince them of a major Soviet invasion of China. Nixon, in a letter to Mao on 16 March, even gave a unilateral commitment that the United States would intervene militarily if the Soviet Union attacked China.[121] Mao remained ever skeptical of Nixon's sincerity, perhaps for the right reasons. Any United States military involvement in support of China would have meant a nuclear war with the Soviet Union, a prospect which no American leader could easily contemplate. Even the West Germans felt that the United States 'could not be counted upon to risk its survival to defend Europe in a nuclear war.'[122] Mao also made this point to Kissinger in one of their meetings.[123] The Chinese, in spite of Kissinger's prodding to put military pressure on India during the Indo-Pakistan war in East Pakistan (now Bangladesh), refused to do so. Nor did they agree to help America extricate itself from the Vietnam War. The groundwork for the normalization of relations with China that the Nixon–Kissinger diplomacy had so assiduously laid did not come to fruition during the Nixon days except in a symbolic sense, with the two countries establishing liaison offices on a reciprocal basis.[124]

The Chinese were not ready to proceed with regular diplomatic relations before the United States discontinued its diplomatic relations with Taiwan. On the other hand, the Watergate scandal had increased the dependence of the enfeebled Nixon presidency on the Republican Right, which was totally opposed to abandoning Taiwan. This stymied Nixon and his successor, Gerald Ford. During Kissinger's visit to China in October 1975 to arrange a meeting between Ford and the Chinese leadership, the draft for a joint communiqué was rejected by the Chinese, and Ford's visit had to be concluded without a communiqué.[125] It was during his October 1975 visit that Kissinger had proposed intelligence and military cooperation.[126] Ford's China visit became a virtual non-event.

Initially, the Chinese rejected proposals for both the sharing of intelligence and military alliance. Mao felt it was premature.[127] The only time a serious military cooperation was considered was during the Ford visit. This referred to a covert military operation in Angola against the Soviet-backed Popular Movement for the Liberation of Angola (MPLA). This decision could not be implemented because news of the CIA covert operation leaked to Washington, and the Senate cut-off its funding. The CIA was asked to terminate its Angola operations.[128] The sharing of military intelligence, in its initial stages, remained unilateral. During the Nixon administration, Kissinger regularly passed on military intelligence to the Chinese ambassador in Washington. Kissinger also took military intelligence with him to Beijing to be passed on to the Chinese.[129]

Carter recognizes China

The Carter administration finally officially recognized China on 1 January 1979, and normalized relations by discontinuing diplomatic relations with Taiwan.[130] The Chinese agreed not to use force to reincorporate Taiwan unless Taiwan took too long to negotiate or if they attempted to negotiate an alliance with the Soviet Union.[131] Carter's recognition of China and the abandonment of Taiwan infuriated the conservatives in Congress; a number of them brought a law suit in federal court challenging the constitutionality of the president's action. The case failed in the Court of Appeals, a verdict also supported by the Supreme Court. Later, Congress passed the Taiwan Relations Act, which has constantly undermined presidential foreign policy regarding China.

The question of Chinese entry into the United Nations had already been resolved by a snap vote in the General Assembly on 25 October 1971. The People's Republic was admitted to the United Nations, and Nationalist China (Formosa) was forced out by a two-thirds majority (76 for and 35 against).[132] George Bush, the American ambassador to the United Nations, desperately tried to postpone such action or at least to secure the continuation of Taiwan in the world body. Kissinger also supported a dual representation; he had worked hard, without much success, to persuade the Chinese leadership to accept a 'two-China' formula.

Deng Xiaoping, who had survived the two purges and returned to seats of power, made his triumphal visit to America during Carter's administration and was given a welcome fit for a head of state, which in the formal sense he was not. In the course of this visit the Carter administration proposed an intelligence co-operation to monitor Soviet strategic missile sites and troop movements. Deng decided to provide a surveillance facility in western China to replace the monitoring station in Iran which the United States lost in the wake of the Khomeini revolution.[133] Deng also obtained the tacit consent of Carter for the Chinese invasion of Vietnam to 'teach [them] a lesson.' Carter also opened the door for China to buy military hardware and advanced technology from the United States. The administration arranged for the Chinese to procure jet engine manufacturing technology and nuclear reactor technology from European sources.[134] The Carter administration also gave China Most Favored Nation (MFN) status, which was denied to the Soviet Union. China and America negotiated a civil aviation agreement allowing airlines to fly directly to the two countries, and a maritime agreement to open the ports to each other's ships. America also agreed to allow increased shipment of textiles from China.[135]

Carter's human rights hypocrisy

Carter had introduced human rights as a tool of American foreign policy and made loud noises about the Soviet Union's infringements of human rights. However, he kept silent on the transgression of human rights in China, even when the leaders of the Democracy Movement were being imprisoned in large numbers. The crackdown lasted for two years; hundreds were imprisoned, many were incarcerated in labor camps.[136] Carter did not say much when the Chinese constitution was amended to take away the peoples' right to 'four freedoms:' speaking out freely, airing views freely, holding great debates, and writing big character posters. The 'four freedoms' were incorporated into the Chinese Constitution in 1975 on Mao's insistence; Deng got them deleted from the Constitution in 1980. Carter remained silent when the Democracy Wall was closed to the public.[137] Until then, the Wall could be used by anyone to post one's grievances against the Party or government officials and remained accessible to people even during the heyday of the Cultural Revolution. Deng closed it.[138] During his presidential visit to Beijing, Carter feigned ignorance when asked by a journalist about Wei Jingsheng, who was serving a 15-year prison sentence for his prodemocracy writings critical of Mao, Deng, and the Communist Party.

Carter also boasted that he would never 'want to do anything as President that would be a contravention of the moral and ethical standard that I would exemplify in my own life as an individual.'[139] Yet Carter supported Pol Pot, a person indiscriminately killing and torturing his fellow Cambodians. The Carter administration and the Chinese had come to support Pol Pot because the Vietnamese had recently joined the Soviet-led Council for Mutual Economic Assistance (COMECON).[140] Raphael Iungerich, the chief Indochina analyst of the State Department, told Nayan Chanda, a veteran Indian journalist, that 'it was the Vietnamese who were being ambushed within Vietnamese territory. It was happening against the Thais also that summer. So we were all looking upon this wild dog Pol Pot as the pariah of the whole region, as the original terrorist.'[141] Yet, the Carter administration voted for the Pol Pot regime retaining the Cambodian seat in the United Nations. The Vietnamese were also keen to normalize relations with the United States, but under the influence of Zbigniew Brzezinski, the president's national security adviser, Carter decided to keep the Vietnamese normalization on hold. Later, the administration provided *post facto* justification in terms of Vietnam's treaty with Moscow, its invasion of Cambodia, and the surge of boat people.[142] This claim was chronologically unjustifiable because, as shown by Nayan Chanda, 'The first two developments took place well after the October 11 decision by Carter, and the boat people exodus reached crisis proportions only in the summer of 1979.'[143] Following in the footsteps of Kissinger, Brzezinski provided intelligence to the Chinese ambassador, Chai Zemin, virtually every night.[144] Thus, for Carter, like many other political heavyweights in America – as seems to be happening currently with George W. Bush in his 'War against Terror' who is in coalition with some of the worst human rights trangressors – the issue of human rights was not a matter of conviction, but another weapon in America's cold war armory.

US–China military cooperation flourishes under Reagan

President Reagan, who succeeded President Carter, had been a supporter of Taiwan for a long time, and reportedly received financial support from Taiwan for his political organization.[145] Initially Reagan was keen to upgrade the United States' official relations with Taiwan, but he was persuaded to drop the idea lest it affect his electoral prospects. Even after his election as president, he maintained his hard line policies against China until he was convinced that China was cooperating in anti-Soviet action in Afghanistan. By this time China was cooperating with the United States and Thailand in supplying weapons to Afghan guerrillas fighting against the Soviet Union. Many of the arms came from China, paid for by the CIA.[146] For this cooperation, China not only earned a considerable amount of foreign exchange against the sale of weapons, but also received Reagan's clearance for buying lethal weapons and advanced technology for its own use. Under his administration the exchange of military personnel flourished. From 1984 onwards, China was declared eligible for America's Foreign Military Sales Program, enabling China to obtain United States government funding for arms purchases in America.[147] Unfortunately, one of the biggest arms deals – to upgrade the Chinese F-8 jets, modeled on the Soviet MIG-21 – floundered and led to financial disputes between the two countries.

Like Ford's visit to China, Reagan's trip also became a virtual non-event; nothing much of substance was achieved. President Reagan was virtually rebuffed; his two speeches mentioning 'faith' and 'freedom,' remarks prejudicial to the Soviet Union, were deleted before being broadcast. The third speech, delivered to the students at Fudan University in Shanghai, was broadcast but only in English, thus ensuring that it would not reach the majority of the Chinese audience. The Chinese also came out frustrated because they failed to persuade the Reagan administration to convince Taiwan to talk about its peaceful re-incorporation into the mainland along the lines of Hong Kong; a 'one country, two systems' deal between Beijing and London had paved the way for the British to hand over the territory in 1997. Deng's proposal for a similar system for Taiwan, remained a dead letter. US sales of arms to Taiwan also continued in spite of Chinese complaints.

China's sales of arms, particularly missiles, to the Middle Eastern countries, became the other bone of contention. In 1987, American intelligence discovered that China sold Silkworm land-to-ship missiles to Iran. Even when confronted with the evidence, the Chinese denied selling any missiles to Iran. In retaliation, the Reagan administration imposed economic sanctions restricting the export of high technology products. Soon thereafter, it came to light that China was selling CSS-2 missiles to Saudi Arabia and planning to sell more advanced M-9 and M-11 missiles to Syria, Libya, Iran, and Pakistan. The sales to Syria, Libya, and Iran – viewed by America as unfriendly countries – were particularly disturbing to the Reagan administration. Delicate bargaining between the two governments secured some concessions from China in exchange for export licenses allowing Chinese Long March rockets to launch American commercial satellites, even though such launches drastically undercut American competitors.[148]

Tiananmen massacre strains Bush's friendship with China

President George Bush, who succeeded Reagan, had cultivated the Chinese leadership over a decade. The uncontrollable events that overtook China during his presidency made his tenure barren of any significant achievement to advance the Sino-American relationship. The Democracy Movement in China, which Deng smothered in the late seventies, had not died but simply gone underground. High prices, unemployment, undermining of welfare provisions, and rampant corruption and nepotism that came in the wake of Deng's economic reform generated a lot of discontent and added significant numbers to the ranks of supporters for the movement from among the Chinese masses.

By this time, news of Mikhail Gorbachev's *perestroika* (reform), and *glasnost* (openness), giving unprecedented personal freedom and freedom of expression to individuals and the media in the Soviet Union, had reached China. This was a matter of hope for the students who, with their long tradition of activism in China, were pressuring the government to institute political reforms together with economic reforms. To impress upon the government the need for political reforms, student activists organized mass demonstrations in 80 cities throughout China.[149] On the occasion of the memorial service for Hu Yaobang, one of the few leaders popular with the students for his liberal views and unpretentiousness, students in Beijing assembled in large numbers in Tiananmen Square.[150] This was a way of expressing their displeasure with Deng's dismissal of Hu Yaobang from his party secretary position. Students had also demonstrated in large numbers on the occasion of the funeral of Zhou Enlai to protest against the treatment meted out to Zhou who, by the time he died, was criticized by Mao and disgraced by the Red Guards. Students assembling in Tiananmen Square at the time of Hu's memorial service were mainly interested in dialogue with the leadership and were not contemplating anything other than passive resistance.

The party old guard, including Deng, with their experience of the chaos and near civil war situation during the Cultural Revolution, saw the student unrest as the ominous sign of further trouble. The economic and political confusion and the partial disintegration of the Soviet Union in the wake of Gorbachev's reforms had presumably further convinced the Chinese leadership of the risks of hasty political democratization in China. They opted for a hard-line response to the students' demand for dialogue. On 19 May the Politburo decided to employ the military to force the students out of Tiananmen Square.[151] The stalemate continued for the next two weeks. On the fateful day of 3 June the troops opened fire, often indiscriminately, killing and maiming hundreds.[152] Most of those killed were workers and bystanders.[153] During the following weeks, thousands of students and intellectuals were interrogated, arrested, and deprived of their jobs, but they were not executed, as were the workers who had participated in the demonstration.[154]

President Bush, like Nixon and Kissinger, more concerned with maintaining the rather fragile link with the Chinese leadership than with human rights or democracy, was not inclined to take drastic punitive measures against China, nor even a symbolic gesture of withdrawing the American ambassador. Nevertheless, he had to act under pressure from Congress and the knowledgeable Americans, who witnessed the massacre on the television screen. The international media happened to be in Beijing at the time to document Gorbachev's visit. Bush suspended all military sales to China, and all visits by American and Chinese military officials in either direction were put on hold. Later, as the arrests and execution of suspected dissidents escalated, Bush suspended all high level official contacts.

In the meantime, both houses of Congress had passed more comprehensive sanctions. However, in his anxiety not to jeopardize the American relationship with China, Bush secretly sent Brent Scowcroft, the national security adviser, and Lawrence Eagleburger, the deputy secretary of state, to Beijing to assure Deng that the sanctions were temporary and that Bush was anxious to preserve the relationship, but needed some help from Deng to do so. Deng met Scowcroft and Eagleburger but made it clear that in the context of the punishments of the dissidents, the Bush administration had little influence. Repression in China continued, yet Bush approved the sale of four Boeing 757 passenger planes to the Chinese national airline.

During Nixon's private visit in the autumn of 1989 Deng indicated that he was prepared to mend fences, but he said that the initiative had to come from the United States. In response, Bush sent Scowcroft and Eagleburger again, this time publicly. Even before martial law was lifted, Bush approved the sale of Hughes Aircraft communications satellites to be launched by Chinese rockets and asked the Export-Import Bank to resume lending to American firms engaged in business in China.[155] The first loan after the resumption amounted to $9.75 million, advanced to China National Offshore Oil Corporation to buy the engineering services of a New Orleans company.[156] With his eyes on reelection, Bush had to keep US big business on his side. To placate both Chinese leadership and US business interests, Bush also renewed China's MFN status, remaining opposed to watering down the provisions of MFN as retaliation for human rights abuses in China. The World Bank and other international agencies were also allowed to resume lending to China. In return the Chinese agreed to issue more exit visas to students completing their jail sentences. Another olive branch to the administration was the Chinese consent for Fang Lizhi, a well-known dissenter, to leave China with his family for the United States. This action followed a pattern long-established in negotiations with the Soviet Union on human rights, in which one or more prominent dissenters were allowed to leave the Soviet Union for residence in the United States.

The most significant outcome was the Chinese agreement not to export M-11 missiles to Syria or Pakistan and commitment to abide by the guidelines of the Missile Technology Control Regime (MTCR), even though it was not prepared to join the regime. The Chinese government also hinted at its willingness to sign the Nuclear Non-Proliferation Treaty.[157] However, to date the Chinese record of abiding by these regimes has remained mixed.[158]

The influence of American big business in US official policy making can clearly be seen from another incident which occurred during President Bush's regime. Taking advantage of the uncertainties of Bush's reelection, American friends of Taiwan virtually conspired with General Dynamics and the Texas congressional delegation to convince Bush that he could not carry Texas in the November elections unless he sanctioned the sale of F-16 fighters to Taiwan. In line with the argument, General Dynamics let it be publicly known that a failure to secure new orders for F-16s would force the company to lay-off 5 800 workers at its Fort Worth factory.[159] For Bush, reelection was more important than the national commitment given to the Chinese on 17 August 1982 that the future 'arms sales to Taiwan will not exceed, either in qualitative or quantitative terms, the levels of those supplied in recent years.' The Chinese leadership has continued to blame the United States government for violating the spirit of the commitment on arms sales to Taiwan and has implicitly taken this as a license for its own undermining of non-proliferation regimes.[160]

Conclusion

The Chinese entry – albeit reluctantly – into the Korean War marked the beginning of Sino-American confrontation. Chinese overtures and the advice of friendly countries for a peaceful settlement were repeatedly rejected by President Truman for fear of conservative backlash in Congress. To appease the Republican Right, Truman not only greatly expanded the US armed forces but created a security apparatus to make the Central Intelligence Agency and others immune from democratic oversight. Truman's 'ideologogical crusade' was not necessarily a reaction to an imminent Soviet threat; at that time the Soviet Union was too weak to challenge the American might. Truman's objectives were mainly domestic; invariably domestic considerations have had much sway on foreign policy formulations with most presidents.

His advisers had come to the conclusion that the president's anti-Communist stand would sit well both with the conservatives in Congress and with the American public, particularly those who had immigrated from Russia and the Eastern European countries. In appeasing the conservatives, Truman unhesitatingly sacrificed American values. He instituted a peacetime loyalty program only nine days after the Truman Doctrine speeech.[161] Government employees were required to prove their patriotism without the benefit of confronting their accusers to knowing the explicit charges against them.[162] Democratic freedom was put at risk, as it was placed in the hands of those 'whose values are the values of dictatorship and whose methods are the methods of the police state.'[163]

The president's electoral prospects in early 1948 were rather dim. With the introduction of the Truman Doctrine and the Loyalty Program, and a hard-line policy toward Communists within America, his rating jumped from 35 per cent to 60 per cent in March.

Both Kennedy and Johnson, fearing the wrath of the conservatives in Congress, failed to normalize relations with China. President Nixon succeeded in initiating the process mainly because of his earlier credentials as a Communist-basher.

Under Carter and Reagan, China, estranged from the Soviet Union, came to be seen as a military ally entitled to advanced military equipment and technology. Even an ardent human rights advocate like Carter remained silent about the Chinese infringement of human rights while voicing serious criticisms of Soviet abuses. Carter's support of the murderous Pot Pol regime left the world wondering whether the issue of human rights was a matter of conscience or convenience for the president. Even the Tiananmen Square massacre brought down only lukewarm sanctions by the George Bush administration.

Since the Nixon administration opened China to US foreign relations, the relationship between China and the United States has progressed, albeit with hiccups, coming to full maturity under the Clinton presidency. The future shape of the policy under the George W. Bush administration remains uncertain; whether it is going to be confrontational or conciliatory on the lines of Clinton's policy of 'engagement.' This is the subject matter of the next chapter.

4
Clinton and Bush: Contrasts in World View

> . . . There is clear evidence that the United States is moving away from its long-established concern for and advocacy of international legal norms of state behavior.
>
> . . . International law changes, just as domestic law changes. We are fully within our rights to propose changes; to limit or withdraw commitments. What we must not do is act as if the subject was optional, essentially rhetorical. For it is a fearfully dangerous thing, the thing most to be feared, to hold that some laws bind the president but others do not.
>
> (Senator Daniel Patrick Moynihan[1])

Introduction

By the time President Clinton took office in 1993, the world had changed immeasurably. In December 1988, Soviet Premier Mikhail Gorbachev gave an assurance that he would withdraw the Soviet forces from Afghanistan within a year in his speech to the United Nations General Assembly. Renouncing 'class-conflict' as the basis for Soviet foreign policy, he stressed that he would convert the Soviet armament-economy into an economy of disarmament. The year 1989 proved to be momentous. It not only saw the withdrawal of the Soviet troops from Afghanistan, but also witnessed the beginning of multi-party elections, ending the political monopoly of the Communist Party in the USSR and in Poland, where the Solidarity-led coalition came to power by defeating the Communists. A peaceful political transition from Communism to democracy came rather quickly in all the Eastern European countries except Romania, where the struggle ended with the execution of Communist dictator Nicolae Ceausescu and his wife. Gradually, Ukraine and other Central Asian republics became independent. As one of his critics later pointed out, 'the Soviet Union that Gorbachev inherited in 1985 was a global power, perhaps somewhat tarnished in that image, but still strong and united and one of the world's two superpowers.

But in just three years, from 1989 to 1991, the political frontiers of the European continent were effectively rolled eastward to the Russian borders of 1653, which were those before Russia's union with Ukraine.'[2] By the time Gorbachev was forced to resign, Russia, the successor state of the Soviet Union, did not pose a real military threat to the United States.

'It's the economy, stupid'

Having 'won' the Cold War, it was natural for the only remaining superpower to maintain its immense technological lead over both friend and foe. During the Cold War years, much of the technological progress, largely subsidized by the defense budget, was geared to the development and production of increasingly sophisticated weapons. Once the Cold War was over, the need for weapons diminished, and a market had to be created for whatever American technology could produce for non-military uses. The export of sophisticated weapons remained a major outlet, but trade with rapidly developing countries for both weapons and non-military equipment became increasingly more important. China, with over a billion people and a rapidly growing economy, became particularly attractive for big business in America. Thus, economy and technology became the main focus of Clinton's policies. President Clinton had, during his election campaign for presidency, blamed President Bush for coddling the Communist regime in China and for extending MFN treatment to it without any human rights conditions attached. Nevertheless, in his own tenure he not only decoupled the renewal of MFN treatment from human rights but also became one of the ardent advocates of granting China permanent MFN status and facilitated its entrance into the WTO. Efforts toward isolating China had barely succeeded in the past and had even less chance of success in coming years. The US allies in Europe and Asia, now free from Cold War worries, were charting their own independent course in matters of trade and diplomacy, taking advantage of increasing liberalization of trade and investment in China. American big business could not sit idly by while its competitors were making serious in-roads into the Chinese market. The businessmen favored decoupling the renewal of the MFN status from human rights or any other conditionality.

Strategic considerations were also important. So long as China was outside international trade and weapons non-proliferation regimes, it could not be made accountable for its infringements of such regimes. China has been transferring weapons of mass destruction and related technologies to Middle Eastern regimes, considered by Washington to be unfriendly. Any hope of moderating China's behavior in these respects depended on whether it was given a legitimate stake in international governance. Prudence required that the Chinese be brought on board and Clinton, with his keen intellect, realized China's importance soon after taking office. After reaching a compromise with the democratic leadership in both houses of Congress, he signed an executive order on 28 May 1993 extending MFN treatment to China for another year with human rights conditionality attached, but with a milder version of the requirements Congress might have written into the law.[3]

President Clinton had hoped that the Chinese leadership would release one or more high-profile dissidents from detention and allow them to migrate to the United States, thus making it easier for the administration to renew MFN status. The Chinese did not oblige. Instead, they began courting US big business. Taking a cue from Taiwan's success lobbying within the United States, China began to engage influential lobbyists, including those who held senior positions in past administrations. One of the important ones has been Henry Kissinger.[4] More recently, others have included Cyrus Vance, Lawrence Eagleberger, Alexander Haig, George Schultz, Edmund Muskie, and Warren Christopher, all of whom have held the office of secretary of state at one time or another. Among other important lobbyists for China have been Dick Cheney, a former defense secretary and now the vice-president in George W. Bush's administration; Brent Scowcroft, a former national security adviser; Carla Hills, Bill Brock, and Robert Strauss, all three former US trade representatives; Howard Baker, former Senate majority leader; former Senator Gary Hart; and former Ambassador to China Leonard Woodcock.[5] Apart from these foreign policy heavyweights, China began to solicit the support of corporate lobbyists working for some of America's largest corporations, among them Boeing, McDonnell Douglas, General Motors, Ford, Chrysler, Proctor & Gamble, Amway, McDonalds, Coca-Cola, Motorola, AT&T, General Electric, and IBM.

China also pursued other sectors of the American business community, such as farmers and agribusiness (particularly those involved with wheat, soybeans, cotton, and corn), and firms involved with financial services (including banking and insurance) which had considerable interest in the China trade. The importers of Chinese apparel, shoes, toys, and plastic gadgets also had a vested interest in retaining China's MFN status. The termination of China's MFN status would, in 2000, have increased the import duty on nearly two-thirds of US imports from China from 3.5 per cent to nearly 43 per cent, increasing the overall costs of importers by almost a third.[6]

The American China policy formulation has become quite complex, as different groups have different interests, reconciling them is not always easy. 'There are too many conflicting institutions, or formal and informal rules, regarding how to play the game of China policy making, particularly regarding Taiwan.'[7] Ramon Myers and David Shambaugh call the complexities an 'institutional gridlock,' yet the influence of big business remains the most important. Clinton's own instincts favored trade expansion as a primary concern; this was symbolized in his election slogan, 'it's the economy, stupid.'

Within a month of his inauguration, Clinton, along with his Vice-President Al Gore, launched the technology policy initiative with a speech at Silicon Graphics in Mountain View in California on 22 February 1993 in which he declared that 'investing in technology is investing in America's future.' The technology policy initiative aimed to ensure that the US trade policy supported high technology industries by guaranteeing 'access to overseas markets and effective protection of intellectual property rights.' [8]

In order to centralize the formulation, coordination, and implementation of domestic and international economic policies President Clinton created a National Economic Council (NEC) with the president as the chairman. As with the NSC, the NEC was to be managed by an assistant to the president with direct authority from the president and with direct access to him. It was hoped that, in time, the NEC would be as important in the economic and technological sphere as the NSC is in security matters. To see his policy through, President Clinton appointed Ronald Brown, the Democratic Party's chief fundraiser, as the secretary of commerce, assigning export promotion as one of his main agendas. The president also appointed William Perry, a Silicon Valley executive, to be the deputy secretary of defense, subsequently defense secretary. Perry was also in favor of export promotion and was opposed to export controls, advocated by the Pentagon on grounds of security. President Clinton also brought John Deutch to a senior post in the Pentagon; Deutch had views similar to Perry's.[9]

According to James Mann, the administration's China policy of 'engagement' came in late September 1993, with a decision to engage China 'at all levels of government and on a wide range of subjects.'[10] Yet in July, the president, against the advice of his security aides, had given the go-ahead to license Motorola and Martin-Marietta to use Chinese rockets for launching commercial communication satellites. However, the sanctions on satellites exported for launch by Chinese rockets were reintroduced in August 1993 when the administration received confirmation that China had sold M-11 ballistic missile components to Pakistan.

In November 1993, President Clinton met President Jiang Zemin in Seattle on the occasion of an APEC summit, the first ever APEC summit. Nothing of substance came out of this meeting, but a thaw had begun. Just before the summit, China had indicated that it might consider allowing the International Red Cross to visit China to look into the conditions of political prisoners. On its part, the Clinton administration decided to approve the sale of Cray supercomputers to China for the purpose of weather forecasting.[11] The administration also decided to lift the ban on the export of components for China's nuclear generators.[12] Military contacts, suspended in the wake of the Tiananmen massacre, were also resumed. On the occasion of his visit to Beijing in January 1994, Treasury Secretary Lloyd Benston also reactivated the China–US Joint Economic Committee, which had not met since 1989. Possibly in response to these American gestures of goodwill, the treasury secretary was informed that the Chinese authorities would allow US Customs officials to visit prisons allegedly producing goods for export to the US.[13] However, Secretary of State Christopher's visit to Beijing to ask the Chinese to make some visible progress on human rights (so as to make it easier for Clinton to extend the MFN status to China) did not go so well. In spite of this, on his final day he was told in confidence that the Chinese government would be releasing two dissidents, Wang Juntao and Chen Ziming, from prison. Subsequently, both were released and Wang was allowed to leave for the United States.[14]

After the Chinese gave an assurance that they would not henceforth export M-11s or related technology, sanctions were lifted again in October 1994. By this time, many of the export controls on telecommunications equipment and computers, except high-performance computers, had already been removed. With the increasing capacity of commercially available computers, it became necessary to revise the threshold for supercomputers. A revision of export policy in January 1996 removed the licensing requirements for most exports of computers with performance levels up to 2000 millions of theoretical operations (MTOPS).[15] Again in July 1999, the threshold for exports for all destinations was raised. To facilitate export of satellites, the Clinton administration transferred the licensing of satellite exports from the State Department to the Commerce Department, leaving the licensing of technical data related to launching with the State Department. Later, in the wake of allegations that the Hughes Space and Communication Company and the Space System Loral had, in course of their launch failure investigations, endangered US security interests by passing on unauthorized technical information to China, Congress returned the satellite export licensing authority from the Commerce Department to the State Department.[16]

Security leaks and the China connection

Whether there was a genuine security leak harming US interests remains controversial. A classified CIA report concluded that Hughes and Loral did not reveal information to China that could have harmed US security interests. However, a Pentagon report claimed the contrary, leading to the launch of a Department of Justice criminal inquiry. The intelligence arm of the State Department also reached a conclusion similar to the Pentagon's.[17] The Select Committee on US National Security and Military/Commercial Concerns with the People's Republic of China (the Cox Committee) could not reach a definitive conclusion; it simply said that 'while the Select Committee's limited review found no witness to confirm that a transfer of controlled US technology has occurred ... it cannot be inferred that no such transfer took place.'[18] The Cox Committee also alleged that the PRC had stolen design information on the US most advanced thermonuclear weapons, including those already deployed, together with classified material on the enhanced radiation weapon (popularly known as the neutron bomb) and missile-related technology.[19]

As early as 1995, both the Department of Energy (DOE) and the CIA independently learned that highly sensitive information on US nuclear weapons, including W-88 missile warheads had been passed on to the PRC. A DOE/FBI administrative inquiry to look into the counter-intelligence failure concluded that the transfer of information took place some time between 1984 and 1988 from the Los Alamos National Laboratory. From among those officials who had visited China frequently, had the opportunity to meet regularly with Chinese scholars visiting the laboratory, and had access to classified information on the laboratory's computer, a list of a dozen people was passed on to the FBI in 1996. From the list, only two people – Wen Ho Lee, a Taiwan-born but naturalized American scientist, and his wife, Sylvia Lee – were selected for further investigation. The FBI's request to the Attorney General for a search warrant for Lee under the Foreign Intelligence Surveillance Act (FISA) was refused. For some inexplicable reason the case remained dormant until December 1998. By this time, it was common knowledge that the Cox committee was about to publish its report, which would be highly critical of the Departments of Justice and Energy for improperly handling the Wen Ho Lee case. The DOE soon sprang to action. Lee's job was terminated in March 1999, and a search warrant was issued in April 1999. After being indicted on 59 counts in December 1999 for illegally copying data on nuclear design, Lee was kept in solitary confinement for nine months. The case against Lee could not be proved to the satisfaction of the court, and Lee was released in September 2000 after pleading guilty to one charge of unauthorized possession of national defense documents. The presiding judge authorized his release and added, 'I sincerely apologise to you, Dr. Lee, for the unfair manner in which you were held in custody by the executive branch.' He further added, 'they have embarrassed an entire nation and each of us who is a citizen of it.'[20]

Congress, with a Republican majority, also alleged that China had tried to influence the outcome of the 1996 presidential election through donations to the Democratic National Committee (DNC). There were certainly some suspicious donations to the DNC and the money so collected had to be returned.[21] However, the Senate Committee on Governmental Affairs inquiry was not able to find a direct link between the donations and the Chinese government.

There were other minor irritants to the Chinese. In July 1993, the CIA Non-Proliferation Center falsely claimed that a Chinese container ship, *Yinhe*, was carrying chemical agents needed for the production of mustard and nerve gases for the chemical weapons program in Iran. In spite of assurances given by Qin Huasun, assistant foreign minister, and subsequently by President Jiang Zemin, the vessel was tailed and searched upon arrival in Saudi Arabia, but no chemicals were found.[22] Additionally, the Chinese had offered to host the 2000 summer Olympics in Beijing; but in the face of active opposition from the administration and much resistance by Congress on grounds of Beijing's poor human rights record, the Olympic Committee decided in favor of Sydney, Australia.

Nevertheless, human rights increasingly became less and less important in Sino-American relations. Secretary of State Warren Christopher and Winston Lord, assistant secretary of state for Chinese affairs, both committed to human rights conditionality, fought for their corner to no avail. The pressures from Clinton's economic team, big business, and above all, Clinton's own preferences, led to the decoupling of MFN status from human rights in May 1994. Of course, the rhetoric continued, and whenever pressure mounted, the Chinese, intending to give the administration a face-saving device, released one or more important dissidents from prison.

Taiwan president's American visit infuriates China

Unexpectedly, in early 1995, the Clinton administration had to confront a rather awkward situation. Encouraged by the Republican Congress, Lee Teng-hui, the Taiwanese president, orchestrated an invitation from Cornell University, his *alma mater*, which had recently accepted a donation from 'friends of Lee' of $2.5 million for creating the Lee Teng-hui Chair of World Affairs.[23] Initially, the administration had no intention of granting a visa to Lee and informed the Chinese authorities likewise. However, under pressure from both the houses of Congress and the media, the administration relented.[24] The administration was worried that if it insisted on denying Lee entrance into the United States, Congress might introduce a binding resolution. Lee was allowed to come on the condition that he would not make a political speech; as it turned out, and as was to be expected, Lee made a political speech at Cornell. The Chinese leaders were furious and in retaliation postponed the planned visit of their defense minister to the United States, recalled the ambassador from Washington, and delayed the approval of Jim Sasser, Clinton's nominee for the ambassadorship to Beijing. It also suspended the dialogue on security, non-proliferation, and human rights.[25] The Chinese authorities also arrested Harry Wu, a Chinese-born naturalized American, as he entered China through the border post of Horgas. Wu had earlier drawn attention to the Chinese practice of exporting goods produced by prison labor in contravention of US laws. Harry Wu was tried for spying and given a 15-year prison sentence.[26] However, to make it acceptable for Mrs. Hillary Clinton to attend the Fourth UN International Women's Conference in Beijing, Wu was expelled from China.

Possibly as a reprisal for Lee's American visit, the PLA began a ten-day naval exercise with live ballistic missiles aimed at Taiwan's coastal waters in the East China Sea. This had a devastating effect on the Taiwanese stock market and its currency, and reportedly support for Taiwanese independence also showed a decline.[27] In order to placate China, Christopher met with Qian Qichen, the Chinese foreign minister, in Brunei on 1 August and passed on a letter from Clinton to Jiang assuring him that the administration did not support Taiwan's independence, nor did it support the creation of two Chinas (or even one China and one Taiwan), or Taiwan's entry into the United Nations. These three assurances, subsequently known as the 'three noes,' given confidentially, were later reiterated publicly by President Clinton during his visit to China.[28] The Chinese foreign minister was also informed that the administration would welcome the visit of Jiang to the United States.[29] In response, the Chinese authorities approved the nomination of Jim Sasser as the new ambassador to China and promised the return of the Chinese ambassador Li Daoyu to Washington. They also suggested that the forthcoming trips of Commerce Secretary Brown and Assistant Secretary of Defense Nye could proceed as planned. China also suspended the sale of nuclear reactors to Iran.[30] This paved the way for the Clinton–Jiang 'summit' meeting in New York.

The lull did not last for very long. On 5 March 1996, *Xinhua*, the Chinese official news agency, reported that the PLA was to hold a new series of training exercises, including some live-ammunition war games, from between 8 March to 15 March. The exercises would include surface-to-surface missiles in two areas, one in the northeast of Taiwan, nearly 21 miles from Keelung, the island's second busiest seaport, and the other 32 miles west of the port of Kaohsiung, the third largest container port in the world.[31] The exercise was, presumably, planned to intimidate the Taiwanese electorate and influence the outcome of the presidential election, scheduled for 23 March. Lee Teng-hui, the incumbent, a keen advocate of independence for Taiwan, had been working hard for a separate international identity (as opposed to a Chinese province as recognized by the United Nations) for Taiwan. Lee denounced the Chinese military exercises as 'state terrorism.'[32] The White House spokesman called the Chinese military exercises 'provocative' and 'reckless.'[33] The upcoming presidential election put Clinton in a quandary; formerly critical of President Bush for being soft on China, he could not be perceived as soft himself. Besides, the Republican-dominated Congress had already introduced a concurrent resolution to 'deplore' China's actions, and called on the president to defend Taiwan in an event of attack or blockade of Taiwan.[34] Clinton was also worried that Congress might pass a binding resolution, leaving no option for him to be flexible. He ordered five American warships, including the aircraft carrier *Independence* and two submarines, to move near Taiwan. He also ordered the aircraft carrier *Nimitz* and its support ships to join the *Independence* group to monitor the Chinese military exercises.

Rapprochement begins again

After Lee was elected with 54 per cent of the votes in a four-candidate contest, rhetoric on both sides of the Strait was toned down. Secretary of State Christopher announced that he would meet his Chinese counterpart, Foreign Minister Qian Qichen, on 21 April in The Hague. Soon thereafter, the State Department announced that the administration would not impose sanctions against China for sending 'ring magnets' to Pakistan in violation of the Treaty on the Non-Proliferation of Nuclear-Weapons (NPT). The Export-Import Bank resumed normal lending to US businesses exporting to China. For its part, China undertook not to provide assistance to unsafeguarded nuclear facilities.[35] The president also decided to extend China's MFN status (without human rights conditionality) for another year. American business vigorously supported granting unconditional MFN status to China. The Business Coalition for United States-China Trade wrote a letter of support to the president signed by 881 businesses and business associations.[36] A joint resolution of the two houses of Congress, however, proposed to disapprove the extension, but the resolution was defeated in the House.[37] Soon thereafter, following the visit of National Security Adviser Anthony Lake to China, several high-level visits, including one by Secretary of State Christopher, took place. Defense Minister Chi Haotian and the security adviser, Liu Huaqiu, made reciprocal visits to the US. At The Hague meeting, Christopher assured Qian that the United States 'remains committed to a "one China" policy and believes that the Taiwan question is a matter for the parties on both sides of the Taiwan Strait to address peacefully.' He further added that 'our furnishing of arms to Taiwan is carefully limited in accordance with the Taiwan Relations Act, and we don't have any intention to go beyond that and as well as our other commitments to restraint in the furnishing of arms of that character.'[38] Qian assured Christopher of China's intention to make progress on CTBT negotiations.[39] In November 1996 Christopher met President Jiang Zemin, Premier Li Peng, and Vice Premier Qian Qichen. This meeting was intended to pave the way for a Clinton-Jiang meeting in the Philippines on the occasion of an APEC meeting. The Chinese side again assured the Americans that they would abide by the 11 May 1996 commitment not to provide assistance to unsafeguarded nuclear facilities. They also showed their willingness to join the Zangger NPT Suppliers Committee and to abide by the guidelines and parameters of the MTCR. Both sides agreed to seek ratification of the Chemical Convention by the end of April 1997. On his part, Christopher assured China that the United States continued to support China's accession to the WTO.[40] The next day, in his speech at Fudan University, the secretary of state once again reiterated that the United States was 'firmly committed to expanding our relationship within the context of our "one China" policy, as embodied in these three [the Shanghai Communiqué of 1972 and those that followed in 1978 and 1982] communiqués' and 'that the PRC and Taiwan must act to resolve their differences between themselves. At the same time we have a strong interest in the peaceful resolution of issues between Taipei and Beijing.'[41]

Clinton and Jiang met in Manila in November 1996; as expected this meeting was no more than a confidence-building effort on both sides after a confrontational situation over Taiwan for nearly two years. Both presidents suggested the need for regular high-level meetings and it was decided that in the next two years the two would exchange state visits.

When Jiang came to Washington in October 1997 he was given the 'red carpet' treatment, the first such welcome extended to a Chinese dignitary since the Tiananmen incident in 1989. Clinton welcomed him at the White House and the two presidents talked about some of the most contentious issues such as Taiwan, trade, nuclear technology, human rights abuses, and religious persecution in Tibet. The next day there was an extraordinary public exchange between the two presidents over fundamental differences relating to human rights and the suppression of pro-democracy demonstrations in Tiananmen Square in 1989. Clinton said that the United States and China had 'profound disagreements' on human rights. As to the Tiananmen massacre, Clinton observed that China was 'on the wrong side of history.' Jiang insisted that the United States and China had 'different historic and cultural traditions' and therefore the differences of approach to human rights were 'just natural.' On the Tiananmen incident, he claimed that for stability in the country the Chinese government was justified in doing what had to be done.[42] On other substantive issues some progress was made. The Clinton Administration reiterated the 'one China' policy and stressed that the United States would abide by the principles enunciated in the three US–China communiqués. On Korea, both sides agreed to work toward a four-party (the two Koreas, the United States, and China) talk to promote peace and stability in the peninsula. They also agreed to establish a 'hot line' between Beijing and Washington for direct contact between the two presidents. As to trade and economy, China showed an interest in participating in the Information Technology Agreement, and in the context of joining the WTO, China promised to offer further concessions and reiterated its commitment to withhold assistance to unsafeuarded nuclear facilities. For its part, the United States agreed to facilitate the sale of nuclear power equipment to China.

The two countries also agreed to reactivate the 1985 US–China agreement on Peaceful Nuclear Cooperation; with this objective in view, the Chinese State Planning Commission and the US Department of Energy signed an Agreement. The two countries also reached an agreement to create a consultative mechanism for strengthening military maritime safety in order to avoid accidents, miscalculations, or misunderstandings between the two navies and air forces.[43] They also agreed to have military exchanges in the context of humanitarian assistance and disaster management.[44] In order to meet its commitments on human rights, China signed the UN International Convention on Economic, Social and Cultural Rights on 27 October 1997, and the Covenant on Civil and Political Rights on 12 March 1998.

Congress votes Permanent Normal Trade Relations (PNTR) for China

While Clinton and Jiang were trying to mend fences, Congress was busy constraining the executive from having any free play in China-policy making. A number of conservatives in Congress had been ardent supporters of Taiwan, and would do anything to undermine Clinton's policy of 'engagement.' The 105th Congress saw a plethora of bills and legislations imposing sanctions or constraints linked to human rights, freedom of religious beliefs, export of goods produced by prison labor, forced abortion, political freedom and democracy, and proliferation of missile technology. Several acts and resolutions aimed at increasing arms sales to Taiwan and facilitating Taiwan's membership in international organizations were also passed.[45] Similar actions continued in the 106th Congress. Congress also proposed a joint resolution to disapprove the president's recommendation for the extension of MFN treatment to China. This resolution was defeated in the House by a vote of 166 to 264.[46] Clearly, a rejection of MFN treatment would have undermined trade between the two countries, jeopardizing US business interests. Subsequently, both houses voted with substantial majorities to extend permanent normal trade relations to China. This was a victory for President Clinton, who actively lobbied Congress to support the bill. He signed the bill on 10 October making it into a law.

The interim between Jiang's visit to Washington and Clinton's impending visit to Beijing was not very propitious for the policy of engagement. In March 1998 the House Governmental Reform and Oversight Committee held hearings on China's role in influencing the presidential election. The House International Committee's East Asia and the Pacific subcommittee urged the government to introduce a resolution in the 54th session of the UN Commission on Human Rights condemning China's human rights abuses. The Senate also passed a similar resolution.[47] In June, the Cox Committee was appointed to look into the Chinese acquisition of missile technology and the transfer of know-how relating to high-performance computers and nuclear technology. Allegations that China had consistently engaged in espionage in US nuclear research establishments surfaced.

Clinton visits China

In this atmosphere of Congressional anti-China frenzy President Clinton visited China in June 1998. Some circles in America had advised against such a trip. Not much was expected from this trip, but Clinton's outspoken comments on human rights were well received by the American audience. On 27 June 1998, a debate between Clinton and Jiang was broadcast live on Chinese television. During this trip President Clinton reaffirmed his 'three noes' about Taiwan, which were not well received by many conservatives in America. In reaction to the president's remarks, the Senate passed two resolutions relating to Taiwan soon after his return. One supported Taiwan's membership in the international financial institutions and the other reaffirmed the American commitment to come to Taiwan's defense when attacked by China and to sell weapons for Taiwan's defense.

The warmth in the relationship between the two countries created by President Clinton's visit began to disappear in 1999. In early February, American newspapers started publishing news regarding the construction of missile sites in China targeting Taiwan. The classified version of the Cox report was issued in January 1999 alleging that China had stolen technical information on advanced missile and nuclear technology, enabling it to improve its design of missiles and nuclear weapons. A declassified version of the report was published in May 1999.[48] In April, the CIA had already reported to Congress that Chinese spies had acquired considerable sensitive information on nuclear technology from American research establishments. In order to prevent the transfer of sensitive satellite technology, the US government disapproved the sale of Hughes satellites to China. As desired by Congress, the United States government also sponsored a resolution denouncing the Chinese record of human rights at the Geneva meeting of the UN Human Rights Commission, but it could not generate the requisite number of votes to censor China.

Chinese embassy in Belgrade bombed by NATO

In the meantime, Secretary of State Madeleine Albright visited China in February, and China's Premier Zhu Rongji visited Washington. The slowly developing rapport suddenly came to an end as a result of NATO's bombing of the Chinese Embassy in Belgrade on 7 May 1999. The bombing killed three Chinese journalists and injured twenty members of the diplomatic staff. The American government claimed that it was an accident; the news from NATO headquarters was mixed. The official NATO version corroborated the US official line. However, on the basis of reliable NATO military sources, the *Observer* reported that the Chinese Embassy was deliberately targeted directly on orders from Washington, because the Chinese Embassy was acting as a rebroadcast station for the Yugoslav army after NATO jets destroyed the transmitters at President Milosevic's residence.[49] The *Observer's* findings were taken seriously by the world media but were ignored by the US media, which continued to tow the official line. On being criticized for this 'deafening silence' by FAIR (Fairness and Accuracy in Reporting), an American public interest group, Andrew Rosenthal, the foreign editor of the *New York Times*, admitted that the reporting of the bombing in his newspaper was 'poorly phrased.' However, Douglas Stanglin, the foreign editor of *USA Today*, said that his paper did not find the *Observer* report credible. As FAIR commented, it was a strange conclusion in the face of the fact that some of the most respected international newspapers, such as *Frankfurter Allgemeine Zeitung*, the *Times*, and the *Globe and Mail* found the story credible enough to print, and the reputed news services, such as the Associated Press, Reuters, *Deutche Presse-Agentur*, and *Agence France Presse* (AFP) had included the *Observer's* findingsin their dispatches. Interestingly, even the German chancellor, Gerhard Schroeder, publicly questioned NATO's official version of the incident.[50]

The Chinese were outraged. There were large demonstrations in Chinese cities. Demonstrators, hurling rocks and chunks of concrete and bottles and screaming anti-American slogans, barricaded the American embassy in Beijing. The embassy building and cars were damaged. The US consulates in Guangzhou and Shanghai also incurred minor damage, and demonstrators burned down the US consul-general's residence in Chengdu.[51] Undoubtedly, the state-controlled media, as the leading US newspapers claimed, fanned some of this resentment but one should not underestimate the rise of nationalism in China. As the AFP reported, some 'ordinary people applauded the students as they passed and genuine nationalistic fervour was much in evidence.'[52] The Chinese government did not believe the US government or the NATO explanation, and as a result cancelled the ongoing military exchanges and halted all port visits of the US navy to Hong Kong. The human rights dialogue between the United States and China was also suspended. The Chinese government also asked for a bombing probe and an apology. President Jiang called the NATO bombing 'absolute gunboat policy.'[53] Nevertheless, China was not prepared for a confrontation with the United States as Deputy Prime Minister Qian Qichen declared on 12 June 1999.[54]

On the American side, efforts at reconciliation continued. Soon after the bombing, Secretary of State Albright went to the Chinese embassy in Washington to express regret, apologies, and condolences. President Clinton spoke personally to President Jiang, expressing sorrow and promised an investigation.[55] In early June, Clinton recommended renewing China's normal trade relations for another year. In mid-June Thomas Pickering, the undersecretary of state, went to China to convince the Chinese authorities that the NATO bombardment was a genuine mistake.[56] His meeting with the Chinese minister for foreign affairs, Tang Jiaxuan, went well, but Tang did not accept the American explanation. In a further effort to mend fences, Secretary of State Albright met Minister Tang in July at the Association of South-East Asian Nations (ASEAN) Forum. In September, the United States paid $4.5 million to the victims of the bombing and began to negotiate with China on a property damage settlement. Clinton himself met Jiang at the APEC summit in Auckland in September. The two leaders had 'a very productive, friendly, non-polemical and quite comprehensive meeting' as Sandy Berger, the president's national security adviser, told the press reporters. He felt that the relationship was 'back on track.'[57]

While the two presidents were meeting in Auckland, a short meeting between Shi Guansheng, minister of foreign trade and economic cooperation (MOFTEC), and Charlene Barshefsky, United States Trade Representative (USTR), revealed the differences between what the USTR thought was on offer and what China thought it had really offered in the trade negotiations. The main differences related to the stipulations regarding foreign participation in telecommunications; the Chinese thought they had agreed to a maximum of a 49 per cent stake for foreigners, while the American side thought the Chinese authorities had offered a ceiling of 51 per cent on foreign ownership. Other main differences related to the period of phasing out protection, particularly for automobiles; the concessions on textiles; and safeguards against import surges from China.[58] Nothing much came out of this meeting. In mid-October and then in early November, Clinton called Jiang for the resumption of trade talks.[59] He also sent Charlene Barshefsky and Gene Sperling, assistant to the president for economic policy, to Beijing to finalize the deal. After a gruelling six-day negotiation, an agreement was reached on 15 November. The agreement became the basis for granting permanent normal trade relations, dispensing with the need for annual renewal of normal trade relations.

President George W. Bush takes a tough stand on China

President George W. Bush deliberately undermined much of the understanding that President Clinton had assiduously created with China within weeks of his election. George W. Bush once said, 'if we make China an enemy, they'll end up being an enemy.'[60] Yet, he made it clear that he did not believe in the Clinton policy of engagement. Even before his election, categorically differentiating himself from the Clinton-Gore administration, he said 'they believe in what's called a strategic partnership. I believe in redefining the relationship to one of competitor.'[61] Arguably, portraying China as the potential enemy justifies spending more money on defense, particularly the National Missile Defense to which Bush (Jr) is passionately committed. Increased expenditure on defense systems creates markets for defense industries; this may be his way of repaying his debt to those who funded his election. President Clinton was doing much the same by opening up the Chinese market for the very same group of businesses, because in electronics, airplanes, space, laser technology, and many other sectors, firms produce equipment for both military and civilian uses. For a president as committed as Bush to the reduction of taxes, a substantial increase in the military budget either for missile defense systems or for other military needs may defeat his tax strategy. An increase in exports to potentially large markets reduces the need to raise domestic revenue, at the same time reducing the ever-increasing trade deficits. So, if the president's aim is to pay back his debt tó big business, Clinton's trade-oriented policy would seem more enlightened than a military-oriented one. Both on over-all trade policy, as well as on supporting China's candidacy for the WTO, Bush conceded in a speech at the Boeing plant in May 2000 that he was 'in complete agreement' with Clinton policies. [62]

Thus, President George W. Bush's China policy has two somewhat contradictory elements. On one hand, normalizing trade relations with China and letting it into WTO's liberalized international trade regime may accelerate Chinese economic development and provide China with the resources to modernize the Chinese armed forces. This comes into direct conflict with the policy of containing Chinese military might, which – as those in the Pentagon assume – poses a strategic threat to American interests. These contradictions are inherent in the president's disparate collection of people in his cabinet. For instance, Secretary of State Colin Powell believes in dialogue and engagement and feels that despite occasional 'ups and downs' in its relations with China, the United States must stay engaged.[63] On the occasion of his first visit to Beijing in July 2001, he categorically said 'my presence here today is an example of trying to let the world see that we are not enemies, and we are not looking for an enemy. We are looking for ways to cooperate.'[64] On the other hand, Defense Secretary Rumsfeld sees China as the principal threat to American interests and advocates that the Pacific Ocean ought to become the main focus of US military deployment.[65] On the eve of Powell's visit to China, Rumsfeld issued 'a strong warning that the US must remain militarily strong in the face of a rising threat from China.'[66] Rumsfeld is also a keen promoter of the National Missile Defense that China looks on with disfavor. The president is also keen on deploying anti-ballistic missiles, even if it means backing out of the 1972 ABM treaty with the Russians.[67] In fact, the United States government gave notice in December 2001 of its withdrawal from the ABM treaty.

If the president feels, as seemingly he does, that economic liberalization will in due course lead to a political liberalization, the administration's efforts to paint China as a 'potential threat' may be self-defeating. Chinese hardliners have always suspected that the United States has been trying not only to undermine Communism and the Communist leadership but also the very unity and the integrity of the country. If China is constantly portrayed as an enemy these suspicions might be intensified, and under pressure from Beijing hardliners, the Chinese leadership might decide to restrict foreign contacts or at least slow down the opening of the country to foreign, particularly American, influence. The portrayal of China as a potential threat does not serve any useful purpose except to fuel Chinese paranoia and may possibly result in an arms race, even though the indications emanating from China suggest that China will avoid a Soviet-style arms race with America.

Unilateralism

Within six months of his taking office, President George W. Bush has, to the utter consternation of the world in general, rejected nearly half a dozen international treaties or negotiations, giving the impression that he is bent on undermining 'the overall system of international agreements and negotiations that has grown up since World War II.'[68] As an editorial in the *New York Times* pointed out:

> . . . he would not seek Senate ratification of the treaty creating the International Criminal Court. In March, the White House announced that the United States was withdrawing from the Kyoto Protocol on

global warming. In May, Mr Bush made clear he was ready to set aside the constraints of the Antiballistic Missile treaty in order to test and build missile defenses.

Earlier this month, American delegates insisted on diluting a United Nations agreement to reduce illegal trafficking in small arms. Last week, Washington pulled out of long running efforts to negotiate enforcement provisions for the convention banning biological weapons. Meanwhile, the administration has indefinitely deferred seeking Senate ratification of the 1996 nuclear test ban treaty and the 1993 nuclear weapons reduction treaty with Russia . . . [69]

The Pentagon is drawing up plans for a 'sub-orbital vehicle' launched like a spacecraft, to drop precision bombs from a height of 60 miles, flying at 15 times the speed and 10 times the height of America's current bomber fleet.[70] Any such weapon would lead to the militarization of space, which has been banned by the ABM Treaty and the 1967 Outer Space Treaty, and is opposed by both China and Russia.

In his disregard for international treaties, the president is ostensibly influenced by the hawks in his administration who do not believe in the policy of security through treaties. As Anthony Lewis, a veteran American journalist with the *New York Times* points out, 'the dislike of treaties reflects an attitude that the United States must be free to do what it wants in the world. Call it unilateralism or whatever, it is a sharp break from our postwar premise that if wisely negotiated, treaties enhance our security.'[71] This unilateralism is applauded by conservatives in the United States. Charles Krauthammer, a distinguished columnist of the *Washington Post*, approvingly suggests that 'we now have an administration willing to assert American freedom of action and the primacy of American national interests. Rather than contain American power within a vast web of constraining international agreements, the new unilateralism seeks to strengthen American power and unashamedly deploy it on behalf of self-defined global ends.'[72] Strangely, the very same people, both inside and outside the administration, are not opposed to binding international trade agreements *á la* WTO; they – the 'rule of law'-loving citizenry – only oppose international agreements that might constrain the gratuitous use of the military might of the United States.

President George W. Bush's missile defense initiative – a sure means of transferring money from the state to the coffers of military contractors – widely questioned within America, has serious implications for Chinese deterrence capabilities. The Chinese leadership thinks – and their fears are not necessarily unfounded – that the missile defense is against them. Defense Secretary Rumsfeld, as mentioned earlier, sees China as a potential enemy and his defense strategy review has made it clear that, in the future, the focus of America's military would shift from Europe to Asia. The conservative wing of the Republican Party – with which Bush (Jr) has a close affinity – has always been pro-Taiwan. A few of them have even advocated reviewing the 'one China' policy and recognizing Taiwan as an independent country.[73] Some members of Bush's administration, such as Vice-President Richard Cheney's chief-of-staff and national security adviser Lewis Labby have been keen supporters of Taiwan. As are Richard Armitage, the deputy secretary of state, and Paul Wolfowitz, the deputy defense secretary. Both advocate closer relations with Japan to balance China's influence in Asia.[74]

Soon after the president took office, the Pentagon claimed that Chinese technical experts were installing a fiber-optic communications network to link Iraqi air-defense radars. It argued that such installations not only threatened US and British planes in the 'no fly' zone in Iraq but also violated the UN Security Council sanctions.[75] The Chinese authorities promised to look into the matter. Subsequently, the United States was privately informed that China did not intend to violate the UN sanctions and had already asked all Chinese companies doing business in Iraq to 'stop working' in areas that might violate UN sanctions.[76]

Another contentious issue between the Bush (Jr) administration and the Chinese government relates to human rights abuses. In late February, the State Department's *Country Reports on Human Rights Practices, 2000* pointed out that the human rights situation in China was becoming worse; first, because of the suppression of religious groups, particularly the Falun Gong movement and some of the Christian groups, and secondly due to the 'strike hard' crime control policies. The administration announced that it would sponsor a resolution condemning China's human rights record at the Geneva meeting of the UN Commission on Human Rights in March 2001. China was not particularly disturbed because it knew that the United States would not be able to muster enough votes to have its resolution passed. Much of the Chinese effort concentrated on dissuading the administration from selling advanced weapon systems to Taiwan. Such efforts did not succeed; even Vice Premier Qian Qichen failed to obtain any assurance on this question.[77]

Bush's first foreign policy test

The first real test of the president's policy toward China came on 1 April 2001 when a US Navy EP-3E Aries II reconnaissance plane and a Chinese F-8 fighter collided in mid-air some 60 miles southeast of China's Hainan Island, destroying the Chinese plane and killing its pilot. The damaged US plane was forced to land on the island. The exact location of the collision was disputed. The American authorities claimed that at the time of collision the plane was over international waters, but it conceded that after the impact the plane was badly damaged and had landed on Hainan Island without permission, thereby intruding into Chinese air space. According to Chinese allegations, the collision occurred over China's

Exclusive Economic Zone (EEZ). Under normal circumstances a foreign plane has the right of innocent passage over the EEZ but since the American plane was involved in electronic surveillance – in plain language, spying, a common practice by both countries – the plane did not have legal immunity. The Chinese leadership held the American side responsible and repeatedly asked for an apology. However, both sides showed considerable restraint. President Bush, after his initial demand of immediate release of the crew and the plane, seemingly cooled down, with the crewmembers still in China, his options were limited. The Iran hostage crisis was never mentioned but memories of what it did to the Carter presidency still linger in America. Besides, the wise men of the Republican Party, including the president's father, Henry Kissinger, and several CEOs who have a lot to lose in a US–China stand-off, reportedly advised the president to cool off demands and concentrate on diplomatic efforts.[78] Secretary of State Colin Powell expressed his regret for the loss of life of the Chinese pilot; subsequently the president did the same. Beijing itself did not want to precipitate the matter. No large-scale mass demonstrations, like the one organized in the aftermath of the Belgrade Chinese Embassy bombing, were mobilized. The *Xinhua* news agency reported some demonstrations by the 'cadres and the masses' in some major cities including Beijing and Shanghai, but there was no sign of mobilizing college students and other residents to demonstrate outside American missions.[79] As to the incident itself, the Chinese authorities had not behaved much differently to what the United States government might have done if a Chinese plane flew over the American EEZ and came that close to the US coast. As the *Boston Globe* reported, 'there is no precise historical parallel, but numerous military historians and analysts said several cases with some similarities, as well as standard US procedures, suggest that Washington would just as vehemently oppose surveillance flights 60 miles off the US coast – and be just as quick to dismantle and delay returning a high-tech Chinese plane if one landed uninvited on US shores or at an overseas US base.' [80] The Chinese *Mingpao Daily News* commented much in the same vein, mentioning the 1976 Soviet MIG-25 incident and pointing out that in the spy plane incident China was following international norms in boarding the plane to make an examination in much the same way the United States had done with the MIG military plane 25 years ago.[81] After expressions of regret by Powell and Bush, the Chinese authorities allowed the crew of the US plane to leave after an 11-day standoff. The plane was subsequently dismantled and allowed to be taken away by a Russian freighter plane. This procedure almost exactly paralleled the 1976 return of the Soviet MIG-25 to the Soviet Union in crates. The hardliners in America were furious at the expression of regret. Robert Kagan and William Kristol wrote in the *Weekly Standard* that President Bush had brought 'profound national humiliation' upon the United States and advised tough actions.[82]

It was in this embittered atmosphere that the decision to sell advanced weapons systems to Taiwan was made. The arms package, decided on 23 April, was the largest in a decade and the most sophisticated that the United States had ever offered to Taiwan. An internal Pentagon review had already concluded that the military balance was moving swiftly against Taiwan and had advocated Taiwan's 'arms upgrade.'[83] Ignoring Chinese protests, the president decided to offer Taiwan, among other things, eight submarines and twelve P-3C Orion anti-submarine patrol aircrafts, as well as four older Kidd-class missile destroyers. The package did not include the Arleigh Burke-class destroyers equipped with advanced Aegis radar systems, the sale of which was strongly protested by China.[84]

So far, previous administrations had avoided selling submarines to Taiwan because submarines are considered offensive weapons, not essential for Taiwan's defense. According to the communiqué signed by President Reagan in 1982, the United States had given China assurances that it would not sell offensive weapons and gradually reduce arms sales to Taiwan. Nevertheless, a substantial amount of arms and related technology continued to be transferred from America to Taiwan, thus making the Communiqué virtually ineffective.[85] However, the transfer of diesel submarines in the arms package may not be so straightforward, as these submarines are not constructed in the United States. They can be produced only in cooperation with Germany and Netherlands, and both countries ban the transfer of weapons to Taiwan.[86] As CNN reported a year earlier, the Taiwan armed forces themselves had been divided over the purchase of Arleigh Burke-class destroyers with the Aegis system. The navy wanted the destroyers, but some high-ranking army and air force officers argued that it would be too expensive to buy the ships. Some Taiwanese military analysts also were not sure about the wisdom of the purchase. Ting Shou-chung, a member of Taiwan's parliamentary defense committee, felt that by the time the ships were delivered, the tensions in the Taiwan Strait could be reduced. Echoing the same point of view, Andrew Yang, military expert and secretary-general of Taipei's Chinese Council of Advanced Policy Studies argued that, apart from the high costs, the delivery of the destroyers might take five years; another three years might be needed to train personnel. Thus, the destroyers could be effectively deployed only after eight years; by that time, the political situation may not require such a deployment.[87]

The very next day, to the utter dismay of the Chinese leadership, President George W. Bush gave press interviews forcefully declaring that the United States had the obligation to defend Taiwan if it was attacked by China. On being asked by the ABC whether the defense of Taiwan 'will involve the full force of American military,' he answered, 'whatever it took to help Taiwan defend herself.' Later, in his Associated Press interview, the president reiterated that the use of force was 'certainly an option.' He further added, 'the Chinese have got to understand that is clearly an option.' After a possible reminder from his advisers that he had gone a bit too far – previous presidents maintained ambiguity on this question – Bush, in his interview with CNN a day later, qualified himself by saying that his statements ought not be seen by Taiwan as an encouragement for a declaration of independence. He stated, 'I certainly hope Taiwan adheres to the one China policy, and a declaration of independence is not the one China policy. We'll work with Taiwan to make sure that that doesn't happen. We need a peaceful resolution of this issue.'[88]

Other symbolic gestures of defiance also followed in quick succession. Ignoring China's request to refuse a visa to Chen Shui-bian, the Taiwanese president, the State Department decided to give him a visitor's visa on 14 May 2001.[89] He visited New York on 23 May; receiving a much more enthusiastic reception than the one he had received the previous year during a stopover in Los Angeles. On that occasion, the Clinton administration had asked him to remain in his hotel and members of Congress were dissuaded from seeing him. During the May visit, Chen met then-New York Mayor Rudolph Giuliani as well as a delegation of 21 Congressmen.[90] A day earlier, Colin Powell met the Dalai Lama, who visited the White House and met the president in a highly publicized fashion, in contrast to an earlier meeting with Clinton. As usual, China protested. At a high-level internal Communist Party meeting President Zemin reportedly called Bush 'logically unsound; confused and unprincipled; unwise to the extreme.'[91] Nevertheless, Jiang advised caution, particularly in view of China's application for membership in the WTO and of its candidacy as host for the 2008 Olympics.

For its part, China continued to indulge in provocative acts, more irritating than having serious diplomatic implications. Security agents picked up Gao Zhan, a Chinese-born sociologist with permanent resident rights in America in February 2001. In early April she was formally charged with spying. Gao's husband and her five-year-old son were also detained and held for 26 days. Since Gao's son was a US citizen, the Chinese government had the obligation to inform the American embassy within four days of the detention – but the Chinese officials failed to do so. This led to a major uproar in the United States.[92] Another scholar, Li Shaomin, a US citizen and a business professor in Hong Kong, was also arrested by the Chinese security service on 25 February while visiting a friend in China. He was later charged with spying for Taiwan which he denied, claiming that he was being penalized for his pro-democracy views. Tan Guangguang (also referred to as Qin Guangguang), a Chinese citizen but a permanent US resident, was arrested in December 2000; at the time of arrest he was working for a US medical group in Beijing. Xu Zerong, a historian with permanent resident rights in Hong Kong, was also arrested in August 2000 in Guangdong.[93] Wu Jianmin, a US citizen and a well-known writer, was also taken into custody on 8 April 2001 on spying charges. In his case, the US embassy was informed that he was being investigated for spying on behalf of Taiwan.

Encouraging signals from both sides

As neither China nor the United States was prepared to precipitate the matter in spite of the goading of hardliners, occasional encouraging signals were sent from both sides. The Bush administration stressed that frustration over the detention of the scholars would not jeopardize the president's support for extending normal trade relations status for China, nor would it adversely affect the president's plans to travel to China in October for the annual Asia Pacific Economic Cooperation summit in Shanghai, followed by a trip to Beijing for bilateral talks with President Jiang Zemin.[94] President Bush also wrote a letter to congressional leaders requesting a one-year extension of normal trade relations on 1 June 2001. On 7 June Robert Zoellick, the US trade representative, speaking at a two-day gathering of the Asia Pacific trade ministers at Shanghai, hoped that China would became a member of the WTO within the year.[95] The administration had also let it be known that the United States would not oppose China's candidacy for the 2008 Olympics. In his first ever telephone conversation with Jiang, Bush 'reinforced the importance of building constructive bilateral relations.'[96]

For its part, the Chinese leadership sent an important signal through an article in the official *China Daily*, stressing that 'future problems in US–China relations could and should be settled through diplomatic means.' It also made the point that China, being 'basically a regional power in the Asia-Pacific region,' did not threaten American international interests. The article also reminded Americans that the two countries shared common interests in 'safeguarding international financial order, fighting against international terrorism, preventing proliferation of nuclear weapons and maintaining peace on the Korean peninsula.' As John Gittings, a veteran China watcher, points out, 'such a public pledge of Chinese cooperation, coupled with the low-profile description of China's regional interests, is a considerable olive branch.'[97] Another favorable signal came when two US navy ships were allowed to visit Hong Kong. Such visits had been denied in the wake of the spy plane crisis.[98] The final goodwill gesture came when three convicted American scholars, Gao Zhan, Li Shaomin and Qin Guangguan – each convicted for ten years for espionage – were expelled from China on grounds of medical parole just a few days before Powell's visit.[99]

On his one-day visit to Beijing on 28 July, Powell met separately with President Jiang Zemin, Premier Zhu Rongji, and Vice-Premier Qian Qichen. Powell discussed the issues of human rights, proliferation of missiles, and missile technology, and the national missile defense. The Chinese authorities disavowed selling missiles or technology to any country, but agreed to have expert level talks on proliferation. They also agreed to reactivate expert level talks on human rights, suspended in the aftermath of the US bombing of the Chinese embassy in Belgrade. The Chinese leaders remained unconvinced on the issue of national missile defense but indicated their willingness to listen to the American arguments in future talks on the subject.[100] However, Powell's interview on Chinese television was broadcast in an edited form in spite of assurances that it would be broadcast in full. The edited version left out Powell's mention of the Taiwan Relations Act of 1979 and the US obligation to sell defensive weapons to Taiwan.[101] Although this soured the otherwise 'productive' visit, the scene was set for the planned October visit of the president, which was the prime objective of Powell's visit.

Bush visits China in the aftermath of September 11

Even before President George W. Bush's visit to China, the Chinese leaders pledged their support to America's counter-terrorism effort. Chinese Foreign Minister Tang Jiaxuan (who was on a two-day visit to the United States in September 2001 to pave the way for President Bush's visit to Shanghai and Beijing in October), speaking at a dinner sponsored by the US–China Business Council and the National Committee on US–China Relations, reaffirmed that China stood by America and the international community in the fight against terrorism. He also revealed that China would soon resume dialogues on human rights with the United States.[102] On the occasion of his first visit to China as the president, Bush did not use his oft-repeated designation of China as a 'strategic competitor' and indicated that he was looking for a 'constructive and cooperative' relationship with China.[103] President Jiang Zemin reiterated his support for the US counter-terrorism efforts but at the same time hoped that the targets of the US anti-terrorism efforts were clearly defined and innocent casualties avoided. He also hoped to see the United Nations brought into full play.[104] Subsequently, the two countries decided to establish semi-annual consultations on freezing the flow of funds between terrorist organizations and a meeting of the group was held in late May 2002.[105]

Other substantial issues were discussed, but on human rights, religious freedoms, proliferation of weapons of mass destruction, national missile defense, and the Taiwan disagreement remained. In the midst of the anthrax scare in America (created by the arrival of anthrax contaminated letters to a number of legislators and media offices and the resulting death of a number of people), Bush cut short his stay in China and did not visit Beijing. However, he went to China again in February 2002 on the thirtieth anniversary of President Nixon's first visit to China. In his opening remarks to the joint press conference on 21 February President Jiang Zemin mentioned his willingness to 'actively carry out exchanges and cooperation in economy and trade, energy, science and technology, environment protection, prevention and treatment of AIDS, law enforcement and other fields, hold strategic dialogues on regional economic and financial issues,' and to 'convene three joint meetings within this year on economy, trade, and science and technology.'[106] During this visit President Bush, speaking to the students of Tsinhua University, stated that 'life in America shows that liberty, paired with law, is not to be feared. In a free society, diversity is not disorder. Debate is not strife. And dissent is not revolution.' He also said 'freedom of religion is not something to be feared, it's to be welcomed. Because faith gives us a moral core and teaches us to hold ourselves to high standards, to love and to serve others, and to live responsible lives.'[107] In this speech Bush reiterated that his administration stood by the 'one China' policy of the previous administrations, but he also underlined his support for Taiwan under the Taiwan Relations Act and hoped for a peaceful settlement of the Taiwan issue. This speech was broadcast in full on China's television network but the *Xinhua*, the oficial news agency, edited out most of Bush's remarks concerning faith and freedom in the published version of the speech.[108] The visit was considered productive by both sides but soon thereafter some signs of discord appeared.

The US-Taiwan defense summit meeting, sponsored by the US–Taiwan Business Council invited Tang Yiau-min, the defense minister of Taiwan, to attend. On the American side, the participants included senior US officials, such as Paul Wolfowitz, the US deputy defense secretary and J. A. Kelly, assistant secretary of state in charge of East Asian affairs. Other participants came from American defense-related industries. The high-profile invitation to Tang Yiau-min irked the Chinese. Chinese Assistant Foreign Minister Zhou Wenzhong was ordered to summon US Ambassador to China Clark Randt to make serious representation with the US government.[109] What irked the Chinese most was the fact that the seminar almost coincided with the fourth China–US conference on armament control, disarmament, and prevention of proliferation of arms. To the Chinese side participating in this conference, the sale of sophisticated weapons to Taiwan not only undermined the assurances given by previous American administrations regarding sales of arms to Taiwan but it also amounted to weapons proliferation. The US side contended that arms sales were conducted under the Taiwan Relations Act; therefore, it was not a weapons proliferation issue. On such a contentious issue no consensus could be reached.

The Chinese leadership was further infuriated by a news item published on 9 March in the *Los Angeles Times* claiming that a secret report of the US Defense Department, forwarded to Congress on 8 January 2002, pointed out that the Bush administration had instructed the US military to draw up a plan for launching nuclear attacks against seven countries, including China and Russia. The report indicated that nuclear weapons could be used against China in the case of a conflict in the Taiwan Straits.[110] Even before this happened, the Pentagon's *Quadrennial Defense Review* published in September 2001 indirectly implied the possibility of China emerging as a military competitor, threatening US interests in Asia.[111] Another Defense

Department report, *Annual Report on the Military Power of the People's Republic of China presented to Congress in Pursuance of the FY2000 National Defense Authorization Act*, argued that the Chinese efforts to modernize the armed forces were narrowing the qualitative gap between China and Taiwan and improving China's ability to counteract third-party [American] intervention, meaning thereby that the United States must see China as a strategic challenge. Another report, *The National Security Implications of the Economic Relationship Between the United States and China*, submitted to Congress by the US–China Security Review Commission in July 2002, not in so many words but by implication presented China as a threat, so much so that one of the commissioners, William Reinsch, wrote a note of dissent suggesting that the report 'fails to present a fair and objective analysis of the US–China security relationship' and that the report 'adds to the level of paranoia about China in this country, and contains recommendations that could make that paranoia a self-fulfilling prophecy.' He further added, 'the commission majority has bent over backwards to avoid describing the Chinese as a "threat," yet the belief that they are permeates every chapter.'[112]

All this unsettles China. The Chinese leadership is also worried about the continuing involvement of the US armed forces in Afghanistan, Pakistan, Uzbekistan, and Kyrgyzstan. If the United States establishes military bases in these countries, China might see it as one additional move to encircle the country. In this context, China has reason to suspect the American involvement in the Philippines against Abu Sayyaf Group (ASG). The group, one of the most radical Islamic separatist groups with a relatively small following, is more interested in receiving ransom payments for foreign hostages rather than a *jihad* against Western interests. Its involvement with *Al-Qaida* is at best tenuous. According to one interpretation, the Bush administration has gone to the Philippines either to claim a quick victory in the face of a likely stalemate in Afghanistan or to regain military influence in the Philippines that was undermined after the loss of a military base in the country. A military presence in the Philippines gives the United States a good opportunity to watch its strategic interests in the resource-rich South China Sea.[113] Recent warming of the relationship between the US and India is also perceived as potentially anti-Chinese.[114]

Nevertheless, both sides seem to be interested in reviving military contacts, which were suspended after the plane collision in 2001. Peter Rodman, the assistant secretary of defense for international security affairs visited Beijing in June 2002 with this end in mind and met with the Chinese Defense Minister Chi Haotian. Reportedly, the talks were constructive but no agreement was reached.[115]

It is too early to predict how the Bush administration might handle its China policy during the rest of his presidency. As mentioned earlier, Reagan and Clinton both came in with a hard line on China but during their respective tenures, each mellowed. It is possible that President George W. Bush of necessity might see China more as an opportunity to expand business markets rather than a strategic challenge. Besides, as long as the president's 'War on Terrorism' continues, he would like to keep China on his side. How long this respite lasts for China depends on how badly the president needs an enemy other than *Al-Qaida* and Saddam Hussein to win the next four years in office.

Conclusion

President Clinton came to power at a time when the Cold War was over and Russia, the successor state of the Soviet Union, did not pose a threat to American security. Taking advantage of such a relaxed international climate, the president decided to concentrate on economic issues such as trade liberalization, promotion of American exports, and protection of intellectual property rights. In this context, he realized the importance of the fast growing China market and adopted a policy of 'engagement' with China. In spite of repeated attempts by the Republican Congressional majority to undermine his policies, his efforts bore fruit in terms of increased access for American products and investments in China. Above all, he succeeded in developing a personal relationship with the Chinese president to an extent that the two could discuss even the most contentious issues in public. Progress on human rights and on proliferation of weapons of mass destruction remained patchy; the Taiwanese question remained as intractable as before, but Clinton laid a foundation for a constructive relationship in economic and diplomatic spheres.

Although it is too early to judge the outcome, the Bush administration began in a position of confrontation with respect to China, portraying it as a potential enemy. Not all the senior members of the administration advocate a confrontational approach – it is mainly those who are close to the Pentagon and the defense industries that push the hard line. For them, the portrayal of China as the enemy justifies planned increases in the military budget and in the deployment of national missile defense. However, the very same industries which gain from an expanded military budget also benefit from exports of high-tech equipment not directly related to military uses. In addition to these industries, sectors such as agriculture, banking, and finance, together with firms that deal in imported goods, tend to prefer 'engagement' rather than confrontation with China. Barring the hardcore conservatives, members of Congress also prefer cooperation to conflict. The administration itself had to change in the wake of September 11, because it needed China's support for its counter-terrorist efforts. China has been prepared to oblige because it not only needed the American market and technology, but also a seat at the table where decisions are being made. So far, while cooperating in intelligence-sharing or restricting the flow of finance to terrorists, China has not been directly involved in decision-making with respect to the war on terrorism. China can have influence on such decision-making only through the Security Council, but the Bush administration has more or less sidelined the United Nations. However, as long as the war against terrorism continues the administration's 'engagement' with China will remain in place; China might be seen once again as a 'strategic competitor' soon thereafter.

5
China as an Economic Threat

> ...The important thing...is not to assume that the relationship is
> inherently adversarial but instead to take what we know is the
> truth – that the world will be a better place over the next 50 years
> if we are partners, if we are working together...
>
> (President Bill Clinton[1])

Introduction

Throughout the first half of the twentieth century, the United States
lacked substantial business interests in China, the British and the
Japanese being the two main forces dominating trade and investment.
The United States was, as evidenced by its 'Open Door' policy, content
mainly with ensuring its access to the Chinese market. US businessmen
saw a much more important trading partner in Japan and regarded the
Japanese invasion of China as a great opportunity to expand US trade
with Japan. Only after the Japanese march into Southeast Asia threatened
the supply of raw materials to the United States did American businessmen change their tune.

After Japan's surrender in World War II, the world situation changed drastically. The United States emerged victorious from World War II as the
world's most dominant economic and military power. Until the European
countries and Japan were able to reconstruct their war-devastated
economies, the United States remained the only source of capital goods
necessary for reconstruction. Mao, fully conscious of the importance of
the United States in the post-war world, wished to keep China's channels
of communication open with the United States. Both Mao and Zhou Enlai
made it clear to the US administration that China's 'leaning to one side' was
no impediment to normalizing economic and diplomatic relations with the
United States. Even the US National Security Council favored continuing
economic relations with China. In spite of the Shenyang incident, in which
the local Communist authorities arrested and harassed US consular officials,

American oil companies were allowed to continue supplying kerosene and gasoline to Communist China almost until the end of 1950. Relations became strained when the United States failed to recognize the new Communist regime, and particularly embittered after China's entry into the Korean War. The United States imposed economic sanctions on China, and asked its allies to abide by the sanctions. This policy led to a near-cessation of trade between China and the Western economies. The action deepened China's dependence on the Soviet Union. However, some trade continued through Hong Kong, then a British colony, because many Japanese and Western companies had established subsidiaries in Hong Kong and began to trade with China through these subsidiaries.

In the mid-1950s, the Chinese relationship with the Soviet Union began to deteriorate further and in 1958, the Soviet Union recalled the technical experts it had previously sent to help Chinese economic development. China's estrangement from the Soviet Union was the end of any hope of China's economic progress as an open economy. It is not often realized that a near-autarchic regime was not imposed on China by its own leadership, but by the two post-World War II superpowers: firstly, because China had intervened in the Korean War (thereby threatening the American sphere of influence) and secondly because China was not prepared to be totally subservient to its Communist big brother.

An autarchic development strategy was the only option left; however, China was never really a closed economy. It continued to trade with France and the Scandinavian countries, the majority of developing countries, and the Eastern European countries (who did not abide by the American sanctions). During the early stages of development, foreign trade usually only accounts for a small percentage of the gross domestic product, and trade among developing countries, by its very nature, remains limited. Because both China and the developing countries in the 1950s and 1960s were mainly exporting primary commodities and textiles, their trade remained limited. Not many developing countries had surplus food and those that did (e.g. Argentina and Thailand) were seen to be both under considerable American influence. China needed machinery and technology, which could be procured either from the Soviet Union or from the countries not party to US sanctions. Furthermore, China did not have the foreign exchange to finance its imports. Admittedly, ideology played a part in the choice of economic strategy, but the scope for adopting an open-economy strategy for China was strictly limited.

President Nixon's visit paved the way for normalizing economic relations. Soon after Nixon's visit, several major plants were imported from the United States and other industrialized countries. The Chinese authorities hoped that by reverse engineering they would be able to improve the quality of their own capital goods. However, this did not occur to any significant extent, possibly due to a shortage of trained engineers and technologists, a general phenomenon in developing countries. The shortage of trained personnel was further exacerbated by the undermining of higher education during the Cultural Revolution. The memories of the Great Leap and the excesses of the Cultural Revolution created a crisis of confidence among the Chinese leadership, and the death of Mao paved the way to alter the economic landscape.

By this time, the rapid growth of the Southeast Asian economies was tilting the balance of thinking in favor of an export-led growth paradigm, so it is no surprise that the Chinese leadership opted for an open-economy strategy. When Deng Xiaoping began implementing economic reforms in 1978, the world situation had changed enough to allow China to enter into foreign trade and import foreign technology in a significant way. US allies, trading mainly through Hong Kong, were already undermining US sanctions. US businesses could not just stand by watching America's trading partners cornering the Chinese market, and exerted pressure on the government to normalize relations with China. American anxiety to extricate itself from the Vietnam War also dictated normalization. With relations between the Soviet Union and China rapidly deteriorating, the US was more willing than ever before to use the 'China-card' as a tool of diplomacy against the Soviet Union, while the Chinese leadership saw in the United States a safeguard against aggressive Soviet designs. Internationally, the United States was increasingly isolated on its China policy. China was voted into the United Nations and Taiwan voted out with the overwhelming support of member countries, including some key US allies. The United Nations officially recognized Taiwan as a province of China. This is the context in which Nixon's initiative to normalize a relation with China has to be viewed. Nixon had also conceded that Taiwan was a part of China. By the time Deng's reforms took hold, the international environment had become more congenial for China than ever before.

The Economic Reforms of 1978 liberalized both foreign trade and foreign capital in China. Between 1980 and 1992, the growth rate of exports rose above 15 per cent per annum, occasionally even higher than 30 per cent. Exports continued to grow by 15 per cent per annum during the 1990s. The rise in imports was faster, reaching 24 per cent per annum during the 1990s. In 2000, China accounted for 3.9 per cent of world exports and 3.4 per cent of world imports.[2]

By this time, the pattern of China's foreign trade was substantially diversified. In 2000, 46 per cent of exports were destined for Asian countries, 30 per cent to North and Central America, and 16 per cent to Western Europe. Of imports, 61 per cent came from Asia, 15 per cent from Western Europe, and only 12 per cent came from North and Central America. Other regions of the world had relatively small shares both for exports and imports. Thus, as much as 92 per cent of China's exports went to Asia, North and Central America, and Western Europe, and 88 per cent of imports came from these areas (Table 5.1).[3] The United States has emerged as China's largest

Table 5.1   Direction of Chinese exports and imports by regions, 2000 ($billion)

Regions	Exports*		Imports**	
	Amount	%	Amount	%
Asia	114.6	46.0	136.6	60.7
Western Europe	39.6	15.9	34.0	15.1
North and Central America	75.5	30.3	26.6	11.8
Middle East	5.2	2.1	5.9	2.6
South America	2.7	1.1	4.3	1.9
Africa	3.2	1.3	4.3	1.9
Oceania	4.5	1.8	6.1	2.7
Rest of the World	3.5	1.4	7.6	3.4
World	249.2	100.0	225.1	100.0

Source: The amount for each region is calculated on the basis of the totals and percentages given in Asian Development Bank, *Key Indicators 2001: Growth and Change in Asia and the Pacific*, (Manila: Asian Development Bank, 2001), Tables 29 and 30, pp. 67–8. (Totals do not add up due to rounding errors.) The amounts for North and Central America and Western Europe in this table are on the low side because, according to the WTO, exports from the United States alone in 2000 totaled $16.2 billion and imports reached $103.3 billion. For the European Union, total imports in 2000 amounted to $61.2 billion. See WTO (2001), *International Trade Statistics, 2001* (Geneva: WTO, 2001) Tables III.17 and III.39, pp. 49 and 64.
Notes: *fob (free on board); **cif (cost insurance and freight).

Table 5.2   China's main trading partners, 2000 ($billion)

Partners	Trading partner data			Chinese data		
	Exports	Imports	Balance	Exports	Imports	Balance
USA	16.2	103.3	−87.1	22.4	52.1	−29.7
Japan	30.4	55.1	−24.7	41.5	41.6	−0.1
EU(15)	27.8	61.2	−33.4	30.8	38.1	−7.3
Germany	8.5	16.8	−8.3	10.4	9.3	1.1
UK	2.3	6.7	−4.4	3.6	6.3	−2.7
France	3.1	7.5	−4.4	3.9	3.7	0.2
Hong Kong	69.9	92.4	−22.5	9.4	44.5	−35.1
Taiwan	26.1	6.2	19.9	25.5	5.0	20.5
South Korea	17.7	11.1	6.6	23.2	11.3	11.9
Singapore	5.2	7.0	−1.8	5.0	5.8	−0.8

Source: USA, Japan, and EU data are from the WTO (2001), op. cit., Tables A12, A14, and A19, pp. 194, 198, and 208. The rest of the data is from Thomas Lum and Dick K. Nanto, *China's Trade with the United States and the World*, Congressional Research Service, 3 May 2002, Table A4, p. CRS-31.

trading partner, followed by Hong Kong, now part of China but is treated as a Special Administrative Region (SAR). Among the other trading partners, the European Union (EU) and Japan are the most prominent. Within the

European Union, Germany, France, and the United Kingdom are China's most important trading partners, and among the Asian developing countries the Korean Republic, Taiwan, and Singapore have emerged as the most important. In 2000, the United States imported as much as $103 billion worth of Chinese merchandise. This was 87 per cent more than Japan's and 69 per cent more than the EU's imports from China. Hong Kong – with its $92.4 billion worth of imports – comes next to the United States (Table 5.2).

The nature of China's trade

China, as one would expect of a developing country, is neither a large market for exports nor a source of imports for the United States, the EU, or Japan. Only 6 per cent of Japan's total exports go to China, and nearly 15 per cent of Japan's total imports come from China. China is even less important for the United States and the European Union in both exports and imports (Table 5.3). Only 2 per cent of the total US exports go to China and nearly 8 per cent of total US imports come from China. The corresponding figures for the EU are lower still. In the case of manufactures, Japan imports much more (21 per cent of total imports) from China than the US (10 per cent), and the European Union (3 per cent). The United States also exports fewer

Table 5.3   China's share in the United States, the EU, and Japanese trade, 2000 (%)

Commodities	China's share in the United States		China's share in the EU (15)		China's share in Japan	
	Exports	Imports	Exports	Imports	Exports	Imports
Agricultural	3.3	2.2	0.7	1.0	14.3	11.3
Food	2.8	2.2	0.4	0.8	–	12.3
Mining Products	3.7	0.8	0.8	0.5	15.8	3.3
Manufactures	1.9	10.2	1.3	3.2	6.2	20.9
Iron and steel	–	–	–	–	14.3	–
Chemicals	2.7	2.5	0.8	1.0	11.3	6.1
Machinery*	2.0	6.3	1.8	2.3	4.7	12.2
Electrical machinery	–	14.5	–	5.5	8.5	28.1
Office & telecom Equipment	2.1	10.2	2.1	3.8	4.9	10.5
Textiles	–	12.0	–	3.8	36.8	41.2
Clothing	–	13.2		9.4	–	74.7
Other consumer goods	1.5	30.2	0.7	8.2	5.0	26.1
Footwear	–	61.9	–	10.0	–	65.0
Toys and games	–	64.6	–	33.1	–	47.1
Total merchandise	2.1	8.2	1.2	2.6	6.3	14.5

Source: WTO (2001), *International Trade Statistics, 2001*, Tables III.75 and III.76, pp. 89 and 90.
Note: *Includes transportation equipment.

manufactures than Japan (i.e. 2 per cent of its exports against 6 per cent in the case of Japan). This is also confirmed by the data given in Table 5.4, which provides the value of manufactures and other exports and imports. It seems that for every dollar of export of manufactures the US imports nearly $8 worth of manufactures from China against only $2 dollars and 50 cents for the European Union and a little more than $1 and 50 cents for Japan.

China's total exports (in terms of value) in 2000 to the EU were only 59 per cent of US imports, and Japan's only 53 per cent. On the other hand, Chinese imports from the United States were a little more than half that Japan and a little less than two-thirds of the European Union. The end result was that China's trade surplus with the United States was as much as

Table 5.4   US, EU (15), and Japanese trade with China, 2000 ($ billion)

Commodities	US–China Trade		EU–China trade		Japan–China trade	
	Exports	*Imports*	*Exports*	*Imports*	*Exports*	*Imports*
Agriculture	2.4	1.5	1.5	2.4	0.6	7.0
Food	1.5	1.1	0.6	1.6	0.1	5.9
Mining Products	1.0	1.3	1.0	1.2	1.2	3.3
Fuels	0.1	0.8	0.2	0.4	0.2	2.2
Manufactures	12.6	99.3	23.9	57.5	27.8	44.4
Iron and steel	0.1	0.6	0.5	0.4	2.1	0.6
Chemicals	2.3	1.9	2.5	2.5	4.0	1.6
Machinery[+]	8.1	36.1	16.9	21.2	15.3	13.0
Other non-electrical	1.8	2.6	5.9	1.8	4.6	1.1
Electrical machinery	0.8	8.9	2.1	6.0	3.4	4.1
Office & telecom equip.	3.2	22.4	5.4	11.9	5.2	6.4
Automotive products	0.2	0.6	1.0	0.2	1.3	0.2
Other transport equip.	1.8	1.6	1.5	0.8	0.3	0.4
Textiles	0.12	1.9	0.33	1.9	2.	2.0
Clothing	–	8.8	0.1	8.1	0.1	14.7
Other consumer goods	1.2	42.3	1.6	18.4	2.1	9.6
Total merchandise	16.2	103.3	27.8	61.2	30.4	55.1
Trade surplus*	−87.1		−33.4		−24.7	
	(− 29.7)		(−7.3)		(−0.1)	
Import cover Ratio**	638		220		181	

Source: WTO (2001), *International Trade Statistics, 2001*, Tables A12, A14, and A19, pp. 194–5, 198–9, and 208–9.
Notes: [+]Includes transport equipment; *Trade surplus figures differ between China's own estimates (within brackets) and foreign estimates because of the treatment of Hong Kong. In Chinese trade statistics, shipments to Hong Kong are treated as exports, while other countries classify imports from Hong Kong as imports from China, **Import Cover Ratio = Import/Exports multiplied by 100 to convert into an index. It simply indicates how many dollars worth of goods are imported for every $100 worth of exports to a particular country.

$87.1 billion against only $33.4 billion with the EU and nearly $24.7 billion with Japan. According to Chinese statistics the corresponding deficits are much smaller (Tables 5.2 and 5.4).[4] On the whole, the estimated import-cover ratio suggests that for every $100 worth of exports from Japan to China, Japan imported only $181 worth of imports from China, and the EU imported only $220, while the United States imported as much as $638 worth of merchandise from China. On a per capita basis, import of manufactures from China amounted to $350 each for both Japan and the United States against only $172 for the EU. Thus, the European Union comes out as the least open to Chinese manufacturing exports. Machinery and transportation equipment constitutes almost one-third of the total imports of the US and the EU, but only around a quarter of that of Japan. Thus, in the context of total merchandise trade or trade in manufactures, the United States market has been more open to Chinese goods than the European Union. It seems that the United States is prepared to take machinery and transport equipment more readily than Japan. Arguably, therefore, the US is not only making a much larger net transfer of resources to China through foreign trade than Japan or the EU but also enabling China to diversify its manufacturing more than other developed trading partners. Although there is controversy about the actual extent of the deficit, the growing US trade deficit with China occasionally becomes a major bone of contention between the two countries. The Clinton administration's support for China's entry into the WTO was intended not only to persuade or force China to open its economy to foreign imports, (which may help to reduce the US trade deficit in the long-run), but also to make China party to a rule-based system so that it would be more accountable for its restrictive trade policies. In any case, leaving China, a founding member of the General Agreement for Trade and Tariffs (GATT), out of the organization does not make sense, less so when its economic and trade potential is taken into consideration.

US–China bilateral trade agreement

According to the November 1999 bilateral agreement between China and the United States, China consented to reduce the tariffs on industrial products from an average of 24.6 per cent in 1997 to 9.4 per cent by 2005 (and on American priority products to 7.1 per cent). When implemented, these rates become comparable to those prevailing in other major trading countries. China agreed to cut tariffs on automobiles from the current rate of 80 to 100 per cent to 25 per cent by 2006. China also agreed to join the International Technology Agreement and eliminate almost all tariffs on information technology products such as semiconductors, telecommunications equipment, computers, and computer equipment by 2005. Under the agreement, the tariffs on agricultural products are to come down from the current levels of 22.5 per cent to 17.5 per cent and from 31 per cent to 14 per cent on America's priority products. China is also aiming at liberalizing purchases of bulk agricultural commodities (wheat, corn, rice, cotton, and soybean oil) through tariff-rate quotas (TRQs), which allows for the import of a prescribed amount of a commodity at very low tariffs. A certain proportion of the quota is to be reserved for imports through the private sector. Agricultural subsidies are also to be phased out. Other provisions relate to state-owned enterprises (SOEs), foreign investment, intellectual property rights, and so on. The Chinese government gave an assurance that when making commercial purchases, the SOEs will base their decisions solely on commercial considerations and will give American firms the opportunity to compete for sales or purchase on a non-discriminatory basis.

When it joined the WTO, China agreed to implement the Agreement on Trade-Related Investment, thereby allowing investment licenses to be issued without performance requirements of any kind. In the sphere of services, China agreed to participate in the Financial Services Agreement covering banking, insurance, and other services. After the accession to the WTO, China will be awarding licenses to foreign insurance companies on prudential criteria and will not impose any economic-needs test or quantitative restrictions on the number of licenses; geographical limitations will also be phased out within three years. Foreign insurance companies will eventually be allowed to offer group, health, and pension insurance. For non-life insurance, a 51 per cent ownership by a foreign company would be permissible; for life insurance only a 50–50 joint venture will be allowed.

Within five years foreign banks will be given the right to conduct business in foreign currency with all their clients and in local currency with foreign clients and gradually with Chinese enterprises and individuals. Non-financial institutions will be permitted to supply finance for automobile purchases. China also gave assurances that it would ease the restrictions on professional services such as accountancy, engineering, medical, and consultancy and information technology. Foreign firms will also be permitted to operate as minority joint ventures in underwriting domestic securities, trade, and other securities, such as debt and equity securities. China also guaranteed the protection of intellectual property rights, and will gradually allow increased access to motion pictures, music, and software.

The agreement allows the United States to treat China as a non-market economy for 15 years after its accession to the WTO, thereby enabling the US government to impose a higher anti-dumping duty on Chinese products than on those of market economies. For the 12 years following the Chinese accession, the United States can more easily use product-specific safeguards against import surges of Chinese products, as against other WTO members. Safeguard provisions against import surges of textiles have also been agreed upon.[5]

China will also abolish quotas and other quantitative restrictions. It also agreed to allow American firms to export, import, and distribute their products in the Chinese market. So far, foreign companies have not been allowed to distribute imported products or to provide distribution services such as repair and maintenance.[6] According to the estimates of the US International Trade Commission (ITC), the US exports to and imports from China will rise by 10 and 7 per cent respectively as a result of China's entry into the WTO. Hence, the American trade deficit will increase.[7]

Even allowing for growth effects, the impact of various tariff cuts on the United States' gross domestic product, consumption, and wages would be rather small, inevitably so, as American trade with China accounts for less than one per cent of the US GDP.[7] The sectors benefiting from the Chinese trade reforms would be agriculture, paper and pulp, chemicals, rubber, plastics, and other transportation equipment including aircraft machinery and equipment. Footwear, apparel, wood products, and other light manufactures would be hurt by increased competition from Chinese products. From within the agricultural sector, the exports of cotton, beverages, tobacco, and vegetable oil to China will have increased significantly, and there may also be some increase in the exports of wheat and corn.[8] The American textile sector will be adversely affected, mainly because of the Agreement on Textile and Clothing (ATC), which stipulates phasing out of all quota restrictions on imports from developing countries. The Chinese share of the US textile market is likely to rise to 11 per cent by 2010, and to nearly one-third of the US apparel market.[9] The Chinese gains are likely to come largely from the displacement of competing products from other developing countries.

The US ITC also estimated that the trade reforms will lead to an increase of nearly 4 per cent in the Chinese GDP, mainly due to efficiency gains resulting from restructuring and from greater availability of more productive capital goods. China's total exports are expected to increase by nearly 12 per cent and imports by 14 per cent.[10] According to a recent report by the Chinese Academy of Social Sciences (CASS), Chinese agriculture will 'be exposed to market risks, unemployment risks and security risks.'[11] The production of corn, wheat, soybean oil, seeds, sugarcane, and cotton is likely to drop because of increased competition from American imports. China, currently a net exporter of corn, may become a net importer of corn.[12] According to the CASS, the steel industry, already suffering from excess capacity, would also be hurt; as would the nascent petroleum and petrochemicals, automobile, and information technology industries. In the case of machinery, the impact of the accession is likely to be small. China has some competitive advantage in metal working equipment, instruments and meters, electrical wire, and cable; these are not likely to be seriously affected. On the other hand, new industries involving high technology, high value-added products, and intensive processing will suffer and so will the industries with low-level technology which have not standardized or attained economies of scale.

All in all, the social consequences of China's entry into the WTO will be enormous in terms of increased unemployment and personal, regional, and rural–urban disparities.[13] One estimate suggests that as many as 11 million Chinese workers, 3.5 to 5 million in industry and 5 to 7.5 million in agriculture, could be displaced through the removal of trade protection in 25 key sectors in China. On the other hand, it is hoped that with liberalization overseas, Chinese exports – particularly of textiles and apparel – will create up to 1.5 million jobs, causing a net loss of employment in China of nearly 10 million.[14]

The future of trade disputes

The US–China Bilateral Trade Agreement has certainly removed the immediate irritant of annual renewal of MFN status and its concomitant criticisms of China, some genuine, by various interest groups. Yet the trade agreement between the two countries may turn out to be only a temporary respite – demonstrated amply by the continuing saga of trade disputes with Japan – for a number of reasons. First, the US trade deficit with China will continue and might even grow for a time, depending on the rate of growth of the US economy. Secondly, those who are critical of China's human rights infringements or laxity in enforcement of environmental regulations will continue to focus on trade issues, though in the absence of annual renewal of MFN status, the chances of doing so would be limited. Thirdly, those conservatives in Congress who support Taiwan will continue to find excuses for criticizing China and its performance concerning trade liberalization. Fourthly, many trade unions, which are likely to be affected by increasing imports from China, would also try to find fault with Chinese trade liberalization. Fifthly, those US civil servants who are responsible for trade negotiations would like to be perceived by the voters as doing something meaningful; therefore, it would be in their interest to keep on criticizing China for not doing enough. Finally, a number of tariff and non-tariff barriers within both America and China will provide ample scope for various groups to keep trade disputes alive.[15] For instance, every time any of the two countries takes recourse to anti-dumping action – most commonly used by the United States as a trade protection measure, and more recently being used by China for the same ends – the other will cry foul, and the dispute will get a new lease of life.

It is also possible that the American foreign investment-related imports might increase with the growth of direct foreign investment by US companies that have been locating some of their more labor-intensive manufacturing in China. These Chinese subsidiaries of American companies supply the home base with parts, accessories, and finished products. One estimate suggests that nearly 40 per cent of Chinese exports to the United States originate from American multinationals operating in China. It is also suggested that a 10 per cent increase in US investments in China leads to a 7.3 per cent decrease in the volume of US imports from China, while the American exports to China decrease by only 2.1 per cent.[16] This means that an increase in American foreign investments in China, resulting from the trade agreement and the Chinese accession to the WTO, may tend to increase the US trade deficit. The increase in imports, by providing commodities at cheaper prices and by necessitating a restructuring of the domestic economy, may increase overall welfare, but the cost of such a transformation is not equitably shared by society; some groups gain, yet others are damaged. As a result of the increase in American imports from China, the work force employed in textiles, apparel, footwear, and toys have suffered most. Women have been hit hardest; minorities such as African Americans and Hispanics have also suffered. Imports from China are gradually encroaching on high-wage manufacturing sectors, such as chemicals, fabricated metal products, electrical machinery, electronic and electrical equipment, and transportation equipment. In 1989, only 27 per cent of the imports from China competed against goods produced by the high-wage industries; by 1999, this share rose to 45 per cent.[17] It is natural in a democratic society that the interest groups involved with the affected population be critical of trade deficit.

Even after China's accession to the WTO, the tariff rates for some industries will remain high. On automobiles, for instance, the import duty will be 25 per cent and for motorcycles of various engine capacities, will range from 30 to 45 per cent. Similarly, duties on magnetic tape recorders and video recorders and parts and accessories of video recorders, color satellite television receivers, color video monitors, and color video projectors will be bound at 30 per cent. Similar levels of import duties will be levied on edible vegetable oils, oranges and orange juice, and much higher levels on cane sugar. Some of these products may be of interest to the United States. However, much more contentious are the NTBs (non-tariff barriers). Chinese NTBs included quotas, import licensing, import substitution and local content policies, export performance requirements, and unnecessarily restrictive certification and quarantine standards.[18] China is committed to abolishing quotas, licensing, local content, and export performance requirements on its accession to the WTO, but some of the products subject to licensing and quotas – such as sugar, rubber, wool, and consumer electronics (color TVs, tape players and cameras) – are not major concerns for American exporters.[19] On the other hand, the requirements with regard to automatic registration and stringent labeling requirements will be restrictive. Those who wish to import have to register in advance each jurisdiction into which they wish to import. Some of the labeling requirements, such as in the case of cosmetics and toiletries, are much more stringent than those prevailing in both developed and developing countries importing these items.

State trading may be another barrier, but it is permitted under the WTO rules, so long as the state trading enterprises (STEs) behave as commercial enterprises. China has already made it clear that it would control imports of 66 products and exports of 18 products through a dozen STEs and similar enterprises. China has been liberalizing the handling of foreign trade, and by 1999 as many as 6000 Chinese manufacturing firms were given permission to engage in export and import activities; 61 private companies had also been given such trading rights. China has already agreed to grant full trading rights to US companies within three years of accession.[20] Offsets in terms of local co-production, license for local production, a training package, or technology transfer as a condition of approval of foreign investment can adversely affect the free flow of investment and trade, and therefore is not viewed with favor by the WTO. Public procurement is acceptable so long as it is for government use and not for commercial sale.[21]

In the bilateral agreement with the United States, China has agreed to abolish these offsets. In practice, these offsets will continue because local co-production often suits the foreign investor due to the lower costs of both skilled and unskilled labor. Training packages and technology transfer makes foreign investment more attractive and therefore provides foreign enterprises investing in China a distinct advantage against competing foreign investors. Therefore, even if China were to fully conform to the WTO discipline, 'it is conceivable that voluntary collaboration will simply replace government-mandated offsets in sales between US firms and the Chinese government and the state-run enterprises.'[22] In any case, China or any other developing country which aims at economic development and gradual transformation to a more technologically oriented economy needs technology transfer and training packages. Under the circumstances, it is inevitable that they will use their bargaining power – and certainly, China has the bargaining power – much of which would be determined by the size of the market to approve the entry of a foreign enterprise.

Subsidies can be another issue on which opinions may differ. China has abolished export subsidies on manufactures, but agricultural commodities, particularly corn and cotton, receive export subsidies; manufacturers receive indirect subsidies in the forms of guaranteed provision for raw materials, energy, or labor or low-interest loans.[23] China has agreed to abolish such indirect subsidies on accession; under WTO rules, subsidies on exports and domestically produced inputs are prohibited. On the other hand, subsidies for research and development, regional development, and environmental improvements are permissible.[24]

Among other barriers, mention is often made of standards, testing, labeling and certification. The United States has complained that in China foreign products have to undergo more rigorous tests than domestic products. Many imported and exported products have to undergo a statutory inspection regarding quality, technical specifications, quantity, weight, and packaging and safety requirements. This inspection can be expensive and time consuming.[25] The procedure of obtaining administrative protection for foreign patents takes months, and in the intervening period it is possible for a domestic firm to register, produce, and legally sell a domestic version of similar pharmaceutical products. The shortage of trained personnel in China makes it difficult for foreign companies to register trademarks easily. Lack of transparency is a continuing problem. Chinese ministries implement policies which are often based on 'guidance' or 'opinions,' and the foreign firms do not have access to such information. Besides, laws and regulations in China are more general than in other countries and therefore are subject to differing interpretations. Procedures for appeal against regulatory decisions are continually insufficient.[26] Many of these complaints are genuine, but a little circumspection will show that, given the fact that the current spate of reforms in China only began in 1978, progress in the creation of a legal infrastructure for dealing with market economies and foreign firms is reasonably impressive.

Foreign investment into China

China is the second largest recipient of foreign investment next only to the United States. The Asian financial crisis caused some decline to the inflow of foreign investment into China, yet it attracted an average inflow of $42 billion (Table 5.5) during the three years 1998–2000. Nearly 40 per cent of all foreign direct investment (FDI) inflow came from Hong Kong.[27] The United States share is only 10 per cent of total FDI. Virgin Islands comes

Table 5.5 Foreign Direct Investment flows into China, 1998–2000 ($ billion)

Country sources	1998		1999		2000		Average 1998–2000	
	Amount	%	Amount	%	Amount	%	Amount	%
Germany	0.74	1.6	1.37	3.4	1.04	2.5	1.05	2.5
Hong Kong	18.51	40.6	16.36	40.5	15.50	38.1	16.79	39.8
Japan	3.40	7.5	2.97	7.3	2.91	7.1	3.09	7.3
Singapore	3.40	7.5	2.64	6.5	2.17	5.3	2.74	6.5
Korean Rep.	1.80	4.0	1.27	3.1	1.49	3.7	1.52	3.6
Taiwan	2.92	6.4	2.60	6.4	2.29	5.6	2.60	6.2
UK	1.18	2.6	1.04	2.6	1.16	2.8	1.12	2.6
US	3.90	8.6	4.22	10.4	4.38	10.8	4.17	9.9
Virgin Islands	4.03	8.9	2.66	6.6	3.84	9.4	3.51	8.3
Others	5.58	12.3	5.27	13.1	5.93	14.6	5.59	13.2
Total	45.46	100.0	40.40	100.0	40.71	100.0	42.19	100.0

Source: Based on Lum and Nanto (2002), op. cit., Table 15, p. CRS-21.

next; in this case, however, the investors may possibly have different origins and are using the island as a tax-haven. The annual inflows from Japan, Singapore, and Taiwan are between 6 per cent and 7 per cent of the total inflow into China, and the Korean Republic contributed around 4 per cent. Thus, nearly 60 per cent of all FDI into China came from only four countries: Hong Kong, Singapore, South Korea, and Taiwan. The European contribution has been rather small; inflow from Germany and the United Kingdom was a little less than 3 per cent each. For foreign resources, China also relied quite heavily on foreign loans; between 1994 and 1997, China borrowed an average of $18 billion a year, a substantial part of which came from commercial banks.

During 1998 and 2001 China paid back nearly $43 billion worth of bank loans. Nevertheless, as of September 2001, China's outstanding bank loans amounted to $59.4 billion. Nearly $12 billion of this total was owed to Japan, between $6–7 billion each to France, Germany, and the United Kingdom, and $5 billion to the United States.[28] Multilateral development banks such as the World Bank, the Asian Development Bank, and the International Development Association (IDA) all provided additional loans. These banks, on average, provided $1 billion a year. Trade credits brought in anywhere between $1–3 billion a year. Foreign concessional loans under foreign aid brought in around $2 billion a year to China during the second half of 1990s, about half of it coming from the Japanese government; such loans have been declining to a virtual trickle since 1996 (Table 5.6).

Thus, since the 1978 economic reforms, China has depended significantly on foreign resources for its economic development. Such resources have come in various forms; trade surplus, direct foreign investment, and borrowing from commercial and development banks, as well as

Table 5.6   Annual private and official international borrowing by China 1996–2001 ($ million)

Type of borrowing	1996	1997	1998	1999	2000	2001
Debt securities issued	1,550	2,515	−774	−729	−19	−123
Total trade credits	3,046	1,824	588	1,022	−312	−1,513
Multilateral bank loan	2,402	2,501	2,338	1,903	1,953	1,789
Official loans	1,703	1,145	561	465	−2,047	705
Borrowing from banks	13,105	11,274	−8,488	−23,361	−7,232	−3,923
Total	21,806	19,259	−5,775	20,701	−7,657	−3065

Source: The Joint Bank for International Settlements (BIS), the International Monetary Fund (IMF), the Organization for Economic Cooperation and Development (OECD), and the World Bank statistics on external debt database, updated in December 2002 (http://www.bis.org).
Notes: Multilateral Loans are from institutions such as the World Bank, the International Development Association, the Asian Development Bank, and bilateral foreign aid.

government-to-government loans on concessional terms. During the period 1998–2000, China had an annual trade surplus of nearly $32 billion. During the same period China received an average annual inflow of $42 billion in terms of FDI. However, during 1998–2000 China paid back nearly $10 billion a year of its loans. Thus, during the period China received net foreign resources of $64 billion annually. This sum was roughly one-fifth of the gross domestic savings of the country.

Technology transfers

China has also borrowed foreign technology and, as a part of granting licenses to foreign firms to operate in China, has insisted that foreign firms transfer technology to their Chinese counterparts. It is generally accepted that American and EU firms more inclined to transfer advanced technology to developing countries than their Japanese counterparts. The transfer of sophisticated technologies from Japanese firms tends to be slow, and the Japanese style of management (along with their methods of technology transfer through on-the-job training and small group discussions) tends to be less effective in transferring cutting-edge technology.[29]

China has sent a large number of Chinese students for advanced training abroad, primarily in science, engineering, and in advanced technology. Around 55,000 Chinese students were being trained in the United States in 1998–99.[30] The number of Chinese students in Japan totals around 11,000.[31] However, a substantial number of Chinese students in Japan are registered in Japanese language schools. An entry into a language school there entitles a student to a visa to live and work in Japan. Unfortunately, some of the best trained Chinese never leave America to go back to China. American salaries and lifestyles are attractive to those coming from developing countries. China has some additional disadvantages in terms of restrictions on personal freedom. Before the current recession, foreign companies enticed well-trained Chinese and Indian technologists to jobs in computing, software, and artificial intelligence; work visas were being granted much more easily in most industrialized countries. However, as a result of the recession, many foreign nationals are finding the job-hunt much more difficult; more so in the cases of young men and women from Middle Eastern countries after September 11.

Intellectual property rights

American firms have been consistently complaining about global infringement of intellectual property rights. Some of the most affected industries include computer software, high technology products, sound recordings, motion pictures, pharmaceuticals, agricultural chemicals, and books. The total losses incurred by American industries have been estimated to be around $2.3 billion in 1995, consisting of $124 million in losses to the motion picture industry, $300 million in losses due to piracy of sound recordings and musical compositions, $1.3 billion in losses to the entertainment software industry, $488 million in losses due to piracy of business software, and $125 million in losses due to book piracy.[32] In an attempt to live up to its commitments, China conducts thousands of raids and arrests, imprisons the violators, and has confiscated millions of pirated CDs, books, audiocassettes, and other trademarked products. It has established a nationwide intellectual property rights (IPR) enforcement structure consisting of enforcement agencies and the police. Moreover, it has decided to provide market access for foreign software companies by allowing them to establish joint ventures and, in some instances, wholly owned ventures.

There is an increasing involvement of the Public Security Bureaus (PSBs) and criminal courts in cases of IPR infringements. Both the intellectual property owners and the Chinese enforcement agencies can file criminal complaints with the PSBs. The PSBs are now authorized to conduct raids on pirates and arrest them. The People's procurators both at local and central levels can prosecute IPR violators under Chinese criminal law.[33] As a result of the National Campaign for the Rectification of Market Disorder, launched in April 2001 to crack down on shoddy counterfeit products, as of July 2001 nearly 115,000 cases have been identified, 13,500 factories producing fake goods closed, and 567 suspects taken to court.[34]

Nevertheless, the record of Chinese enforcement remains mixed. Millions of pirated CDs, videos, and high-value-added CD-ROMs containing computer software not only circulate within China but also flood the Southeast Asian, European, and Latin American markets. The reasons are not far to seek: the pirate factories can go underground; there is a shortage of trained staff with the enforcement agencies; and with the multiplicity of enforcement agencies coordination becomes difficult. In the face of widespread corruption and inefficiencies within China, enforcement can at best be incomplete.

According to an OECD report, China leads the top five sources (China, Korea, Taiwan, Hong Kong, and the Philippines) in supplying counterfeited goods to the US market.[35] American pressures on China to ameliorate the situation are understandable. On the other hand, counterfeiting is a major world problem, and no amount of unilateral or bilateral negotiations or actions can bring about a meaningful solution. The same OECD report suggests that nearly one-third of the music CDs, half of the videos, and 43 per cent of software sold are pirated products. Almost all software producers are based within the United States.[36] The global sale of counterfeit music recordings is estimated at $4.5 billion by one EU report, including the sale of nearly 370 million CDs and 1.6 billion cassettes.[37] Many of the counterfeit CDs sold within the EU are manufactured within EU countries.[38] The largest proportion of optical polycarbonate manufacturers and replicators are also located in the United States and in the EU.[39]

Counterfeit clothing and footwear are produced on a large scale in France, Greece, Italy, Spain, Portugal, and the United Kingdom. Half of all counterfeit clothing is produced in EU member countries. Counterfeit vehicle spare parts are produced in Germany, Italy, Spain, Portugal, and the United Kingdom. Counterfeit pharmaceuticals are produced in Germany, Italy, Greece, Spain, and Portugal. Nearly all counterfeit perfumes and video film are manufactured in the EU member state where it is sold.[40] No country within the European Union is immune; the incidence in Greece and Italy is much higher than in Germany, the Netherlands, or the United Kingdom.

In spite of vigorous anti-piracy law enforcements within the United States and Canada, the piracy rate of software in North America is estimated to be around 28 per cent; in Europe it is as high as 43 per cent.[41] One of the major problems is that organized crime has become involved with trade in counterfeit goods. The other is that consumers are willing to buy counterfeits knowingly. A recent Mori Poll suggested that as many as 40 per cent of the respondents would buy counterfeits even if they knew the products were counterfeit.[42] Most desired counterfeits included clothing, watches, and perfumes, but also children's toys, pharmaceuticals, car parts, and electrical switchgear, which may have serious adverse consequences for safety and health. However, it is the desire, fueled incessantly by high-pressure advertising, to own and be seen in designer-labeled clothes and accessories that lead people to purchase imitations. Enforcement at the consumer level is not easy. Even at production levels enforcement is difficult because it can go underground or move to a more convenient country. In countries with long borders with a neighboring country, border control presents immense problems. Even within the United States, the experiences of policing and eliminating traffic in drug, vice rings, child pornography, and money laundering have at best a mixed record. In most countries, there is a provision for raids, imprisonment, confiscation of counterfeits, court cases, and fines, but the penalties imposed are not always sufficient to deter counterfeiting. It is getting easier to sell counterfeits through the Internet. Under the circumstances, Chinese commitments to enforce the IPR regulations can bear fruit only slowly. Besides, some of the methods, such as summary trials and firing squads, adopted by China for crime control and for elimination of corruption, smuggling, etc., come directly into conflict with human rights and cannot be advocated or morally condoned.

International implications of the high rates of growth

As the Chinese economy is growing fast, it will inevitably generate a rising demand for food, raw materials, and energy. China is also facing some other problems. With the opening up of the country to market forces and other foreign influences, the power base of the Chinese Communist Party and its popularity has been undermined. The crumbling of the Soviet empire and the demise of the Communist parties in the Soviet Union and Eastern Europe have convinced the leadership in Beijing that it can retain its legitimacy – in fact its very survival – mainly on delivering visible improvements in the living conditions of the people. It is for this reason that China's leadership has been giving primacy to economic over security considerations. The future growth rate of the Chinese economy will inevitably depend on both social and political stability at home and a congenial international environment. The pace of economic reform itself might determine the domestic as well as the international situation. If the Chinese authorities are tempted, under either foreign influence or foreign pressures, to accelerate the pace of reforms, it is possible that social distress in terms of increasing unemployment and widening income disparities between people and regions might be further aggravated, leading to social and political unrest at home. Rising disparities in income levels – among both individuals and regions – are divisive and can be detrimental to political stability and consequently to the future rate of growth.

The growing income inequality

In market-oriented economic reform, growing equality of income is almost inevitable. With the rapid increase in income, there is an initial tendency in all market economies for inequality to grow until such time as the government, by various policy measures, decides to reduce the disparities. In fact, the wealthier echelons of communities in the United States as well as the United Kingdom have been growing faster since the Reagan-Thatcher market revolution aimed at the privatization of public enterprises, often at the cost of public expenditure on welfare provisions. The privatization of public sectors benefits bankers, financiers, and speculators on the stock market, while the workers lose jobs, subsidized food, housing, and medical facilities. The distribution of income in rural China, as reflected by the Gini-coefficient (one of the most commonly used measures of income distribution) rose only marginally between 1988 and 1994, but urban income distribution became markedly unequal.[43] Primarily because of the concentration of modern industries in the coastal areas, regional disparities have also increased. While some 'trickle down' effect from the eastern coastal region through migrant workers has helped other regions, regional differences have nevertheless grown. Between 1978 and 1995, income differentials between the eastern and western regions increased from 1.2 times to twice as much.[44] Such disparities create resentment among the poorer regions, some of which are inhabited predominantly by ethnic minorities. In 1989, China's western and central regions also had the highest incidence of poverty, ranging from 18.4 per cent in the west to 11.2 per cent in the central region, against only 3.6 per cent in the coastal region.[45] Nearly half of the counties in the western and central regions had per capita incomes below the poverty line (defined at 300 Yuan in 1989). These are the areas which have a considerable Muslim population, which is being greatly influenced by the surging tide of Islamic fundamentalism in the Central Asian republics and in the Middle East. All this does not auger well for the continued social and political stability of China.

Increasing unemployment

Further disenchantment is being created by growing unemployment in the wake of privatization and rationalization of the Chinese industries, particularly the SOEs. The currently estimated number of 'floating population' (or temporary and illegal rural migrant workers) at around 100 million is probably an underestimate. The number of rural labor surplus was expected to have reached 200 million by the year 2002.[46] The WTO accession by China, providing for increased agricultural imports, may further add to rural unemployment and lead to an increased flow of urban migrants with all the social and political consequences of uncontrolled urbanization and urban slums.

The problem of unemployment and underemployment may also be exacerbated by the market-oriented reform of China's SOEs.[47] On 'efficiency' criteria, the very touchstone of a capitalist enterprise, about half of the SOEs are unprofitable and are not able to pay back bank loans. With a view to restoring the viability of the Chinese industrial sector and the banking system, the government is closing down some of the unprofitable SOEs and privatizing and streamlining many others through a massive retrenchment of labor. This goes hand-in-hand with the retrenchment of social services (housing, health, and education) so far provided by the SOEs. By the year 2025, China's natural increase in population itself may add another 190 million people to its labor force.[48] This would be in addition to the currently estimated unemployed and underemployed population of over 155 million.[49] Thus China, by the end of the first quarter of the twenty-first century, may have to provide meaningful job opportunities for nearly 350 million people. The prospect of a viable solution to the problem, particularly under a market-oriented development strategy, is not very bright. Under the circumstances, many potential workers will have to subsist in low paid jobs in small-scale industries, handicrafts, small shops and other services. Growing unemployment is already creating social unrest and will have serious implications for the social and political stability of the country in coming years.

Environmental degradation

The indiscriminate pursuit of rapid growth in most developing countries has had serious deleterious effects on the environment. China is no exception. Chinese official sources concede that overall pollution levels in Chinese cities are high. Among the 47 key cities, 13 have very poor air quality. Nearly a third of the country is affected by acid rain. Organic pollution is universal in the surface water of the seven major river basins in China.[50] With rising incomes and the removal of restrictions on car ownership – as well as the ready availability of cars in China – the number of cars rose from 2.4 million in 1984 to 9.4 million in 1994. By 2020, it is estimated to increase by 13–22 times. Chinese vehicles, considered to be the most polluting in the world, are said to be responsible for nearly three-quarters of the carbon monoxide emissions in Beijing, Shanghai, Hangzhou, and Guangzhou.[51] The energy and industrial sectors are the other major polluters in terms of causing smoke, acid rain, and poor water quality, particularly in waters close to the industrially advanced cities and towns. According to Chinese National Environmental Protection Agency estimates, the economic costs associated with ecological destruction and environmental pollution may add up to nearly 14 per cent of the Chinese GDP.[52] Any significant progress on the environment front would require a considerable diversion of funds from directly developmental expenditure to environmental protection, which can possibly slow down the rate of growth in the short-run, even though in the long-run it might increase social welfare.

Another major source of disquiet is the unsatisfactory state transportation and communications systems that lead to frequent bottlenecks in these sectors. Unless considerable financial resources and technological expertise are diverted to transportation and communications, it is inevitable that frequent bottlenecks and breakdowns will impede economic growth. The massive diversion of financial resources to these sectors is needed at a time when Beijing's ability to collect tax revenue is eroding under the growing clamor for tax autonomy by the regions; those regions that are growing fast are reluctant to subsidize the slowly growing or laggard ones. Besides, not unlike other developing countries, tax evasion is quite rampant. While the economy has grown, government revenues as a share of GDP dropped from 28 to 11 per cent between 1978 and 1995.[53] Under the circumstances, maintaining a high rate of growth in the coming decades seems problematic. On the other hand, if China fails to maintain adequate growth, social cohesion and political stability may be threatened, with all the consequences for the future rates of growth.

Unfortunately, if the pace of reform is too slow, it may risk trade conflicts with major trading partners and disenchantment among foreign investors, adversely affecting in-flow of foreign funds. A compromise on the pace of economic reforms will tax the ingenuity of China's leadership for the foreseeable future. One thing is almost certain: the pace of reform will be relatively slow, at times even halting. The Chinese leadership has learned its lessons from the economic and political collapse of the Soviet Union and will try its utter best to avoid the same mistakes.

Projections for future growth rates

The projections of future growth rates, even the most sophisticated ones, are largely extrapolations of past trends into the future. Of course, some alternative scenarios based on the subjective judgments of the researcher are also examined, which makes most projections somewhat conjectural. Yet for most policymaking, some ideas of the likely trends of growth and its direction are essential starting points. Most available projections of Chinese economic growth over the next quarter century range between 5 and 7 per cent per year.[54] Perkins, a leading China scholar, suggests that even under unfavorable circumstances, such as a hostile international economic environment, China could attain an annual growth rate of no less than 4.5 per cent, which might even be as high as 8 or 9 per cent per annum if the circumstances were favorable.[55] Taking his best and worst scenarios, it is possible to expect China to grow by 7 per cent per annum, a rate consistent with the World Bank projection of 5.5 to 7.5 per cent between 2002 and 2010 and the 6.7 per cent growth forecast for the period 2006 to 2020 by Standard & Poor's Data Resources, Inc.[56]

With a 5 per cent rate of growth over the next twenty-five years, by 2025 China's nominal GDP would reach around $3.5 trillion, against $7.3 trillion for Japan and $15.5 trillion for the United States, assuming a 2 per cent growth rate for both Japan and the US. At a higher rate of growth of 7 per cent per annum, the Chinese nominal GDP in 2025 would be around $5.8 trillion, a little more than half of Japan's $9.4 trillion or a little more than a quarter of the United States' at $19.9 trillion, assuming the higher 3 per cent growth rate both for Japan and the United States. Even at the high rate of 7 per cent per annum, the Chinese nominal per capita income at $4587 will not exceed that of a middle-income developing country in 1999. In terms of per capita income (GDP) China's would be an estimated $2809 (at 5 per cent growth) as compared with $57,764 for Japan and $56,710 for the United States (at 2 per cent growth).[57] At these growth rates of 5 per cent for China and 2 per cent for Japan and the United States, the absolute gap in per capita incomes would have grown.[58] Even if China were to grow at 7 per cent per year, its per capita income in 2025 would be somewhat higher at $4587 but still relatively low.[59]

In terms of PPP[60] the Chinese GDP would range between $18 and $30 trillion, thus exceeding the gross domestic products of the United States, the European Union, and Japan. In an aggregate sense, China will have emerged as an economic superpower. Yet the Chinese per capita GDP (PPP) will remain much below those of the United States, the European Union, and Japan. (Table 5.7)

China's emergence as a major economic power carries several implications for US economic and security interests. A question for the United States, and the world as a whole for that matter, is whether the magnitude of China's future demand for food and energy will disrupt world markets. Most industrialized and developing countries depend heavily on imported food, raw materials, and energy. With more rapid economic growth of developing countries, such demands are likely to rise faster. First, we consider the Chinese demand for food grains and its consequences.

Table 5.7   GDP and per capita GDP, 1999 and projections for 2025 at selected growth rates ($)

	China	Japan	USA	EU
1999 base year figures				
Nominal GDP (billion)	997	4,370	9,256	8,361
GDP (PPP) (billion)	5,201	2,935	9,256	7,986
Nominal GDP per capita	790	34,519	33,889	22,285
GDP per capita (PPP)	4,228	23,465	33,889	21,286

			Projections for 2025 at selected growth rates					
	%	Amount	%	Amount	%	Amount	%	Amount
Projected nominal GDP (billion)	5	3,545	2	7,313	2	15,452	2	13,715
	7	5,790	3	9,424	3	19,914	3	1 7,504
Projected GDP (PPP) (billion)	5	18,493	2	4,911	2	15,452	2	13,102
	7	30,204	3	6,330	3	19,914	3	16,720
Projected nominal per Capita GDP	5	2,809	2	57,764	2	56,710	2	3 7,473
	7	4,587	3	74,443	3	73,085	3	47,823
Projected per capita GDP (PPP)	5	15,033	2	39,267	2	56,710	2	35,797
	7	24,553	3	50,604	3	73,085	3	45,683

Source: Nanto and Sinha (2000), op. cit., Table 6, CRS-20.
Note: Projections by CRS assuming alternative growth rates for China of between 5 and 7 per cent per year over the next 25 years and at 2 and 3 per cent per year for both Japan and the United States. Projected amounts are in 1999 prices.

China's future food demand

For most developing countries, the future demand for food in international markets depends on the likely rates of economic growth, changes in income distribution, the rates of growth of population, the pace of urbanization, income-generated changes in food habits, and the relative prices of substitutes or complementary goods. Future long-term domestic supplies of food depend largely on increased investment in agriculture and agricultural inputs (e.g. fertilizer), research and development, the availability of water, relative prices, and infrastructural developments (transportation, communications, and storage), while the short-run supply situation is greatly influenced by the vagaries of the weather.

Although there are wide differences among the available estimates of grain import requirements for China, the current consensus indicates that by 2025, annual import of grain in China may range between 40 and 50 million tons. A recent study by the OECD suggests a baseline projection of annual net imports of 43 million metric tons by the year 2020.[61] Other estimates suggest imports of between 20 and 30 million metric tons per year.[62] On the other hand, as the OECD estimates indicate, if China does not invest significantly in agriculture or fails to implement appropriate agricultural policies, its imports could rise to as much as 106 million metric tons annually. The OECD study suggests that even this magnitude of Chinese import demand of over 100 million tons may not have a significant impact on world food grain markets, as there is sufficient potential in food-exporting countries to increase domestic production; the rise in prices resulting from the Chinese demand in itself provides an incentive for increased production.[63]

However, grain imports of this magnitude, roughly equivalent to a sixth of the Chinese annual food demand, may be viewed as an unacceptable vulnerability by the Chinese leadership, mainly because it is the United States and its allies (namely Canada, Australia, Argentina, and Thailand) who are the main suppliers to the world markets. Past experience shows that the United States does not hesitate to use food as a political weapon. On the other hand, increasing Chinese demand for food creates new opportunities for American farmers and agri-businesses, so they would conceivably use their influence against America using food as a political weapon. In April 1999, the Clinton Administration decided to lift prohibitions on US commercial sales of most agricultural commodities and food products to Iran, Libya, and Sudan and indicated that these products would not be included in future sanctions on other countries.[64] Nevertheless, particularly in view of the potential risk of military confrontation with the Unites States on the question of Taiwan, China will certainly aim at a much lower level of import dependence, possibly not much more than the currently acceptable level of 5 per cent. Whether this level can be successfully maintained only time can tell.

Petroleum demand

As an inevitable consequence of rapid economic development, the demand for energy in China has been rising fast; domestic production is already failing to keep pace with demand.[65] China's estimated demand for crude petroleum in 2001 was 4.9 million barrels a day against a domestic production of 3.3 million barrels per day.[66] Thus, the Chinese dependence on imported petroleum was as high as one-third of the total demand. Nearly half of the current Chinese oil imports comes from the Middle East, a figure that is expected to rise to 80 per cent by the year 2010.[67] Such high levels of imports from a region that is controlled directly or indirectly by the United States or its client states, with the exception of Iran, Iraq, and Libya, will certainly be seen as a strategic vulnerability by China, and it will try to diversify its sources of supply. It is in this context that China has been transferring weapons technology to Iran and is supportive of Iraq. This certainly irks American policymakers, who are keen to prevent the transfer of technology related to weapons of mass destruction and missiles to these countries.

There is another problem, a purely economic one, which may create a confrontational situation between the United States and China. China's rapidly rising petroleum demand may raise world petroleum prices – unless OPEC decides to increase production – creating potential risks of inflation within the United States, EU, Japan, and South Korea, which are also major importers of oil as are some of the major developing countries. This may slow down the growth rates of the world economy, affecting not only world trade but also China's future exports, standard of living, and poverty. China is fully conscious of the dilemma and is exploring the possibility of opening up oil fields, particularly in its neighboring countries in Central Asia. China recently acquired the right to develop two oil fields in Kazakhstan and is planning to build a 3000-kilometer pipeline from the Kazakhstan oilfields into China's western Xinjiang province and a 250-kilometer pipeline to the borders of Iran.[68] China National Petroleum Corporation (CNPC) also holds oil concessions in Venezuela, Sudan, Iraq, Iran, Peru, and Azerbaijan.[69] China is also giving high priority to offshore developments and has signed contracts with Western companies for exploration and product sharing. China's effort to diversify its sources of petroleum supply has increasingly brought it into closer contact with Islamic countries; this has worried US policymakers. As seen earlier, some international relations experts see this development as a Sino-Islamic conspiracy to undermine American hegemony. Chinese offshore development in the East and South China Seas has the potential to exacerbate territorial disputes with neighboring countries, which can also be seen as undermining American interests.

Conclusion

On the economic front, since 1978, China has become significantly dependent on the United States and its allies not only for trade, but also for foreign investments, loans and technology transfers. Since the very legitimacy of the Chinese Communist Party depends on delivering continued perceptible improvements in the living standards of the Chinese people, it does not seem logical for it to adopt a confrontational posture towards the United States. In fact, from the establishment of the Communist regime in Beijing, the leadership tried to create a *modus operandi* by which a meaningful economic and diplomatic relationship could be established between the two countries. Communist China did not intentionally opt for an autarchic regime. It was forced upon it by the United States and the Soviet Union; by America as a reprisal for the Chinese involvement in the Korean War and by the Soviet Union as a punishment for not towing the Soviet line in its entirety. As seen in the previous chapters, mistakes were made on both sides, but America and its anti-communist obsessions must be apportioned a larger share of the blame for the embittered relationship between China and the United States for over a quarter of the last century. With unparalleled economic and military might in the post-World War II years, America became 'entrapped and enthralled,' as Senator Frank Church stresses, in the 'fantasy that it lay within our power to control other countries through the covert [and sometimes overt] manipulation of their affairs.'[70] This tendency has distinctly reemerged since the demise of the Soviet Union and is reflected in the increasing unilateralism of the George W. Bush administration.

From the Nixon days of normalizing diplomatic relations, economic relations and occasional anti-Soviet security cooperation between the two countries have progressed with some short-term interruptions and came to full bloom during the Clinton presidency.

Neither of the two sides, barring a possible confrontation on the Taiwan issue, is prepared to rock the boat. For China, the economic gains from the relationship are impressive; for America too, the lure of the Chinese market is tempting. There have been continuing disputes with regard to trade deficits, infringements of intellectual property rights, the pace of market opening, environmental issues, and above all, human rights, but both sides concede the preeminence of economic over other considerations. There is an underlying fear in America that the rapidly increasing income in China and, consequently, its rising demand for grains, oil, and other resources might create international market situations detrimental to US interests. However, the Chinese resource demand at the current or projected levels of income over the next quarter century is not of the order that might threaten the American lifestyle. In fact, the increase in the demand for food might provide additional market opportunities for American farmers. Despite the United States disavowing use of food as a political weapon, China may wish to keep its food imports within manageable proportions. The rapidly increasing Chinese energy demand may have inflationary consequences for America and its allies, but this can be averted if the United States uses its influence with its Middle Eastern client states to persuade them to increase supply commensurate with rising world demand. China sees a high dependence on imported oil as a strategic vulnerability and is trying to diversify its sources of supply. This is bringing China into closer cooperation with the Muslim countries in Central Asia and the Middle East, which may potentially undermine American interests in these regions. For the foreseeable future, however, China is more of an economic opportunity than a threat for America.

6
Human Rights – a Tool of Diplomacy

What a calamity it must be to have 300 millions unemployed, several millions becoming degraded every day for want of employment, devoid of self-respect, devoid of faith in God. I may as well place before the dog over there the message of God as before those hungry millions who have no lustre in their eyes and whose only God is their bread. I can take before them a message of God only by taking the message of sacred work before them. It is good enough to talk of God whilst we are sitting here after a nice breakfast, and looking forward to a nicer luncheon, but how am I to talk of God to the millions who have to go without two meals a day?

(Mahatma Gandhi[1])

Introduction

The defense of human rights and fundamental freedoms has been one of the basic responsibilities of the United Nations since its very inception. But the great powers behind the formation of the United Nations saw the respect for human rights and fundamental freedoms as 'merely an incidental aspiration of the new organization.' Only pressure from American non-governmental organizations such as the American Jewish Congress and the National Association for the Advancement of Colored People led to human rights being given a prominent place in the UN Charter.[2]

The human rights ideas incorporated in the UN Charter were inspired by H.G. Wells and a few of his 'well-meaning middle-class socialist' friends. They felt that adequate nutrition, housing, clothing, shelter, and medical attention sufficient to realize one's full potential in terms of physical and mental health must be guaranteed to everybody irrespective of race or color. They also felt that sufficient education for making an individual a responsible and involved citizen was critical. To this list they also added civil and police protection to lawfully acquired property, safeguards against torture, beating or any bodily punishment or maltreatment in prisons, particularly subjecting a prisoner to excessive silence, noise, light or darkness as to cause mental suffering or to unsanitary conditions in prisons.[3]

President Franklin Roosevelt, deeply impressed by Wells' ideas, made some of them a basis for his declaration of the 'four essential freedoms' of the Atlantic Charter. These were: the freedom of speech and expression; the freedom of religion; the freedom from want; and the freedom from fear. The idea of promoting and encouraging respect for human rights and fundamental freedoms for all without distinction as to race, sex, language, or religion was incorporated in the United Nations Charter both in the preamble and in Article 1.[4]

However, as Geoffrey Robertson indicates in his book, *Crimes Against Humanity*, none of the major allied powers were in favor of including a bill of rights in the Charter – Britain and France had no intention of granting self-determination to their colonies, America had its 'Jim Crow Laws' supporting American apartheid – as the smaller countries wished, nor was a human rights convention prepared because such a convention after ratification would have legal validity. However, a Universal Declaration of Human Rights was adopted by the General Assembly on 10 December 1948.[5] The Declaration did not involve any legal obligation and was 'flouted without regard to geography, by governments of every creed and color and often by or with the connivance of the US and its European allies'[6] The Declaration, along the lines of Wells' ideas and of the 'freedom from want' of the Atlantic Charter, incorporated 'a basic standard of living' as 'rights' which were 'indispensable for dignity and the free development of personality.' Yet they were consigned to a separate treaty – the International Covenant on Economic, Social and Cultural Rights – and it was decided that this covenant should have no adjudicatory body like the Human Rights Committee.[7] Subsequent attempts to annex an Optional Protocol to the Economic Covenant were consistently opposed by the United States.[8] Interestingly, even Friedrich Hayek, the archpriest of free-market capitalism, has been in favor of 'a social safety net guaranteeing all citizens a basic minimum of food, shelter, and clothing.'[9] Nevertheless, President Truman, in his economic policy speech given a week before the Truman Doctrine speech, narrowed down Roosevelt's 'four freedoms' to three, replacing the old 'freedom from want' and 'freedom from fear' to a new 'freedom of enterprise' to accompany the 'freedom of speech' and 'freedom of worship.'[10] In much the same tradition, the present debate on human rights invariably revolves around political and religious freedoms, neglecting economic freedom.

Seen in the context of the UN Declaration or the criteria set by Wells, the human rights record of the People's Republic of China is certainly a mixed one: although it did succeed in providing basic needs, it deprived the Chinese of basic political freedoms. In the wake of economic reforms that began in 1978, while some personal freedoms are gradually being made available, economic guarantees are disappearing fast. Nevertheless, the PRC record might still be better than the records of its predecessors. The PRC might also come out better in terms of providing the basic needs of the Chinese people than those of contemporary developing countries, such as Brazil or India – two countries that can be legitimately compared with a nation the size and diversity as China – which have not been able to provide the basic necessities to a substantial proportion of their citizens. On the criterion of liberty, India is certainly way ahead of China, but the same may not be said with confidence about Brazil. Arguably, if Wells' economic criteria are taken as the touchstone, even the richest countries of the world including the United States may not come out unscathed. Many of their citizens are still inadequately provided for in terms of sufficient 'nourishment, housing, covering, medical care and attention' for realizing their 'full possibilities of physical and mental development.'

Pre-communist China

There is a long tradition of Confucian scholars expressing concern over the conditions in which Chinese people lived and advocating reform of land ownership, redistribution of land, and appropriate levels of taxes. Mencius, the great Confucian philosopher, went so far as to suggest that the people had the right to revolt against a tyrant and to overthrow him.[11] Many Chinese rulers adopted policies to improve the economic and social conditions of peasants. Particular mention may be made of the southern Sung government, which 'sought to strengthen its economic position by a policy of official encouragement for more skilful husbandry.'[12] Nevertheless, the fate of the peasants varied over time and was linked not only to natural disasters, but also to man-made conditions such as types of tenure, landlord's share of rent, level of wages and working conditions, nearness to cities, commercialization of agriculture, and, above all, peace and order and the general prosperity of the country.[13] However, the economic condition of peasants over long stretches of time was not always satisfactory. A University of Nanking study suggested that in the 2019 years between 108 BC and AD 1911, 1828 years experienced famines.[14] During the nineteenth century alone, an estimated one hundred million people died of famine.[15] In a survey of twenty-two provinces in China during 1929–33, an informant told Lossing Buck about four famines in northern wheat regions and three in the rice regions of the south within the informant's lifetime.[16] As Ramon Myers points out, 'in the famine-ridden northwest great masses of peasants were perpetually on the verge of starvation; the human spirit frequently broke under these conditions, and the family disintegrated.'[17]

As in many developing countries, even in normal times, let alone in times of shortages, Chinese women suffered the most. A preference for a male child made female infanticide quite common. Wives and daughters did not possess rights of inheritance. Many women were subjected to concubinage, adultery, foot binding, sale into prostitution, and other subjugating fates.[18] All this was reflected in the demographic statistics collected during Buck's survey of China. In both North and South China there were as many as 108 males per 100 females.[19] The rural poverty in China translated into a relatively high death rate estimated at 27 per thousand. Infant mortality rates reached highs of 156 per thousand live births. Less than 60 per cent of the babies born alive survived their tenth year. Forty per cent of the babies born in China did not live to be five, mainly due to insufficient food consumption. According to Buck's survey, the people in as many as 30 per cent of the localities in China had an intake below the recommended scale; in wheat regions this proportion was as high as 40 per cent.[20]

Mao's China

For the rural poor, the land reforms (1949–52) which came in the wake of the Communist take-over of China in 1949 'came as a tremendous, and most welcome, revolutionary change. They became owner-peasants, even if very small ones. In addition the crushing burden of rent was reduced over the whole country by some 25–30 million tons of grain. The combined effect on millions of peasants was one of deeply felt satisfaction.'[21] On the other hand, for many landlords and rich peasants the land reform was a disaster. Those who resisted the confiscation of their property lost their lives; death estimates have ranged between 2 and 20 million.

Unlike the Soviet Union's dependence on technocracy for rapid economic development, Mao firmly believed in unleashing the massive energy of the masses for increased production and raising the standard of living in China. The considerable addition to the rural infrastructure in the initial years and an increase in agricultural production during the First Five Year Plan were achieved simply by means of labor power. Mao had no doubt that mobilizing under-utilized labor power throughout the Chinese countryside could add much more to the rural infrastructure and production.[22] However, the process became over-ambitious when the Advance Production Cooperatives (APCs) were quickly converted to People's Communes, combining all aspects of rural life: economic, social, political, and military. Such aspirations, already stretched beyond credibility, were taken further during the Great Leap Forward's unattainable targets for steel production, a part of it in 'backyard furnaces.' Chinese blacksmiths have been forging iron tools for agriculture, manufacturing, transportation, and warfare for centuries. Therefore, a campaign for producing tools needed in rural China should not have been such a disaster; it failed, however, because the targets were too unrealistic.

Had the Great Leap and communization come in successive stages and with more modest targets they might have worked, but, as it was, both programs failed. The cadres responsible for implementing these programs were not trained to do what was expected of them, and cared more about meeting numerical targets than for the spirit of the program: an experience repeated all too often in developing countries striving for social change. Too many people were mobilized for the production of backyard steel, leaving too few to harvest the ripening crops. At the same time, the country also faced one of its worst natural disasters. Drought in the spring and summer affected every province in China except Tibet and Xinjiang, while Shandong and other coastal provinces such as Guangdong, Fujian and Jiangsu were ravaged by typhoons and floods. All this caused immense human suffering. On all of the three core issues – the formation of the communes, the mass steel campaign, and the launching of the Great Leap – Mao admitted his responsibility.[23]

Nevertheless, Mao remained concerned about the growing elitism, bureaucratization, and erosion of ideological commitment within the party as well as the growing inequality between people in China.[24] Liu Shaoqi, the State Chairman, and Deng Xiaoping, the General Secretary of the Party, agreed with Mao 'that the party had suffered badly in its prestige among the people, that corruption had increased and morale was low.'[25] Mao favored a mass campaign for rectification of the lower levels of rural cadre, while Liu and Deng preferred to do so within the organizational structure of the Communist Party. In 1964, the party launched a 'four cleanups' movement. It involved cadres being sent to the rural areas, collecting evidence against corrupt rural cadres, compiling charges, interrogating, and obtaining confessions for the struggle meetings.[26] Clearly, such witch-hunts led to massive human rights abuses.

Mao, a keen student of Chinese history, had known that even in those dynasties which rose as a result of peasant rebellions, with time, decadence set in and the new rulers reintroduced the old social forms once again.[27] Much the same had happened to the Taiping leadership. The Taiping rebellion 'did not lead to social equality. Privileges were quick to arise. The higher members of the hierarchy exploited their position to take more than an equal share of rice, meat, oil, etc. from the public granaries and storehouses. They soon began to dress in rich and costly clothes, to wear gold and jewel-studded crowns and to live in luxurious palaces.'[28] While the Heavenly King began to be carried in the sedan chair by sixty-four porters, the people in the streets had to kneel down at the roadside.[29] The talk of women's equality was also forgotten and by a decree of 1861 high princes were allowed to have eleven wives; high ranking officers three; middle ranking officers two; other officers and soldiers one.[30] The egalitarian concerns usually gave way to a new privileged ruling class.

By the mid-1960s, China was returning to normal. Seemingly restructured communes became increasingly acceptable to the people. Collective farming at the team-level turned out to be more manageable. The surplus labor that could be released from farming helped create rural infrastructure, roads, irrigation, flood control, small-scale industries, and electricity. On purely economic criteria, such small enterprises were probably inefficient, but in the face of transport bottlenecks, a local production with low efficiency was certainly preferable to no local availability of power, chemicals, and agricultural implements. Agricultural output increased and grew faster than the population. Industrial output rose even faster. A near-egalitarian distribution of employment and food led to a substantial increase in life expectancy to levels not reached by many contemporary developing countries.

Perhaps it was wrong of Mao to sacrifice economic and political stability to an elusive search for a cure for elitism, but for Mao, time was running out simply because he was getting on in age. Therefore, he gambled once again and launched the Great Proletarian Cultural Revolution (GPCR), directly challenging the Party about its growing elitism. At the height of the movement, between August and November 1966, ten million Red Guards rampaged through Beijing, humbling, torturing, and demeaning intellectuals, party officials, and bureaucrats. Ultimately, the Mao-inspired 'seizure of power' degenerated into armed warfare between various factions of the Red Guards, and the regional military began to take sides in factional fighting. The country hovered on the brink of a civil war. Mao had to demobilize the Red Guards and to call upon the PLA to restore order. The rebuilding of the Party and the government began with the official termination of the GPCR by the Ninth Congress of the Chinese Communist Party, with the PLA still playing a dominant role. The military committed some of the worst excesses in 1970–71.[31] Mao lost his gamble once again. The GPCR brought immense suffering to party officials, intellectuals, and bureaucrats. An estimated 60 per cent of party officials were purged, nearly 400,000 people died as a result of maltreatment, and many committed suicide.[32]

Clearly, Mao and the Communist Party he led until 1976 must bear the responsibility for those killed, starved, and humiliated during the initial land reforms (1949–52), the Great Leap, and the GPCR. Other political purges, such as the Anti-Rightist Campaign of 1957–59, deprived 400,000 to 700,000 educated people of their jobs. These 'campaigns' certainly amounted to gross human rights violations. On the other hand, there were some positive aspects to the revolutionary changes brought about by Mao.

The unification of the country and the establishment of peace and security in China after the turbulent hundred years since the Opium War remains one of the most important contributions of the Mao era. The political changes in the wake of the Republican Revolution in 1911 proved to be short-lived and the mandate of the central government rarely affected the rural areas, which continued to be ruled arbitrarily by warlords. Among the social reforms during the Mao era, pride of place must go to the 1950 law that gave women equal rights in matrimony, divorce, and property ownership and the freedom of choice in marriage.[33] In purely economic terms, China did achieve an annual growth rate of six per cent between 1952 and 1978 despite the turbulence of the land reforms, the Great Leap, and the Cultural Revolution. Inflation was kept under control and the budget and trade deficit was rarely large.[34] Production of most major crops rose a little faster than population growth.[35] China's industrial base in the 1970s was comparable to those of Japan and the Soviet Union in the 1960s. It had a relatively low foreign debt. The rise in expectation of life at birth from 35 years in pre-1949 China to 65 in the mid-1970s itself suggests that the level of nutrition, healthcare, and hygiene in China had improved dramatically.[36] In a country of a over half a billion people, with 10 to 12 million additions each year, such appreciable increases in economic and social indicators were major achievements. Mao certainly died a frustrated man, but he gave the Chinese masses a rarely possessed dignity.

Post-reform China

Soon after coming back to power, Deng Xiaoping[37] quickly introduced some drastic changes to the Chinese economic system. His agricultural reforms aimed at decentralization of decision-making and diversification of crops; emphasis on economic incentives; and greater commercialization of agriculture.[38] With a view to decentralize decision-making, provinces were given more active roles in agricultural planning. On the local level, teams were given autonomy in their choice of crops and crop-mix within targets for major crops set by the state. Restrictions on private plots, rural markets, and sideline activities were relaxed, enabling households to grow foods such as vegetables, pork, and poultry to supplement their income. Procurement prices of agricultural products were raised in March 1979 by 20 to 26 per cent to provide production incentives. Prices paid for above-quota deliveries were considerably more.[39] By 1992 the market fixed prices of almost 70 per cent of agricultural products and by mid-1993 controls on the prices of grain and other foods were also removed in much of the country.[40] In order to provide personal incentives, the household responsibility system, with household as the decision-making unit, was introduced initially in 1978 as an experiment on a limited scale. However, by 1982, official sources claimed that the household responsibility system had been introduced in 90 per cent of production teams.[41] Under the new system, a team contracted out a piece of land, initially for 5 years, now for 50, to individual households. The household receiving land was required to pay an agreed proportion of output to the team. In theory, both land and agricultural equipment continued to be collectively owned; in practice, the agricultural equipment was also divided among the households.[42] Now, the contracted land can be inherited, bought and sold, or mortgage. This has created a *de facto* free market in land and has led to much speculation in real estate by the more affluent Chinese peasants.[43] Specialized households producing commercial crops such as tea, silk, meat, fish, and poultry manage a fifth of the rural farms. Naturally, these farms tend to be richer than other peasant households. One of the major consequences in the face of land scarcity and growing population is that a significant proportion of the rural labor force is now redundant. As mentioned earlier, nearly 100 million 'illegal' rural migrant workers 'float' in the cities in search of work. Without permanent resident certificates these 'floating workers', depending largely on low-paid temporary jobs, are deprived of housing, medical care, welfare support, and schooling, which must be seen as retrogression in the context of human rights.

The industrial enterprise reforms introduced by the Central Committee of the Chinese Communist Party in 1978 gave enterprises new decision-making powers with regard to their production processes, marketing and pricing of products, and investment funds. Enterprises were allowed to retain a certain percentage of profits to be used for renovation or expansion of production capacity, construction of welfare facilities (e.g. dormitories, canteens, and nurseries) for workers, and the provision of cash bonuses to workers. Managers were given the sole authority to hire and fire workers.[44] While it cannot be denied that reforms since 1978 gave primacy to economic incentives and profits over ideology, the fact remains, as Andrew Watson has shown, that the role of professional management was already being emphasized by 1972. The system of material rewards and punishments was reintroduced in many places, bringing management practices closer to the pre-1965 situation.[45] The post-1978 industrial reforms included the policy of closing down some of the loss-making SOEs even if this exacerbated unemployment. To ameliorate the situation, small-scale enterprises received encouragement in both rural and urban informal sectors.

The reforms in agriculture, aided by the return to normality after the Cultural Revolution and favorable weather conditions in the early 1980s, resulted in an annual rate of growth of about 9 per cent between 1978 and 1984.[46] After 1985, growth of agricultural production slowed to 6 per cent per annum for the 1980s and 4 per cent per annum during the first half of the 1990s. Thus, the rate of increase in food production throughout the Deng years remained significantly higher than the population growth, which had come down to 1.1 per cent per annum.

The post-1978 reforms also led to an impressive increase in industrial output, particularly in the non-state owned enterprises such as individual township and village enterprises and enterprises funded by foreign investments. Industrial production rose to 18 per cent per annum in 1990–95 against 11 per cent during the 1980s. During the early 1990s, exports grew at an annual rate of 16 per cent. The exports of goods and services in 1995 were as high as 21 per cent of the GDP against only 6 per cent in 1980. In 1995, gross international reserves stood at $80.3 billion.[47] Total external debt, however, rose from less than $5 billion in 1980 to $118 billion by 1995, but the debt-servicing ratio as a proportion of export earnings at

10 per cent remained reasonable.[48] Thus, in terms of economic performance, the post-1978 reforms certainly brought impressive gains.

The achievements of the post-Mao reforms turned out to be mixed in terms of social indicators. According to the official statistics, between 1978 and 1984 the incidence of poverty in China fell from 28 to 9 per cent and rural poverty from 33 to 11 per cent.[49] According to the United Nations Development Program (UNDP) *Human Development Report, 1997*, the number of the rural poor increased from 97 million in 1985 to 103 million in 1989.[50] This is most likely the result of the change in the nature of decision-making under the household responsibility system. During the commune days, the teams tended to employ all the available labor, sharing limited employment among them. In contrast, on a family farm (to which a household responsibility system household closely approximates) additional employment stops when the additional cost of hiring of one more worker (marginal cost) is equal to the additional income (marginal revenue) generated by the employment of that worker. Therefore, the household responsibility system creates less employment than a system of the commune-type sharing employment equitably. Much the same happens on specialized farms and in rural industries. Therefore, it is highly likely that under the new system, total employment will rise more slowly (or may even decline) than under a system dominated by communes. Specialized farms and rural industries, which can hire available workers, do not have any statutory requirements about the level of wages or acceptable working conditions; therefore, it is also likely that wages in rural areas with surplus labor will remain low. The redundancy of labor resulting from rationalization of SOEs may lead to additional unemployment and a consequent rise in the number of people below the poverty line. In search for profit, the SOEs are also giving up welfare provisions such as runnig of schools, hospitals and dispensaries. Despite the government's efforts to create alternative institutions, it is highly likely that overall social welfare is curtailed.

In situations when overall unemployment increases, women suffer most. As a result of the economic reforms in China, as many as 59 per cent of workers laid-off are women. Women are also discriminated against in recruitment. Many young women who fail to secure regular jobs end up in prostitution and are exposed to a high risk of drug abuse, AIDS, and other sexually transmitted diseases. Eighty per cent of massage parlors in Beijing are involved in the sex trade. Trafficking in women, a flagrant abuse of human rights, continues unabated despite government crackdowns because crime groups, businessmen, police officers, and the army are reportedly involved in this business. Continuing indiscretions of government officials include bribery, nepotism, and smuggling. Unfortunately, official crackdowns on criminal activity lead to draconian measures of crime control that exacerbate human rights abuses.

Income distribution in China is now more unequal than it has been since 1949. The Chinese Gini-coefficient – one of the most-used indicators of the distribution of income – indicated a not-particularly-high rate of 0.42 in 1995. It compares favorably with Brazil at 0.63, but it is higher than India's 0.34. The lowest 20 per cent of the households in China now accounts for only 5.5 per cent of the income, and the highest 20 for 47.5 per cent.[51] This means that the highest 20 per cent households receive 8.6 times the income than the lowest 20 per cent. The corresponding figure for India is only 5 times. If the rate of economic growth is rapid, increasing inequality will not increase poverty. However, increasing polarization of society between haves and have-nots might lead to discontent with serious implications for social stability, law, and order.

Human rights violations in China

Political purges in communist countries have always been endemic. Mention has already been made of the lives lost during the land reforms of 1949–52. The atrocities committed during the Cultural Revolution and the witch-hunt in 'rectification' campaigns have also been mentioned. Such witch-hunts and political purges continued even after Deng's rise to power in 1976. Under the guise of 'streamlining' the Party, its members, bureaucrats, and members of the PLA with 'leftist' inclinations were purged in large numbers, many being assigned to manual labor in factories.[52] Clearly, such political purges must be considered human rights abuse.

Nevertheless, the early years of Deng's regime introduced some liberalization in political spheres. A large number of party leaders, intellectuals, bureaucrats, and lower- and mid-level cadres, persecuted during the Cultural Revolution and before, were rehabilitated. Some freedom of expression was also tolerated. Even the Democracy Movement – essentially a network of young dissidents demanding greater freedom of expression and transparency in administration – was allowed to operate with some restrictions. The Communist Youth League, disbanded during the Cultural Revolution, reappeared and began publishing its magazine, *China Youth*, with articles critical of the Party. Wall posters, a popular mode of criticism of the Party and its bureaucracy flourished again, highlighting the grievances of people and asking for the democratization of administration, the enhancement of human rights, and the creation of a modern legal system. The Third Plenum of the Communist Party also hinted at some concessions toward political changes demanded by the Democracy Movement. However, the overriding emphasis of the party remained focused on maintaining political stability to successfully implement economic modernization.[53]

The fortunes of the Democracy Movement changed with its criticisms of the Chinese invasion of Vietnam. The invasion, a fiasco and personal defeat for Deng, was meant to 'teach a lesson' to Vietnam. Deng presumably took the criticisms by the Democracy Movement as a personal affront and moved swiftly to silence the movement. The suppression of the Democracy Movement – mass arrests of youths and their subsequent banishment to labor camps – continued for almost two years. The publication and circulation of unofficial journals became increasingly restricted. Already in August 1980 Deng had persuaded the Fifth National People's Congress to remove the 'four greats' (speak out freely, air views freely, hold great debates, and write big character posters) from Article 15 of the state constitution.[54] Thus, China entered a period when freedom of expression was in some ways more limited than in Mao's China.

In early 1989, in violation of the official prohibition of the freedom of organization and expression, some student activists decided to commemorate the seventieth anniversary of the May Fourth Movement.[55] As seen earlier, the situation was mishandled by the old guard, whose decision to use the army who indiscriminately fired at the demonstrators, resulting in the Tiananmen massacre and the subsequent suppression of dissent. The overall human rights record of Deng's China was possibly as dark as Mao's China; in any case Deng had taken part in most of Mao's purges, except, of course, of his own.

Continuing human rights abuses

In response to increasing world criticism, the Chinese government signed the United Nations Covenant on Economic, Social and Cultural Rights in 1997 and ratified it in February 2001. It also signed the International Covenant on Civil and Political Rights in 1998.[56] In some respects, the Chinese government is now a little more tolerant of open dissent than in the immediate aftermath of the Tiananmen incident. These days many articles critical of the government appear in the popular press and academic journals. In recent years, the Chinese government has also attempted to improve its legal system, to train more lawyers, and to provide remedial measures in cases of gross abuse.[57] It is also trying to promote the building of democracy at the grass-roots levels in urban and rural areas.[58] Under the Organic Law of the Village Committees, appointments to the village committees are now conducted by direct elections. Nearly 90 per cent of villages have conducted such elections and the verdict of foreign observers, including the Carter Center and International Republic Institute, is that the elections, on the whole, have been fair.[59] In urban areas too, the majority of urban neighborhood committees have held direct elections to elect members for such committees.[60]

Yet, human rights abuses in China are many. As the US State Department's *Country Reports on Human Rights Practices, 2000* stated:

> Abuses included instances of extrajudicial killings, the use of torture, forced confessions, arbitrary arrest and detention, the mistreatment of prisoners, lengthy incommunicado detention, and denial of due

process.... In many cases, particularly in sensitive political cases, the judicial system denies criminal defendants basic legal safeguards and due process.... The Government maintained tight restrictions on freedom of speech and of the press and increased its efforts to control the Internet; self-censorship by journalists continued. The Government severely restricted freedom of assembly and continued to restrict freedom of association. The Government continued to restrict freedom of religion and intensified controls on some unregistered churches. The Government continued to restrict freedom of movement.[61]

Extra-judicial killings

Extra-judicial killings, based on confessions extracted under torture, and summary trials for both political reasons and for criminal acts are quite common in China. According to the Amnesty International *Annual Report, 2001*, at least 1511 death sentences were passed and 1000 executions were carried out in 2000.[62] Death sentences in the 1990s totaled more than 27,120 and an estimated 18,000 were executed. The true figure could be even higher. The number of such executions in China is a state secret.[63] In March 1997, the National People's Congress (NPC) amended the Criminal Procedural Law and passed a new Administrative Punishment Law in order to provide legal protection to detainees and defendants. Laws relating to summary trials in cases of death penalties were repealed. Yet under the anti-crime *yanda* ('strike hard' or 'severe crackdown') campaign, commenced on 28 April 1996, summary trials and executions continued, making a mockery of the new laws. The death penalty is given not only to criminal gangs but also to those involved in corruption, financial crimes, and offenses undermining the social order and, above all, 'separatist' activities in Tibet and Xinjiang.[64]

The State Department's *Country Reports* mentioned that in 2000, nearly 100 adherents of *Falun Gong*, a spiritual group now outlawed by the Chinese government, died in police custody; in many cases their bodies showed signs of severe beatings or torture, or were cremated before relatives could examine them. Much the same seems to have happened to several members of underground house churches who also died in custody, as a result of beatings by prison authorities. According to press reports, in June 2000, in an attempt by almost 500 police to suppress a protest by 2300 inmates at the Shangrao labor camp, three people were killed and over 70 were injured. This was followed by numerous executions carried out after summary trials.[65]

Extra-judicial killings of political prisoners labeled as 'separatists' or 'terrorists' are quite common in Xinjiang, the only region of China where political prisoners continue to be executed on the basis of secret or summary trials, and on confessions extracted under torture.[66] According to Amnesty International, political prisoners are often tried in secret, summary trials being a mere formality with pre-determined convictions. In October 2000, China's highest court issued a judicial interpretation authorizing the aggressive use of the death penalty for those who smuggled arms, counterfeited currency, and endangered species, and for the government officials aiding them.[67]

Arbitrary arrests, torture, and other cruelties

Although China's 1997 legal reforms provide for various kinds of protection against arbitrary detention, torture, and other cruelties inflicted on prisoners, such practices are widespread in police stations, detention centers, prisons, labor camps, repatriation centers, and drug rehabilitation centers.[68] The administrative detention of dissidents may involve detention without charges or trials and the accused being assigned to labor camps for up to three years. The use of electric shocks, prolonged periods of solitary confinement, incommunicado detention, beatings, and the use of shackles are common phenomena in Chinese prisons. A recent report by Tibet Centre for Human Rights and Democracy (TCHRD) alleged that, 'Almost all of the [Tibetan] prisoners arrested have at some stage undergone severe physical abuse at the hands of either Public Security Bureau officers or prison guards – or often by both. Torture is a prevalent occurrence in detention centers and prisons in Tibet resulting in many deaths.'[69] The incidence of torture often increases during periodic 'strike hard' campaigns during which police are expected to achieve quick results in the fight against crime.[70] The Amnesty News Service reported in July 2001 that at least 2960 people were convicted and 1781 executed within the previous three months in a 'strike hard' campaign. Executions are reported from all over China for crimes including bribery, pimping, embezzlement, tax and financial fraud, currency counterfeiting, robbing of petrol, selling harmful foods, drug offences, and other serious crimes. Of late, the press has been reporting cases of policemen being punished, even with execution and life sentences in prison, for extorting confessions through torture and for causing death.[71]

Cruelty to women and children

In theory, Chinese women have equal rights with men and are entitled to equal pay for equal work. They have the right to take part in the political process on equal terms with men. Yet in practice, women are discriminated against in workplaces, both in the private and the public sectors and their earnings are no more than three quarters of those of men. In order to avoid paying for maternity benefits and child care expenses, some private employers do not employ young women. In many cases women are coerced into retiring at 40 even when the statutory age of retirement for women is 55 years. Besides, much of the progress in the status of women since 1949, is gradually whittling away and women's status in society has regressed in the 1990s because of primacy of material gains over ideology – *á la* Deng's adage 'it does not matter whether the cat is black or white so long as it catches the mice' – and the increasing permissiveness and widespread corruption in officialdom. 'Women are also suffering disproportionately in terms of redundancies and unemployment as a result of the economic reform of the state-owned enterprises.'[72]

On the social level too, the position of women is far from satisfactory. One in five women is a victim of domestic abuse. There are numerous cases of abduction or kidnapping of women by criminal gangs for the purpose of selling them into prostitution or into marriage. The social preference for a male child still continues. Although it is illegal to terminate pregnancies based on sex of the fetus, the majority of pregnancies terminated are female fetuses.[73] The existence of female infanticide is widely acknowledged but there is no real statistical evidence. However, the national ratio of male to female births of 117 to 100 for 1994 against the worldwide statistical norm of 106 to 100 is very likely the result of sex bias in termination of pregnancies.[74] Furthermore, on the statistics compiled in 1994, as many as 1.7 million children are abandoned every year in China, the vast majority of them female or disabled. Abandoned children end up in poorly managed orphanages, where the children are inadequately fed and medical care is almost nonexistent. The kidnapping, buying, and selling of children persists in many rural areas despite government regulations against these practices.[75]

Enforced birth control – Chinese official sources deny such policies, and of late there is some relaxation in the 'one child' policy[76] – also leads to considerable suffering for women throughout the country. There is much greater suffering in ethnic areas, where religious beliefs as well as family needs for children (for instance for farming and looking after parents in old age) are different. Refugee testimonies mention many Tibetan women suffering permanent disabilities and deaths as a result of forced abortions and inferior procedures of sterilization and contraception as well as poor healthcare facilities.[77]

Gender-based torture, including rape, is reportedly quite common in Tibet. Many nuns suffer torture and other forms of repression for their religious beliefs and are often expelled from their nunneries; many others face lengthy prison sentences.[78] Young Tibetan girls searching for employment frequently end up as prostitutes in urban centers.[79] The official Chinese position is that prostitution is under control in Tibet. However, according to the Department of State *Country Reports on Human Rights Practices, 1999*, hundreds of brothels with as many as 10,000, 'commercial sex workers,' mainly of Han extraction, operate openly in Lhasa alone, largely on properties owned by the Party or the Government and under military patronage.[80]

Despite their age, children in Tibet also suffer harsh treatment. Children, as young as nine years old, suffer confinement, torture, beatings, and verbal abuse. Children suspected of being involved in Tibetan nationalist activities are often subjected to the same tortures that adults suffer: beatings with metal rods; electric shocks with cattle prods; solitary confinement; forced labor; deprivation of food, light and water; and suspension in painful or contorted positions.[81]

Freedom of expression, assembly and association

The Chinese government also severely restricts the freedoms of expression, assembly, and association. It also regulates publications, controls the broadcast media, and censors foreign television broadcasts. Sometimes it jams radio signals from abroad. In 2000, several publications were shut down for publishing material perceived to be objectionable by the Government.[82] There were reports of journalists, authors, and researchers being harassed, detained, or arrested.[83] According to Human Rights Watch, in 1999 regulations were introduced to prevent web operators from linking up with foreign sites and or hiring their own reporters. In March 2000, China-based web sites were forbidden to use materials from 'independent news groups.' In January 2000, the Ministry of State Security decided to close down web sites, chat rooms, and Internet news groups posting 'state secrets' and banned e-mail being used for transmitting 'state secrets.' The use of encryption technology is also being restricted.[84]

The government has also intensified restrictions on freedom of religion. Harsh treatment, in terms of detention, unfair trials, torture and imprisonment, of *Falun Gong*, continues.[85] In October 1999 the group was declared a cult, banned under the Chinese Criminal Code, thus enabling the authorities to justify severe punishments to the followers of *Falun Gong*. As stated earlier, many followers of the group are reported to have died in police custody as a result of forced feeding, suicide, and torture. Other groups such as *Qi Gong*, evangelical Protestants and Roman Catholics, not belonging to the official 'patriotic' churches have also been added to the 'heretical organizations' and are subjected to repressive measures.[86]

The government continues to restrict freedom of movement. Independent domestic non-governmental organizations (NGOs) are still not allowed to monitor human rights abuses. Workers' right to organize is also severely restricted. Forced labor in 'education through labor camps' and in prisons continues. Child labor continues to be a serious problem, particularly in rural areas where children work to supplement the family income.[87]

In conclusion, it must be said that in any objective assessment of China's human right records one has to concede the positive aspects of government policies towards improvements in nutrition, health, and education of the people in general, and women and children in particular, although the record of such achievements in ethnic minority areas still leaves much to be desired. Notwithstanding the human costs of socio-economic and political strategies of the last fifty years, one might venture to suggest that an average Chinese national is much better off today than his or her counterpart in the early twentieth century. The Department of State's *Country Reports* for 1998 concedes that at present an average Chinese citizen goes about his or her daily life without significant interference from the government. They now face looser economic controls, have increased access to outside sources of information, a greater availability of individual choice, and far more diversity in cultural life. However, the authorities quickly suppress any person or group – whether religious, political, or social – deemed 'to be a threat to government power or national stability. Citizens who seek to express openly dissenting political and religious views continue to live in an environment filled with repression.[88]

Human rights violations are more common in minority regions such as Inner Mongolia, Tibet, and Xinjiang. A concerted attempt has been made by the Chinese authorities to import the Han Chinese from other parts of the country and settling them in these areas to dilute the Inner Mongolian, Tibetan, and Uighur populations and cultures. The Chinese government denies this. Reportedly, the government gives preferential treatment to the Han Chinese in education, health, housing, and employment and the educational system is being used to undermine the history, languages, and culture of the minorities. The imposition of the Chinese language as the main language of education, at the neglect of the mother tongue of the children, basically thwarts the educational progress of the children. Many of these policies followed by the Chinese authorities in Inner Mongolia, Tibet, and Xinjiang are reminiscent of policies followed by European colonizers in their respective colonies in the nineteenth and the first half of the twentieth centuries.

As the Chinese authorities point out,[89] and as the American government itself readily acknowledges, human rights violations are quite common in the United States. The continuation of human rights abuses in America is not a matter for gloating for China, for that matter any other developing country, but for circumspection.[90] If abuses still exist in an open society such as America, with high levels of literacy, media exposure, active public interest groups monitoring and exposing such violations, legal and constitutional safeguards, and judicial reviews, China has a long way to go before it can claim to have any meaningful progress on the human rights front. In the immediate future, China runs the risk of experiencing increasing unemployment, widening gaps in income and wealth, and the resulting discontent of those who suffer from economic reform and the liberalization of trade. If China's leadership, in search of political stability, decides to take draconian measures to suppress dissent, human rights transgressions will multiply further.

Human rights violations in the USA

There are many federal and state laws – the Constitution and the Bill of Rights being the most important – and safeguard mechanisms designed to protect human rights within America, yet violations of human rights, both in public as well as private spheres, are quite common. As far as the international arena is concerned, the human rights record of the United States – even after considering the positive aspects of individual and state acts of charity – could easily be described as appalling. American human rights transgressions began early in its history, continued through the Cold War years and is still continuing in the conduct of wars, such as the Gulf War, war in Kosovo and Afghanistan and the war against drugs in Colombia. Some transgressions of this type have already been mentioned before. In this chapter attempt is made to highlight some of the major human rights abuses within America. NGOs such as Amnesty International and Human Rights Watch regularly monitor and report on the areas of concern. This section draws extensively on their reports. However, one of the most instructive documents is the State Department's *Initial Report* submitted to the UN Committee Against Torture in October 1999. This report candidly concedes that 'there continue to be areas of concern, contention, and criticism. These include instances of police abuse, excessive use of force and even brutality, and death of prisoners in custody. Overcrowding in the prison system, physical and sexual abuse of inmates, and lack of adequate training and oversight for police and prison guards are also cause for concern.'[91]

In 1994, the US Congress responded to growing concerns by enacting legislation authorizing the Attorney General to initiate civil lawsuits obtaining remedies for misconduct by law enforcement and other agencies responsible for the incarceration of juveniles. The Department of Justice is actively enforcing this statute, together with older laws that provide for criminal prosecution of law enforcement and correctional officers who willfully deprive individuals of their constitutional rights. The department is also enforcing statutes that enable the Department of Justice to obtain civil relief for abusive conditions in state prisons and local jails.[92] Nevertheless, the progress on the human rights front is slow. As Amnesty International's *Report 2001* covering the year 2000 points out, police brutality continues. In 2000, police shot unarmed suspects at the end of vehicle pursuits, during traffic stops, or during police street patrols. A disproportionate number of the victims came from ethnic minorities. The use of dangerous restraint holds or pepper sprays has also led to deaths of several suspects. As one example of excessive use of force by the police, Amnesty International quotes the highly publicized case of Amadou Diallo, an unarmed West African immigrant, who in 1999 was shot forty-one times outside his home. The four New York Police Department (NYPD) officers were acquitted of all criminal charges.[93] According to the Human Rights Watch (HRW) most police officers violating departmental rules or the law go without punishment for lack of adequate investigative and disciplinary arrangements. Victims who complain are subjected to overt intimidation. During fiscal year 1999, of nearly 12,000 civil rights complaints brought to the

Department of Justice, only 31 officers were either convicted or pleaded guilty to crimes under the civil rights statute.[94]

Death penalty

According to the AI *Report 2001*, in 2000 as many as 85 convicts were executed in 14 states. Since 1976 when the Supreme Court lifted a moratorium on executions, a total of 683 convicts have been executed in the United States. The report also pointed out that 'the USA continued to violate international standards by using the death penalty against the mentally impaired, individuals who were under 18 years of age at the time of the crime, and defendants who received inadequate legal representation.'[95]

According to the State Department's report to the UN Committee on Torture, the death penalty is permissible in 38 states of which 29 have conducted executions since 1977; the majority of death penalties have been given in the states of Texas, Virginia, Florida, Louisiana, Maryland, and Georgia. In fourteen states, offenders aged less than 18 at the time of committing capital offenses cannot be subjected to the death penalty. A total of 20 states allow the death penalty if a prisoner convicted of a capital crime has reached the age of 16; in 4 others, the age is 17. Although US law prohibits the execution of the legally insane, the standard for judging mental competence varies among states. Only 12 states and the federal government specifically prohibit the execution of the mentally retarded.[96]

Cruelty in prisons

The AI *Report 2001* also mentions wide spread cases of torture and ill treatment, of both adults and juveniles, in prisons and in juvenile detention facilities. Such cases include beatings, use of excessive force, sexual misconduct, misuse of electro-shock weapons and chemical sprays, and the cruel use of mechanical restraints, including holding prisoners for prolonged periods in a four-point restraint. The conditions are particularly cruel in super-maximum security (supermax) prisons, where prisoners are kept in prolonged isolation. Most prisons in the United States use electro-shock weapons, including stun belts, stun shields, and stun guns. Contrary to the claims of manufacturers of such weapons, experts suggest that such weapons 'can be harmful, even lethal, for people with high blood pressure, for pregnant women and for those suffering epilepsy and some other conditions. In light of this, stun weapons have been banned for law enforcement use by a number of countries, including Canada and most West European countries, as well as some US states.'[97] One of the devices, remote controlled electro-shock stun belts for use on US prisoners, is of particular concern. Pushing a button from a distance activates this belt, causing severe pain and instant incapacitation; when activated it can cause the person to defecate or urinate. This belt is being used by the US Bureau of Prisons, the US Marshall's service, and more than 100 county agencies and 16 state correctional agencies. It is also used on prisoners during judicial hearings, which is a contravention of international standards on the treatment of prisoners.[98]

The AI *Report 2001* also notes that the use of excessive force, restraint devices and stun-devices has led to deaths of prison inmates. One of the grimmest cases reported was of Corcoran State Prison, California, where eight prison guards were accused (and later acquitted of criminal charges after jury trial) of staging 'gladiator style' fights among prisoners between 1989 and 1995. In breaking up the fights, 31 prisoners were shot by the guards, seven of them fatally. An independent panel found that 80 per cent of the shootings had been unjustified. The state legislative hearings in 1998 also confirmed a pattern of brutality at the prison.[99]

Cruelty to women

The AI *Report 2001* also referred to the ill treatment of women inmates, including sexual abuses by male guards, including rape, parading partially naked in front of male inmates; forced strip searches by male guards, and fondling by male officers while dressing. AI's *Rights for All* report points out that it is not only female inmates who are coerced into having sex by male staff; sexual coercion by female staff against both male and female inmates, and by male staff against male inmates are not uncommon. This happens because the US prisons employ both men and women to supervise prisoners of the opposite sex, allow them to undertake searches involving body contact, and to be present where inmates are naked. The practice of employing male staff to supervise female inmates is contrary to international standards.[100]

Women inmates have to suffer the indignity of being shackled even when they are pregnant; sometimes they remain shackled while in labor or are re-shackled shortly after. This practice has been denounced by a Washington, DC court as 'inhumane' – yet the practice continues.

Cruelty to children

In as many as 20 states, children can be convicted as adults and be imprisoned in adult prisons and housed with adult inmates in violation of the International Covenant on Civil and Political Rights (ICCPR) and other international standards, which require that juvenile prisoners be kept separate from adults. Juveniles can be treated as adults only in exceptional circumstances. Nevertheless, many states are legislating to broaden the circumstances in which children may be prosecuted as adults and held in adult prisons.[101] A special AI report on the ill-treatment of children in US prisons states that children are often held in cruel conditions in overcrowded facilities, deprived of adequate mental health care, education and rehabilitation programs. They are also subjected to cruel punishments, including shackles, chemical sprays and electro-shock devices. Children are also kept in solitary confinement in violation of international standards.[102]

In a lawsuit against the State Training School in Plankinton, South Dakota, a juvenile detention facility, it was alleged that children were placed in puni-tive handcuffs and shackles and forced to lie spread-eagled in four-point restraints for hours at a time, even through the night. It was common for male staff to forcibly strip girls while held in four-point restraint. Children, including those who were mentally ill, were routinely held in isolation for 24 hours a day, sometimes for months at a time.[103]

Inadequate health care

Many prisons and jails fail to meet not only the international standards but also fall below the Supreme Court ruling that the inmates have a right to adequate medical care for 'serious' medical needs. The AI *Rights for All* report mentions, among the major deficiencies, the 'lack of screening for tubercu-losis and other communicable diseases in overcrowded and insanitary jails; too few medical and psychiatric staff; failure to refer seriously ill inmates for treatment; delays in treatment or failure to deliver life-saving drugs; inad-equate conditions for prisoners with HIV/AIDS; lack of access to gynaeco-logical and obstetric services; and grossly deficient treatment for the mentally ill.'[104] The report also notes that many states and local jails have started charging inmates fees for medical consultations, which contravenes the international standards that medical care for prisoners should be free.

Prison labor

A new development in the American penal system is the rapid growth of joint ventures between public correction services and private firms. The prison industry now employs as many as half a million people. At both the state and federal level such enterprises are seen as instruments for transfer-ring part of the burden of the inmate's upkeep to the inmates. For private firms it is an attractive proposition because it saves rent, the cost of heating and lighting, and of social security. On top of all this, they have access to cheap captive labor, supervised by armed prison guards, and devoid of the rights of association, if not in law, at least in practice. In seasonal or cyclical downturn, this labor can be easily shed. From the human rights point-of-view this is probably a grey area, because this labor is 'voluntary' and is paid for by the companies. The inmate is arguably learning a skill, which can become the basis for his rehabilitation after release. Therefore, whether there is a transgression of human rights can be judged only on the basis of the wage levels paid and other conditions of work.

Available reports suggest that the private firms generally pay the inmates a wage, which may compare favorably with the statutory minimum wage. However, the correctional service makes several deductions. For instance, in one Washington State reformatory, inmates making aircraft parts and accessories are paid $7 an hour, out of which the Department of Correction (DOC) deducts 20 per cent for the 'cost of correction.' Ten per cent goes to a mandatory savings fund, which is largely devoted by the DOC to victim notification and awareness programs. The inmate has also to pay federal taxes, social security, and up to 20 per cent for victim restitution, child support, trial costs, and other court ordered financial obligations. The inmate also pays $3 per visit in medical charges for access to medical care. After all these deductions, the inmate receives nearly $1.50 per hour, which is less than half of the minimum wage. However, it compares favorably with the $0.38 to $0.42 per hour paid for working in the prison kitchen and laundries, or for janitorial work.[105] The presumption, at least as claimed officially, is that the labor is voluntary. However, there is some evidence that 'prisoners in Oregon, like those virtually everywhere else in the US, get time subtracted from their sentences for working in prison industries. If prisoners don't work, they serve longer sentences, lose privileges, and risk solitary confinement.'[106] If this is the general case, the practice may violate the international norms because if an inmate is directly or indirectly forced into work, it virtually becomes forced labor. Charging a fee for medical care, which has been mentioned above, is certainly against international standards that require free medical care. It is interesting to note that the US government is critical of China for exporting prison-made things; American laws now prohibit such imports. Yet the states of California and Oregon are reported to be exporting prison-made clothes to Asia. Federal law prohibits inter-state trade in prison goods unless the prisoner is paid 'prevailing' wages, but there are no such restrictions on exports.[107] The fact remains that many reputed companies are the ultimate beneficiaries of prison labor employed by their subcontractors; their products are sold both at home and abroad.[108] The situation is akin to China's where transnational corporations take advantage of sweated labor through subcontractors.

Ethnic minorities

In view of the widespread geographic and racial disparities in the application of the federal death penalty nationwide, the AI report, *Rights for All*, calls the application of the death penalty 'to be racist, arbitrary, and unfair.'[109] The American criminal justice system's vulnerability to personal or social prejudice is clearly unfair to minorities, particularly to African Americans. The fact that such an injustice takes place is confirmed by the State Department's report to the UN Committee on Torture. It concedes that 'African Americans are disproportionately more likely to be sentenced to death and executed than other racial or ethnic components of the US population.'[110]

The minorities have also suffered disproportionately as a result of the war on drugs. African Americans, constituting only 12 per cent of the total population accounted for 47 per cent of state prisoners and 40 per cent of federal prisoners convicted mainly for drug offenses. For the US, as a whole, African American men were eight times more susceptible to imprisonment than white men, with an incarceration rate of 3408 per 100,000 African American male residents, as against only 417 per 100,000 for white males. In eleven states, the African American incarceration rates ranged between twelve and twenty-six times those of white men.[111] In September 2000, in its Initial Report to the United Nations Committee on the Elimination of Racial Discrimination, the US Department of State conceded the persistence of racism, racial discrimination, and *de facto* segregation in the United States. It pointed out that 'while the scourge of officially sanctioned segregation has been eliminated, *de facto* segregation and persistent racial discrimination continue to exist. The forms of discriminatory practices have changed and adapted over time, but racial and ethnic discrimination continues to restrict and limit equal opportunity in the United States.'[112]

Asylum-seekers

Highlighting the human rights violations of asylum-seekers in the United States, *Rights for All* pointed out that an increasing number of asylum-seekers are, on arrival in the USA, often detained indefinitely, confined with criminal prisoners and are held in inhuman and degrading conditions. They are liable to be stripped and searched; shackled and chained; sometimes verbally or physically abused. They are often denied access to their families, lawyers and NGOs and even telephones. They cannot even receive letters.[113] The passing of the new Illegal Immigration Reform and Immigrant Responsibility Act (IIRIRA) in 1996 has led to a considerable rise in detentions. People without valid documents can be summarily sent back under the 'expedited removal provisions' of the act[114] International law provides an opportunity for a review of the decision to detain depending on the merits of the case, taking into account the overall circumstances of the asylum-seeker, not just procedural correctness. US practice does not allow for such an examination.[115]

Foreign nationals

In violation of the Geneva Convention, foreign nationals have been executed in the United States without being given their treaty-based consular rights. These rights have been denied to as many as 90 foreign nationals on death row in the USA. In a case brought to the International Court of Justice in The Hague by Germany in the context of the execution of two German nationals in Arizona in 1999, the Court, with an overwhelming majority, found the United States in violation of the Vienna Convention on consular relations.[116]

Child labor

The United States is also in violation of international laws prohibiting exploitative and harmful work by children, against the standards set by the

Convention on the Rights of the Child. It might even contravene the 1999 ILO Worst Forms of Child Labor Convention, which requires member governments to prohibit and eliminate 'the worst forms of child labor.' This convention came into effect in the US in December 2000. According to HRW, hundreds of thousands of children and teenagers (estimated to range between 300,000 to 800,000) work under appalling conditions in fields, orchards, and packing sheds. They pick lettuce and cantaloupe, cherries, 'pitch' heavy watermelons, weed cotton fields, and bag produce. Wages are often below the minimum wage, sometimes only two or three dollars an hour. They are made to work under hazardous conditions, exposed to dangerous pesticides, sometimes even in fields still wet with poison. They are often made to eat lunch without washing their hands still contaminated with deadly pesticides. Their employers fail to provide enough water, commonly exposing the child farm workers to heat exhaustion and dehydration. Injuries from sharp knives, accidents with heavy equipment, and falls from ladders are common. Female farm workers frequently suffer from sexual abuse by farm labor contractors and field supervisors, refusal leading to retaliation in the form of discharge, blacklisting of the worker and her family members, and even physical assault and rape.[117]

These child or teen farm workers have little protection under United States laws. The Fair Labor Standards Act (FLSA) allows the employment of children of 12 (or even younger) to work on farms as opposed to fourteen in other occupations. In Oregon, the minimum age is as low as 9; in Illinois, 10. Children younger than 18 are not allowed to work in mines. A total of 18 states have no minimum age requirement for juvenile farm workers. In non-farming occupations children under 16 are allowed to work only 3 hours a day on a school day, with a total of 18 hours in a school week. On a non-school day the total hours allowed per day is 8–40 hours in a non-school week. For farm work, there is no limit to the number of hours a child is made to work. Without regard for educational or health considerations, employers normally make them work for 12 hours a day, 6 to 7 days a week, going up to 14, 16, or even 18 hours a day, 7 days a week during peak harvesting seasons. The FLSA provides for overtime pay for other occupations but not for farm work.

In farm work, juveniles can be given hazardous work at the age of 16 as opposed to 18 in other occupations. As HRW points out, 'the Fair Labor Standards Act claims to prohibit "oppressive child labor." Yet the FLSA permits oppressive child labor in agriculture to continue. The FLSA's bias against farmworker children amounts to de facto race-based discrimination: an estimated 85 percent of migrant and seasonal farmworkers nationwide are racial minorities; in some regions, including Arizona, approximately 99 percent of farm-workers are Latino. In addition to raising serious concerns under the Equal Protection clause of the US Constitution, this discrimination may violate numerous provisions of international law.'[118]

Since the US laws relating to child farm workers are discriminatory with regard to the minimum age, hours of work, and conditions of work and effectively provide a lower standard of protection for child farmworkers than for children working in other occupations, they violate various international treaties forbidding discriminatory laws and practices. They are certainly in contravention of Article 26 of the ICCPR, providing for equal protection of the law without any discrimination, to which the United States has been a state party since 1992. The US laws are also contrary to Article 2 of the Convention on the Rights of the Child, which requires state parties to respect and ensure all rights enumerated in the Convention without discrimination of race, color, language or national, ethnic, or social origin. Since the United States has only signed but not yet ratified the Convention, it is not legally bound by its articles. On the other hand, the International Labour Organization (ILO) Convention Concerning the Prohibition and Immediate Elimination of the Worst Forms of Child Labour (Worst Forms of Child Labor Convention), which the United States has already ratified, will certainly be violated if the federal and state laws are not amended accordingly. Unfortunately, the United States government, rather disingenuously, contends that it is already in full compliance with the Worst Forms of Child Labour Convention, requiring no changes in US law and practice. As HRW candidly points out, 'while eager to point out abusive child labor practices in Guatemala, Brazil, Pakistan, and other developing countries, the United States is myopic when it comes to domestic abuses.'[119]

Labor Rights Violations

The Human Rights Watch *Report 2001* pointed out that 'each year thousands of workers in the United States are spied on, harassed, pressured, threatened, suspended, fired, deported, or otherwise victimized by employers in reprisal for their exercise of the right to freedom of association.'[120] Loopholes in the law and feeble enforcement prevent millions of workers, especially farm workers, household domestic workers, and low-level supervisors from obtaining protection under the law guaranteeing the right of workers to organize. In absence of the right to organize, workers are left to the mercy of the employers with regard to labor contracting, subcontracting, and working conditions; employers have the veto to permanently replace workers who dare to exercise the right to strike.[121]

In another investigation into working conditions of migrant workers, the Human Rights Watch found that the rights of migrant domestic workers, mostly women, with special temporary visas, were often violated. Since the special visas are employment-based, workers on such visas lose their legal immigration status in the US if they leave abusive employers, and therefore they face deportation. So far the US government has not established procedures to ensure that employers comply with employment contracts or the humane treatment of workers and other mandatory terms for these workers' special visas.[122]

Felony and Disenfranchisement

The violation of human rights in America also comes in the form of lifetime disenfranchisement arising out of felony convictions even for petty crimes. Felony disenfranchisement leads to an estimated 3.9 million US citizens being deprived of their voting rights. This includes one million people who have completed their sentences. The incidence of felony disenfranchisement affecting African Americans males is disproportionately high. Nearly 1.4 million African American men, 13 per cent of the total African American adult male population, are disenfranchised. No democratic country other than America debars those who have served their sentences. A few countries restrict the right to vote for a short period after the completion of the prison term. Others, such as Germany and France, permit disenfranchisement only when it is imposed by a court order. In many countries, such as Denmark, France, and Germany, even prisoners are allowed to vote. In Germany, the law requires the prison officials to encourage prisoners, except those convicted of electoral crimes or of treason or those subject to court-imposed disenfranchisement, to vote. The US felony disenfranchisement laws may fall foul of the international human rights standards. Article 25 of the ICCPR provides for voting rights for every citizen without discrimination or 'unreasonable restrictions.' The UN Human Rights Committee, which reviews adherence to the ICCPR, affirms that restrictions on the right to vote should only be based on grounds that are 'objective and reasonable' and in the case of disenfranchisement related to conviction for an offence, the period of such suspension should be proportionate to the offence.[123]

Democracy and human rights

Americans rightly emphasize the need for the rule of law, elections, free press and the independent judiciary as safeguards for human rights. However, it is not widely appreciated that the rule of law, elections and independent judiciary are, at best, *necessary* but not *sufficient* conditions for ensuring constitutional or human rights of citizens. These *necessary* conditions are the 'superstructure;' the *sufficient* conditions involve the 'spirit.' Unless the spirit of the law is respected, the mere existence of the rule of law does not provide sufficient safeguards against injustice. American history is full of injustices despite the rule of law, regular elections, free press and an independent judiciary. Until recently, it was under the façade of democracy in the southern states of America that African American people were denied the right to vote, and hundreds were lynched. Thousands of white men, women, and children, including the members of legislatures, gathered at such lynchings. 'Leading white journalists, churchmen, and politicians, either passively ignored or actively justified lynching.'[124] A South Carolina governor, upon receiving the severed finger of a lynched black, appreciatively planted it in the gubernatorial garden. A US senator from Mississippi boasted that he was proud of leading a lynch party. There were some southern politicians who opposed lynching and forced anti-lynching legislation in their states but such laws were rarely implemented.[125] Only three of the more than two hundred anti-lynching bills proposed to Congress passed the House of Representatives; in the face of opposition from white supremacist senators, not one bill ever reached the Senate. Even President Franklin D. Roosevelt simply considered the issue too hot to touch.[126]

It was not unusual for newspapers to defend or even to incite or advertise a lynching. In one case reported in the *New York Tribune*, after the victim was burned at the stake, his body, liver, and heart were cut into pieces, bones crushed into small pieces and sold at extravagant terms as souvenirs.[127] Remember that all these oppressions continued in spite of the Fourteenth and Fifteenth Amendments and the Civil Rights Bill of 1875. In fact, in civil rights cases, the Supreme Court said that 'the Fourteenth Amendment forbade *states*, not individuals, from discriminating.' It declared the Civil Rights Act of 1875 (which had given the black population the right to equal treatment in inns, public conveyances, theaters, and other places of public amusement) to be unconstitutional.[128] The only dissenting judge, Justice John Marshall Harlan, commented that the Court had gutted the Fourteenth Amendment 'by a subtle and ingenious verbal criticism.'[129] This Court decision became the very basis of all the Jim Crow laws in the South except Tennessee, which passed its segregation laws two years before the judgment.

Examining the contemporary situation one finds that three decades after the Civil Rights Act of 1968, in spite of significant progress, equality between the races is far from achieved. Particularly with regard to equality before law, it is now acknowledged by the federal government that the African Americans, the Hispanics, and other minorities are much more vulnerable to the death penalty for capital crimes. As seen earlier, for drug offences they have much greater chance of imprisonment than their white counterparts. Recently, Supreme Court Justice Sandra Day O'Connor pointed out in a public speech that 'serious questions are being raised about whether the death penalty is being fairly administered in this country.' She further noted that last year six death row inmates were exonerated, bringing the total to 90 since 1973. She also pointed out that 'defendants with the resources to hire their own lawyers are considerably less likely to be convicted than those with appointed counsel.' She further added, 'perhaps it's time to look at minimum standards for appointed counsel in death cases and adequate compensation for appointed counsel when they are used...'.[130] This reaches the crux of the matter. In a society with a high inequality in the distribution of income and wealth, the rich can obtain justice by paying for it, while the poor are often denied justice because they do not have the resources to hire expensive lawyers. With overwhelming white control of the organs of the state, and with their prejudices against non-whites, a poor African American or Hispanic is presumed to be guilty unless proven innocent.

India may be taken as another example of a fully-fledged working democracy with regular elections at the federal, state and local levels, independent judiciary, and a vibrant and fairly independent media. Indian citizens have constitutional guarantees against any form of discrimination. India also has a large positive discrimination program to assist the *harijans* (God's people), a euphemism for so-called untouchables, members of various tribal groups, and other groups economically and socially left behind. There are obvious successes. Several members of minorities such as the Muslims, *harijans* and other social groups so far left behind, as well as women have attained high offices including the presidency, the highest office in the country, in the federal and state governments, state-owned enterprises, universities and so on. Yet, as the State Department *Country Reports – 1998* points out, serious human rights abuses continue. The human rights transgressions are not limited to Kashmir, where a cycle of violence and counter violence has destroyed the judicial system, but in the entire country. Human rights violations include extra-judicial killings, torture and rape by police and other agents of government, death in police custody, arbitrary arrests, prolonged detention while undergoing trial and so on. As to the treatment of women, the report pointed out the persistent 'societal discrimination against women; extensive societal violence against women; female bondage and prostitution; trafficking in women; child prostitution, trafficking, and infanticide. It also reported 'violence against indigenous people and scheduled castes and tribes; widespread intercaste and communal violence, increasing societal violence against Christians; and wide spread exploitation of indentured, bonded, and child labor.'[131] As more recent State Deprtment reports point out some of the worst human rights abuses have continued.[132]

Conclusion

Thus, both China and the United States have many areas of concern relating to human rights violations. In American criticisms of China, there is an emphasis on political rights, while in the Chinese criticisms of the United States importance is primarily given to economic and social rights.[133] How a person can maintain human dignity and aspire for democratic freedoms while deprived of basic needs such as adequate food and shelter is a question not realistically answered yet. Certainly neither H.G Wells nor the framers of the UN Charter saw democratic freedoms independent of economic freedoms. The 'freedom from want' was one of the basic tenets also of the 'Four Freedoms' of the Atlantic Charter.

Although the leaderships in both countries cannot escape the blame for policy related human rights violations such as the existence of the death penalty, one can legitimately presume that the leaderships in both countries is committed to safeguarding human rights, but domestic constraints prevent speedy implementation. In China, the leadership, worried about political instability leading to national disintegration and the demise of the Communist Party, is becoming somewhat paranoid of any kind of dissent, political or religious. It is also worried about the rampant nature of corruption and nepotism in the political and bureaucratic hierarchy. The practice causes hardships for the people, feeding their resentment against the leadership and ultimately undermining the authority of the Party. In their anxiety to root out corruption and nepotism, the leadership opts for draconian methods of punishment that violate the very essence of human rights despite strict regulations against some of the abuses. In America it is largely the disproportionate influence of the conservatives in politics, government and the media that accounts for the continuation of the death penalty. More recently, it is the 'War on Terrorism' that may account for various attempts by the Bush administration to adopt policies that might undermine human rights in America (and elsewhere). Ultimately, however, it is the lack of proper training and inadequate supervision of the lower level staff in the police and in prisons that accounts for the majority of human rights violations. The lack of appropriate punishment of the officials for such violations is another cause of the continuation of such abuses. The government's campaigns to obtain quick results (such as 'striking hard' or 'iron fist' in China and zero-tolerance in policing in New York, for instance) invite abuse of power by ill-trained and corrupt officials at various levels of government. Target-oriented programs in the hands of over-zealous cadres spell disaster. Many of the violations of human rights in China and police brutalities in the United States fall into this category.

In America, crime prevention has received greater priority than meeting the minimum basic needs of the poor. The American leadership fails to fully appreciate that deprivation often leads to crime. Arguably, if some of the financial and human resources devoted to policing, prisons, and the judiciary were diverted to improving the living conditions and the quality of education in the inner cities, the incidence of crime might be reduced. However, the privileged in America are more interested in protecting their property than in improving the living conditions of the poor. In fact, when the security conscious rich move out of inner cities to suburbs with their private security arrangements, cities are deprived of resources to adequately fund their services.

As far as America is concerned there is another problem too. The conservatives in Congress and in the media and the intelligentsia, over-concerned about their country's sovereignty, see any international regime as a threat and often try to undermine UN-sponsored regimes and enter reservations into international treaties and conventions, including those on human rights. For instance, the US has not ratified the Convention on the Elimination of All Forms of Discrimination Against Women. It ratified the International Covenant on Civil and Political Rights, but with reservations on the death penalty, torture and other cruel and degrading treatment or punishments. The US has not ratified the International Covenant on Economic, Social and Cultural Rights, even after 25 years of signing it. It also attached several reservations at the time of ratifying the Convention Against Torture and Other Cruel, Inhuman and Degrading Treatment or Punishment. In addition, the USA has not ratified the Convention on the Rights of the Child.[134] There are several other instances. While asking other nations to abide by international standards, the United States fails to do the same. This has led even British journalists, almost always partial to America, to call the country a 'rogue' state.[135]

All this is a recipe for a human rights disaster. Sadly, there is a wide gulf between human rights promises and practices both in America and China. The fundamental difference, of course, is that in America, thousands of public interest groups are allowed to operate freely enough to expose the weaknesses of the legal system and the implementation of law, while such freedom is very nearly absent in China. However, American human rights credentials are often tarnished as a result of the government condoning the violations by countries seen as friendly and sanctioning those which are inconvenient in one respect or another. This is clearly reflected in the American tolerance of the present Afghan regime which has, in the past (and in some instances such as in Mazar-i-Shareef even currently) been blamed for gross human rights violations, and of the Indonesian Army which has been blamed for such violations in East Timor. The United States government is also showing an uncanny tolerance for General Pervez Musharraf, the president of Pakistan who is seriously undermining whatever limited democracy there exists in Pakistan. Unfortunately, as the *New York Times* editorial points out, 'the United States has a nasty habit of embracing foreign dictators when they seem to serve American interests. It is one of the least appealing traits of American foreign policy.'[136]

Ultimately, whether constitutional and legal efforts towards ensuring human rights progresses in both the countries would depend largely on how soon the two countries succeed in providing the requisite training to local officials such as police, prison officials, and immigration officers. At the same time attempt has to be made to enforce the regime of punishments – in both cases already provided by law – for government officials for human rights abuses practiced by them. In the case of China additional efforts toward human rights monitoring by independent non-governmental organizations may have to be encouraged by the government.

7
China as a Security Threat

> If you look at world history, ever since men began waging war, you will see that there's a permanent race between sword and shield. The sword always wins...We think that with these systems, we are just going to spur swordmakers to intensify their efforts.
>
> (President Jacques Chirac[1])

Introduction

China's rapid economic growth over the next two or three decades may enable the country to catch up with the United States or possibly overtake it. Obviously, China would be able to devote considerably more financial resources to the modernization of its armed forces, possibly undermining America's role as the global superpower or threatening US interests in East Asia. This chapter examines whether China will have the capability of fielding a military comparable to the United States' and posing a military threat to US interests.

With rapid economic development, China could dramatically increase its military spending. However, the total amount it would be devoting to its armed forces in the year 2025 or later is difficult to speculate. Much would depend on the perceived external threat of regional or international alignment of forces outside China's control. Additionally, China must consider the internal risks of disintegration arising from domestic discontent – particularly among the minority nationalities living on the borders of northwest China and the newly emerging Central Asian republics. Islamic fundamentalist groups have been gaining influence in some of these republics, which might have spillover effects among the Islamic populations within China. The risk of a major upheaval may also come from the dissatisfaction among the Chinese population in general, arising from growing unemployment and inequality of income and wealth within China. Nothing can be said with certainty about either of these risks, internal or external. There is a general consensus among China watchers that the chances of China disintegrating from within are rather limited, but one must remember that China has a long tradition of peasant revolts against the excesses of the rulers; Confucian teachings support such uprisings if the rulers are unjust. Mao further politicized the population. With the wider availability of mass media, particularly television and the Internet, gaps in the standard of living are more visible than ever before. By the year 2025, China may have added another 190 million to the labor force. To this number, one must add the currently estimated surplus of over 155 million un- and underemployed population. Some more people will be laid-off with the restructuring of large-scale state-owned enterprises and trade liberalization as a result of China joining the WTO. Thus, China may have to provide employment to over 350 million people by the year 2025. It is highly unlikely that China will be abe to provide meaningful employment to all its surplus population, a significant part of which would have to depend on the small scale industries, small shops, tea stalls, domestic service and the likes. This has implications for overcrowding in cities, rise of slums, increased crime, and social unrest. To avoid a high level of discontent, a substantial portion of China's financial resources will have to be allocated to basic needs-related programs, including a social safety net for those who lose jobs in the course of economic reforms. The risk of internal political instability, particularly in the border areas, would also have a military dimension. The intensity of discontent and its violent expression, either in regional revolts, peasant revolts, or inner city troubles, will determine whether the military's involvement would be necessary. In the cases of large-scale regional revolts that threaten the integrity of the country it is almost certain that the military will be involved, as is already the case in Xinjiang.

Economic development in itself will create the need for additional food, raw materials, and energy. Many of these resources can be procured through trade; however, a substantial dependence on foreign sources (especially on the US and its allies) could be seen by the Chinese leadership as a strategic vulnerability. This means that China will attempt to obtain some of its essential resources from within the country or from the 200-mile EEZs. As a corollary, China may actively claim its rights to disputed islands, which might intensify territorial disputes with neighboring countries. Even if such disputes are settled by peaceful means, it is conceivable that China will develop a capacity to project its military power in the East and the South China Sea as well as in the Indian Ocean, because it may have to depend on the Middle East for a substantial part of its energy needs. In order to protect foreign trade and safeguard off-shore oil or non-oil mineral production against the growing menace of piracy on the high seas in China's periphery, China may have to deploy its navy or organize a collective naval presence.

Chinese military expenditure

With the expanding scope of military activities, it is inevitable that Chinese military expenditure will increase. Any estimation of these increases after two or three decades will be highly speculative; even estimating China's current military spending is a matter of guesswork. Table 7.1 gives four estimates of total military expenditure of selected countries. The Department of State Bureau of Arms Control data for China and Russia are in PPP terms; as such, they are not directly comparable to other estimates for these countries or with estimates for other countries.

Excluding the Bureau of Arms Control's PPP estimate (as it is not comparable to others), the IISS estimate of $36.7 billion is almost twice the estimate of $18.4 billion given by SIPRI and two and a half times that of the $14.6 billion suggested by Chinese official sources for the year 2000.[2] Recently, the US Department of Defense gave an estimate of $65 billion against the Chinese official figure of $20 billion for 2002.[3] If one accepts the Defense Department estimate, China is the largest military spender in Asia and is only second to the United States in the world. However, some defense experts feel Chinese military expenditure to be about equal to Japan's.[4] It is difficult to say which of the estimates are nearer the truth. Chinese expenditures on five activities – 'military R&D, the militia, People Armed Police, subsidies for the production of weapons and earnings from arm sales' – ought to be considered a part of the total military expenditure but are not included in the Chinese official estimates.[5] As such, the Chinese official figures are possibly an underestimate. On the other hand, the Department of Defense estimate of $65 billion is possibly an overestimate. Currently, the defense secretary sees China as a potential enemy, as such the department may possibly have an interest in

Table 7.1 Military expenditure in selected countries, 1998 or 1999 ($ billion)

Country	Total military expenditure (CIA) *	Total military expenditure (IISS) **	Total military expenditure (SIPRI) ***	Total military expenditure (US Bureau of Arms Control) ****
China	12.6 (1.2)	36.7 (5.3)	18.4 (1.9)	74.9 (2.2) (PPP)
USA	276.7 (3.2)	265.9 (3.2)	259.9 (3.2)	276.0 (3.3)
Japan	42.9 (1.0)	36.9 (1.2)	51.2 (1.0)	40.8 (1.0)
France	39.8 (2.5)	39.8 (2.8)	45.8 (2.8)	41.5 (3.0)
Germany	32.8 (1.5)	32.4 (1.5)	39.5 (1.5)	32.9 (1.6)
UK	36.9 (2.7)	36.6 (2.8)	31.8 (2.7)	35.3 (2.7)
Russia	N/A (N/A)	53.9 (5.2)	22.4 (3.2)	41.7 (5.8) (PPP)
Taiwan	8.0 (2.8)	F13.9 (4.6)	9.3 (3.5)	13.1 (4.6)

Notes: *CIA *World Factbook*. The data is for 1998; **IISS, *The World Military Balance, 1999/2000*. The data is for 1998 with prices and exchange rates in 1998; ***SIPRI, *SIPRI Yearbook 2000: Armament, Disarmament and International Security* (Oxford: Oxford University Press, 2000) Tables 5.2 and 5.A4, pp. 236, 238. Data is in 1995 prices and exchange rates. The data is for 1999 (at 1995 constant prices and exchange rates: ****U.S. Department of State, Bureau of Arms Control, *World Military Expenditures and Arms Transfer, 1998*, Washington, DC, 2000, Table 1. The figures are for 1997. The figures given in parenthesis represent military expenditure as a percentage of GDP.

exaggerating the Chinese military expenditure. Such exaggerations have occurred before. For instance, in 1957 both the Gaither and Rockefeller reports had exaggerated the 'missile gap' between the Soviet Union and the United States.[6]

However, even at $65 billion, Chinese military expenditure is only one-quarter of the current US military expenditure. Unlike America, China does not maintain military bases abroad therefore its strategic needs are limited, yet China has common borders with 16 countries; with a few of them, boundary disputes have not yet been settled.[7] Other than Russia, China has the longest land boundary; its coastline is a little smaller than the United States. China may also face the risk of Islamic fundamentalism from the neighboring Central Asian republics spilling over to the Muslim minority areas of western China. With its long history of foreign invasions (including the European military interventions in the nineteenth century and the Japanese in the twentieth), China has reason to be somewhat paranoid about the US military presence in Japan, South Korea, and the Western Pacific and Indian Oceans, and now in Afghanistan, Pakistan and in Central Asia. American commitment to undermine communism and the continuing support of Taiwan also worry China.

Yet, possibly learning from the experiences of the now-defunct Soviet Union, the Chinese leadership has consciously decided not to enter into an arms race against the United States. As the report from the secretary of defense, the *Annual Report on the Military Power of the People's Republic* (henceforth *Defense Report 2000*) points out, 'over the last decade, senior PLA strategists periodically have cautioned China's leaders to avoid being goaded by the United States into a lopsided arms race that could derail China's economic modernization.'[8] Deng explicitly advised against 'confrontation with the hegemon.' President Jiang also holds similar views.[9] This is clearly reflected in a rather low-key military modernization in China.

Even if one assumes that China may be spending as much as 5 per cent of its GDP on military expenditure in 2025, and further assuming that China's GDP will grow by 7 per cent annually, the total Chinese military expenditure will be around $290 billion in 2025. This compares favorably with the *Defense Report 2002* speculation of a fourfold increase.[10] Even at the current rate of US military expenditure of 3.2 per cent of the GDP with a growth rate of 3 per cent annually, the United States may be spending $637 billion or almost two and one-half times as much as China in the year 2025. Thus, in terms of military expenditure, China will not overtake or even catch up with the United States. Even so, the growth in military expenditure is a rather poor indicator of fighting capabilities; with increased sophistication of weapon systems, a modern military requires a very solid base of techno-industrial systems and a regular flow of scientific and technological innovations. The United States will continue to make further advances in weapon systems and it is highly likely that the gap between the levels of weapons technology between China and the United States will widen further. It is unlikely that China will be anywhere near the United States in this sphere within the next 25 years. Because of its dire financial state, even Russia – the successor state of the former superpower, the Soviet Union – will fall further behind the United States. As a result, China will not have the opportunity to procure the most advanced weapons and technology from sources other than America. It is highly unlikely, therefore, that China will risk open confrontation with US military might.

Chinese military too weak to be a threat

In its assessment of the strengths and weaknesses of the Chinese military and the defense strategy as a whole, the *Defense Report 2000* suggests that the 'fundamental objective of China's military modernization program is to create a force sufficient to defend against any regional opponent, maintain the credibility of territorial claims, protect national interests, maintain internal security, deter any moves by Taiwan toward *de jure* independence, and deter aggression.'[11] With these objectives in mind, Beijing is downsizing its armed forces and streamlining it into three components: (1) a small number of highly trained and technology-based rapid deployment forces that can be deployed at relatively short notice in regional conflicts; (2) the bulk of the forces equipped with medium technology weapons largely geared to internal security, particularly at the border regions; and (3) a modest nuclear capability to act as a deterrent against nuclear powers.[12]

The *Defense Report 2000* candidly points out that China's defense industrial complex is too far behind that of the West and is not capable of producing weapons that could challenge a technologically advanced country like the United States or Japan in the foreseeable future.[13] According to American military analysts, the Chinese defense industry's inability 'to produce modern weaponry and equipment means that the Chinese armed forces can field only the small numbers Beijing has purchased abroad. Newer armaments produced by China's defense industries are usually based on technologies acquired abroad in the 1980s and represent, at best, 1970s levels. Since the late 1970s, senior military officials have made public their dissatisfaction with this situation and have cited obsolescent equipment as one of the most significant factors constraining the development of operational doctrine and the PLA's ability to successfully perform its missions.'[14]

In view of the resource constraints and the relative backwardness of the defense industries, the leadership favors creating selective 'pockets of excellence' to exploit the critical vulnerabilities of adversary defenses. This strategy is reflected in the presence of a small number of rapid reaction units (RRUs) armed with modern equipment, logistics, and mobility.[15] An all out modernization of the PLA, which would require a substantial diversion of resources from developmental to military expenditure, is currently considered unacceptable. In this respect, Chinese military thinking seeks to place an increased emphasis on 'electromagnetic warfare,' particularly combined with information warfare (i.e., computer hacking combined with irregular guerilla operations to undermine or destroy the enemy's operational systems without a head-on confrontation). The PLA's information warfare capabilities are certainly growing, but 'they do not match even the primitive sophistication of their underlying strategies, which call for stealth weapons, joint operations, battlefield transparency, long-range precision strike, and real time intelligence.' Although the PLA is 'acquiring advanced telecommunications equipment through its commercial operations, even BC41 gear... it is not clear that this equipment or subcomponents are being incorporated into PLA units, much less integrated into the military's system as a whole. Therefore, IW [the information warfare] may currently offer the PLA some attractive asymmetric options, some of which may be decisive in narrowly circumscribed situations, but the Chinese military cannot reasonably expect anything approaching "information dominance" for the foreseeable future.'[16]

The *Defense Report 2000* also points out that the Chinese capability to launch military photoreconnaissance satellites is 'outdated by Western standards.' So far, much of the system development efforts in the field of reconnaissance, surveillance, and targeting have been indigenous; expediting the programs may require foreign technology. China has recently attached a high priority to manned space operations, but such efforts would not lead to improvements in military space systems before 2010, or even 2020.

According to the *Defense Report 2000*, China's ability to defend itself against cruise missiles is extremely poor; it has virtually no capability to counteract against theater ballistic missiles. China may be able to develop state-of-the-art surface-to-air missile (SAMs) over the next 20 years but current developments in this field are the derivatives of existing systems. Though China has procured state-of-the-art Russian SAM systems, they have limited defense capabilities against aircraft and cruise missiles. By Western standards, Chinese subsurface warfare capabilities are modest. The PLA's navy equipment is older, noisier, and less sophisticated than that possessed by its Western counterparts. With new acquisitions, particularly from Russia, the quality of China's submarine warfare capability will certainly improve, but its effectiveness will be hindered by a lack of well-educated and well-trained personnel.

By contrast, China's electro-optic industry is highly developed and can produce sophisticated tactical laser weapons capable of hitting aircraft. China is investigating the feasibility of ship-borne laser weapons for air defense. China's CSS-4 Intercontinental Ballistic Missile (ICBM) is the only missile capable of reaching the continental United States; there are reportedly 18 CSS-4 silos. The CSS-3 ICBM can reach Alaska but is intended mainly for Russia or Asian countries. China has one regimental-sized CSS-6 SRBM unit deployed in Southern China. It is a solid propellant road-mobile missile that can deliver a 500-kilogram conventional payload to a maximum range of 600 kilometers. The CSS-7 SRBM, again, a solid propellant road-mobile missile with a range of 300 kilometers, will supplement this unit. According to the *Defense Report 2000*, in the event of a military confrontation with Taiwan, these missiles could target air defense installations, airfields, naval bases, C-41 nodes, and logistics facilities. China may successfully develop an air-launched land-attack cruise missiles (LACMs) by the middle of this decade.

According to the *Defense Report* 2002, the PLA Air Force (PLAAF) and PLA Naval Air Force (PLANAF) possess 3400 fighters, most of obsolete design. The attempted modernization is reflected in the purchase of Su-27 and Su-30 fighters from Russia.[17] China lacks a confirmed capability to utilize precision-guided munitions (PGMs). Only the PLANAF's B-6D bombers and its FB-7 fighter-bombers have a standoff strike capability. China does not have a comprehensive, integrated national air defense network. The heavy lift capability of the Chinese air force is also limited; the PLAAF has only about a dozen heavy lift aircraft and its aerial refueling and airborne early warning programs are yet in infancy. The PLANAF so far has achieved only 'a very limited, clear weather, daytime aerial refueling capability.'[18]

The *Defense Report 2000* noted that, particularly with reference to the threat to Taiwan, until at least 2005 the limitations of the PLAAF and PLANAF would make it difficult for China to achieve air superiority over the Taiwan Strait. Taiwan will continue to have a technological edge over China in terms of the quality of its aircraft. Nearly 300 Taiwanese fighters are fourth-generation aircraft, while the number of PLA fourth-generation fighter aircraft may reach 150 by 2005. Although China's pilots have become somewhat more competent during the past five years, professionally they still lag behind their counterparts in Taiwan.[19] The *Defense Report 2002* suggests that the Taiwan Navy has a qualitative edge over the PLA Navy but 'China has a much larger number of submarines that could pose a considerable torpedo and mine threat.'[20] China could also use commercial merchant ships as well as fishing vessels to block ports with mines.

All in all, the *Defense Report 2002* concludes that the Chinese success in a military offensive against Taiwan will succeed only if China can remove some of the obstacles it faces. It said, 'the PRC faces roadblocks and challenges in implementing doctrinal changes; fielding new equipment and operating it to its full potential; executing combined or joint operations; and assimilating technology. China's main weaknesses today in sustaining extended campaign beyond its coastal waters include an inability to protect air and sea lanes of communications against superior naval and air forces; poor ASW capabilities; limited ground force amphibious lift assets; a limited number of missiles; significant logistic and training weaknesses...and a lack of real- time intelligence. China also is challenged by difficulties in absorption of technology. Its Navy is highly vulnerable to attack.'[21] The *Defense*

Report 2000 felt that in the mid-term (2005–2010) the PLA's capability to conduct integrated operations against Taiwan will certainly improve. However, major weaknesses in several areas mentioned above will force China to bear considerable losses in terms of men and material in case of an invasion of Taiwan. A massive invasion of the island will also have economic, political, and diplomatic costs for China since much of its trade surplus and technology come from the United States and its allies such as Japan and the European Union.

The opinions of some other American analysts are similar. For instance, Andrew Nathan and Robert Ross refer to the Taiwanese advantages in terms of 'better fighter planes, navigational equipment, and pilot training.' They also add that 'the mainland's acquisition of Su-27s from Russia...will merely slow the rate at which Taiwan's air superiority grows.'[22] Similarly, Frank Moore, an analyst at the Institute of Defense and Disarmament Studies in Cambridge, Massachusetts, concludes that,

> In theory, China could launch a combined arms amphibious and airborne assault on Taiwan. China's current forces do not include enough transport assets to accomplish such a task, however; and there is no evidence that China is building up larger numbers of amphibious assault ships or large cargo aircraft. Current military doctrine calls for a 5-to-1 attacker to defender ratio for amphibious assaults. Today China can only transport 1 armored or infantry brigades with its amphibious ships, which would be completely inadequate for an attack on Taiwan. The use of commercial and fishing vessels (for example, splitting a company of troops among 4 fishing trawlers) could not substitute effectively due to communication problems and the resulting inability to coordinate units. An amphibious assault would only be conducted with control [of] the skies over the Strait, which the Chinese Air Force probably cannot accomplish.[23]

Such amphibious assaults are also constrained by the fact that air strips and naval facilities in Fujian province, opposite Taiwan, are still underdeveloped and exposed to Taiwan's counterattack.[24] Moore believes that military modernization in China is rather slow and is being done in a piecemeal manner; the new systems are purchased in small batches or singly and cannot change the power balance in the region. This also applies to the recent acquisitions from Russia, which are relatively modern in relation to the existing Chinese systems but are not as effective as the comparable systems fielded by the United States or even Japan, South Korea, or Taiwan. According to Moore, 'for the foreseeable future, China's potential for military action in Taiwan and other areas will remain limited. China may take a more active military role in its region, but the overall balance of power in East Asia will remain unchanged.'[25] Bates Gill and Michael O'Hanlon have similar views. They point out that 'both China and Taiwan are modernizing their forces. But Taiwan will surely do so much faster, especially given its high-tech economy, its willingness to purchase weapons abroad, and a modernization agenda that emphasizes capabilities such as precision strikes, maritime reconnaissance and integrated air defense.'[26]

So far, opinion in China is divided on military action against Taiwan. The Chinese armed forces seem to be in favor of military action against Taiwan even if it means confrontation with the United States. However, the political leadership still gives priority to economic modernization and the cultivation of friendly relations with the United States. The defense policy announced by the State Council of the People's Republic of China in July 1998 clearly stated that 'China is now confronted with the extremely heavy task of economic construction, so the work in defense must be subordinate to and in the service of the nation's overall economic construction.' It further reiterated that the 'armed forces actively participate in and support the nation's economic construction.'[27] More recently, Chinese Premier Zhu Rongji, at a Beidahe meeting in September 1999, categorically objected to the idea of invading Taiwan. He stressed that attacking Taiwan would make it harder for China to deal with the United States. Any deterioration of Sino-American relations may result in a trade war with serious implications for the Chinese economy.[28] The leadership in Beijing feels that ensuring growth and modernization of the Chinese economy is essential for the stability of the social environment, and foreign trade and investment links are the keys to the development of China's material component of national power. The leadership also feels that assigning a high priority to defense will provide a justification for the United States to intensify its efforts to contain China, at the same time providing Japan an excuse for improving its force projection capabilities.[29]

National missile defense

The idea of defending against incoming enemy ballistic missiles has been a constant challenge for American scientists and military planners from the very day the Soviet Union succeeded in exploding its first nuclear weapon. The general consensus has been that it is not easy to mount 'an effective defense against nuclear warheads.'[30] In 1969, the Johnson Administration decided to deploy Sentinel, a ballistic missile defense (BMD) also known as the ABM defense. Since the interceptors would have nuclear payload, cities were unwilling to house the warheads within their geographic areas. President Nixon deployed Sentinel to defend American land-based ICBMs stationed in North Dakota. As Richard Garwin, nuclear weapons and national security expert and consultant to the US government since 1950 stresses, even an elaborate system of missile defense could be made ineffective simply by destroying the radars. 'This prospect of an enormous force directed against the defense itself kept us from building any kind of effective system against the Soviet Union.'[31] Garwin, like many other scientists, feels that the decision to deploy a national missile defense (NMD) system as planned by the Bush administration is unworkable, rather premature, unnecessarily expensive and counterproductive – it gives the wrong signals to Russia and China.

A recent report by the Union of Concerned Scientists (UCS) and the MIT Security Studies Program[32] suggests that if the system is deployed according to the time schedule suggested by the Bush administration, it would be deployed virtually untested. As the UCS report points out, the first three tests (out of a total of nineteen) before the Deployment Readiness Review 'will not even begin to address the question of how well the system would work... these tests will be limited to demonstrating the basic functioning of the system in a relatively benign test environment.'[33] None of the 19 tests would be using credible countermeasures. The General Accounting Office (GAO) is also critical of the project. In its 1998 review of the national missile defense, GAO pointed out that the system entailed 'high technical risk because the associated compressed schedule will permit only limited testing of the system.'[34] In its 2000 report, the GAO went into further details. It pointed out that the development of a 'highly reliable hit-to-kill capability is a difficult technical challenge. In various missile defense programs, this capability has been demonstrated in about 30 per cent of the attempted intercepts outside the atmosphere, and a panel of experts convened by the Department [of Defense] noted in 1998 that the difficulty of performing the hit-to-kill capability very reliably had been underestimated.'[35]

The system is expensive too. According to the estimates of the National Missile Defense Program office, the first phase (capability I) would cost $36.2 billion over the life of the capability I system; this estimate is already $7.5 billion more than the 1999 estimate. The GAO warns that the likely schedule delays will involve much greater costs, almost as much as $124 million per month of delay.[36] The Department of Defense has not prepared the cost estimates of capability II and capability III systems. However, the Congressional Budget Office (CBO) has made an estimate. It suggests that the cost of expanded capability I would be $29.5 billion and the costs of capability II and III would be $6.1 and $13.3 billion respectively. The total cost of the entire system may possibly be as much as $48.8 billion.[37]

The UCS report, considering the political and strategic risks, emphatically warns that the deployment of such a system will be seen by Russia as a threat to its deterrent capabilities, and it would be provoked into taking compensatory actions. It could easily equip its missiles with countermeasures to ensure that its warheads could have a high probability of entering the NMD shield. It could equally increase its capacity to launch its missiles on warning of attack or maintain a larger number of ballistic missile warheads than it would have otherwise done. It could also plan for alternative means of delivery – by bombers or by placing them on ships or submarines – of nuclear weapons, or it could create its own NMD. Reactivating the arms race would increase the risks to America's security. Russia may also be more willing to sell nuclear weapons and technology to other countries, thus jeopardizing the non-proliferation regime. Nevertheless, the Bush administration formally informed Russia on 13 December 2001 that the United States would withdraw from the IBM treaty in six months time. The message also indicated that 'the United States has concluded that it must develop, test, and deploy anti-ballistic missile systems for the defense of its national territory, of its forces outside the United States, and of its friends and allies.'[38] Senior democrats in Congress expressed their concern over Bush's decision, both with respect to the withdrawal from the IBM treaty and the decision to deploy a NMD system. Senate Foreign Relations Committee Chairman Joseph Biden stressed that the move could induce China to develop many more intercontinental ballistic missiles than it would have otherwise done; this would put pressure on India and, in response, Pakistan to add to their nuclear capabilities. Even Japan may have to consider becoming a nuclear power.[39]

The UCS expert group has misgivings similar to those of Senator Biden. In their views the US NMD system has some serious implications for China. The system, with only 250 interceptors, could not destroy many of Russia's 5000 or more warheads (this number is to be reduced to nearly 2000 according to the recent agreement between the United States and Russia). But China has barely eighteen single-warhead missiles that can reach the mainland of the United States. These could be easily countered by the 250 interceptors. China has already indicated that if the United States goes ahead with the deployment, China will cease to cooperate in non-proliferation regimes and add to its nuclear arsenal by placing multiple warheads on mobile missiles. The UCS expert group warns that 'those who believe that the proposed NMD would fundamentally shift the strategic balance in favor of the United States, freeing the United States to act with impunity against China's perceived vital interests, are engaged in wishful thinking. China has the resources, knowledge, and incentive to maintain a credible strategic deterrent into the foreseeable future, and there is every indication that it will do just that.'[40] If China begins to add significantly to its nuclear arsenal, it is inevitable that India would feel threatened and do the same, sparking a chain reaction in Pakistan. As to the 'rogue states' with first generation nuclear weapons, it would be more convenient to carry the weapon via either ship or passenger plane to the United States and launch it inside the country or from a port. The UCS report concludes that, contrary to the expectation of its promoters, the deployment of the system would decrease the overall security of the United States. A similar view was expressed in a report, *Toward True Security: US Nuclear Posture for the Next Decade*, published jointly by the Center for Defense Information, the

Federation of American Scentists, the Natural Resource Defense Council and the Union of Concerned Scientists. It categorically states that 'the United States should recognize that deployment of a U.S. missile defense system that Russia or China believes could intercept a significant portion of its survivable long-range missile forces would trigger reactions by these countries that could result in a net decrease in US security. The United States should therefore commit to not deploy any missile defense system that would decrease its security in this way.'[41] Other analysts see the deployment of missile shields as an open invitation to the multiplication and possibly proliferation of nuclear weapons. Mike Moore quotes the statements of two academicians of the Russian Academy of Sciences, Yevgeniy Aleksandrovich Fedosov and Igor Dmitriyevich Spasskiy who wrote that 'high-tech precision weapons create "incentives for the proliferation of nuclear weapons as a 'cheaper' response to challenges that are arising 'because of the' uncontrolled development of non-nuclear strategic arms."'[42] Moore also quotes a similar view from a Russian military expert, Igor Khripunov, that 'with the growing prowess of US conventional weapons, which Russia cannot afford, some of Russia's key defense experts are beginning to advocate a rebuilding of Russia's nuclear arsenal.'[43]

Most concerned observers feel that the deployment of the American NMD would generate a new arms race. US allies in Europe and the citizenry of Europe are opposed to the idea and made that clear to George W. Bush during his first visit to Europe. Yet, the president has already decided to deploy a modest anti-missile shield within two years. This decision has come in spite of the failure of the latest test of ground-based system. This decision to deploy a system that has not been tested properly and has been shown to be working has been derided by Senator Carl Levin, the Chairman of the Armed Service Committee, as violating common sense[44] Much in the same vein, the *New York Times* editorial called the rush 'to construct a system based on the present unreliable technology' as premature.[45]

There is a growing fear worldwide that a national missile defense is just the beginning; American military planners are thinking in terms of militarizing space, currently banned under the Outer Space Treaty of 1967. Before his appointment as secretary of defense, Donald Rumsfeld chaired a congressional commission examining the military issues relating to outer space. The commission came to the conclusion that space war is inevitable and the United States must prepare for such an eventuality if it is to avoid 'a space Pearl Harbor.' The commission recommended that 'the present extent of U.S. dependence on space, the rapid pace at which this dependence is increasing and the vulnerabilities it creates all demand that US national security space interests be recognised as a top national security priority.'[46] Similarly, a US Space Commands document called 'Vision 2020' advocates that 'space operations must be fully integrated with land, sea and air operations,' and that the 'U.S. Space Command must assume a dynamic role in planning and executing joint military operations. Included in that planning should be the prospects for space defense and even space warfare.'[47] It is for this reason that the United States did not join other nations in reaffirming the Outer Space Treaty and has blocked negotiations at the UN Conference on Disarmament. Both Russia and China have advocated demilitarization of outer space. Only the United States has consistently opposed even the start of negotiations in the UN Disarmament Conference on preventing an arms race in outer space. Thus, national missile defense is not about defense against a few 'rogue' states, but 'a system designed to enhance America's war fighting capability, reducing the risk of U.S. casualties while optimizing conditions for U.S. cruise missiles and jets to hit their targets.'[48] Above all, the NMD is designed to provide public welfare for American big business, a fraternity to which Bush, himself, belongs. In the words of Noam Chomsky, 'promoting advanced industry has been a leading objective of military planning since World War II, when it was recognized by business leaders that high-tech industry could not survive in a competitive "free enterprise" economy and that "the government is their only possible savior". . . . Reagan's SDI [Strategic Defense Initiative] was peddled to the business world on these grounds. Maintaining "the defense industrial base" – that is, high-tech industry – was one of the factors brought to congressional attention by President Bush [Sr.] when he called for maintaining the Pentagon budget immediately after the fall of the Berlin Wall had eliminated the Russian pretext. Militarization of space is a natural next step, which will be propelled further by the anticipated arms race.'[49] Interestingly, even though official Chinese policy opposes militarization of outer space, some Chinese military leaders advocate integrating the air force with space forces.

Territorial disputes in East and South China Sea

East Asia has two main sea lines of communication, one in the north through the East China Sea and the Sea of Japan to the Pacific Ocean and the west coast of North and South America. The other, in the south, is through the South China Sea to the Indian Ocean and to the Middle East. Both in terms of commercial and military traffic the East Asian sea routes are among the busiest in the world.[50] Most of the imports of oil, food, and essential raw materials such as iron ore and coal for Japan, Taiwan, and South Korea pass through these routes. They are as vital for two-way trade between the East Asian countries and Australia, New Zealand, North and South America, South Asia, Africa, and Europe as for the inter-regional trade between ASEAN, China, Japan, South Korea, and Taiwan. More than 41,000 ships pass through the South China Sea annually; this number is twice the number passing through the Suez Canal and three times the number passing through the Panama Canal.[51] The sea route through the Malacca Strait, which connects the Bay of Bengal with the Singapore Strait and the South

China Sea, is the shortest between Aden (the representative port of origin for oil from the Persian Gulf) and the principle destinations of Hong Kong, Shanghai, and Yokohama.[52] The Sunda Strait connecting the Indian Ocean and Java Sea is an alternative to the Malacca Strait, but is still inadequately charted and not particularly suitable for the deeper draught ships. Ships destined for the Torres Strait, eastern Australian ports, and the South Pacific may find this route appropriate, particularly during the South West Monsoon season.[53] The Lombok Strait, connecting the Makassar Strait and the eastern Philippines, is wide and deep and considered navigationally safe. However, during the North East Monsoon, ships prefer to go through the Basilan Strait to the west of the Philippines. The Lombok Strait is the main route for ships larger than 250,000 dwt. from the Middle East, the Suez, and Southern Africa to Japan, Korea, and China.[54]

Another route via the Thai Land Bridge, connecting the Andaman Sea with the Gulf of Thailand, is still a matter for the future. The 112-mile land bridge would consist of a road, high-speed rail link, and petrochemical pipeline across the peninsula. The Thai government is hoping to build port facilities at Krabi as an entry point from the Andaman Sea and another one at Khanom on the Gulf of Thailand. Krabi will also have refineries, storage, and a natural gas petrochemical complex; a container repacking facility would be built at Khanom. It is hoped that when the project is completed it will reduce the distance between Europe and the Far East by more than 1700 miles.[55]

More than half the world's annual merchant fleet tonnage is routed through the three straits of Malacca, Sunda, and Lombok. Oil, liquefied natural gas, coal, and iron ore are the main commodities passing through these straits and the South China Sea. It is estimated that the oil flow through the Malacca Strait into the South China Sea is three times greater than through the Suez Canal and 15 times greater than through the Panama Canal.[56] As much as 80 per cent of crude oil imports from the Middle East, Africa, Indonesia, and Malaysia into Japan, South Korea, and Taiwan pass through the South China Sea; as does coal from Indonesia, South Africa, and Vietnam.[57]

Although no accurate estimate of the potential capacity is available yet, it is believed that the offshore areas of most of the East Asian countries have substantial hydrocarbon deposits. In 1995, the Russian Research Institute of Geology of Foreign Countries estimated that the Spratly area might have a potential capacity of 6 billion barrels of oil, nearly two-thirds of which may be natural gas. However, Chinese estimates put it as high as 130 billion barrels of oil and natural gas.[58] The Sea of Japan and the East China Sea are also believed to have 'copper, zinc, lead, nickel, cobalt, manganese, iron, gold, and silver associated with geographical faults and spreading zones.'[59] These seas are also a source of fish, one of the main sources of food in East Asia. With the rapid economic development of the countries in the region, the need for these resources has been increasing, leading to an intense competition for control of the seabeds. The problem has also been complicated by the provisions of the 1982 UN Law of the Sea Convention (LOS Convention) which allows for twelve miles of territorial sea and an additional 200 nautical miles of EEZ in which a country has 'sovereign rights for the purpose of exploring and exploiting, conserving and managing the natural resources, whether living or non-living, of the waters superjacent to...the seabed and of the seabed and its subsoil...'. The law also gives a nation sovereign rights 'over the continental shelf' for the 'purpose of exploring it and exploiting its natural resources.'[60]

The problem, of course, is that the countries in the region are located in close proximity, thereby creating many overlapping EEZ claims by various countries in the region. None of the boundaries has been delimited.[61] Bateman mentions that as many as twenty-eight boundaries are open to disputes between 15 countries including India, Myanmar, and Russia. Both China and Vietnam claim sovereignty over the Paracel Islands, which were occupied by South Vietnam until 1976. In 1976, China took them by force, but Vietnam continues to claim sovereignty over these islands. Several hundred miles south are the Spratly Islands, which are claimed by six countries: Brunei, China, Malaysia, the Philippines, Taiwan, and Vietnam. The latter five occupy some of the islands, rocks, and reefs; Brunei has not occupied any.[62] Until 1985 only 13 locations on these islands were occupied but by 1992 as many as 42 locations were occupied. China has six, Vietnam twenty-four, the Philippines eight, Malaysia three, and Taiwan had only one.[63] There have been several skirmishes between the armed services of different countries, one of the worst between China and Vietnam in Fiery Cross reef (Yung Shu Jiao), in which the Chinese Navy sank 3 Vietnamese vessels and killed 72 Vietnamese.

China has been asserting its territorial claims in various other ways. In February 1992 the Standing Committee of the Chinese National Congress adopted *The Law on the Territorial Sea and Contiguous Zone of the People's Republic of China* [henceforth Chinese Territorial Law]. Article 2 of the Law stated that, 'the territorial land of the People's Republic of China includes the mainland and its offshore islands, Taiwan and the various affiliated islands including Diaoyu [Sengaku, claimed by Japan] Islands, the Penghu (Pescadores) Islands, the Dongsha (Pratas) Islands the Xisha (Paracel) Islands, the Nansha (Spratly) Islands and other islands that belong to the People's Republic of China.'[64] It also conducted a seismic survey to explore oil, and signed a contract with a US company for exploration of oil and the construction of a military installation on the Mischief Reef.[65] However, the Chinese government never published the coordinates of its claims to the South China Sea; a chart published by the South China Institute produced in 1984 shows nine broken lines, now claimed by China as representing its claim to the South China Sea. If this claim is taken at its face value, it would seem that China claims the entire South China Sea except for a narrow belt, varying between 12 and 80 miles in breadth, which China is prepared to concede to other countries around the sea.[66] Thus, China seems to be claiming virtually all of the South China Sea except approximately 60 nautical miles of Vietnam's continental shelf.

Neighboring countries have disputed the Chinese claims and detailed arguments have been provided in a paper by Brice Clagett of Covington & Burling, a Washington, D.C. law firm, based on an opinion commissioned by the Government of Vietnam.[67] Clagett questions Chinese assertion that sovereign claims to the Paracels and the Spratly Islands entitle it to use these islets as base points in an equidistance delimitation and that it is also entitled to connect them by 'archipelagic' straight baselines. Clagett argues that both the arguments are unjustifiable under the LOS Convention. Firstly, China does not occupy any high-tide elevations in the Spratly, while Vietnam occupies at least nine such elevations. China has established military installations on a number of locations, but all of them are low-tide elevations and international law does not allow maritime space for such locations. Article 60(8) of the LOS Convention specifies that 'artificial islands, installations and structures do not possess the status of islands. They have no territorial sea of their own, and their presence does not affect the delimitation of the territorial sea, the exclusive economic zone, or the continental shelf.' The legal consensus seems to be that the Spratly's' high-tide elevations would be entitled only to a narrow belt within the 12-mile territorial system.[68] Secondly, the Chinese contention of using the Paracels and Spratlys as the base point to connect them by 'archipelagic' straight baselines has also been questioned for two reasons: one that under the Convention only a state comprised entirely of islands may draw archipelagic baselines; two, that 'even if the Spratlys and Paracels were independent states and thus could qualify under Article 46(a), no such baselines could be drawn that would meet the first and principal requirement of Article 47, for such baselines: that the area enclosed by such baselines be "an area in which the ratio of the area of the water to the area of the land, including atolls, is between 1 to 1 and 9 to 1."'[69] According to Clagett, a South China Sea delimitation based on the lines suggested by China would have a 'disproportionately distorting effect' and therefore, under the Convention, would not be acceptable in a court of law. China's 'historic waters' claim is also questioned because China will have to prove that it had 'clearly, effectively, continuously, and over a substantial period of time, exercised sovereign rights over the area claimed.' Clagett did not find any evidence of China exercising sovereign rights on 'any, let alone all of the waters' in the South China Sea.[70]

China and its Southeast Asian neighbors have indicated that they would like to settle the dispute in a peaceful way, and the Convention also provides for third-party mediation. China prefers a bilateral negotiation and does not wish to get the United Nations or International Court of Justice involved.

On an Indonesian initiative, several rounds of regional workshops met and decided the number of topics on which cooperation was feasible. The Indonesian effort was geared largely toward confidence building measures.[71] The 1991 Workshop issued a statement stating that the jurisdictional disputes in the South China Sea ought to be settled by 'peaceful means through dialogue and negotiations.' This statement became the basis for the ASEAN Declaration on the South China Sea in Manila in July 1992. The Workshops encouraged negotiations between the parties and such negotiations took place between China and the Philippines; Vietnam and the Philippines; between China, Malaysia, and Vietnam; and between Malaysia and other claimants. In these negotiations the parties decided upon bilateral codes of conduct. There is an increasing emphasis on joint development, an idea that China supports. China has also ratified the 1982 Convention on the Law of the Sea and has indicated that it would be willing to resolve the disputes on the basis of the Convention. China has also agreed to discuss the South China Sea issues informally with the ASEAN in the context of ASEAN Regional Forum (ARF).

On the question of the dispute settlement between the Asian countries, the United States supports the idea of peaceful negotiations but it has serious misgivings about China's 1992 Territorial Sea Law provisions regarding the innocent passage of military vessels. The Law stipulates that 'to enter the territorial waters of the People's Republic of China, foreign military vessels must obtain permission from the government of the People's Republic of China.'[72] The United States government argues that such a provision goes against the Convention's stipulation that the ships of all nations 'enjoy the right of innocent passage.' However, the Geneva Convention on the Territorial Sea and Contiguous Zone, 1958 provides for 'innocent passage' but is silent on the issue of prior notification or authorization of such a passage. In the discussions of the Convention on the Law of the Sea serious differences emerged and the question of prior notification or authorization remained inconclusive. China reserved the right to require prior notification or authorization in its security interests.[73]

The United States government also objects to Indonesian interpretations of 'innocent passage' of warships. Under the Indonesian interpretation, outside the designated sea-lanes 'submarines must sail on the surface, weapons and surveillance radars must be switched off and aircraft-carriers must keep their planes deck-bound.'[74] There are other controversial issues, such as military maneuvers by a foreign state in the EEZ of another state that might jeopardize the right of the EEZ state to fully enjoy its privileges in the area. The United States and the other nuclear states also have misgivings about the Southeast Asian Nuclear Weapons Free Zone (SEANWFZ) and the inclusion of the EEZs and continental shelves in this zone. There is also a controversy regarding the shipment of nuclear waste through the EEZs, territorial seas, and straits. The littoral states of the Malacca Strait have been uneasy about the shipment of nuclear waste through the Strait. Several coastal states expressed their strong reservations regarding the shipment of nuclear waste from Europe to Japan. Malaysia denounced this traffic and Indonesia asked the Japanese government not to pass through Indonesian waters.[75] Nevertheless, there are issues such as piracy, maritime highjacking, drug trafficking, pollution control, and disaster relief in which fruitful cooperation between nations can easily take place. The IMO reports that the number of acts of piracy and armed robbery against ships in 2000 increased by more than 50 per cent. Over the same period the number of incidents went down in the Mediterranean and West Africa but increased considerably in the Malacca Strait, the South China Sea, and the Indian Ocean: 72 crew members were killed, 5 were missing, and 129 wounded. One ship was destroyed, two were highjacked, and three ships 'went missing.'[76] Oil pollution resulting from deliberate emissions from ships has become a much greater long-term threat than those from shipping accidents. On the basis of an analysis of intermediate resolution European Remote Sensing (ERS) space-borne synthetic aperture radar (SAR) quick look images, it has been found that 'the main shipping routes with high incidences of oil spills include the routes through the Straits of Malacca, the Singapore–Java route, the numerous routes crossing the South China Sea and the Singapore–Bangkok route. Another route with relatively high incidences of pollution is the Jakarta–Manila route, which also runs parallel to the coast of East Malaysia and Brunei where intensive exploitation activities exist. The most polluted waters are found in the Gulf of Thailand and the South China Sea off the coast of Southern Vietnam.'[77] These issues, affecting all the countries in the region, need immediate attention – cooperation in more contentious areas can come only slowly.

Arms trade and proliferation of advanced weapon technology

The United States is, by far, the largest exporter of weapons accounting for almost half of the world arms exports. Russia, France, the United Kingdom, and Germany are the other large exporters of weapons (Table 7.2). China's trade in armaments is currently rather insignificant in value. Its share in the export of weapons is only around 2 per cent of total export and a little more than 4 per cent of the US export of arms (Table 7.2), but its transfer of arms and weapons technology, particularly to Iran, Iraq, Pakistan, North Korea, and Myanmar has caused serious concern in the United States.[78] Other Middle Eastern countries that purchased Chinese arms include Egypt, Libya, Saudi Arabia, and Syria. China sold tanks, armored personnel carriers, combat aircrafts, small warships, air-to-air missiles, surface-to-air missiles, anti-cruise ship missiles, and other missile technology to Iran. It also agreed to provide assistance for the development of Iran's nuclear, chemical, and biological weapons-related technology.[79]

Table 7.2 Arms exports by selected countries, 1995–99 ($ billion)

Countries	Total Arms Exports (1995–99)	Arms exports as % of total arms export (1995–99)
USA	53.4	48.0
UK	7.3	6.6
France	11.7	10.5
Russia	14.6	13.1
China	2.2	2.0
Netherlands	2.2	2.0
Germany	6.1	5.5
Italy	2.0	1.8
Ukraine	2.0	1.8

Source: SIPRI, *SIPRI Yearbook 2000*, (Oxford: Oxford University Press, 2000) Table 7A.2, pp. 372–3.

China has also sold entire chemical plants to Iran for the production of legitimate items, but these can easily be used for the production of poison gas and industrial chemicals that can be used as nerve agents. Chinese firms have also provided supplies to Iran for its chemical weapons program and dual-use equipment and vaccines for biological weapons. China's transfer of civilian nuclear technology, legitimate under the International Atomic Energy Agency (IAEA) guidelines, has helped Iran mine and enrich uranium, build research reactors and production facilities, and train personnel. In 1997, China gave an assurance to former US Secretary of State Madeleine Albright that it will not assist Iran with any new nuclear program but will complete its existing programs of building a small research reactor and a plant producing zirconium cladding to encase fuel rods in nuclear reactors.[80] It seems that China is keeping that promise.

China's assistance in missile production has ranged from helping building missile plants to the construction of a test range and provision of guidance technology and precision machine tools. In January 2002, the Director of Central Intelligence reported to Congress that China continued to supply ballistic missile goods, technology, and expertise during 2001.[81] In July 1998, Iran tested a *Shahab-3* missile with a range of 1300 kilometers. Another test was held in July 2000. Iran is now developing *Shahab-4*, which is likely to have a reach of up to 2000 kilometers. Iran also has plans for a '*Shahab-5.*'[82]

China's help to Pakistan in terms of nuclear weapons and missile technology has been quite substantial, and has included the transfer of a proven nuclear design and ring magnets to be used for enriching uranium and dual-use equipment that can be used in nuclear weapons. In 1996, China issued a statement that it would not assist unsafeguarded nuclear plants, but there is some evidence confirming China's assistance in the construction of a plutonium producing nuclear reactor at Khushab, a facility that is not safeguarded. China is also helping Pakistan construct a nuclear power plant at Chashma, which will be safeguarded.[83] There is no doubt that China's assistance was essential for Pakistan's nuclear program, which was tested in May 1998.

China has transferred M-11 short-range ballistic missiles and related equipment to Pakistan to help develop its missile program. According to the Director of Intelligence Report to the US Congress, China has continued assisting Pakistan's ballistic missile program. Pakistan is moving toward serial production of solid fuel short-range ballistic missiles (SRBMs). China is also assisting the development of Pakistan's two-stage medium-range ballistic missile (MRBM), *Shaheen II*. China is reportedly building a second missile plant for Pakistan and providing specialty steel, a guidance system, and expertise.[84]

Among the other major recipients of China's arms and weapons technology in the Middle East have been Egypt, Saudi Arabia, and Syria. China is reported to have assisted Egypt in upgrading its domestic missile production facilities, including an improved version of the SA-67 SAM, (Ayn al-Saqr), in improving indigenously built SCUD-B SSM and the licensed production of Silkworm Anti-Ship Missiles.[85] China also sold a number of long-range ballistic missiles (2700 kilometer-range DF-3 or CSS-2) to Saudi Arabia. China agreed to sell Syria a 30 kilowatt neutron source research reactor for which the approval of the International Atomic Energy Agency (IAEA) was obtained. China has also assisted the Syrian missile and WMD program, including the chemical weapons program. China reportedly assisted Syria in the construction of an underground facility for the production of chemical and biological weapons near Damascus. There is also a cooperative agreement with Libya but whether it is connected with WMD or a missile development program is not known.[86] However, it is known that China declined to sell nuclear weapons to Libya.[87]

China's nonproliferation non-compliance

The Chinese attitude toward nonproliferation regimes has changed over the years. Beginning with total opposition during the 1950s, China began to agree to a conditional acceptance of the principles behind nonproliferation regimes in the 1980s, so long as they did not compromise China's independence regarding the manufacture of nuclear weapons during the quarter of a century until the mid-1980s. Since the mid-1980s, China has gradually moved toward conforming to the international nonproliferation regimes.[88] However, when the United States and the Soviet Union negotiated the Limited Test Ban Treaty (LTBT) in 1963, the Treaty on the Nonproliferation of Nuclear Weapons (NPT) in 1968, and the Threshold Test Ban Treaty (TTBT) in 1974, even though China considered these regimes a conspiracy of the nuclear powers to maintain their monopoly, it supported the ban on transference of nuclear weapons or technical information related to it. This could be seen as a tacit acceptance of one of the main provisions of the LTBT; yet it did not support the treaty.[89] Even after developing its own nuclear weapons, China declined to join the NPT but gave an assurance that it would not assist any other country in the development of nuclear devices. It had already announced its 'no first use' policy. However, in 1984 China joined the IAEA, which assists research and development relating to the peaceful uses of atomic energy. The IAEA also administers safeguards designed to ensure that the activities supported by the Agency are not used for military purposes. It also has the responsibility to oversee the mandatory safeguards under the NPT and some other international treaties. China joined the NPT in 1992. The NPT imposes a treaty obligation on the member Nuclear Weapon States (NWS) not to transfer nuclear weapons or other nuclear explosive devices and not to assist Non-Nuclear Weapon States (NNWS) to manufacture or acquire them. It also obliges the NNWS not to obtain nuclear weapons or other nuclear explosive devices, nor to manufacture them. Peaceful uses of atomic energy under IAEA safeguards are permitted.

China is also a signatory of the CTBT but has not ratified it. The treaty requires each member state 'not to carry out any nuclear weapon test explosion or any other nuclear explosion;' to prohibit and prevent any such nuclear explosion at any place under its jurisdiction or control; to 'refrain from causing, encouraging, or in any way participating in' any nuclear weapon test explosion or any other nuclear explosion by any other state. The CTBT prohibits only nuclear explosion but not other activities involving nuclear power or research reactors, nor does it prohibit site preparation or the management of existing stockpile.[90]

China signed the Chemical Weapon's Convention (CWC) in 1997. The Convention obliges member nations not to develop, produce, acquire, stockpile, or retain or use chemical weapons, or transfer chemical weapons to anyone. It also requires the member nations to destroy, in three stages within a maximum of fifteen years, all chemical weapons and chemical weapons production facilities. The Convention provides for routine inspection as well as 'challenge' inspections of both military and commercial sites. China claims to have destroyed all its chemical weapons stockpile and three former production facilities, but Western intelligence sources suggest that it still possesses a moderate stockpile and chemical weapons production capability.[91] China joined the Zangger Committee in 1997. The Committee, an informal group whose decisions are non-binding on its members, produces a 'trigger list' of fissionable materials, and equipment or materials especially designed or prepared for the processing, use, or production of special fissionable materials. Items on the 'trigger list' are subject to IAEA safeguards if supplied by NPT parties to any NNWS. China is not a member of the MTCR. MTCR is an informal association of member governments, aimed at combating the proliferation of missile technology (not missiles). It hopes to limit the spread of WMD by controlling the delivery systems, especially rockets, with a capacity to deliver a payload of 500 kilograms to a distance of at least 300 kilometers. China has given an assurance that it will abide by the guidelines of MCTR. China is not a member of the Australia Group (AG), an informal group aiming to limit the spread of Chemical Weapons (CW) and Biological Weapons (BW) through the control of chemical precursors, equipment, and BW agents and organisms. However, China has agreed to abide by its guidelines.

China is gradually introducing an export control system with regard to nuclear equipment and technologies. It has imposed export control on dual-use material and technology consistent with the Nuclear Suppliers Group (NSG) regulations but has not joined the group. It has introduced export controls on chemical and related technology and banned the export of 10 of the 24 chemicals banned by the Australia Group (AG). In its White Paper, *China's National Defense, 2000*, China reiterates its commitment to 'the issue of arms control and disarmament,' and promises to work hard 'to promote the sound development of the international disarmament process.'[92] On the other hand, China's compliance record is not unblemished. China is a signatory to the Biological Warfare Convention (BWC) and the CWC, yet it did export equipment and materials to Iran. However, it did not export chemical and biological technology. As stated earlier, China has not joined the MTCR, although it has agreed to abide by the MTCR guidelines; but it has consistently supplied missile technology to Egypt, Iran, Pakistan, and Syria. China is a member of the NPT and the CTBT. Nevertheless, it did violate the NPT by transferring ring magnets to Pakistan. China not only provided nuclear weapons technology to Pakistan but also possibly participated in Pakistan's test explosion. Beijing sees its own violations in the same light as the United States' sales of arms to Taiwan. Further to the Shanghai Communiqué the US government gave an assurance in the 'August 17' communiqué that 'its arms sales to Taiwan will not exceed, either in qualitative or quantitative terms, the level of those supplied in recent years.'[93] In reality, transfer of military technology has more than compensated the reduction in US arms shipment to Taiwan.

America's nonproliferation non-compliance

America, together with the Soviet Union, has initiated and negotiated bilateral and multilateral nuclear arms reduction and nonproliferation regimes. It negotiated, with the Soviet Union, the Treaty Banning Nuclear Weapons Tests in Atmosphere, in Outer Space and Underwater (LTBT) in 1963 and the Treaty on the Limitation of Underground Tests (TTBT) in 1974, followed by a companion treaty, the Treaty on Underground Nuclear Explosions for Peaceful Purposes (PNE Treaty) or PNET in 1976. The US has been a member of the Conference on Disarmament (CD), which primarily aims to prevent a nuclear arms race and encourage nuclear disarmament and the prevention of nuclear war. In 1993, the United States supported the CD's establishment of an ad hoc Committee on the Nuclear Test Ban Treaty with a mandate to negotiate a treaty. The negotiations began in 1994. The United States extended the test ban moratorium to facilitate the negotiations. The UN General Assembly adopted the text of the CTBT and recommended signature in September 1996. President Clinton was the first world leader to sign the treaty.[94]

Nevertheless, the US record on nonproliferation compliance has its blemishes too. For instance, the United States joined the CWC and destroyed its quota of chemical weapons well ahead of the CWC timetable but remained in technical violation of the regime because it did not submit the declaration for chemical industry facilities until May 2000, nearly three years after the deadline.[95] Congress' dithering about implementing legislation needed to apply the CWC provisions to the domestic chemical industry caused the delay. This hesitancy was surprising because the American chemical industry and the Chemical Manufacturing Association supported the CWC.[96] Interestingly, the issue of implementing legislation became a victim of presidential election politics. Since President Clinton seemed supportive of nonproliferation regimes, Robert Dole, the Republican presidential candidate and a former Senate majority leader, wrote to his former colleagues that since the CWC was effectively unverifiable it provided an 'illusory' arms control. President Clinton, instead of fighting for the implementing legislation, simply withdrew CWC from Senate consideration. When President Clinton resubmitted it for Senate consideration just before CWC came into force, Robert Dole had changed his views and became supportive of the Convention.

The Senate approved the Convention in April 1997 but introduced three exceptions that effectively diluted the provisions of the CWC. Firstly, that the president could refuse an on-sight inspection if he felt that it would compromise national security. Secondly, that the samples collected by an inspection could not be taken out of the United States for analysis, and finally, the third exception narrowed the scope of CWC by reducing the number of industry facilities that were required to declare their mixture or solutions or be inspected.[97] Another reason for the delay was the jurisdictional infighting between the State and the Commerce departments as to which was the most appropriate agency to oversee the coordination of industry declarations and inspections.[98]

When the inspectors arrived to inspect US chemical weapons stores, the officials of the US On-site Inspection Agency (OSIA) refused to lend or sell even simple equipment such as electrical adapters to the inspectors, and contested every single request made by the visiting inspectors. The attitude of the US officials throughout the inspection remained unhelpful, dilatory, and confrontational.[99] One is reminded of American complaints about the uncooperative and confrontational attitude of Iraq toward the United Nations Special Commission (UNISCOM) for overseeing the destruction of the Iraqi WMD. The difference, of course, was that Iraq was dealing with enemies and had harbored a suspicion, subsequently substantiated, that William Butler, the head of the inspection team, was cooperating with American espionage in Iraq.[100] There was another major difference: the CWC inspectors came from an organization of which the United States was a leading member, while the enemies of Iraq dominated the UNISCOM. Some of the arguments used by the US officials during the CWS inspection were subsequently copied by India, Russia, and South Korea, thereby undermining the objectives of the CWC.

The prospect of BWC being approved by the U.S. government is also bleak. An internal review by the Bush administration has already concluded that 'since verification of the treaty will be extremely difficult, the protocol will jeopardize US secrets while doing nothing to stop cheaters from developing biological weapons.'[101] Another case in point is the Ottawa Convention banning anti-personnel land mines, which the Clinton administration did not sign. However, President Clinton asked the Defense Department to end the use of all anti-personnel land mines outside Korea by 2003 and to have alternatives to such mines in Korea by 2006.[102] The Comprehensive Test Ban Treaty fared worse. President Clinton referred the CTBT to the Senate in September 1997 for advice and consent for ratification. The Senate sat on it for almost two years and then allotted two days of hearings in the Senate Arms Services Committee, one day in the Senate Foreign Relations Committee, and a closed briefing in the Select Committee on Intelligence. The allotment of such a short time to a major arms control program was unprecedented.[103] President Clinton, engrossed with Kosovo and his impending impeachment, had little time to campaign for the CTBT. Meanwhile, the Republican Senate majority leader, Senator Trent Lott, together with the Chairman of the Senate Foreign Relations Committee, Senator Jesse Helms (also Republican), campaigned feverishly against the ratification of the CTBT to further embarrass the president. On 13 October 1999 the Senate, by a narrow majority, rejected the president's ratification request for the CTBT.

The chances of the ratification of the treaty under the Bush administration are even bleaker. In his presidential election campaign, President Bush supported the continuation of the moratorium on testing but asserted that the 'CTBT does not stop proliferation, especially by renegade regimes. It is not verifiable. It is not enforceable. And it would stop us from ensuring the safety and reliability of our nation's deterrent, should the need arise. On these crucial matters, it offers only words and false hopes and high intentions – with no guarantees whatever. We can fight the spread of nuclear weapons, but we cannot wish them away with unwise treaties.'[104]

Apart from the direct non-compliance of nonproliferation regimes, some other US policies indirectly undermine international efforts toward nonproliferation. On one hand, the United States complains about missile technology being transferred to countries like Iran but it does not hesitate in transferring such technology to Taiwan. It also sells surface-to-air and anti-ship missiles to countries in the Middle East, particularly to Saudi Arabia. It is only natural for Iran to procure missiles from wherever it can to counter the increasing missile threat from Saudi Arabia.[105] Russia and China, as well as the Western European countries, stand ready to oblige. Since depending entirely on foreign supplies for strategic weapons creates strategic vulnerability, it is natural for a country to produce missiles domestically if it has the requisite scientific and industrial capacity. Thus, the import of missiles leads, in a natural progression, to domestic production or co-production. The U.S. efforts toward nonproliferation are also undermined by its implicit acceptance of Israel's nuclear weapons.[106] The US government also allows its armed forces to use weapons banned under international protocols, further undermining nonproliferation efforts. For instance, US armed forces used fuel-air explosive bombs in the Persian Gulf War. These bombs, by burning the oxygen over a surface of one or two square-kilometers, destroy human life by asphyxiation, which is explicitly outlawed by The Hague and Geneva Conventions.[107]

Conclusion

Regardless of what some American scholars and journalists would like us to believe, there is no real evidence that China, in the foreseeable future, will catch up with America either in economic or in military terms. The gap between both the organizational and technical competence of the Chinese and the American military machines is so enormous that the very idea of China being a threat to United States security in the next two or three decades seems to be simply untenable. Except for a small number of elite groups, Chinese soldiers are ill-trained and are equipped with largely out-of-date weapons. Their education is inadequate to help them use sophisticated imported weapons systems. The industrial support system, an essential prerequisite of a modern army, is outdated and under-developed. The Chinese army has a very limited forward projection capability, so much so that short of total destruction by showering Taiwan with missiles, it cannot conquer Taiwan. The destruction of Taiwan by missiles is not really an option open to China because of the high civilian casualty and the economic and diplomatic costs internationally. China would probably be prepared to pay the price if Taiwan declared independence, but Taiwan cannot take American support of such direct provocation for granted. China could wage a small military encounter with one of its neighbors in Southeast Asia in connection with disputed islands in the South China Sea. Even this may have economic and diplomatic costs, which China would like to avoid. For this reason China wishes to settle these disputes peacefully by bilateral negotiations. China values the contribution the United

States makes toward its economic development, without which both the integrity of the country as well as the legitimacy of the Communist Party of China can be threatened.

Those who predict an impending threat from China must realize that if their dire warnings are taken at face value, they will spur a new world arms race. This may be good for the Pentagon and the military machines of China as well as other countries, but is certainly not in the interest of mankind. Even within America, considerable financial resources are needed to eradicate poverty and raise the standard of health care and education. Those who paint China as the next enemy may conceivably think that by doing so they may trigger an arms race between the United States and China of the Cold War vintage in which the Soviet Union destroyed itself. However, they may be in for a surprise. Undoubtedly, China will increase military expenditure but so far there is no indication that it will extend itself beyond a limited deterrence. It will not compete, at least in the foreseeable future, with the United States globally; even the Chinese army does not want that kind of competition. China has always learnt from Soviet mistakes, and it is not likely to make the biggest Soviet mistake of competing globally and exporting revolutions. What the Chinese, with a long history of subjugation and humiliation by the West, want is to regain self-respect as a large nation. China aspires for a proper place in the international hierarchy in a multipolar world with one superpower and a number of major powers.

8
Conclusion

As we peer into society's future, we – you and I, and our government – must avoid the impulse to live only for today, plundering for, for our own ease and convenience, the precious resources of tomorrow. We cannot mortgage the material assets of our grandchildren without asking the loss also of their political and spiritual heritage. . . .

Down the long lane of the history yet to be written America knows that this world of ours, ever growing smaller, must avoid becoming a community of dreadful fear and hate, and be, instead, a proud confederation of mutual trust and respect.

(President Dwight Eisenhower[1])

At the dawn of the twenty-first century the sole superpower, America, possesses an undoubted superiority in science and technology; it has an impressive lead in the weapons of mass destruction. In many ways the situation today is reminiscent of the period just after World War II when America was the undisputed world leader. It emerged from the war enormously wealthy and militarily powerful, with none to dispute its world dominance. Western European countries and Japan needed funds for post-war reconstruction and American assistance came via the Marshall Plan and other types of foreign aid. This reflected American high-minded humanitarianism as much as self-interest, both economic (the vastly expanded production capacity within America needed markets) and political (continuation of the alliance in the post-war world). Funds for post-war reconstruction were needed for the Soviet Union too and its leaders looked to the United States for such funding. It is difficult to tell whether the granting of such loans would have made a difference to Soviet–US relations but it is undoubtedly true that the mishandling of the loan request embittered relations and hardened the Russian attitude toward post-war diplomacy.[2] The Soviet Union was given the choice to join the Marshall Plan but it found the attached conditions unacceptable. It launched its own 'Molotov Plan' for the Eastern European countries, thus confirming the division of Europe into two power blocks. By this time the Truman Doctrine had been unveiled so there was little or no reason for the Soviet Union to believe that the invitation to join the Marshall Plan was a genuine one.

While the division of Europe was progressing the sun was setting on the European colonial empires in Asia and elsewhere. The independence of India and Pakistan in August 1947, to some extent aided by the Roosevelt administration, heralded the emergence of independent non-European countries, which drew inspiration from the American War of Independence, and looked to America as a role model. Thus, in terms of both military might and as an inspiration, the United States of America was the unchallenged world leader at the mid point of the twentieth century. It had two choices: to assist the post-war reconstruction of the Eurasian sub-continent (the Western hemisphere and much of Sub-Saharan Africa remained physically unaffected by the Second World War) or alternatively to enter into an arms race with the Soviet Union with the ultimate objective of a 'roll back' of Communism. In fact America pursued both objectives, but post-war reconstruction essentially became a spin-off of the military containment of the Soviet Union. The Western European countries, Japan, South Korea and Taiwan – the allies in the American crusade against Communism – largely owe their economic reconstruction in the post-war period to that crusade.[3] The newly emerging countries that modelled themselves on America and adopted neutral positions ('non-alignment' as it came to be known) became *bête noir* in American eyes. A country which had proclaimed freedom as the eternal right of mankind and had launched a crusade to free those enslaved behind the 'iron curtain' readily came to the assistance of dying colonialism, thus prolonging the enslavement of people struggling for their freedom in Asia and elsewhere. Unfortunately, as Sinha pointed, the United States leadership had taken over European fears and prejudices against Russia, with roots in European history much before the emergence of Communism in Russia.[4] The American crusade against Soviet Communism was not necessarily against its totalitarian tendencies but its agnosticism to private property; after all the American leadership had shown an uncanny tolerance before World War II not only for Fascist Italy and Nazi Germany but also after the war for totalitarian dictatorships all over the world.

In the name of saving the world from Communism, democratic America organized the overthrow of democratically elected regimes, replacing them with ruthless military dictatorships. It initiated state-sponsored assassinations of nationalist leaders of newly emerging countries. It masterminded massive pogroms of innocent people. Above all, it launched and conducted wars with inhuman ferocity, violating international laws with impunity in the process. Ideological blinkers prevented it from realizing that in the process of fighting Communism it was losing many of the ideals on which the new republic of the United States was founded. Sadly, millions of innocent people were sacrificed to safeguard the interests of American big business or to guarantee the short-term electoral advantage of political leaders.

Truman's containment of Communism by massive mobilization and rearmament of peace-time America was not necessarily a reaction to an imminent Soviet threat; at that time the Soviet Union was too weak to confront America and was seeking American assistance for its reconstruction. Truman had domestic considerations in mind. He had to appease the conservatives in both parties in Congress and he also wanted to be re-elected. His advisers had come to the conclusion that the President's anti-Communist stand would go down well with both the conservatives in Congress and with the American public.[5] Many voters migrated from the Soviet Union and the eastern European countries to escape oppression.

In appeasing the conservatives Truman unhesitatingly sacrificed American values. He instituted a peacetime loyalty program only nine days after the Truman Doctrine speech.[6] Government employees were required to prove their patriotism even without confronting their accusers or knowing explicitly the charges against them.[7] This created, as a leading American historian said, an atmosphere rife with 'spying, suspicion, defamation by rumor' and in which 'democratic freedom' was put at risk, placed as it was in the hands of those 'whose values are the values of dictatorship and whose methods are the methods of the police state.'[8] The Department of Justice brought out a list of 'subversive' organizations. Aliens living in the United States for long periods were deported because of their association, one way or another, with the Communist Party. Hostile reporters were prevented from covering military activities; credentials of many newsmen were revoked or denied. The administration proposed loyalty tests for journalists, a provision that had to be modified after considerable opposition.[9]

Many of these onslaughts on freedom also came as part of Truman's election strategy. The president's electoral prospects in early 1948 were rather dim. Henry Wallace, a third-party candidate, was quite popular and in January, Truman's Gallup Poll approval rate was only 35 per cent.[10] By March however, with the implementation of the Truman Doctrine, the introduction of the Loyalty Program, and the tough stance against Communists within America, his rating had jumped to 60 per cent.

President George W. Bush faces the same choices: cooperation or confrontation. Initially, he was determined to set aside the policy of a constructive dialogue with China, developed under all presidents since Richard Nixon, and was tending more towards confrontation than cooperation. To his defense secretary, Donald Rumsfeld, China is the potential enemy threatening American interests in Asia. The truth, of course, is that like the Soviet Union in 1950, China at the beginning of the twenty-first century is too weak to challenge American might. Even if the Chinese economy sustains a rapid rate of economic growth for the next quarter of a century, it is almost certain that China will remain (except perhaps in total gross domestic product as expressed in terms of purchasing power parity) considerably behind the United States, the European Union, and Japan in terms of economic and technological capabilities. Rapid growth of the economy will certainly provide China with the means to modernize its armed forces but, barring islands of excellence, the Chinese military will significantly lag behind the United States, both organizationally and technologically. With increasing demands for food, fuel, and raw materials, China's dependence on foreign supply, particularly on the United States and its close allies such as Argentina, Australia, New Zealand, Thailand, and Saudi Arabia, may be seen by the Chinese leadership as strategic vulnerability. Therefore China will aim to diversify the source of foreign supply while at the same time developing sources of supply in its own EEZs. This runs the risk of military skirmishes erupting in disputed areas, which may possibly lead to American military involvement. So far China and its neighbors have preferred a cooperative approach and joint development. The Chinese leadership has made it clear that its present priorities – economic development and internal political stability – require international peace and constructive dialogue with neighboring countries and with the United States and its allies. Consequently China has shown an uncanny willingness to compromise in trade negotiations and to allow foreign capital to operate in the country on terms at which many other developing countries might balk. Apart from rhetoric, China has not questioned the continued stationing of American troops in the region and at least tacitly sees the US presence in the region as a counterbalance to the re-emergence of Japanese imperialism. Barring a few episodes of confrontational posturing, China has shown considerable restraint on the Taiwan question. Although there is a considerable difference of opinion within the country, the Chinese political leadership is not contemplating a military take-over of the island. It may possibly be in recognition of the inherent weaknesses of the Chinese armed forces, but a more likely explanation is the economic and diplomatic consequences it may have to suffer in terms of its alienation from America and its allies. It has shown its readiness to cooperate in the management of international regimes against proliferation of weapons of mass destruction, though the Chinese record remains imperfect. In this respect, the American record too has its blemishes.

On other matters of dispute, such as human rights and the environment, China is taking halting steps toward amelioration. However, it is unrealistic to expect rapid progress in these areas in light of the lack of financial resources, trained manpower, and low levels of public acceptance of the seriousness of the problem. All in all, China, given a choice, would prefer cooperation to confrontation. Of course, national interests of America and China do not always coincide; therefore, differences will arise. Resolving them will require mutual understanding and constructive dialogue.

The events of September 11 brought a great respite for China. The administration – not necessarily the defense secretary and his team – in search of an international coalition to fight the 'War on Terrorism,' needed China's support and began to look for a productive relationship instead of strategic competition. China, for its own reasons (most likely a desire to suppress its own 'terrorists'), was ready to accommodate but voiced strong reservations against American unilateralism; America's withdrawal from the IBM treaty; the deployment of the national missile defense; and particularly against the US–Taiwan policy.

President George W. Bush, whose election to the presidency was legally disputed, needed an 'enemy' to justify his proposed massive investments in missile defense. The reality is that investing in defense and its attendant industries is one of the easiest ways of showing gratitude to American big business, which funded Bush's election campaign. The search for an enemy had begun in America soon after the end of the Cold War. In fact, the present author had quoted Godfrey Jansen claiming as early as 1981 that 'today Islam and the modern Western world confront and challenge each other. No other major religion poses such a challenge to the West.'[11]

September 11 gave the president the enemy he was looking for. His clarion call for his 'War on Terror' and bringing Osama bin Laden 'dead or alive' to justice raised his popularity rating to an unprecedented height. The country, numb from watching the demolition of the two citadels of American economic and military power and the mass live burial of over 3000 innocent lives under the rubbles of the twin towers of the World Trade Center and the Pentagon, gave the administration a *carte blanche* to move forward with defense spending.

Not unlike Truman, Bush (Jr)'s administration, supported by Congress, has ncreased the defense budget significantly and may be susceptible to dragging the country down the slippery slope of a renewed arms race. It has also increased the budget of the secret services, giving them considerable freedom to organize covert operations, including assassinations abroad and domestic spying. At home, many democratic freedoms are being curtailed. The Patriot Act, as David Cole suggests in an article in the *Nation*:

> imposes guilt by association on immigrants, rendering them deportable for wholly innocent non-violent associational activity on behalf of any organization blacklisted as terrorist by the Secretary of State....This provision in effect resurrects the philosophy of McCarthyism, simply substituting 'terrorist' for 'communist.' Perhaps not realizing the pun, the Supreme Court has condemned guilt by association as 'alien to the traditions of a free society and the First Amendment itself.' Yet it is now the rule for aliens in our free society.[12]

Cole further added that under the Patriot Act the Attorney General can lock up aliens almost indefinitely, 'on mere suspicion, without any hearing and without any obligation to establish to a court that the detention is necessary to forestall flight or danger to the community.' The Justice Department added insult to injury by refusing to provide basic information about the identity of the detainees – most of them detained on the basis of racial, ethnic, and religious profiling – the nature of their crimes, or even their whereabouts, were withheld. This refusal came in spite of the requests for such information by Representatives John Coneyers Jr, Sheila Jackson Lee, Jerrold Nadler, and Robert C. Scott, and Senators Patrick Leahy, Edward Kennedy and Russell Feingold, the only person to vote against the Patriot Act in the Senate. This unprecedented 'blanket practice of secret incarcerations,' as Cole called it, was challenged in the District Court of Columbia under the Freedom of Information Act (FOIA) by the Center for National Security Studies, *Nation* magazine, the American Civil Liberties Union, and a number of public interest groups connected with civil liberties and human rights. In her verdict, District Judge Gladys Kessler not only ordered the Justice Department to reveal some of the information but also noted that 'secret arrests are "a concept odious to a democratic society"...and profoundly antithetical to the bedrock values that characterize a free and open one such as ours.'[13]

The George W. Bush administration has failed to realize, as Stanley Hoffmann reminds Bush (Jr) in an article in the *American Prospect*, three key points: 'first, the war against terrorism cannot be the alpha and omega of a foreign policy; second, it cannot be waged by military means alone, and finally, even a state endowed with overwhelming superiority in all the ingredients of "hard" force cannot substitute that for eyes, ears and brains. Decisions based on dubious assumptions, overconfidence and intelligence reports risk ending in impudence and fiasco.' Hoffmann rightly points out, America needs allies for the war against terrorism, countries that would be ready to arrest, try, or deliver terrorists to the United States and, if military action was needed, cooperate with it.[14] Alas, President George W. Bush's unilateralism and his decisions to spurn key international treaties and agreements have increasingly isolated America. Hoffman's second point, regarding the inadequacy of military means alone in fights against terrorism, is also voiced by Joseph Nye in his recent book, *The Paradox of American Power*, in which he makes the case for what he calls 'soft power' as opposed to military intervention and economic coercion. In his view, 'a country may obtain the outcomes it wants in world politics because other countries want to follow it, admiring its values, emulating its example, aspiring to its level of prosperity and openness.'[15] This is what Brand's exemplarists have been advocating for a long time.[16] If America wishes to lead it has to resurrect the values which might make it into John Winthrop's shining 'city upon a hill.'

Zbigniew Brzezinski, at one time President Carter's security adviser, in a recent article in the *Washington Post*, has raised another related point. He complains that, 'missing from much of the public debate is discussion of the simple fact that lurking behind every terrorist act is a specific political antecedent. That does not justify either the perpetrator or his political cause. Nonetheless, the fact is that almost all terrorist activity originates from some political conflict and is sustained by it as well. That is true of the Irish Republican Army in Northern Ireland, the Basques in Spain, the Palestinians in the West Bank and Gaza, the Muslims in Kashmir.'[17] Pope John Paul II also called for giving attention to 'the underlying causes that lead young people especially to despair of humanity, of life itself and of the future, and to fall prey to the temptations of violence, hatred and a desire for revenge at any cost.'[18] Soon after September 11, the *Al Ahram Weekly* of Egypt and the *Dawn* of Pakistan, two of the most prestigious newspapers of the Islamic world, published some very perceptive articles making similar points. Hassan Nafaa, a professor of Political Science at Cairo University, while categorically condemning the attacks on New York and Washington, candidly pointed out that by its 'blind' and 'absolute' support for Israel, 'the U.S. has actively contributed to isolating the forces of peace and, consequently, exacerbating Islamic extremism. 'Once it realizes this,' it will have begun the true war on terror.'[19] Similarly, Ali Mazrui, a leading Muslim thinker, wrote in the *Dawn* that 'a global coalition against terrorism would only make sense if it included addressing the causes of terrorism.' In his view, 'the single most explosive cause of anti-American terrorism is the perceived alliance between the United States and Israel against major Muslim concerns.'[20] Writing in the same vein, Maqbool Ahmad Bhatty, a retired Pakistani diplomat, stressed that 'it has to be realized that in most cases terrorism is the manifestation of a deep-seated and throbbing political or any other problem.... Durable and stable international order can be established only by addressing the root cause of ... anti-social acts.'[21] Jihan Alaily, a journalist writing from Washington, pointed out that 'the crucial issue is about how to address the desperation and resentment that breeds terrorism and suicide bombers. This is the best prevention against terrorism. Yet debate in America currently centers on the massive use of force as a counter measure to such terrorism and offers few, if any, clues on how to address the deep-rooted causes that fuel deadly acts of vengeance.'[22] In the same issue of the *Al Ahram Weekly*, Gamal Nkrumah stressed that 'economic well being, poverty eradication and improved health and educational standards are the surest means of fighting terrorism. Unfortunately, Washington appears uninterested in the Third World's predicament – an indifference that many of the world's poor cannot help feeling is tinged with racist hues. Until that changes, it seems, terrorism will continue to pose a global threat.'[23] President Hosni Mubarak, highlighting the difficulties [deprivation and humiliation] facing an average family living in a Palestinian town or city under occupation pointed out that if someone had to struggle even to feed and educate children, one would decide to commit suicide and kill someone along with oneself.[24] Neutral observers such as Reverend Desmond Tutu, a Nobel Peace

Prizewinner and a leading member of the anti-apartheid struggle in Africa have corroborated the fact of daily humiliation of ordinary Palestinians by the Israeli armed forces.[25]

The deprivation and humiliation of the Palestinians increased immensely as a result of Prime Minister Sharon's drive against terrorists, using sophisticated American weapons supposedly given to allies for defensive purposes. Yet, President Bush continues to call him a 'man of peace,' an adjective many Israelis would hesitate to use for their prime minister. Such a statement by the president at the time of the siege of Jenin, when human rights violations by the Israeli armed forces were rampant, was insensitive to say the least. In its callousness it compares with an earlier statement by Madeline Albright to a question from Leslie Stahl about the 500,000 Iraqi children killed by American bombs, stating that 'we think the price is worth [it].'[26] President Bush (Jr) may not realize that his close association with Prime Minister Sharon has not only cost America the 'role of an honest broker,' but it might exacerbate Arab grievances and add to future numbers of terrorists. In an interview with Dina Ezzat, an *Al Ahram* journalist, Amr Moussa (the Arab League secretary general) voiced his frustrations. He stated that, 'it would be unrealistic to ignore the overwhelming ... tendency to support Israeli policy indiscriminately, even during the most glaring cases of blatant Israeli aggression against the Palestinian people, and Israeli's outright violation of international law. ...'[27] Whatever President George W. Bush is doing to settle the Arab-Israeli conflict is too little too late. If he and some of the members of his administration are deluding themselves by convincing themselves that force is *the* answer to terrorism, then they should heed the warning of Jon Utley of the Ludwig von Mises Institute, that 'for the US, this war is unwinnable because our policy makers refuse to address its causes, and fear that doing so would make us look like we are caving in to terrorism. Until we do, for every terrorist killed, 10 more will take his place.'[28]

Another cause of Arab frustration – also shared by other countries including US allies – has also been aired by Hassan Nafaa who pointed out that 'on both occassions [the Gulf War and Afghanistan War], too, although the Arab and Muslim peoples were the most immediately affected by the crises, they were never in a position to choose the place or time of the ensuing battle or the methods of conducting it. Indeed, it almost seemed that they were dragged helplessly to the front in a war they did not want.'[29] This complaint has the same resonance as the one expresssed by Helmut Schmidt, former German Chancellor, regarding the American leadership imposing their 'solo adventures' on the allies without consulting them, even if such a decision affects them.[30] The best contemporary example is George W. Bush's misplaced determination regarding the 'preemptive' invasion of Iraq aimed at a 'regime change' in spite of the growing opposition to such a policy at home and abroad.

In its fight against terrorism, the American leadership needs to seriously rethink its attitude toward two major policy issues; one relates to the export of arms either commercial or foreign policy-related and the other the policy of covert operations. The export of arms, whatever its rationale, leads to proliferation. If the adminstration introduces arms into a volatile region by selling or through miliatry aid to friendly countries, it is almost certain that the 'unfriendly' countries will buy from other sources, including the black-market. There are several examples. In the Cold War years, America began to sell or give arms to Pakistan, resulting in India's increased dependence on the Soviet Union. The same is true of arms sales to Taiwan. Beijing had to counter this by procurring from other sources such as Russia. Arms sales to Israel or to Saudi Arabia will have similar reactions as far as Iran is concerned.

While collecting information and intentions of potential enemies is legitimate intelligence work, covert operations to destabilize or overthrow regimes or to assassinate foreign leaders are neither legally nor morally justifiable. Covert operations breed terrorists. All those who are trained by the CIA (and similar other organizations run by other countries) are taught the tricks of the trades of sabotage and subversion. The Taliban and Osama bin Laden are not the only examples; the Contras, the operatives trained in Sudan, and elsewhere, are of the same genus. They all cannot be liquidated when their services are no longer needed by the CIA. Some come back to haunt the United States.

If America really believes in the 'rule of law,' as it certainly does in the domestic sphere, it must appreciate that it cannot operate in the world as if it was beyond the law. In a globalized world with rapid dissemination of news and views internationally, discrepancies in domestic and foreign behavior are glaringly obvious. These discrepencies are at the root of the world's disenchantment with America. Much more so, these are the discrepancies which make American values sound hollow. Those within America or elsewhere who advocate policies contrary to American values are to be feared more than the terrorists, because the latter kill only people and destroy property – those who destroy values kill the soul.

Notes

1 Why Does America Need Enemies?

1. Quoted in Faisal Islam, 'Soros: May Day Protestors Do Have a Point, *Observer*, 6 May 2001.
2. George W. Bush did not obtain a majority of popular votes in the presidential election. Bush won Florida as a result of the Supreme Court intervention which by a one-vote majority stopped counting votes in Florida. It was subsequently found that the Republican establishment in Florida meticulously removed a large number of black voters from the electoral roll depriving Al Gore, the Democratic presidential candidate of a large number of votes. See Greg Palast, *The Best Democracy Money Can Buy*, (London: Pluto Press, 2002) pp. 10–43.
3. Samuel P. Huntington, *The Clash of Civilizations and the Remaking of World Order*, (New York: Simon & Schuster, 1997) p. 183. The thesis of the book was originally published in an article titled 'The Clash of Civilizations?' in the journal *Foreign Affairs*, Summer, 1993. Huntington borrowed the title of his article from an earlier article by Bernard Lewis, 'The Roots of Muslim Rage' *Atlantic*, September (1990), in which Lewis tries to explain the reasons for the conflict between Islam and the West.
4. Huntington (1997), op. cit., p. 185.
5. Ibid., p. 13.
6. H. W. Brands, *What America Owes the World: The Struggle for the Soul of Foreign Policy* (Cambridge: Cambridge University Press, 1998) pp. 304–5. The quote is from Brands, who summarizes Kennan's views.
7. Edward W. Said, *Covering Islam: How the Media and the Experts Determine How We See the Rest of the World* (New York: Vintage Books, 1997) p. xix.
8. Immanuel Wallerstein, 'Islam, the West and the World', A lecture given in the 'Islam and World System' series at the Oxford Centre for Islamic Studies, Michaelmas term, 21 October 1998 (*fbc.binghamton.edu/iwislam.htm*).
9. Ibid.
10. *The New Encyclopædia Britannica* (Chicago: Encyclopædia Britannica Inc., 1998) p. 15. A moderate group of the *Khawarij* that rejected aggressive methods still survive and live in North Africa, Oman and other parts of East Africa, including Zanzibar Island. (p. 16).
11. Martin Kramer, 'Fundamentalist Islam at Large: The Drive for Power', *Middle East Quarterly*, June 1996.
12. J. S. McClelland, *A History of Western Political Thought* (London: Routledge, 1996) p. 298.
13. Eric Foner, *The Story of American Freedom* (New York: W. W. Norton & Company, 1998) pp. xxi and 22.
14. McClelland (1996), op. cit., p. 360.
15. Quoted in Foner (1998), op. cit., p. xxi.
16. Samuel Eliot Morison, *The Oxford History of the American People* (Volume One: Prehistory to 1789), (New York: Meridian, 1994) p. 383.

17. Abigail Adams letter to her husband, John Adams on 31 March 1776 reproduced in Jerome B. Agel., *Words that Make America Great* (New York: Random House, 1997) pp. 13–4.
18. Quoted in Foner (1998), op. cit., p. 33.
19. Bradford Perkins, *The Cambridge History of American Foreign Relations, Volume I: The Creation of a Republican Empire, 1776–1865*, (Cambridge: Cambridge University Press, 1995) p. 48.
20. William Appleman Williams, *The Tragedy of American Diplomacy* (New York: W. W. Norton & Company, 1972) p. 14. See also Brands (1998), op. cit., p. viii.
21. Michael Lind, *The Next American Nation: The New Nationalism and the Fourth American Revolution* (New York: Free Press Paperback, 1996) p. 3.
22. Brands (1998) op. cit., p. vii.
23. Ibid. p. viii.
24. Joseph E. Fallon, 'The Dangerous Myth of American Exceptionalism', (http://www.vdare.com/fallon/exceptionalism.htm).
25. George W. Ball, *Diplomacy for a Crowded World: An American Foreign Policy* (London: The Bodley Head, 1976), p. 9.
26. Ibid.
27. Helmut Schmidt, *Men and Powers: A Political Retrospective* (translated from the German by Ruth Hein) (New York: Random House, 1989) p. 280.
28. Ibid., p. 279.
29. *New York Times*, 'Dancing With Dictators,' (Editorial), 1 September 2002.
30. Department of State, *The Convention on the Elimination of All Forms of Racial Discrimination: Initial Report of the United States of America to the United Nations Committee on the Elimination of Racial Discrimination*, September 2000, p. 4.
31. Ellen C. Collier, *Instances of Use of United States Forces Abroad, 1798–1993*, Congressional Research Service. Library of Congress (Washington, DC: CRS, 1993) p. CRS-1.
32. For a list of attempted assassinations, see William Blum, *Killing Hope: U. S. Military and the CIA Interventions Since World War II* (Monroe, Maine: Common Courage Press, 1995,) p. 453.
33. Daniel Patrick Moynihan, *On the Law of Nations* (Cambridge, Mass.: Harvard University Press, 1990) pp. 143–4.
34. Ibid., pp. 145–6.
35. Peter Dale Scott, 'U.S. Counterinsurgency Tradition: Two Indonesias, Two Americas,' 9 June 1998 (http://www.consortiumnews.com/archive/lost22.html).
36. Ibid.
37. John Morgan Gates, *Schoolbooks and Krags: The United States Army in the Philippines, 1898–1902*, quoted in Scott (1998).
38. Golo Mann, *The History of Germany Since 1789* (Translated from the German by Marian Jackson) (Harmondsworth: Penguin Books, 1990) pp. 788, 794.
39. Jean-Paul Sartre, 'Summary and Verdict of the Stockholm Session' in Ken Coats, Peter Limqueco and Peter Weiss, *Prevent the Crime of Silence: Report from the Sessions of the International War Crimes Tribunal Founded by Bertrand Russell* (London: Allen Lane The Penguin Press, 1971) p. 185.
40. Ramsey Clark and Others, *War Crimes: A Report on United States War Crimes Against Iraq* (Washington, DC Maisonneuve Press, 1992), pp. 14–15.
41. Michael Dobbs, 'Bombing devastates Serbia's infrastructure' quoted in Noam Chomsky, *The New Military Humanism: Lessons from Kosovo* (Monroe, ME, Common Courage Press, 1999) pp. 93, 175 n 25.

42. Ibid. p. 65.
43. Amnesty International, 'Memorandum to the US Government on the rights of people in US custody in Afghanistan and Guantánamo Bay, AI Index AMR 51/053/2002, 15 April 2002. See also Human Rights Watch, 'U.S.: Bush Errs in Geneva Convention Rules (*Human Rights News*), New York, 7 February 2002 (http://hrw.org/press/2002/02/geneva0207.html).
44. Schmidt (1989), op. cit., p. 283.
45. Ibid. pp. 280–1.
46. Allan Bloom, *The Closing of the American Mind: How Higher Education Has Failed Democracy and Impoverished the Souls of Today's Students* (New York: Simon and Schuster, 1987) p. 142. See also Daniel Bell who is critical of such tendencies. He feels 'The tendency to convert concrete issues into ideological problems, to invest them with moral color and high emotional charge, is to invite conflicts which can only damage a society' – (Daniel Bell, *The End of Ideology* (Cambridge, MA: Harvard University Press, 1988) p. 121).
47. Mann (1990), op. cit., p. 804.
48. Schmidt (1989), op. cit., p. 283.
49. Noam Chomsky, 'The United States is a Leading Terrorist State,' in an interview with the *Monthly Review*, November 2001. see also Noam Chomsky, 'Who are the Global terrorists?' in Ken Booth and Tim Donne (eds), *World in Collision: Terror and Future of Global Order* (Basingstoke: Palgrave Macmillan, 2002).
50. Timothy Lynch, 'Breaking the Vicious Cycle: Preserving Our Liberties While Fighting Terrorism', *Cato Policy Analysis*, No. 443, 26 June 2002, p. 2.
51. Ibid., p. 13.
52. John Gunther, *Inside U.S.A.* (New York: Harper & Brothers, 1947) p. xii.
53. Mark Nord, Nadar Kabani, Laura Tiehan, Margaret Andrews, Gary Bickel and Steven Carlson, *Household Food Security in the United States, 2000*, Rural Economic division, Economic Research Service, US Department of Agriculture, Food and Nutrition Research Report No. 21, p. iii (http://www.ers.usda.gov/pub-lications/fanrr21/fanrr21fm.pdf).
54. National Coalition Of Homeless, Fact Sheet No. 2, February 1999 (http://nch.ari.net/numbers.html).
55. BBC News, 30 July 1998 (http://news.bbc.co.uk/2/hi/health/142327.stm).
56. Disaster Center, United States Crime Statistics, (www.disastercenter.com/crime).
57. Senate Committee on the Judiciary, *Crimes Committed with Firearms: A Report for Parents, Prosecutors, and Policy Makers*, 15 September 1999; prepared by Majority Staff (http://judiciary.senate. gov/oldsite/guns106.html).
58. Lind (1996), op. cit., p. 152.
59. Ibid., p. 169.
60. Ibid., p. 170.
61. Center for Responsive Politics, 'Campaign Finance Reform,' (http://www:open-secrets.org/news/campaign.finance.asp).
62. Elizabeth Drew, *The Corruption of American Politics: What Went Wrong And Why* (Secaucus, NJ: Drew Carol Publishing Group, 1999) p. 56.
63. Ibid., p. 50.
64. Quoted in David C. Korten, *When Corporations Rule the World* (West Hartford, Conn.: Kumarian Press, Inc. and San Francisco, CA: Berrett-Koehler Publishers, Inc., 1996) p. 58.
65. Henry Demarest Lloyd, *Wealth Against Commonwealth* (New York: Greenwood Publishing Group Inc., 1976) pp. 17–19. Edited by Thomas C. Cochran.

66. Drew (1999), op. cit., pp. 46–7.
67. Ibid., p. 47.
68. The Center of Responsive Politics, 'Long-Term contribution Trends', (http://www.opensecrets.org/payback/issue.asp?issueid = CFR).
69. The Center of Responsive Politics, 'Long-Term contribution Trends', (http://www.opensecrets.org/basics/thesite/index.asp).
70. Common Cause, the Campaign for Tobacco-Free Kids, the American Heart Association and the American Lung Association, *Buying Influence and Selling Death: How Big Tobacco's Campaign Contributions Harm Public Health*, 14 March 2001, p. 1 (http://www.commoncause.org).
71. The Center of responsive Politics, 'Long-Term contribution Trends', (http://www.opensecrets.org/basics/thesite/index.asp).
72. The Center for Responsive Politics (http://www.opensecrets.org/bush/cabinet.asp).
73. G. William Domhoff, *Who Rules America?: Power and Politics in the Year 2000*, (London: Mayfield Publishing Company, 1998) p. 253.
74. Committee for the Study of the American Electorate, 2000 (http://www.fairvote.org/turnout/preturn.htm).
75. Federal Election Commission (FEC) (http://www.fec.gov/pages/reg&to98.html).
76. Jeffrey H. Birnbaum, *The Money Men: The Real Story of Fund-Raising's Influence on Political Power in America* (New York: Crown Publishers, 2000) p. 10.
77. International Institute for Democracy and Electoral Assistance (IDEA), *Voter Turn Out from 1945: a Global Report on Political Participation* (http://www.idea.int/voter_turnout/index.html).
78. Lind (1996), op. cit., p. 159.
79. John Kenneth Galbraith, *The Culture of Contentment* (Boston: Houghton Mifflin, 1992) p. 137.
80. Alan Wolfe, 'Afterword,' in C. Wright Mills, *The Power Elite* (New York: Oxford University Press, 2000) p. 372.
81. Galbraith (1992), op. cit., pp. 137–8.
82. Includes France, Germany, UK, Italy, and Spain. The source of information is Stockholm International Peace Research Institute (SIPRI), *SIPRI Yearbook, 2000*, Stockholm (on the Internet).
83. Galbraith (1992), op. cit., p. 140.
84. Ibid., p. 141.
85. Brian Becker, 'U.S. Conspiracy to Initiate War Against Iraq,' in Clark *et al.* (1992) p. 80.
86. Chomsky (1999), op. cit., pp. 110–16.
87. Prime Minister Tony Blair's statement in the British Parliament, Quoted in Chomsky (1999), p. 134.
88. Ibid., p. 134.
89. Robert W. McChesney, 'The Global Media Giants: The nine firms that dominate the world,' *Extra*, November/December (1997a) (http://www.fair.org/extra/9711/gmg.html).
90. Robert W. McChesney, *Corporate Media and the Threat to Democracy*, the Open Media Pamphlet Series (New York: Seven Stories Press, 1997b) p. 24.
91. The statement of a Westinghouse CEO, in ibid.
92. Statement made in a 'The Erosion of Values' Forum debate among journalists under the auspices of the *Columbia Journalism Review*. See *Columbia Journalism Review*, March/April, 1998. (http://www.cjr.org/year/98/2/value.asp).
93. McChesney (1997a), op. cit.

94. Edward S. Herman and Noam Chomsky, *Manufacturing Consent; The Political Economy of the Mass Media* (New York: Pantheon Books, 1988) p. 19.

95. Quoted in Noam Chomsky, *Necessary Illusions: Thought Control in Democratic Societies* (Boston, MA: South End Press, 1989) p. 75.

96. Quoted in Noam Chomsky, *Deterring Democracy* (London: Verso, 1991) p. 120.

97. Chomsky (1989), op. cit., p. 75.

98. Andrew Kohut, 'Self-Censorship: Counting the Ways', *Columbia Journalism Review*, May/June (2000) (http://www.cjr.org/year/00/2/2/may-juneindex.asp).

99. Ibid.

100. Ibid.

101. John R. MacArthur, *Second Front: Censorship and Propaganda in the Gulf War* (Berkeley: University of California Press, 1993) p. 32.

102. Ibid., p. 152.

103. Ibid., p. 162.

104. Paul Walker, 'U.S. Bombing – the Myth of Surgical Bombing in the Gulf War' in Clark *et al.* (1992) p. 87.

105. MacArthur (1993), op. cit., pp. 184–6.

106. Ibid., pp. 175–6.

107. Ben H. Bagdikian, 'Foreword,' in Macarthur (1993), op. cit., p. xvi.

108. Ibid., p. 199.

109. Ibid., p. 217.

110. Adeeb Abed and Sara Flounders, 'The Final Judgement: The International War Crimes Tribunal' in Clark *et al.* (1992), op. cit., p. 2.

111. Norman Solomon, 'Terrorism, Television and the Rage of Vengeance,' *Media Beat* (http://www.fair.org/media-beat/010913.html).

112. Norman Solomon, 'When Journalists Report for Duty,' *Media Beat* (http://www.fair.org/media-beat/010920.html).

113. Quoted in ibid.

114. Joan Biskupic, 'Election decision still splits the court', *USA Today*, 13 April 2001.

115. Mollie Dickenson,' Lawyers Protest U.S. Supreme Court', Based on Mollie Dickenson show at WPFW, 89.3 FM (http://www.consortiumnews.com/2001/011501a.html).

116. Derek Brown, 'A court divided: what the Supreme Court said', *Guardian*, 13 December 2000.

117. Lind (1996), op. cit., pp. 141–61.

118. Gore Vidal, 'The iron law of oligarchy prevails', *Independent*, 15 December 2000.

119. William Keegan, 'The Herbert Hoover factor', *Observer*, 17 December 2000.

120. Chomsky(1991), op. cit., p. 400.

121. Ibid., pp. 400–1.

122. Foner (1998), op. cit., p. 325.

123. Ibid., p. 301.

124. Brian Glick, *War Home: Covert Action Against U.S. Activists and What We Can Do About It* (Boston, MA: South End Press, 1989) p. 11.

125. Ibid., p. 11.

126. Michael Parenti, *Dirty Truths* (San Francisco: Cty Lights Books) p. 36.

127. Joshua Muravchik, *The Imperative of American Leadership: A Challenge to Neo-Isolationism*, (Washington, DC: The AEI Press, 1996) p. 34.

128. Joseph S. Nye Jr, *The Paradox of American Power: Why the World's Only Superpower Can't Go It Alone* (New York: Oxford University Press, 2002) pp. 8–12.

129. Peter Preston, 'The US must learn that to lead you have to be loved', *Guardian*, 7 May 2001.

2   America's Discovery: the Globalization of Trade and Misery

1. John K. Fairbank, *China Perceived: Images and Policies in Chinese–American Relations* (New York: Vintage Books, 1976) p. 94.
2. H. A. L. Fisher, *A History of Europe*, Vol. 1, Seventeenth Impression (Glasgow: Fontana/Collins, 1977) p. 428.
3. J. M. Roberts, *The Triumph of the West* (London: British Broadcasting Corporation, 1985) p. 140.
4. J. M. Roberts, *The Pelican History of the World* (Harmondsworth: Penguin Books, 1981) p. 510.
5. Roberts (1985), op cit., p. 141.
6. Caroline Blunden and Mark Elvin, *Cultural Atlas of China* (New York: Facts on File, Inc., 1983) p. 220. Among the main transfers from Europe, the authors mention Western hydraulics, astronomy and mathematics, perspective drawing and improved casting of cannon (p. 144).
7. Fisher (1977), op. cit., p. 430.
8. Roberts (1981), op. cit., pp. 506–7.
9. Slavery was not new to the old world; slaves were traded by the Arabs in large numbers but much of it was what one can call the domestic slavery. What emerged in the new world was the plantation slavery, slaves to be used for large scale production in cotton and sugar plantation and in mines. This point was made to me by Mark Elvin.
10. Roberts (1981), op. cit., p. 507.
11. Roberts (1985), op. cit., pp. 207–10.
12. Ibid. p. 210.
13. Ward Churchill, *A Little Matter of Genocide: Holocaust and Denial in the Americas 1492 to the Present* (San Francisco: City Lights Books, 1997) p. 87.
14. Basil Davidson, *The Story of Africa* (London: Mitchell Beazley Publishers and Mitchell Beazley Television, 1984) pp. 137–8.
15. Christopher Hill, *Reformation to Industrial Revolution: British Economy and Society 1530–1780* (London: Weidenfeld & Nicolson, 1969) p. 186.
16. Braudel mentioned estimates ranging between 12 and 20 million, but he thought the 20 million estimate as unrealistic. See Fernand Braudel, *A History of Civilizations* (translated by Richard Mayne), (New York: Penguin Books, 1995) pp. 131–2.
17. Hill (1969), op. cit., pp. 186–7.
18. Roberts (1981), op. cit., p. 612.
19. Fernand Braudel, *The Mediterranean and the Mediterranean World in the Age of Phillip II* (two vols), (translated from the French by Siân Reynolds), (London: Fontana/Collins, 1976) Vol. I, p. 476.
20. Joseph A. Schumpeter, *History of Economic Analysis* (edited by Elizabeth Boody Schumpeter), tenth printing (New York: Oxford University Press, 1978) pp. 311–12.
21. Hill (1969), op. cit., pp. 65–8.
22. Ibid., p. 136.
23. Ibid. p. 190.
24. Ibid. p. 130.
25. Braudel (1976), op. cit., p. 464.
26. Hill (1969), op. cit., p. 193.
27. Samuel Eliot Morison, *The Oxford History of the American People: Volume One, Prehistory to 1789* (New York: Meridian, 1994) p. 85.

28. Ibid., p. 236.
29. Ibid., pp. 245–6.
30. Ibid., p. 296.
31. Ibid., p. 351.
32. Perkins (1995), op. cit., p. 170.
33. Michael Lind, *The Next American Nation: The New Nationalism & the Fourth American Revolution* (NY Free Press Paperback, Simon & Schuster, 1996) p. 44.
34. Churchill (1997), op. cit., pp. 154–7.
35. Ibid., pp. 156, 261, note 139 quoted from 'Exciting News from Tehema-Indian Thefts – Terrible Vengeance of the Whites', *Daily Alta California*, 6 March 1853 quoted in Robert F. Heizer (ed.), *The Destruction of California Indians* (Lincoln: University of Nebraska Press, 1993) p. 251.
36. Documents from the Continental Congress and the Constitutional Convention, 1774–1789, 'Instructions to Superintendent of Indian Affairs for the Department, Item 43 of 201, The Library of Congress Collections.
37. Quoted in Morison (1994), op. cit., p. 265.
38. Lind (1996), op. cit., p. 45.
39. William Brandon, *Indians* (Boston: Houghton Mifflin Company, 1987) p. 229.
40. Ibid. p. 229.
41. Ibid., p. 239.
42. Ibid., pp. 376–7.
43. Ibid., p. 383.
44. Morison (1994), op. cit., p. 46. Recent studies suggest the total North American Native American population of anything between 12.5 to 18.5 million, 15 million as being a close approximation for 1500. See Churchill (1997), op. cit, pp. 134–5.
45. Samuel Eliot Morison, *The Oxford History of the American People, Volume Two: 1789 Through Reconstruction* (New York: Meridian, 1994) p. 227n.
46. Samuel Eliot Morison, *The Oxford History of the American People, Volume Three: 1869 Through the Death of John F. Kennedy, 1963* (New York: Meridian, 1994) p. 336. There were exceptions too. The 'Five Civilized Nations' – Cherokee Chickasaw, Choctaw, Greek and Seminole – who decided to settle as farmers, did not escape forced rewriting of the treaty requiring relinquishing Oklahoma, the western half of their territory, which was opened to white settlement in 1889. In 1890, the Five Civilized Tribes were given American citizenship and received a compensation of $1.1 million for forced removal in 1838. See Morison (1994), Vol. III, p. 64.
47. Brandon (1987), op. cit., p. 395.
48. James Chace and Caleb Carr, *America Invulnerable: The Quest for Absolute Security from 1812 to Star Wars* (New York: Summit Books, 1988) p. 13.
49. Perkins (1995), op. cit., p. 87.
50. William Appleman Williams, *The Tragedy of American Diplomacy* (New York: W. W. Norton & Co., 1972) p. 22.
51. Jenny Pearce, *Under the Eagle: US Intervention in Central America and the Caribbean* (London: Latin American Bureau, 1982) p. 8.
52. Peter H. Smith, *Talons of the Eagle: Dynamics of U.S.–Latin American Relations* (New York: Oxford University Press, 1996) p. 25.
53. Ibid., pp. 25–6.
54. Pearce (1982), op. cit., p. 10. See also Smith (1996), op. cit., p. 36.
55. Pearce (1982), op. cit., pp. 11–12.
56. Ibid., p. 12.
57. Chace and Carr (1988), op. cit., p. 128.

58. Stanley Karnow, *In Our Image: America's Empire in the Philippines* (New York: Ballantine Books, 1990) p. 194. A close Chinese parallel was the Chinese attempt to subjugate the Kingdom of Dali set up by Du Wenxiu from 1855 to 1872. As Blunden and Elvin point out, 'after many years of mutual killing by both sides, it ended with the slaughter of perhaps 30,000 Muslims by the troops of Cen Yuying.' See Blunden and Mark Elvin (1983), op. cit., p. 38.
59. Stuart Creighton Miller, *'Benevolent Assimilation': The American Conquest of the Philippines, 1899–1903* (New Haven: Yale University Press, 1982) p. 188.
60. Pvt. Hambleton to his brother, 26 May 1900 quoted in Ibid., p. 188.
61. Quoted in Chace and Carr (1988), op. cit., p. 133.
62. Harold U. Faulkner, *The Decline of Laissez Faire 1897–1917*, Volume. VII, *The Economic History of the United States* (Armonk, New York: M. E. Sharpe Inc., 1951) p. 69.
63. McKinley's speech published in *The Boston Herald*, 17 February 1899, quoted in Faulkner (1951), op. cit., p. 69.
64. Quoted in Walter LaFeber, The *Cambridge History of American Foreign Relations, Vol. II: The American Search for Opportunity, 1865–1913* (Cambridge: Cambridge University Press, 1995), p. 100.
65. Ibid., pp. 157–8.
66. E. J. Hobsbawm, *Industry and Empire: An Economic History of Britain Since 1750* (London: Weidenfeld and Nicolson, 1968) p. 104.
67. Jerald A. Combs, *American Diplomatic History: Two Centuries of Changing Interpretations* (Berkeley, University of California Press, 1986) p. 84.
68. Charles Conant, *The United States in the Orient: The Nature of the Economic Problem* (Port Washington, NY: Kennikat Press, 1971) (The book was first published in 1900), pp. 79–80. See also Alfred Thayer Mahan, *Lessons of the War with Spain* (New York: Books for Libraries Press, 1970) p. 16.
69. Alfred Thayer Mahan, *The Problem of Asia and its Effect on International Policies* (Boston: Little Brown & Co., 1900) p. 180.
70. Theodore Roosevelt, writing in the *Independent* in 1899, quoted in Combs (1983), op. cit., p. 87.
71. Ibid., p. 87 quoted from Henry Cabot Lodge, Speech in Senate, Congressional Record, 7 March 1900.
72. Combs (1983), op. cit., p. 87.
73. D. P. O'Brien, *The Classical Economists* (Oxford: Clarendon Press, 1975) p. 289.
74. Bernard Semmel, *The Rise of Free Trade Imperialism: Classical Political Economy the Empire of Free Trade and Imperialism 1750–1850* (London: Cambridge University Press, 1970) p. 28.
75. Ibid., pp. 10–11.
76. A. Owen Aldridge, *The Dragon and the Eagle: The Presence of China in the American Enlightenment* (Detroit: Wayne State University Press, 1993) p. 23.
77. Ibid., p. 87.
78. Quoted in Aldridge (1993), op. cit., p. 93.
79. Ibid., p. 96.
80. Ibid., p. 268.
81. Ibid., pp. 109–10.
82. Peter Ward Fay, *The Opium War, 1840–1842: Barbarians in the Celestial Empire in the Early Part of the Nineteenth Century and the War by Which They Forced Her Gates Ajar* (Chapel Hill: The University of North Carolina Press, 1997) p. 45.
83. Richard W. Van Alstyne, The *United States and East Asia* (London: Thames and Hudson, 1973) p. 28. See also Fay (1997), op. cit., p. 45.

84. George M. Beckmann, *The Modernization of China and Japan*, A Harper International Student Reprint, (New York: Harper & Row and John Weatherhill, Inc, Tokyo, 1965) p. 123. The figure of 40,000 chests of 133lb each quoted by Van Alstyne (1973), op. cit., p. 28, works out at 5.3 million pounds.
85. John King Fairbank, *The Great Chinese Revolution, 1800–1985*, (London: Chatto a Windus, 1987) p. 85. See also Wolfram Eberhard, *A History of China* (Berkeley: University of California Press, 1977) pp. 298–9.
86. Barbara W. Tuchman, *Sand Against the Wind: Stilwell and the American Experience in China 1911–45* (London: Macdonald Futura Publishers, 1981) p. 34.
87. Quoted in Semmel (1970), op. cit., p. 152.
88. 'The Opium War' *Spectator*, XIII, no. 613, 28 March 1840, p. 297 quoted in Semmel (1970), op. cit., p. 224 n 1.
89. Fay (1997), op. cit., p. 338.
90. Perkins (1995), op. cit., p. 203.
91. Tuchman (1981), op. cit., p. 35.
92. Fairbank (1987) op. cit., pp. 92–3. See also J. Y. Wong, *Deadly Dreams: Opium, Imperialism, and the Arrow War (1856–1860) in China* (Cambridge: Cambridge University Press, 1998). Wong mentions that as many as 300 firms, mostly concerned with the cotton industry had also petitioned Lord Palmerston, then foreign secretary to intervene in China. (p. 311).
93. Ibid., p. 416.
94. In fact, there were two Opium Wars, one between 1849 and 1852 and the other between 1856 and 1860. The second is more commonly known as the *Arrow War*. The Chinese call it the Second Opium War. The British, together with France, the United States, and Russia had gone to the Second Opium War (1856–60) to complete what remained undone in the first Opium War. Opium had remained illegal in China. The Chinese conversion into a semi-colonial country and the legalization of traffic in opium came only after the Chinese defeat in the *Arrow War* (Ibid., pp. 38–9).
95. As Tuchman suggests 'The wealth of Venice and Genoa was made in trade with the infidels of Syria and Egypt despite papal prohibition.' in *A Distant Mirror: The Calamitous 14th Century* (New York: Alfred A. Knopf, 1979) p. 38. See also Roberts (1981), op. cit., pp. 349–50. Roberts suggests that the immediate beneficiaries of the Fourth Crusade 'were the Venetians and Genoese to whose history the wealth and commerce of Byzantium was now annexed.' p. 350).
96. Ibid., pp. 500–1.
97. Fairbank (1987), op. cit., p. 93.
98. Ibid.
99. Tuchman(1981) op. cit., p. 38.
100. Quoted in Tuchman (1981), op. cit., p. 40.
101. Subsequently, having been inspired by the Christian missionaries, the U.S. Congress decided to devote half of the Boxer indemnity for the education of Chinese scholars in the United States. By 1925, nearly a thousand young Chinese were sent to America for higher education. See Fairbank (1987), op. cit., p. 187.
102. Ibid., p. 177.
103. Beckmann (1962), op. cit., p. 353.
104. Ibid., p. 354.
105. Ibid., p. 357.
106. Chace and Carr (1988), op. cit., p. 164. It was feared that Japan, a British ally in the First World War, might change sides and take possession of whatever it wanted.

107. Ibid., p. 165.
108. Ibid.
109. Ibid.; see also Beckmann (1962), op. cit., p. 360.
110. Memorandum of The American Minister Paul S. Reinsch, 14 August 1918 quoted in Stephen J. Valone, *'A Policy Calculated to Benefit China': The United States and the China Arms Embargo, 1919–1929* (New York: Greenwood Press, 1991) p. 30.
111. Ibid., p. 20.
112. Initially, the arms embargo was undermined by the Italian exports of arms to China. See Valone (1991), op. cit., p. 58. Next came the British exports of commercial planes (Ibid., p. 62). Subsequently, Germany, Czechoslovakia and the Soviet Union began to supply arms to China (Ibid., p. 96). The Soviet aid in the mid-twenties included money, armament and advisers. See Fairbank (1987), op. cit., p. 210.
113. Valone (1991), op. cit., p. 130.
114. The Kwantung Army began the Manchurian onslaught on 18 September 1931 without formal orders from, but with the connivance of, headquarters in Tokyo. See Saburō Ienaga, *The Pacific War, 1931–1945: A Critical Perspective on Japan's Role the World War II* (New York: Pantheon Books, 1978) pp. 62–3. See also W. G. Beasley, *Japanese Imperialism, 1894–1945* (Oxford: Clarendon Press, 1987) pp. 192–3.
115. Beckmann, (1962) op. cit., p. 445.
116. Chace and Carr (1988), op. cit., p. 202.
117. Paul Kennedy, *The Rise and fall of the Great Powers: Economic Change and Military Conflict from 1500 to 2000* (London: Unwin Hyman, 1988) p. 334.
118. Iris Chang, *The Rape of Nanking: The Forgotten Holocaust of World War II* (New York: Basic Books, 1997) p. 6.
119. Chang (1997), op. cit., p. 146.
120. This doctrine, announced by the Japanese Foreign Minister Eiji Amau in April 1934 stipulated that Japan had a special interest in Asia, and it precluded other foreign powers providing any assistance to China.
121. For instance, see William Johnstone, *The United States and Japan's New Order* (Oxford: Oxford University Press, 1941) pp. 216–17. The author suggests that as late as 1940 even US businessmen living in China were opposed to a total embargo on Japan, and even fewer supported going to war against Japan. For some other references see Jonathan Marshall, 'Southeast Asia and US–Japan Relations: 1940–1941', *Pacific Research & World Empire Telegram*, March–April, 1973, Vol. IV, no. 3, p. 4n. Some American scholars held similar views. For instance, Whitney A. Griswold, in his book *Far Eastern Policy of The United States* (New York: Harcourt, Brace and Company, 1938) argued in favor of a conciliatory policy towards Japan because any war either to preserve the territorial integrity of China or the Open Door would obstruct 'the most profitable trend of American commerce and investment in the Far East which, since 1900, had been toward Japan, not China.' (pp. 466–7) quoted in Combs (1983), op. cit., pp. 194–5.
122. Dennet Tyler (1938), 'Alternative American Policies in the Far East', *Foreign Affairs*, April 1938, p. 392.
123. Quoted in Marshall (1973), op. cit., p. 4.
124. Antony C Sutton, *Wall Street and The Rise of Hitler* (Seal Beach, California, '76 Press, 1976) p. 128.
125. Mark Fritz, 'The Secret History of the World War II: Cloaked Business,' *The Boston Globe*, 19 November 2001.

126. David F. Schmitz, *The United States and Fascist Italy, 1922–1940* (Chapel Hill, North Carolina University Press, 1988) p. 65.
127. Donald R. McCoy, *Calvin Coolidge: The Quiet President* (New York: Macmillan – now Palgrave Macmillan, 1967) p. 181.
128. Schmitz (1988), op. cit., p. 138.
129. Ibid., pp. 160–1.
130. Ibid., p. 196.
131. Quoted in David F Schmitz, *Thank God They're On Our Side: The United States & Right-Wing Dictatorships, 1921–1965* (Chapel Hill, North Carolina University Press, 1999) p. 116.
132. C. F. Remer, (1933), *Foreign Investment in China* (New York: Macmillan – now Palgrave Macmillan, 1933) Table 7, p. 77. During this period the total US foreign investment abroad was estimated by the Department of Commerce at $15,000 million. In China, it amounted to only $196.8 million or equivalent to only 1.3 per cent of total foreign investment of the United States.
133. Ibid., pp. 282–90.
134. Ibid., Calculated on the basis of Table 10, p. 86.
135. Richard Storry, *Japan and the Decline of the West in Asia 1894–1943* (London: Macmillan, 1979) pp. 15–16.
136. Fairbank (1987), op. cit., p. 268. There were a few exceptions. The most well known was Professor Owen Lattimore, who certainly knew a lot about China. He lived there in various capacities, as businessman, newspaperman, traveler and scholar, since 1920 and had written books on Mongolia, Manchuria and China's outer provinces. Lattimore's report at the time of the Atlantic Conference 'gave a revealing view of China's resentments' against the United States and Britain. See Tuchman (1981), op. cit., pp. 289–90.
137. Tuchman (1981), op.cit., p. 622. Contrary to Tuchman's views, Chen Jian argues that China's pro-Soviet and anti-American policies in 1949–50 had deeper roots, particularly, the humiliation by the West, and a more flexible attitude of the United states leadership would not have moderated Chinese behavior. But in the three pages where he claims that America's 'lost chance' in China is a myth, he provides little evidence to support his assertions. See Chen Jian, *Mao's China and the Cold War* (Chapel Hill: North Carolina University Press, 2001) pp. 46–8. If the humiliation by the West was the main cause of China's displeasure with America, China had been humiliated in much the same way by Russia before the Russian Revolution and the Communist leadership in Soviet Union after the Russian Revolution. Chen seems also to underestimate Mao's intelligence; Mao knew perfectly well that war devastated Soviet Union could not provide the resources for China's development. In 1949–50 no country other than America had the capacity to provide such resources. Even Japanese technology, on which much of the Chinese industry and the railway system were initially based, could not be made available to China without American consent. It is in this context that one has to see the overtures of the Communist leadership to the United States.
138. What Schmitz (1999) writes of the members of the State Department in charge of the European diplomacy is also true of those responsible for the China policy. Most of the career foreign service officers' 'shared outlook on the world centered around the dangers of communism. All studies of the US Foreign Service at this time draw a similar composite portrait of these men. White, Protestant, and middle-class or wealthy men primarily educated in elite schools, they held a patrician's disdain for labor, minorities, and immigrants and a deep-seated fear of radical change. Most came to the Foreign Service around the time of World

War I and adopted the prevalent hostility toward the Soviet Union and belief that any political upheavals were communist-inspired.' See Schmitz (1999), op. cit., p. 88.

139. The 'China Bloc' was a group of mostly conservative congressmen who consistently supported the Nationalists and were opposed to the recognition of the Peoples' Republic of China or its entry into the United Nations. See Foster Rhea Dulles, *American Foreign Policy Toward Communist China 1949–1969* (New York: Thomas Y. Crowell Company, 1972) p. 70. On the other hand, the 'China Lobby' consisted of Nationalist officials from their embassy in Washington and their propaganda agents, some rabid anti-Communist businessmen, retired army officers, and conservative 'old China hands' (ibid., p. 85). This group acted in close association with the 'China Bloc.' One of the ardent supporters of the Nationalists was Henry Luce, the founder of Time, Incorporated, which published the magazines *Life, Time* and *Fortune*. See T. Christopher Jespersen, *American Images of China: 1931–1949* (Stanford: Stanford University Press, 1996) p. 12. Born and brought up in China in a Christian missionary family, Luce firmly believed that if Christianity came to China, it might bring democracy and in the wake of democracy trade would follow (ibid., p. 35). Luce felt that Chiang represented all the Christian values and had come as the savior of China. Luce's faith in Chiang did not waver even when Chiang was engaged in the extermination of the Chinese Communists, in fact, his magazines consistently approved Chiang's efforts in eliminating the Communists (ibid., p. 28). See also Patricia Neils, *China Images: In the Life and Times of Henry Luce* (Savage, MD: Rowman & Littlefield Publishers, 1990).

140. Sergei N. Goncharov, John W. Lewis and Xue Litai, *Uncertain Partners: Stalin, Mao, and the Korean War* (Stanford: Stanford University Press, 1993) p. 121. It is now known that 'as early as April 1956, Mao told Mikoyan 'the secret deals on Xinjiang and Manchuria were "two bitter pills" that Stalin forced him to swallow, and the next year he complained to Gromyko that "only imperialists" would think of imposing such a deal on China' (p. 122).

141. Ibid., p. 125.

142. Ibid., p. 33.

143. Jian Chen, *China's Road to the Korean War: The Making of the Sino-American Confrontation* (New York: Columbia University Press, 1994) p. 34.

144. Quoted in Goncharov et al. (1993) p. 35.

145. Ibid., p. 34.

146. June M. Grasso, *Truman's Two-China Policy 1948–1950* (Armonk, NY: M. E. Sharpe Inc., 1987) p. 66.

147. Goncharov *et al.* (1993), op. cit., p. 35.

148. Ibid., p. 54.

149. Ibid., p. 45.

150. Chen (1994), op. cit., p. 38.

151. Grasso (1987), op. cit., p. 62.

152. Ibid., p. 73.

153. Richard M. Freeland, *The Truman Doctrine and the Origins of McCarthyism: Foreign Policy, Domestic Politics, and Internal Security, 1946–1948* (New York: New York University Press, 1985) p. 134.

154. Ibid., p. 344.

155. Ibid., pp. 131–2.

156. Derrik Mercer, *Chronicle of the 20th Century* (London: Chronicle Communications, 1988) p. 675.

157. Alonzo L. Hamby, *Man of The People: A Life of Harry S. Truman* (New York: Oxford University Press, 1995) p. 523.
158. Ibid., p. 531.
159. Richard Hofstadter, *The Paranoid Style in American Politics* (New York: Alfred Knopf 1965) quoted in Warren I. Cohen, *The Cambridge History of American Foreign Relations, Volume IV: America in the Age of Soviet Power, 1945–1991,* (Cambridge: Cambridge University Press, 1995) p. 76.

3   Enemies Become Strategic Partners

1. Robert S. McNamara, *In Retrospect: The Tragedy and Lessons of Vietnam* (New York: Vintage Books, 1996) pp. 30–3.
2. Warren I. Cohen, *The Cambridge History of American Foreign Relations Volume IV: America in the Age of Soviet Power, 1945–1991* (Cambridge: Cambridge University Press, 1995) p. 63.
3. Ian Nish, *The Origins of The Russo-Japanese War* (London: Longman, 1996) p. 33.
4. Sergei N. Goncharov, John W. Lewis and Xue Litai, *Uncertain Partners: Stalin, Mao, and the Korean War* (Stanford: Stanford University Press, 1993) p. 130. Recently released classified papers from the Russian Federation throw further light on the involvement of Stalin and Mao in the Korean War. See Alexandre Y. Mansourov, 'Stalin, Mao, Kim and China's Decision to Enter the Korean War Sept. 16, Oct. 15 1950: New Evidence from Russian Archives, Article and Translation,' Cold War History Project, Woodrow Wilson International Center for Scholars. (http://cwihp.si.edu/cwihplib.nsf).
5. Ibid.
6. Nikita Khrushchev, *Khrushchev Remembers: The Glastonost Tapes* (edited and translated by Jerrold L. Schecter and Vyacheslav V. Luchkov (Boston: Little Brown Co., 1990) p. 147.
7. Paul Kennedy, *The Rise and Fall of the Great Powers* (London: Unwin Hyman, 1988) p. 362.
8. J. R. Millar, 'Conclusion: Impact and Aftermath of World War II,' in S. J. Linz (ed.), *The Impact of World War II on the Soviet Union* (Totowa, N. J.: Rowman & Allanheld, 1985) p. 292.
9. S. J. Linz, 'World war II and Soviet Economic Growth' in Ibid., pp. 11–34.
10. Alec Nove, *An Economic History of the U.S.S.R.* (Harmondsworth: Penguin, 1982) pp. 286–7.
11. Thomas B. Inglish to Forrestal, 21 January 1946, James Forrestal Papers Princeton University Library Quoted in Thomas G. Paterson, *Soviet–American Confrontation: Postwar Reconstruction and the Origins of the Cold War* (Baltimore: John Hopkins University Press, 1975) p. 9.
12. C. L. Sulzberger, *A Long Row of Candles: Memoirs and Dairies, 1934–54* (New York: Macmillan, 1969) p. 313.
13. George Kennan, 'The Long Telegram', 22 February 1946, classified in Thomas Etzold and John Lewis Gaddis, *Containment: Documents on American Policy and Strategy, 1945–1950* (New York: Columbia University Press, 1978) pp. 50–63.
14. Alonzo L. Hamby, *Man of the People: A Life of Harry S. Truman* (New York: Oxford University Press, 1995) p. 537.
15. Goncharov *et al.* (1993), op. cit., p. 145.

16. Jian Chen, *China's Road to the Korean War: The Making of the Sino-American Confrontation* (New York: Columbia University Press, 1994) pp. 178–9.
17. Ralph W. McGehee, *Deadly Deceits: My 25 Years in the CIA* (Melbourne: Ocean Press, 1999) pp. 120–1. This book was first published in 1983 by Sheridan Square Publications. See also Jonathan Kwitny, *Endless Enemies: The Making of an Unfriendly World* (New York, Penguin Books, 1987) p. 275.
18. Goncharov *et al.* (1993), op. cit., p. 153.
19. Derrik Mercer (ed.), *Chronicle of the 20th Century* (London: Chronicle, 1988) p. 703.
20. Stephen E. Ambrose, *Rise to Globalism: American Foreign Policy Since 1938* (New York: Penguin Books, 1985) p. 86.
21. Of the few dissenting voices, Roger D. Lapham, at one time chief of the Economic Cooperation Administration in China, refuted that the Chinese Communists had compromised their independence by accepting Soviet aid. To him, the Chinese were 'more Chinese and anti-foreign than tools of Moscow.' Similarly Edgar Snow, who was in close touch with Mao, felt that 'China will become the first Communist-run major country independent of Moscow dictation.' Not unlike Lapham and Snow, John Fairbank, underlining the uniqueness of Chinese society, pointed out the error in looking at China as a part of the Russian expansion. See Dulles (1972), op. cit., pp. 40–1.
22. Ho Chi Minh had approached the U.S. government at least eight times between October 1945 and February 1946 for American help in Vietnamese independence. With the outbreak of hostilities in South Vietnam in September 1945, he made 'formal requests for U.S. and U.N. intervention against French aggression, citing the Atlantic Charter, the U.N. Charter, and a foreign policy address of President Truman in October, 1945, endorsing national self-determination.' His letters went unreplied. *The Pentagon Papers: Defense Department History of the United States Decisionmaking on Vietnam*, The Senator Gravel edn (Boston: Beacon Press 1971), Vol. 1, p. 50.
23. Foster Rhea Dulles, *American Foreign Policy Toward Communist China 1949–1969* (New York: Thomas Y. Crowell Company, 1972) p. 39.
24. Ibid., p. 38.
25. Goncharov *et al.* (1993), op. cit., p. 2. Dulles (1972), op. cit., p. 38. See also Russell D. Buhite, *Nelson T. Johnson and American Policy Toward China, 1925–1941* (East Lansing: Michigan State University Press, 1968) p11. Buhite points out that Johnson, who had recently retired as the Ambassador Extraordinary and Plentipotentiary for China, was disillusioned by President Roosevelt and found surrenderring 'of Chinese territory morally indefensible and in violation of American policy'.
26. Congressional Research Service, *The U.S. Government and the Vietnam War: Executive and Legislative Roles and Relationships, Part I, 1945–1961* (Washington: US Government Printing Office, 1984) pp. 64–5.
27. Ibid., p. 67.
28. Ibid., p. 66.
29. Mercer (1988), op. cit., p. 703
30. Ibid.
31. According to Goncharov *et al.* Andrei Gomyko had advised Stalin to ask Iakov (Jacob) Malik, the Soviet Representative to the UN to return to the Security Council and use the Soviet veto but Stalin disagreed. Goncharov *et al.*, (1993), op. cit., p. 161.
32. Chen (1994), op. cit., p. 164.

33. Richard M. Freeland, *The Truman Doctrine and the Origins of McCarthyism: Foreign Policy, Domestic Politics, and Internal Security, 1946–1948* (New York: New York University Press, 1985) p. 355.
34. Hamby (1995), op. cit., p. 542. See also Chen (1994), op. cit., p. 168.
35. Ambrose (1985), op. cit., p. 121.
36. Chen (1994), op. cit., p. 147.
37. Hamby (1995), op. cit., p. 542.
38. George Kennan, *Memoires, 1950–1963* (New York: Pantheon Books, 1972) p. 25.
39. William Blum, *Killing Hope: U.S. Military and CIA Interventions Since World War II* (Monroe, Maine: Common Courage Press, 1995) pp. 23–4.
40. A transcript of the conversation between Zhou Enlai and K. M. Pannikar is reproduced in Goncharov *et al.* (1993), op. cit., pp. 277–8.
41. Stephen E. Ambrose, *Ike's Spies: Eisenhower and the Espionage Establishment* (Jackson: University Press of Mississippi, 1999) p. 170. The book was originally published in 1981 by New York, Doubleday & Company.
42. Freeland (1985), op. cit., p. 356. In his memoir Dean Rusk counters such suggestions that President Truman ever in any way countenanced the use of the atom bomb against China.
43. Ambrose (1985), op. cit., p. 124.
44. Ibid., p. 125.
45. Ibid., p. 125.
46. Alexandre Y. Mansourov, 'Stalin, Mao, Kim, and China's Decision to Enter the Korean War, Sept. 16–Oct. 15, 1950: New Evidence from Russian Archives' Cold War International History Project, Woodrow Wilson International Center for Scholars (http://cwihp.si.edu/cwihplib.nsf).
47. Ambrose (1985), op. cit., p. 126.
48. The peace treaty was signed in San Fransisco by forty-nine nations. The Soviet Union and the People's Republic of China were not among them. See Warren. S. Hunsberger and Richard B. Finn, 'Japan's Historical Record' in Warren S. Hunsberger (ed.), *Japan's Quest: The Search for International Role, Recognition and Respect* (Armonk, NY: M. E. Sharpe, 1997) pp. 25–7.
49. Daniel Patrick Moynihan, *Came the Revolution: Argument in the Reagan Era* (San Diego: Harcourt Brace Jovanovich, 1988) pp. 207–8.
50. For instance George Ball, who was the undersecretary of state to both Presidents Kennedy and Johnson stresses that, 'For many years, under the Truman, Eisenhower, Kennedy, and Johnson Administrations, our policy of trying to exclude Peking from taking over the representation of China in New York had made no sense…'. See George W. Ball, *Diplomacy For a Crowded World: An American Foreign Policy* (London: The Bodley Head, 1976) p. 26. George Kennan also 'thought it unwise on the part of our government to oppose their [Chinese Communists] admission [into the U.N.].' See *Memoirs 1950–1963*, p. 54.
51. See for instance John Prados, *Presidents' Secret Wars* (New York: Quill William Morrow, 1986). See also Christopher Andew, *For the President's Eyes Only: Secret Intelligence and the American Presidency from Washington to Bush* (New York: Harper Perennial, 1996); Peter J. Schraeder (ed.), *Interventions into the 1990s: U.S. Foreign Policy in the Third World*, (Boulder: Lynne Rienner Publishers, 1992); Ralph W. McGehee, *'Deadly Deceits: My 25 Years in CIA'* (Melbourne: Ocean Press, 1999); and Blum (1995), op. cit.
52. Ambrose (1985), op. cit., p. 42.
53. Freeland (1985), op. cit., pp. 359–60. See also Eric Foner, *The Story of American Freedom* (New York: W. W. Norton and Company, 1998) pp. 252–6.

54. Ambrose (1985), op. cit., pp. 134–5.
55. Stephen E. Ambrose, *Eisenhower: Soldier and President* (New York: Simon & Schuster, 1990) p. 285.
56. Mercer (1988), op. cit., p. 720.
57. Dwight D. Eisenhower, *The White House Years: Mandate for Change, 1953–56* (New York. Doubleday & Company, 1963) p. 181.
58. McGeorge Bundy, *Danger and Survival: Choices About the Bomb in the First Fifty Years* (New York: Random House, 1988) p. 240.
59. Ibid., pp. 240–1.
60. Both Truman and Acheson continued to believe and tried to convince Clement Attlee, that China took orders from the Soviet Union. See 'U.S. Minutes: Truman–Attlee Conversations', 4 December 1950, Chen (1994), op.cit., pp. 171, 278 n 47.
61. For instance see Hamby (1995), op. cit., p. 354.
62. Ambrose (1991), op. cit., p. 273.
63. Cohen (1995), op. cit., p. 86.
64. Ambrose (1991), op. cit., p. 297.
65. It is possible that Eisenhower was influenced by the secret memorandum, now declassified, written by Gerard Smith, the then Director of Policy Planning in the State Department, for Christian Herter, Eisenhower's undersecretary of state. Smith had stressed that the bombing of major Chinese cities would not only involve the death of millions of innocent civilians but also lead to a nuclear war with the Soviet Union with disastrous consequences for the United States itself. See Gerard Smith to Christian Herter, S/P-58231–3A, Discussion of Taiwan Straights, 13 August, 1958, p. 1–2.
66. Ambrose (1991), op. cit., p. 379. First in April when the situation in Dien Bien Phu was getting out of hand; second in May at the time of the fall of Dien Bien Phu; third in June when it was being rumored that the Chinese were at the point of entering the Vietnam war; fourth in September when the Chinese armed forces began to shell Quemoy and Matsu and fifth in November when the Chinese gave prison sentences to American airman (ibid.).
67. Ambrose (1999) p. 176.
68. Ibid., p. 168.
69. Blum (1995), op. cit., p. 70.
70. Peter H. Smith, *Talons of the Eagle: Dynamics of U.S.–Latin American Relations* (New York: Oxford University Press, 1996) p. 135. See also Jenny Pearce, *Under the Eagle: U.S. Intervention in Central America and the Caribbean* (London: Latin American Bureau, 1982), p. 29, and Blum (1995), op. cit., p. 75.
71. Audrey R. Kahin and George McT. Kahin, *Subversion as Foreign Policy: The Secret Eisenhower and Dulles Debacle in Indonesia* (Seattle: University of Washington Press, 1997) pp. 181–5.
72. Roger Hilsman, *To Move A Nation; The Politics of Foreign Policy in the Administration of John F. Kennedy* (New York: Doubleday, 1967) p. 377.
73. Marion Wilkinson, 'Indonesia: Hidden Holocaust of 1965', *Sydney Morning Herald*, 10 July 1999.
74. *New York Times*, 12 March 1966.
75. Kathy Kadane, 'Ex-Agents say CIA compiled the death lists for Indonesians: After 25 Years, Americans speak of their role in exterminating Communist Party' *Herald-Journal*, 19 May 1990. See also Peter Dale Scott, 'The United States and the Overthrow of Sukarno, 1965–67', *Pacific Affairs*, Vol. 58, no. 2, Summer 1985, pp. 239–64. See also *Sydney Morning Herald*, 10 July 1999.

76. Quoted in Kadane (1990), op. cit.; see also Blum (1995), op. cit., p. 194.
77. The other main reason was Sukarno's non-alignment and Sukarno's access to the Chinese and the Soviet Union, which was unacceptable to Dulles. Sukarno's 'tolerance' of the Indonesian Communist Party was another irritant for the Americans.
78. Lisa Pease, 'JFK, Indonesia, CIA & Freeport Sulphur', *Probe Magazine*, Vol. 3, No. 4, May–June 1996.
79. For the details of the development from someone near President Kennedy see Theodore C. Sorensen, *Kennedy* (New York: Konecky & Konecky, 1965) pp. 291–309.
80. Stephen G. Rabe, *Eisenhower and Latin America: The Foreign Policy of Anticommunism* (Chapel Hill: North Carolina University Press, 1988) pp. 122–4.
81. Blum (1995), op. cit., p. 24. See also Kahin and Kahin (1995), op. cit., pp. 10–12.
82. Prados (1986), op. cit., pp. 156–7.
83. Ambrose (1999), op. cit., p. 285; see also Christopher Andrew, *For the Presidents Eye Only: Secret Intelligence and the American Presidency from Washington to Bush* (New York: Harper Perennial, 1996) pp. 244–6; also, Blum, (1995), op. cit., pp. 114–15.
84. Ambrose (1991), op. cit., pp. 381–2.
85. Ibid., p. 383.
86. Ibid., p. 384.
87. Sorensen (1965), op. cit., pp. 661–2, see also Dulles (1972), op. cit., pp. 200–1.
88. *Public Papers of the Presidents*, John F. Kennedy, 1963, p. 659 quoted in the Congressional Research Service, *The U.S. Government and the Vietnam War: Executive and Legislative Roles and Relationships, Part II, 1961–94* (Washington: U. S. Government Printing Office, 1985) p. 163.
89. Ibid., p. 6.
90. Ibid., p. 4.
91. Quoted in Sorensen (1965), op. cit., p. 665.
92. McNamara (1996), op. cit., pp. 79–81.
93. Congressional Research Service, *The U.S. Government and the Vietnam War: Executive and Legislative Roles and Relationships, Part II, 1961–94* (Washington, DC: US Government Printing Office, 1985) p. 163.
94. A detailed account of the Chinese involvement in Vietnam war efforts is given in newly released documents from the Chinese archives translated into English by Qiang Zhai. See Qiang Zhai, 'Beijing and the Vietnam Conflict, 1964–1965: New Chinese Evidence,' Cold War International History Project Bulletin., Woodrow Wilson International Center for Scholars. (http://cwihp.si.edu/cwihplib.nsf).
95. Ball (1976) op. cit., p. 67.
96. For example, Bill Colby, the director of the Phoenix program, himself told a Senate hearing that 20,587 had been killed, 28,978 imprisoned, and 17,717 converted to act as agents for the South Vietnamese Government. To this, one must add over 40,000 killed by South Vietnam's own covert operation called *Phung Hoang*, a mythical bird, a harbinger of peace. Many American veterans claim that the Phoenix Program was literally an assassination program. Prados (1986) p. 309. See also. Ralph W. McGehee, *Deadly Deceits: My 25 Years in the CIA*, (Melbourne: Ocean Press, 1999), pp. 141–3.
97. Richard A. Falk, 'War Crimes: The circle of responsibility', *The Nation*, 26 January 1970, p. 80. In fact, the International War Crimes Tribunal (established by Bertrand Russell), after a detailed inquiry and hearings from witnesses from

various countries pronounced the United States as guilty under international law for committing aggression against Vietnam, bombarding purely civilian targets, and repeatedly violating the sovereignty, neutrality and territorial integrity of Cambodia. See Jean-Paul Sartre, 'Summary and Verdict of the Stockholm Session' in Ken Coates, Peter Limqueco and Peter Weiss (ed.), *Prevent the Crime of Silence*: Reports from the Sessions of the International War Crimes Tribunal founded by Bertrand Russell, (London: Allen Lane, the Penguin Press, 1971) p. 185.

 98. C. L. Sulzberger, *The World and Richard Nixon* (New York: Prentice Hall Press, 1987) p. 112.
 99. Richard Nixon (1967), 'Asia after Vietnam', *Foreign Affairs*, Vol. 46, no. 1, (1967) p. 121.
100. James Mann, *About Face: A History of America's Curious Relationship with China, From Nixon to Clinton* (New York: Alfred A. Knopf), 1999) p. 18.
101. A. Doak Barnett, *China and the Major Powers in East Asia* (Washington, DC: The Brookings Institution, 1977) pp. 178–9. See also Ball (1976), op. cit., p. 75.
102. Barnett (1977), op. cit., p. 190.
103. Ibid.
104. Ibid., pp. 190–1.
105. Mann (1999), op. cit., p. 18.
106. Mann (1999), op. cit., p. 28. Senator Mike Mansfield had been trying to go to China for sometime, he had been writing to Zhou Enlai asking his permission to visit China. During the Johnson Administration he had argued that a normalization of relationships with China might help the United states to extricate itself from the Vietnam war with Chinese help. (p. 28).
107. Ibid., p. 29. See also Patrick Tyler: *A Great Wall: Six Presidents and China: An Investigative History* (New York: Public Affairs, 1999) p. 101. Nixon also wanted James Reston, a *New York Times* columnist, who had secured a Chinese visa to go to China and interview Zhou, stopped from going to China. (p. 96). See also, James Reston, *Deadline: A Memoir*, (New York: Random House, 1991) pp. 381–7.
108. The total number of American boys dead in combat during the entire period of the Vietnam War was 58,000 and 300,000 wounded.
109. Ball (1976), op. cit., p. 6.
110. Quoted in Sorensen (1965), op. cit., p. 515.
111. Ibid., p. 515.
112. Richard J Barnet., *The Alliance: America–Europe–Japan: Makers of the Postwar World* (New York: Simon and Schuster, 1983) p. 239.
113. Dennis L. Bark and David R. Gress, *A History of West Germany: Democracy and Its Discontents, 1963–1988* (volume 2), (Oxford: Basil Blackwell, 1989) pp. 20–1.
114. Dennis L. Bark and David R. Gress, *A History of West Germany: From Shadow to Substance, 1945–1963* (Volume 1) (Oxford: Basil Blackwell, 1989) p. 509.
115. William Burr (ed.), *The Kissinger Transcripts: The Top Secret Talks with Beijing and Moscow* (New York: The New Press, 1999) p. 16.
116. Quoted in Barnet (1983), op. cit., p. 198.
117. Ball (1976), op. cit., p. 7.
118. Sulzberger (1987), op. cit., p. 190. See also Mann (1999), op. cit., p. 79.
119. Ball (1976), op, cit., p. 13. See also Tyler (1999), op. cit., p. 149.
120. The visit was arranged through the good offices of Romania and Pakistan; Japan was not even consulted. Until then, Japan had conformed to the US policies towards China; the Nixon-visit set the scene for Japanese independent diplomacy towards China.

121. Tyler (1999), op. cit., pp. 158–9.
122. Burr (1999), op. cit., p. 35.
123. Tyler (1999), op. cit., p. 212. See also Burr (1999), op. cit., p. 396.
124. In fact, these offices were, as Ross Terrill suggests, 'embassies in all but name.' See Ross Terrill, *Mao: A Biography* (New York: Harper & Row, 1980) p. 372. The chiefs of the office were to be treated as ambassadors; and the personnel had diplomatic immunity. They had their personal secure communications as well. See Henry Kissinger, *Years of Upheaval* (Boston: Little, Brown and Company, 1982) p. 62.
125. Mann (1999), op. cit., pp. 70–1.
126. Ibid., p. 73.
127. Ibid., p. 74. See also Burr (1999), op. cit., p. 400.
128. Tyler (1999), op. cit., pp. 217–19.
129. Mann (1999), op. cit., p. 65.
130. The United States retained the right to sell defensive weapons to Taiwan. The Congress rewrote the bill sent by Carter to downgrade the status of Taiwan and passed, with overwhelming majority, the Taiwan's Relations Act confirming the security relationship with Taiwan. See Tyler, (1999), op. cit., pp. 273–4.
131. Ibid., p. 277.
132. Mercer (1988), op. cit., p. 1037. See also Tyler (1999), op. cit, p. 116.
133. Mann (1999) op. cit., p. 98.
134. Tyler (1999) op. cit., p. 164.
135. Gaddis Smith, *Morality, Reason and Power: American Diplomacy in the Carter Years,* (New York: Hill and Wang, 1986) pp. 94–5.
136. Maurice Meisner, *The Deng Xiaoping Era: An Inquiry into the Fate of Chinese Socialism 1978–1994* (New York: Hill and Wang, 1996) p. 114. For the details regarding the suppression of the Democracy Movement in 1970s. See Chapter 5.
137. Ibid., pp, 112 and 122.
138. However, wall posters could be placed in a remote park so long as the persons putting up such posters registered their posters with the police and gave the details of their whereabouts to the police. See ibid., p. 122.
139. Smith (1986) p. 29.
140. Nayan Chanda, *Brother Enemy: The War after the War* (San Diego: Harcourt Brace Jovanovich, 1986) p. 286. See also Tariq Ali, 'The Ignoble Noble', *Guardian,* 7 Dec. 2002.
141. Raphael Iungerich, chief Indochina analyst of the State Department's Bureau of Intelligence and Research, quoted in Chanda (1986) op.cit., p. 286.
142. Ibid., p. 291.
143. Ibid.
144. Mann (1999), op. cit., p. 100. See also Tyler (1999), op. cit., p. 281.
145. Ibid., p. 290.
146. Mann (1999), op. cit. p. 137.
147. Ibid., p. 141.
148. Ibid., pp. 167–72.
149. Ibid., p. 186.
150. Hu was not a 'liberal' in the Western sense, he simply belonged 'to the democratic and libertarian strains in the Marxist tradition. Hardly a "liberal" or a representative of "liberal thought," Hu Yaobang was in fact a democratic Marxist and a dedicated Communist who devoted his life to realizing his vision of socialism.' See Meisner (1996), op. cit., pp. 352.
151. Zhao Ziyang had objected to the use of force and was in favor of dialogue with students. On being overruled by the politburo he resigned from the post of

general secretary. See Merle Goldman, *Sowing the Seeds of Democracy in China: Political Reform in Deng Xiaoping Era* (Cambridge, Mass: Harvard University Press, 1994) p. 322.

152. The estimates of dead range between 700 and 2700. The Chinese government puts the figure much lower at 310. See Mann (1999), op. cit., p. 395 n 43.
153. Meisner (1996), op. cit., pp. 456–467. See also Goldman (1994), op. cit. p. 337.
154. Ibid., pp. 336–7.
155. Tyler (1999), op. cit., p. 370.
156. Mann (1999), op. cit., p. 234.
157. Tyler (1999), op. cit., pp. 373–4.
158. Daniel L. Byman and Roger Cliff, *China's Arms Sales: Motivations and Implications*, Project Air Force (Santa Monica, RAND, 1999) p. 42.
159. Mann (1999), op. cit., pp. 266.
160. Byman and Cliff (1999), op. cit., pp. 43–4.
161. Freeland (1985), op. cit., p. 241.
162. Eric Foner, *The Story of American Freedom* (New York: W. W. Norton & Company, 1998) p. 255.
163. Howard K. Beale, quoted in Foner (1998), op. cit., p. 255.

4   Clinton and Bush: Contrasts in World View

1. Daniel Patrick Moynihan, *On the Law of Nations: A Historical and Personal Account of the Role of International Law in Foreign Policy* (Cambridge, Mass.: Harvard University Press, 1990) pp. 176–7.
2. Anatoly Dobrynin, *In Confidence: Moscow's Ambassador to Six Cold War Presidents (1962–1986)* (New York: Times Books, Random House, 1995) p. 615.
3. China was required not only to comply with the freedom-of-emigration requirements of the Jackson–Vanik amendment, 1992 US–China prison labor agreement, and the Universal Declaration of Human Rights, but also to release and account for political prisoners detained for the non-violent expression of political and religious beliefs, to ensure humane treatment of prisoners by providing easy access to international humanitarian organizations such as the International Red Cross to visit prisons, to protect Tibet's cultural and religious heritage, allow international radio and video broadcasts into China, to end non-discriminatory trade practices against US businesses, and to adhere to the Nuclear Non-proliferation Treaty and the Missile Technology Control Regime. See Vladimir N. Pregelj, *Most-Favored-Nation Status of the People's Republic of China*, CRS Report for Congress, updated 21 July 2000, Congress Research Service, Library of Congress, Washington, DC, pp. CRS-4.
4. Some of these leading former officials are not strictly lobbyists; the traditional foreign relations firms have to register with the Justice Department under the Foreign Agents Registration Act. 'Unlike the ex-officials who have lobbied for Japan and Japanese corporations, these former officials don't work directly for China or for Chinese businesses, and most have no personal investments in China.... What all of them have to offer is not so much knowledge of China as clout with its government – clout based in part on the statements they have made about U.S. policy toward China.' See John B Judis, 'China Town', *The New Republic*, 10 March 1997, p. 18.
5. Ibid.

6. Pregelj, op. cit., p. CRS-7.
7. Ramon H. Myers and David Shambaugh, 'Introduction: The Legacy of U.S. China Policy, 1989–2000,' in Ramon H. Myers, Michel C. Oksenberg and David Shambaugh (eds), *Making China Policy: Lessons from the Bush and Clinton Administrations* (Lantham, MD: Rowman & Littlefield Publishers Inc., 2001) p. 12.
8. Office of the Press secretary, the White House, 'Technology for America's Economic Growth: A New Direction to Build Economic Strength' – the Technology Policy Initiative, launched at a speech delivered by President Clinton at Silicon Graphics Inc., Mountain View, California, 22 February 1993 (http://clinton6.nara.gov/).
9. Jeff Gerth and Eric Schmitt, 'The Technology Trade: A special report; Chinese Said to Reap Gains In U.S. Export Policy Shift', *New York Times*, 19 October 1998.
10. James Mann, *About Face: A History of America's Curious Relationship with China, from Nixon to Clinton* (New York: Alfred A. Knopf, 1999) p. 290.
11. Kerry Dumbaugh, *China–U.S. Relations: Chronology of Developments During the Clinton Administration*, CRS Report for Congress, updated 25 July 2000, Library of Congress, Washington, DC, p. CRS-4.
12. Elain Sciolino, 'U.S. Will Allow Computer Sales to Court China', *New York Times*, 19 November 1993.
13. Dumbaugh (2000), op. cit., p. CRS-5.
14. Mann (1999), op. cit., p. 303.
15. US General Accounting Office (GAO), *Export Controls: Statutory Reporting Requirements for Computers Not Fully Addressed, GAO/NSIAD 0045* (Washington, DC: Government Accounting Office, 1999) p. 5. Export destinations were grouped into four categories: category one consisting of Western Europe and Japan requiring no license; group two consisting of countries in Asia, Africa, Latin America, and Eastern Europe requiring license for computers with a capacity above 10,000 MTOPS; and group three consisting of fifty countries including China, India, Israel, and Russia, requiring license for computer capacity exceeding 7000 MTOPS for civilian uses, and exceeding 2000 MTOPS for the military end-uses.
16. US General Accounting Office, *Export Controls: Better Coordination Needed on Satellite Exports*, GAO/NSIAD 99–182 (Washington, DC: Government Accounting Office, 1999) p. 5.
17. Eric Schmitt, 'Arguments Over Whether Satellite Companies Illegally Aided China', *Austin American Statesman*, 6 June 1998.
18. US House of Representatives, *Report of the Select Committee on U.S. National Security and Military/Commercial Concerns with People's Republic of China* (Cox Committee Report), (Washington: Government Printing Office, 1999) p. 228.
19. Ibid., Overview, pp. III–V and XII–XIII.
20. ABC News and Associated Press, 13 September 2000.
21. Jeff Gerth, 'Democrat Fund-Raiser Said to Detail China Tie', *New York Times*, 15 May 1998. See also Jeff Gerth, David Johnston and Don Van Natta Jr., 'Evidence of Broad Plan by China to Buy Entree to U.S. Technology', *New York Times*, 15 December 1998.
22. Patrick Tyler, *A Great Wall: Six Presidents and China: An Investigative History* (New York: Public affairs,1999) pp. 398–400.
23. Mann (1999), op cit., p. 322. Mann gives a detailed account of events relating to the developments in China and the United States in connection with Lee's visit (See ch. 17, pp. 315–38).
24. The House of Representatives voted unanimously in favor of Lee's being allowed to come, and the Senate had voted 97 to one in favor of Lee.

25. Statement of Winston Lord, assistant secretary of state, Bureau of East Asian And Pacific Affairs, before the Senate Foreign Relations Committee, Asia and Pacific Affairs Subcommittee, 11 October 1995 (http://dosfan.lib.uic.edu/ERC/bureaus/eap/951011Lord USPolicyChina.html).
26. Dumbaugh (2000), op. cit., pp. CRS-7–8.
27. Ibid.; see also Mann (1999), op. cit., pp. 328–9.
28. Bruce Herschensohn, 'President Clinton and the Republic of China on Taiwan', *Los Angeles Times*, 9 July 1998.
29. Mann (1999), op. cit., p. 330.
30. Shirley A. Kan, *Chinese Proliferation of Weapons of Mass Destruction: Current Policy Issues*, CRS Issue Brief, updated 10 July 2000, Congressional Research Service, Library of Congress, Washington, DC, p. CRS-5.
31. Compiled for the Internet by Kristie Wang, Program Director, Center for Taiwan International Relations, (http://www.taiwandc.org/hst-9596.html).
32. Reuters (Taipei) and Nando.net, 17 March 1996.
33. Reuters (Washington, DC) and Nando.net, 12 March 1996.
34. House of Representatives, H. Con. Res. 148, 7 March 1996, *Congressional Record*, p. H 1971, see also pp. H 2342–2350; H. Con. Res. 140, 31 January 1996; Thomas (and others) Amendment No. 3562, Senate, 21 March 1996, *Congressional Record*, pp. S-2688–9.
35. Dumbaugh (2000), op. cit., p. CRS-10.
36. The letter is included in the 'Announcement by the Speaker Pro Tempore (House of Representatives, 27 June 1996), *Congressional Record*, pp. H 7004–6.
37. See H. J. Res. 182, *Congressional Record*, pp. H 6985–7026.
38. US Department of State, Office of the Spokesman, 19 April 1996. It may be noted that the meeting took place on 19 April and not 21 April, as was originally planned.
39. Ibid.
40. US Department of State, Office of the Spokesman, 'Remarks by U.S. Secretary of State Warren Christopher', Beijing, 20 November 1996.
41. Department of State, Office of the Spokesman, An Address by US Secretary of State Warren Christopher, 'The United States and China: Building a New Era of Cooperation for A New Century', Shanghai, 21 November 1996.
42. Ann Scott Tyson, 'Human Rights in the Back Seat During Summit,' *Christian Science Monitor*, 31 October 1997. See also White House, Office of the Press Secretary, Press Conference by President Clinton and President Jiang Zemin', 29 October, 1997.
43. White House, Office of the Press Secretary, 'Joint US–China Statement,' 29 October 1997.
44. Harry Harding, 'The Clinton–Jiang Summits: An American Perspective', A Keynote Speech to the Asia Society, Hong Kong Center, 28 May 1998. (http://www.asia-society.org/speeches/harding.html).
45. For the details of such bills and legislations see Kerry Dumbaugh, *China and the 105th Congress: Policy Issues and Legislation, 1997–1998*, 21 October 1999, CRS Report for the Congress, CRS, Library of Congress, Washington, DC.
46. Ibid., p. CRS-18. A similar resolution (SJ Res 27) failed in the House on 27 July 1999 by 170–260 votes (*Congressional Record*, p. H 6475). Similarly, a resolution disapproving normal trading relations to China (SJ Res. 17) failed in the Senate on 20 July 1999, by 12–87 votes (*Congressional Record*, S 8851). In fact, joint resolutions of disapproval have been introduced each year since 1990; none has passed both houses. See Dumbaugh (2000), op. cit., CRS-7.

47. Dumbaugh (2000), op. cit., pp. CRS 25–6.
48. Shirley A. Kan, *China's Technology Acquisitions: Cox Committee Report – Findings, Issues and Recommendations*, 8 June 1999, CRS Report for Congress, The Library of Congress, Washington, DC, p. CRS-2.
49. John Sweene, Jens Holsoe and Ed Vulliamy,' NATO bombed Chinese deliberately', *Observer*, 17 October 1999.
50. FAIR, 'Chinese Embassy Bombing Update: Media Reply, FAIR Responds', 3 November 1999 (http://www.fair.org/activism/china-response.html); See also FAIR, 'Action Alert: U.S. Media Overlook Exposé on Chinese Embassy Bombing', 22 October 1999 [http://www.fair.org/activism/embassy-bombing.html].
51. Stanley O. Roth, 'The Effects on U.S.–China Relations of the Accidental Bombing of the Chinese Embassy in Belgrade,' Testimony Before the Senate Committee on Foreign relations, Subcommittee on East Asian and Pacific Affairs, Washington, DC, 27 May 1999 (http://www.state.gov/www/policy_remarks/1999/990527_roth_china.html).
52. AFP (Beijing) 9 May 1999.
53. Andrew Browne, 'China Demands Bombing Probe and Apology,' Reuters (Beijing), 10 May 1999.
54. *Xinhua*, 12 June 1999. See also Joseph Fewsmith, 'China and the W.T.O.: The Politics Behind the Agreement', *NBR Analysis*, Vol.10, No. 5, National Bureau of Asian Research, November 1999 (www.nbr.org/publications/analysis/vol10no5/essay2.html).
55. Roth (1999), op. cit.
56. Dumbaugh (2000), op. *cit.*, p. CRS-30.
57. Edwin Chen, and Mark Magnier, 'US–China relations "Back on track" after Clinton, Jiang mend fences', *Los Angeles Times*, 12 September 1999. See also David E. Sanger, 'Clinton–Jiang Heal Rift and Set a New Trade Course,' *New York Times*, 12 September 1999.
58. Fewsmith (1999), op. cit.
59. Press Conference by US Trade Representative Charlene Barshefsky and Gene Sperling, assistant to the president for economic policy, Hong Kong International Airport, 16 November 1999 (http://www.usconsulate.org.hk/uscn/trade/general/ustr/1999/1116a.html).
60. GOP Debate, Phoenix Arizona, 7 December 1999 (http://www.issues2000.org/Celeb/More_George_W__Bush_China.html).
61. GOP Debate, Phoenix Arizona, 7 December 1999, op. cit.
62. Speech at Boeing plant, part of 'Renewing America's Purpose' 17 May 2000 (http://www.issues2000.org/George_W__Bush_China.html).
63. Merle D. Kellerhals, Jr., 'Powell Says U.S. Must Stay Engaged with China,' Office of International Information Programs, US Department of State (http://www.fas.org/news/china/2001/china-010503zss.html).
64. Damien McElroy and James Langton, 'Powell's warm words highlight White House rift on handling China', *Sunday Telegraph*, 29 July 2001. See also Secretary Colin L. Powell's remarks to the press, Beijing, 28 July 2001 (http://www.state.gov/secretary/rm/2001/4327.html).
65. Martin Kettle, 'US told to make China its No. 1 enemy', *Guardian*, 24 March 2001.
66. Damien McElroy and James Langton (2001), op. cit.
67. *New York Times*, 'Renewing America's Purpose,' 24 September 1999.
68. Jim Hoagland, 'The danger of Bush's Unilateralism', *Washington Post*, 29 July 2001.

69. *New York Times*, 'America on the Sidelines,' (Editorial), 29 July 2001.
70. Ed Vulliamy, 'Bush plans "space bomber",' *Observer*, 29 July 2001.
71. Anthony Lewis, 'Bush the Radical,' *New York Times*, 21 July 2001.
72. Charles Krauthammer, 'The New Unilateralism,' *Washington Post*, 8 June 2001.
73. See for instance Representative Sherrod Brown from Ohio who stated that 'I dream of a day when the US will replace its one China policy with a policy of one China, one Taiwan and one Tibet.' See 'Expressing Sense of Congress Regarding Taiwan's Participation in the United Nations,' House of Representatives, 3 October 2000, *Congressional Record*, p. HR 8726. See also Dalrymple, Mary S., 'Taiwanese President's Comments Inspires GOP to Renew Attack on Clinton's "One China" Policy', *Congressional Quarterly*, 24 July 1999.
74. Murray Hiebert, and Susan V. Lawrence, 'Dangerous Brinkmanship,' *Far Eastern Economic Review*, Issue Cover – 15 March 2001.
75. CNN, 'Pentagon sources say China helping Iraq,' 20 February 2001.
76. CNN. 'Powell: China agrees to stop helping Iraq,' 8 March 2001.
77. Willy Wo-Lap Lam,'Qian fails in his mission,' CNN 23 March 2001.
78. Jay Taylor, '*Top Clique Shifts the Basics on China.*' *Los Angeles Times*, 30 April 2001.
79. CNN, 4 April 2001.
80. Indira A. R. Lakshmanan 'Some See Double Standard in China Flap', *Boston Globe*, 18 April 2001.
81. *Mingpao Daily News*, 4 April 2001 (in Chinese). In 1976 a Soviet air force officer had defected to Japan with a MIG 25. CIA took control of the plane and the plane was thoroughly examined for its potential by American experts. The dismantled parts of the plane were handed over to the Soviet Union in crates after 67 days.
82. Robert Kagan and William Kristol,' A national humiliation,' *Weekly Standard*, (editorial), 16 April 2001.
83. CNN, 'U.S. Navy Study "backs Taiwan's arms upgrade,"' 1 April 2001.
84. James H. Nolt, 'Assessing New U.S. Arms Sales to Taiwan,' A Global Affairs Commentary, World Policy Institute, April 2001, p. 1 (http://www.foreignpolicy-infocus.org/pdf/gac/0104taiwanarms.pdf).
85. Ibid., p. 2.
86. Martin Kettle, and John Hooper, 'Military force an option to defend Taiwan, warns Bush,' *Guardian*, 26 April 2001.
87. CNN, 'Taiwan's military split over buying US warships,' 3 March 2000.
88. Kettle and Hooper (2001), op. cit.
89. CNN, 'U.S. approves Taiwan visitor's transit,' 14 May 2001.
90. Julian Borger, 'China protests as Bush welcomes its foes,' *Guardian*, 23 May 2001.
91. CNN, 'Jiang issues hard critique of Bush,' 26 May 2001.
92. John Pomfret, 'Another Academic Detained by China,' *The Washington Post*, 10 April 2001.
93. Associated Press, 'China detains American writer for suspected spying,' 19 June 2001.
94. CNN, 'Bush asks China for 'fair treatment' of detainees,' 5 July 2001.
95. CNN, 'U.S. wants China to join WTO this year,' 7 June 2001.
96. CNN, 5 July 2001.
97. John Gittings,, 'The China–U.S. olive branch exchange,' *Guardian Unlimited*, 10 July 2001.
98. CNN, 'China allows U.S. warships into Hong Kong,' 9 July 2001.
99. BBC News 25 July 2001.

100. Steven Mufson and Philip P. Pan, 'U.S., China Set For More Talks: Powell Raises Rights, Arms Issues', *Washington Post*, 29 July 2001.
101. CNN, 'U.S. protests Chinese television edit Powell interview', 31 July 2001.
102. *People's Daily*, 21 September 2001.
103. Bonnie S. Glaser. 'Fleshing out the Candid, Cooperative and Constructive relationship,' *Comparative Connections*, Pacific Forum, Center for Strategic and International Studies, Second Quarter 2002 (http://www.csis.org/pacfor/cc/0202Qus_china.html).
104. White House, Office of the Press Secretary, 'U.S., China Stand Against Terrorism', Press Release, 19 October 2001.
105. Glaser (2002), op. cit.
106. Embassy of the People's Republic of China in the United States of America,' President Jiang Zemin's Opening Remarks at the Joint Press Conference of Chinese and US Heads of States 21 February 2002 (http://www.china-embassy.org/eng/25341.html).
107. *Washington Post* (On Politics), 'Text: Bush Touts Free Society to Chinese,' 23 February 2002.
108. June Teufel Dreyer, 'Mr. Bush Goes to China,' *China Brief*, Volume 2, Issue 5, 28 February 2002, The Jamestown Foundation (http://china.jamestown.org/pubs/view/cwe_002_005_001.html).
109. *People's Daily*, 'U.S. Taiwan Secret Talks on Arms Sales: Analysis', 18 March 2002.
110. Paul Richter, 'Pentagon Broadens Nuclear Strategy: Bush Lists 7 Nations as Potential Targets', *Los Angeles Times*, 9 March 2002.
111. Department of Defense, *Quadrennial Defense Review Report* (Washington, DC: Defense Department, 2001), p. 4.
112. US–China Security Review Commission, *The National Security Implications of the Economic Relationship Between the United States and China* (Washington, DC: US–China Security Review Commission, 2002) p. 206.
113. Raymond Bonner, 'Anti-terror Fight: Why the Philippines?,' *New York Times*, 10 June 2002.
114. Venu Rajamony, 'India–China–U.S. Triangle: A 'Soft' Balance of Power System in Making,' Center for Strategic and International Studies, 15 March 2002, pp. 20–24 (http://www.csis.org/saprog/venu.pdf).
115. Glaser (2002), op. cit.

5 China as an Economic Threat

1. Bill Clinton, in his Hong Kong *Fortune* Forum speech reported by Willy Lam, CNN Web, 10 May 2001 (http://cgi.cnn.com/2001/WORLD/asiapcf/east/05/10/willy.clinton/index.html).
2. WTO, *International Trade Statistics, 2001* (Geneva: WTO, 2001) Table 1.5, p. 21.
3. These percentages would be different if calculated on the basis of statistics derived from Chinese sources.
4. As Gary Clyde Hufbauer and Daniel Rosen indicate, this number represents a gross overestimation because of the accounting procedures involving Hong Kong. For 1999, they provide a corrected figure of $43.2 billion, against an original estimate of $64.1 billion for the US trade deficit with China. See Gary Clyde Hufbauer and Daniel H. Rosen, *American Access to China's Market: The Congressional Vote on PNTR*, International Economics Policy Briefs no. 00–3, Washington, DC, International

Institute of Economics, April 2000 (*http://www.iie.com/policybriefs/news00–3.html*). Similarly, Nicholas Lardy has shown that after proper adjustment of Hong Kong trade, the US trade deficit for 2000, would be only $68.8 billion against the Department of Commerce figure of $83.8 billion. See Nicholas Lardy, quoted in US–China Business Council, 'Understanding the US–China Balance of Trade,' May 2001 (*http://www.uschina.org/public/wto/uscbc/balanceotrade.html*).

5. Nicholas Lardy, *Permanent Normal Trade Relation for China*, Policy Brief no. 58 (Washington, DC: Brookings Institution, May 2000) Figure 2, p. 4. See also Testimony of Charlene Barshefsky, 'Hearing on the China-WTO Agreement and Financial Services,' US Senate Committee on Banking, Housing, and Urban Affairs, 106th Congress, 2nd Session, 9 May 2000.

6. Ibid.

7. US International Trade Commission (USITC), *Assessment of the Economic Effects on the United States of China's Accession to the WTO*, Investigation no. 332–403 (Washington, DC, USITC, 1999) Table ES4, pp. xix–xx.

8. Ibid., p. xx.

9. Ibid., p. xxiii.

10. Ibid., Table ES 8, p. xxvi.

11. Yongding Yu, Zheng Bingwen, and Song Hongren (eds), *China After WTO Entry*, (in Chinese) (Beijing: Social Sciences Archive Publishing House, 2000). Excerpts translated by *ChinaOnline* (http://www.chinaonline.com).

12. Shaoguang Wang, 'The Social and Political Implications of China's WTO Membership,' *Journal of Contemporary China*, 2000, Vol. 9, no. 25, p. 397.

13. Ibid., pp. 397–9.

14. Shuguang Zhang, Yansheng Zhang, and Wan Zhongxin, *Measuring the Costs of Protection in China* (Washington, DC, Institute of International Economics, 1999) p. 28.

15. Although the United States is much more open than the European Union or China, many trade barriers – both tariff and non-tariff – continue in America both at the state and federal levels. See for instance European Commission, *Report on United States Barriers to Trade and Investment* (Brussels: European Commission, 2000).

16. James Burke, *U.S. Investment in China Worsens Trade Deficit*, Economic Policy Institute, Briefing Paper, no. 93, May 2000, p. 8.

17. Ibid., p. 6.

18. USTR, *National Trade Estimates Report on Foreign Trade Barriers, 2000 (China)* (www.ustr.gov) p. 44.

19. USITC (1999), op. cit., ch. 3, p.10.

20. Ibid., ch.3, p. 12.

21. Offsets can be negotiated by developing countries at the time of accession and are permissible for being used as a qualification for participating in government procurement, but not as criteria for awarding contracts. See USITC (1999), pp. 3–23.

22. Ibid.

23. USTR (2000), op. cit., pp. 49–50.

24. Alice H. Amsden, 'Industrialization Under New WTO Law,' a paper prepared for the United Nations Conference on Trade & Development 10 (UNCTAD X), High Level Round Table on Trade and Development: Directions for the Twenty-First Century, Bangkok, 12 February 2000, pp. iii and 6 (http://www.unctad 10.org/pdfs/ux_tdxrt1d7.en.pdf).

25. USTR (2000), op. cit., pp. 49–51.

26. Ibid., p. 46.
27. It is possible that some of these come from Japanese or US subsidiaries operating in Hong Kong.
28. Bank for International Settlements, *International Consolidated Banking Statistics for the Third Quarter of 2001*, Press Release 03/2002E, 28, January 2002 (Basle: BIS, 2002), Table 9, pp. 24–25 (http://www.bis.org).
29. Shujiro Urata, 'Japanese Foreign Direct Investment and Technology Transfer in Asia,' in Dennis J. Encarnation (ed.), *Japanese Multinationals in Asia: Regional Operations in Comparative Perspective* (NY: Oxford University Press, 1999) p. 160.
30. According to the Institute of International Education in 1998–99, a total of 55,000 Chinese students were studying in the United States, 53 per cent were studying physical and life sciences, engineering, or mathematics, while another 17.5 per cent health sciences, business, or agriculture. See Institute of International Education, 'Opendoors' Table 1 (http://www.opendoorsweb.org/); See Wendy Frieman, 'The Understated Revolution in Chinese Science and Technology' in James R. Lilley and David Shambaugh (eds), *China's Military Faces The Future* (Armonk, NY: M. E. Sharpe, 1999) pp. 255–6.
31. *People's Daily*, 6 June 2002.
32. USTR, Fact Sheet, 15 May 1996. Some of the following details are from this fact sheet.
33. Pitman B. Potter and Michel Oksenberg, 'A Patchwork of IPR Protection,' *The China Business Review*, Jan.–Feb. 1999, pp. 8–11.
34. USTR, *2002 National Trade Estimate Report on Foreign Trade Barriers*, p. 58 (http://www.ustr.gov/reports/nte/2002/index.html).
35. OECD, *The Economic Impact of Counterfeiting* (Paris: OECD, 1998) p. 3.
36. Ibid., p. 8. See also International Federation of Phonographic Industry (IFPI), *Music Piracy Report, 2000* (London: IFPI, 2000).
37. European Commission, *Report on Responses to the European Commission Green Paper on Counterfeiting and Piracy* (Brussels: European Commission, 1999) p. 14.
38. Ibid., p. 10.
39. Ibid., p. 14.
40. Ibid., p. 10.
41. OECD (1998), op. cit., p. 9.
42. European Commission (1999), op. cit., p. 16.
43. The Gini-coefficient for urban areas rose from 0.23 in 1988 to 0.37 in 1994. During the same period the Gini-coefficient for rural areas marginally increased from 0.38 to 0.41. See: Amei Zhang, 'Economic and Human Development in China', UNDP Occasional Paper no. 28, 1996, pp. 11–12 (http://hdr.undp.org/docs/publications/ocational_papers/oc28a.html).
44. Yongzheng Yang and Yiping Huang, *China's Economy: The Impact of Trade Liberalisation on Income Distribution in China*, (Canberra: Research School of Pacific and Asian Studies, Australian National University, 1997) Table 2, p. 7.
45. The coastal region consists of Guangdong, Jiangsu, Zhejiang, Fujian, Shandong, Liaoning, and the three municipalities of Beijing, Shanghai, and Tianjin. All these are the most prosperous areas and attract the lion's share of foreign capital and state investment. This region also includes the relatively poor, but now rapidly developing, provinces of Hebei, Hainan, and Guangxi. The coastal region accounts for 42 per cent of China's population and 58 per cent of GDP. The central region consists of Heilongjiang, Jilin, Inner Mongolia, Shanxi, Henan, Anhui, Hubei, Hunan, and Jiangxi. These are middle and lower-middle income provinces accounting for 31 per cent of population and 28 per cent of GDP. The Western

region consists of Sichuan, Guizhou, Yunnan, Shaanxi, Gansu, Qinghai, Ningxia, Tibet (Xizang), and Xinjiang. This region accounts for 27 per cent of the population and 14 per cent of the GDP.

46. Carl Riskin, 'Social Development, Quality of Life and the Environment,' in US Congress, Joint Economic Committee. *China's Economic Future: Challenges to US Policy* (Washington, DC: Government Printing Office, 1996) p. 366.

47. In 1995 SOEs employed 40 per cent of the industrial workers and produced 33 per cent of the industrial output. See East Asia Analytical Unit (EAAU), *China Embraces the Market: Achievements, Constraints and Opportunities* (Canberra: EAAU, Department of Foreign Affairs and Trade, 1997) p. 333.

48. According to the World Bank, the labor force in China in 1998 was around 743 millions, projected to grow to 822 million by 2010. If one assumes that the same rate continues up to 2025, the labor force will have reached 932 million, thus adding nearly 190 million people over 1998.

49. Riskin (1996), op. cit., p. 366. See also EAAU (1997), op. cit., which mentions that according to the Chinese Ministry of Labor, during 1995–2000 as many as 54 million workers will be looking for jobs in the urban sectors. This will include 18 million school leavers, 17 million new rural migrants with urban residency rights, 5 million currently unemployed, and 14 million made redundant by the SOEs. Of these, only 36 million will be absorbed in urban jobs, while 18 million will be remain unemployed. According to these forecasts, by 2000 labor surplus in rural areas will total 137 million (p. 400).

50. State Environmental Protection Administration of China, *Report on the State of the Environment in China 2000* (http://www.wri.org/wri/wr98–99.index.html).

51. World Resource Institute, 'China's Health and Environment: Air Pollution and Health Effects,' *1998–99 World Resources: A Guide to the Global Environment* (New York: Oxford University Press, 1998) p. 118. (http://www.igc.apc.org/wri/wr-98–99/prc2air.html).

52. Ibid., pp. 118–24.

53. Nicholas Lardy, 'When Will China's Financial System Meet China's Needs?,' Center for Research on Economic Development and Policy Reform in China, Working Paper no. 54, April 2000 (Stanford: Stanford University, 2000) pp. 15–16 (http://www.brook.edu/views/papers/lardy/19991118.html).

54. CASS, in its estimation of Comprehensive National Power (CNP) assumes a rate of growth of GDP at 5.8 per cent for China, 2.7 per cent for the United States, and 3.2 per cent for Japan for the period 2000 to 2020. See Michael Pillsbury, *China Debates the Future Security Environment* (Washington, DC: National Defense University, 2000), Table 9, p. 130.

55. Dwight H. Perkins, 'Future Economic and Social Development Scenarios for the Twenty-first Century,' in OECD, *China in the 21st Century: Long-term Global Implications* (Paris: OECD, 1996) pp. 30–5.

56. Standard & Poor DRI *Country Outlook*, vol. I. third quarter, 2000. See also World Bank, *East Asia, Recovery and Beyond* (Washington, DC: IBRD, 2000), p. 146 and Vincent Cable, 'The Outlook for Labor-Intensive Manufacturing in China' in OECD (1996), op. cit., pp. 48–50. Cable also suggests a high growth rate of 8–10 per cent and a low rate of 6 per cent.

57. Dick Nanto and Radha Sinha, 'China: A Major Economic Power?' *Post Communist Economics*, Vol. 13, no. 3, September 2001. An earlier version of this paper was published as a CRS Report for Congress, Dick Nanto and Radha Sinha, *China's Emergence as a Major Economic Power: Implications for U. S. Interests*, CRS, Library of Congress, 20 November 2000.

58. UN population projections for 2025 are 1.48 billion (medium projection) for China, 314 million for the United States, and 115 million for Japan. See United Nations, Population Division, *Long-term Population Projection Based on 1998 Revision*, Table 2, p. 6.

59. This is broadly consistent with the expectations of the Beijing leadership, which hopes that China will become a 'medium sized' great power by 2050. See US Secretary of Defense, *Annual Report on the Military Power of the People's Republic of China, FY2000*. The Report points out that, 'If the present trends continue, Beijing believes that it will achieve the status of a "medium sized" great power by 2050 at a minimum' (http://www.defenselink.mil/news/Jun2000/china06222000.html) Chinese scholars have recently developed the concept of CNP, which incorporates unconventional economic variables. It includes gross domestic product and foreign trade, natural resources, social development, science and technology, military affairs, and government and foreign affairs capabilities. For a detailed description in English see Michael Pillsbury, *China Debates the Future Security Environment*, (Washington, DC: National Defense University Press, 2000) ch. 5, pp. 203–58.

60. The *gross Domestic Product* GDP in PPP terms allows for price differentials between two or more countries and gives a broad indication of the overall size of the domestic market and the average levels of living. The measurement of PPP is anything but precise. For instance, estimates by Nicholas Lardy put China's per capita PPP at only around $1000 to $1200 as compared with the $3220 above. See Cable (1996), op. cit., p. 44. See also, Nicholas Lardy, *China in the World Economy* (Washington, DC: Institute of International Economics, 1994). Differences in estimates arise because of the arbitrariness in selecting domestic prices of non-traded goods. Also, certain data regarding agricultural products, particularly for self-consumption, are not very reliable in any developing country. PPP measures also do not operate well for GDP as a whole because it contains numerous non-traded items, which are not comparable among countries.

61. Justin Yifu Lin, Jikun Huang, and Scott Rozelle, 'China's Food Economy: Past Performance and Future Trends,' in OECD (1996), op. cit., pp. 84–6.

62. The range suggested by the World Bank for 2020 is 28 to 89 million tons. The US Department of Agriculture put the import requirement for 2006 at 20 million tons. See World Bank, *China 2020: Development Challenge in the New Century* (Washington, DC: IBRD, 1997) Table 5.3, p. 68.

63. Lin *et al* (OECD, 1996), op. cit., p. 85.

64. See Remy Jurenas, *Exempting Food and Agriculture Products from U.S. Economic Sanctions: Current Issues and Proposals*, CRS Issue Brief, No. IB 10061, updated 16 September 2002, CRS, Library of Congress, Washington, DC, p. CRS-1.

65. US Department of Energy, Energy Information Administration, *China*, April 2000 ([http://www.eia.doe.gov). See also Robert Priddle, OECD (1996), op. cit., p. 118.

66. Energy Information Administration, *China Country Analysis Brief*, June 2002 (www.eia.doe.gov/emeu/cabs/china.html).

67. Sergei Troush, 'China's Changing Oil Strategy and Its Foreign Policy Implications,' Center for Northeast Asian Policy Studies, Working Paper (Washington, DC, The Brookings Institute, 1999) pp. 2–4 (http://www.brookings.edu/dybdocroot/fp/cnaps/papers/1999_troush.html). Another estimate suggests that China's oil import levels would be between 2 and 4 million barrels a day over the next ten years. This will roughly represent 17 to 23 per cent of Asian oil demand and 5 to 7 per cent of the world demand for oil. See Kenneth B. Madoc III and Ronald Soligo, 'Factors Shaping Asian Energy Markets: The Composition and Growth of Energy

Demand in China,' a study produced jointly by the Center for International Political Economy and the James A. Baker III Institute for Public Policy, Rice University (http://www.bakerinstitute.org/).
68. Troush (1999), op. cit., pp. 3, 6.
69. Energy Information Administration (2002), op. cit.
70. Senator Frank Church quoted in Prados (1986), op. cit. p. 337.

6 Human Rights – a Tool of Diplomacy

1. US Mohan Rao (ed.), *Message of Mahatma Gandhi*, quoted in Radha Sinha, *Food and Poverty: The Political Economy of Confrontation* (London: Croom Helm: 1976) p. 81.
2. Geoffrey Robertson, *Crimes Against Humanity: The Struggle For Global Justice* (London: Allen Lane, The Penguin Press, 1999) p. 23.
3. Ibid. p. 21.
4. Ibid. pp. 23–4.
5. Ibid. p. 26.
6. Ibid. pp. 29–30.
7. Ibid. pp. 145–6.
8. Ibid. p. 148.
9. Eric Foner, *The Story of American Freedom* (New York: W.W. Norton 1998) p. 236.
10. Ibid. p. 262.
11. William Theodore de Bary, *The Trouble with Confucianism* (Cambridge, Mass.: Harvard University Press, 1991) Vol. 1, p. 87.
12. Mark Elvin, *The Pattern of the Chinese Past* (London: Eyre Methuen, 1973) p. 114.
13. Ramon H. Myers, *The Chinese Peasant Economy: Agricultural Development in Hopei and Shantung, 1890–1949* (Cambridge, Mass.: Harvard University Press, 1970) pp. 225–40.
14. Walter H. Mallory, *China: Land of Famine* (New York: American Geographical Society, 1926). p. 1.
15. G. Cressey, *Asia's Lands and People*, quoted in Y. Gluckstein, *Mao's China: Economic and Political Survey* (London: George Allen & Unwin, 1957) p. 118.
16. John Lossing Buck, *Land Utilization in China* (New York: Paragon Book Reprint Corp., 1964) p. 125.
17. Myers (1970), op. cit., p. 294.
18. The women in the upper classes had a considerable influence on the way children were raised and on matters concerning family affairs. See Ruth Sidel., *Women and Child Care in China* (London: Sheldon Press, 1972) pp. 8–12.
19. Buck (1968), op. cit., p. 375.
20. Ibid., pp. 386–93, 407 (calculation based on table 3).
21. Gluckstein (1957), op. cit., p. 96.
22. Several leading Western scholars like (Sir) Arthur Lewis and Ragnar Nurkse advocated the use of surplus labor as a source of capital formation in labor-surplus developing countries. See for instance, W. Arthur Lewis, 'Economic Development with Unlimited Supply of Labour', *Manchester School*, May 1954 and Ragnar Nurkse, *Problems of Capital Formation in Underdeveloped Countries* (Oxford: Basil Blackwell, 1953).
23. Roderick MacFarquhar, *The Origins of the Cultural Revolution: 2: The Great Leap Forward* 1958–1960 (New York: Columbia University Press,1983) p. 220.
24. Maurice Meisner, *The Deng Xiaoping Era: An Inquiry into the Fate of Chinese Socialism 1978–1994* (New York: Hill and Wang, 1996) p. 48.

25. John King Fairbank, *The Great Chinese Revolution: 1800–1985* (London: Chatto & Windus, 1987) p. 308.
26. Ibid. pp. 308–9.
27. Gluckstein, op. cit., p. 175.
28. Ibid., p. 176.
29. Ssu-yü Teng, *New Lights on the History of the Taiping Rebellion* (Cambridge: Mass.: Harvard University Press, 1950) p. 123.
30. G. S. Kara-murza. *The Taiping* (in Russian) quoted in Gluckstein (1957), op. cit., p. 177.
31. Fairbank (1986), op. cit., pp. 317–18.
32. Ibid., p. 320.
33. Gilbert Khoo and Dorothy Lo, *Asian Transformation: A History of South-East, South and East Asia* (Singapore: Heinemann Educational Books Asia, 1992) p. 847.
34. Michael W. Bell, Hoe Ee Khor, and Kalpana Kochhar, 'China at the Threshold of a Market Economy,' Occasional Paper 107 (Washington, DC: International Monetary Fund, September 1993) p. 6.
35. Frederic M. Surls and Francis C. Tuan, 'China's Agriculture in the Eighties' in Joint Economic Committee, Congress of the United States, *China Under the Four Modernizations*, Part 1, (Washington: US Government Printing Office, 1982) p. 421.
36. Meisner (1996), op. cit., p. 194.
37. Deng Xiaoping was first condemned as a 'capitalist roader' during the GPCR and thrown out of office, he was rehabilitated in 1973 as a result of Mao's, or even more so Zhou's, intervention. Deng was once again removed from office in 1976 by the so-called 'Gang of Four' (Mao's wife Jiang Qing and three of her compatriots). He outmaneuvered them and came to become the 'paramount leader' in 1978.
38. Surls and Tuan (1982), op. cit., p. 425.
39. Ibid., p. 427.
40. Michael W. Bell, Hoe Ee Khor and Kalpana Kochhar (1993), op. cit., p. 27.
41. Michel Chossudovsky, *Towards Capitalist Restoration?: Chinese Socialism after Mao* (London: Macmillan – now Palgrave Macmillan, 1986) p. 45. Meisner (1996) mentions the 98 per cent of peasant households covered by the new system by 1983. (pp. 228–29).
42. Ibid., (1996), op. cit., pp. 227–30. Chossudovsky (1986) mentions that most of the new small machinery and much of the large machinery had fallen into the hands of the individual households or producer's cooperatives (pp. 50–1).
43. Maisner (1996), op. cit., p. 231. Legally, land belongs to the state; it is only the right to use land, which can be transferred. This is consistent with the practice in pre-communist China.
44. Bruce L. Reynolds, 'Reform in Chinese Industrial Management: An Empirical Report' in Joint Economic Committee, Congress of the United States, *China Under The Four Modernizations*, Part 1 (Washington: US Government Printing Office, 1982) pp. 126–8.
45. Andrew Watson, 'Industrial Management – Experiments in Mass Participation' in Bill Brugger (ed.), *China: The Impact of the Cultural Revolution* (London: Croom Helm, 1978) p. 181.
46. Michael W. Bell, Hoe Ee Khor and Kalpana Kochhar (1993), op. cit., pp. 58–9.
47. World Bank, *The World Development Report, 1997: The State in a Changing World* (Washington, DC: Oxford University Press, 1997) Tables 11, 13, 15 and 17.

48. In the case of India the corresponding rate was 28 per cent, and for Brazil 38 per cent. World Bank (1997), op. cit., Table 17.

49. World Bank, *China: Strategies for Reducing Poverty* (Washington, DC: World Bank, 1992) quoted in Michael W. Bell, Hoe Ee Khor, and Kalpana Kochhar (1993), op. cit., p. 60. *The World Development Report, 1997*, however, mentions an estimated poverty incidence of 29 per cent between 1981–95 these estimates are based on a person's living on less than $1 a day on the PPP basis. (p. 214, Table 1).

50. UNDP, *The Human Development Report, 1997* (New York: Oxford University Press, 1998) p. 49.

51. World Bank (1997), op. cit., pp. 222–3, Table 5. The corresponding figures for the lowest 20 per cent for India is 8.5 per cent, and for the highest 20 per cent 42.6; and in Brazil, the lowest 20 per cent receive only 2.1 per cent, while the highest 20 per cent 67.5.

52. Chossudovsky (1986), op. cit., pp. 15–16.

53. Meisner (1996), op. cit., pp. 94–8.

54. Ibid., pp. 123–4. These freedoms were included in the constitution on the insistence of Mao in 1975.

55. This student movement was organized on 4 May 1919 against the decision of the Versailles peace conference, which had allowed Japan to retain Shantung. Three thousand Beijing (then Peking) students from thirteen institutions demonstrated in front of the Gate of Heavenly Peace (Tiananmen). The resonance of this demonstration was felt over the entire country. The merchants closed their shops; workers went on strike. The Peking warlords were forced by public pressure to release 1150 students they had arrested. The Chinese see this incident as the triumph of Chinese nationalism. See Fairbank, (1986), op. cit., pp. 182–3.

56. Information Office of the State Council, People's Republic of China, *Progress in China's Human Rights Cause in 2000*, 27 February 2001, Section VII (www.chinadaily.com.cn/highlights/paper).

57. Information Office of the State Council, P.R. China, *White Paper – Progress in China's Human Rights Conditions in 1998*, 13 April 1999, Section III. Similar information was given also in the White Paper on *Progress in China's Human Rights Cause in 2000*, 9 April 2001, Sec. III (Beijing: Information Office of the State Council of the PRC, 2001).

58. Information Office of the State Council, *White Paper – Progress in China's Human Rights Cause in 1996* (Beijing: Information Office of the State Council, 1997) [http://www.china.embassy.org/eng/c.2864.htm].

59. US Department of State, *Country Reports on Human Rights Practices for 1998*, Vol. I, (Washington, DC: Government Printing Office, 1999) p. 860.

60. Information Office of the State Council (1997), op. cit.

61. US Department of State, *Country Reports on Human Rights Practices for 2000*, Vol. 1 (Washington, DC: Government Printing Office, 2001) p. 738.

62. Amnesty International, *Report, 2001* (New York: Amnesty International, 2001) p. 72.

63. Ibid.

64. Xinhua News Agency, Beijing 20 March 1997. See also Amnesty International, *The Death Penalty in China: Breaking Records, Breaking Rules*, pp. 1–2, AI Index ASA 17/038/1997, pp. 5–10.

65. US Department of State, *Country Report for 2000*, p. 740.

66. AI, *Report 2001*, p. 72.

67. See, for example, the highly publicized executions of two high CCP officials, Cheng Kejie, former vice-chairman of the Standing Committee of the National

People's Congress and Hu Changqing, former governor of Jiangxi province and former deputy director of Religious Affairs Bureau. Both were convicted of taking bribes and the executions were performed as lessons to other officials. HRW, *Human Rights Watch World Report 2001* (New York: HRW 2000), p. 185.

68. AI, *Report, 2001* p. 71.
69. TCHRD, *Annual Report, 2000: Enforcing Loyalty*, (Dharamsala: TCHRD, 2001) p. 14.
70. US Department of State, *Country Reports on Human Rights Practices for 2001*, Vol. I (Washington: Government Printing Office, 2002) p. 849.
71. US Department of State, *Country Reports for 2000*, op. cit. p. 741.
72. Department of State, *Country Report on Human Rights Practices for 1999*, Vol. 1 (Washington: Government Printing Office, 2000) pp. 1054–5.
73. Ibid., p. 1036.
74. John Gittings, 'Growing sex imbalance shocks China,' *Guardian*, 13 May 2002.
75. US Department of State, Country Reports for 1999, op.cit., pp. 1055–6.
76. John Gittings, 'China moves away from one China policy,' *Guardian*, 27 July 2002.
77. TCHRD, *Annual Report, 2000*, op. cit, p. 46. See also TCHRD, *Report of Racial Discrimination in Tibet*, 2000, 'Discrimination in Healthcare: Forced Sterilization' (Dharamsala: TCHRD, 2000) pp. 37–44. However, a recent study by a team of experts from the United States Case Western Reserve University, Cleveland, Ohio, point out that their survey did not find evidence of forced abortions. See John Gittings, 'Claims of forced abortion in Tibet is untrue,' *Guardian*, 25 February 2002. See also Melvyne Goldstein, Ben Jiao (Benjor), Cynthis M. Beall and Phuntsog Tsering, 'Fertility and Family Planning in Rural Tibet,' *The China Journal*, No. 47.
78. TCHRD, *Annual report, 2000*, op. cit., pp. 44–52.
79. Ibid., p. 57.
80. Department of State, *Country Report for 1999*, op. cit., p. 1071.
81. International Committee of Lawyers for Tibet, *A Generation in Peril: The Lives of Tibetan Children Under Chinese Rule* (Berkeley: International Committee of Lawyers for Tibet, 2001) p. 2.
82. For instance in May 2000, China Finance Information Network was shut for publishing a report on official corruption. In Shandong province New Cultural Forum web site was closed for publishing pro-democracy activities. In January 2000, the Chinese Cultural renaissance Movement's publication *Bulletin* was suspended after its first issue and four members were taken into custody. In April, 2000, the publishers of the *China Business* and *Jingping Consumer's Guide* were removed. In July editors of about a dozen publishing houses were removed, demoted or transferred. See HRW, *Annual Report, 2001*, pp. 183–4.
83. US Department of State, *Country Reports for 2001*, op. cit. p. 861.
84. HRW, *Report 2001*, p. 183.
85. Amnesty International, *Report 2001*, p. 70.
86. Ibid.
87. US Department of State, *Country Report for 2001*, pp. 884–5, There is also some evidence that children are made to work under very difficult conditions even in urban areas. John Gittings mentions the case of teenagers working in garment factories in the garment district of Wuhan, one of China's biggest industrial cities, where the children are made to work round the clock under very unhygienic conditions. See John Gittings, 'China's children labour round the clock,' *Guardian*, 26 September 2001.

88. US State Department, *Country Reports for 1998*, op. cit., p. 839.
89. Information Office of the State Council of the People's Republic of China, *Human Rights Record of the United States in 2001* reproduced in *People's Daily*, 12 March 2002.
90. The Chinese report, *Human Rights Record of the United States in 2001* unjustifiably accuses the United States government for 'turning a blind eye to its own human rights-related problems' (ibid.). The Chinese authorities must appreciate the fact that in the United States there are many safeguard mechanisms open to those who are subjected to human rights abuses. There are many instances when the government at various levels have paid significant amounts of compensation to those who have suffered.
91. Department of State, *Initial Report of the United States of America to the UN Committee Against Torture*, Submitted by the United States of America to the Committee Against Torture, October 15, 1999 (http://www.state.gov/www/global/human_rights/torture_intro.html).
92. Ibid.
93. Amnesty International, *Annual Report 2001* (New York: Amnesty International Publications, 2001) p. 258.
94. Human Rights Watch (HRW), *World Report, 2001*, United States (New York: Human Rights Watch, 2001) p. 430.
95. AI, *Annual Report, 2001*, p. 260.
96. US Department of State, *Initial Report of the United States of America to the UN Committee Against Torture*, op. cit., Annex III.
97. *United States of America: Rights for All* (henceforth *Rights for All*) (NY: AI USA, 1998), p. 73.
98. Ibid.
99. Ibid. p. 260.
100. Ibid., p. 64. See also AI, *Broken Bodies, Shattered Minds: Torture and Ill-Treatment of Women* (New York: Amnesty International Publications, 2001) p. 43. See also AI annual reports.
101. AI. *Rights for All*, pp. 79–80.
102. AI, *Hidden Scandal, Secret Shame, Torture and Ill-Treatment of Children* (New York: Amnesty International Publications, 2000) p. 76.
103. AI, *Report 2001*, p. 259.
104. AI, *Rights for All*, p. 78.
105. Paul Wright, 'Profiteering from Punishment,' *Prison Labor News*, 1 March 1997.
106. Reese Erlich, 'Prison Labor: Workin' for the Man' in *Covert Action Quarterly*, no. 54, Fall, 1995 (http://www.prop1.org/legal/prisons/labor.html).
107. Ibid.
108. Dan Pens, 'Out-Celling the Competition', *North Coast Xpress*, 1 May 1996.
109. AI, *Rights for All*, p. 102.
110. US Department of State, *Initial Report of the United States of America to the UN Committee Against Torture*, op. cit., Annex III.
111. Human Rights Watch, *Report 2001*, p. 431.
112. US Department of State, *The Convention on the Elimination of All Forms of Racial Discrimination: Initial Report of the United States to the United Nations Committee on the Elimination of Racial Discrimination*, September 2000, p. 5 (http://www.state.gov/www/global/human_rights/cerd_report/cerd_report.pdf).
113. AI, *Rights for All*, pp. 87, 91.
114. Ibid., p. 89.

115. Ibid., p. 93.
116. AI News Service, 'No More Excuses: The U.S.A. Must Obey International Court Decision on Prisoner's Rights', Nr. 110, 27 June 2001.
117. HRW, *Fingers to the Bone: United States Failure to Protect Child Farmworkers* (New York: Human Rights Watch, 2000) pp. 2–3, 50–1. What follows in this section on child farm workers is drawn from this report.
118. Ibid., p. 3.
119. Ibid., p. 76.
120. HRW, Annual *Report 2001*, p. 435.
121. Ibid., p. 436.
122. Ibid., p. 436. See also HRW, *Unfair Advantage: Workers' Freedom of Association in the United States Under International Human Rights Standards* (New York: Human Rights Watch, 2000) p. 5.
123. The Sentencing Project (HRW), *Losing the Vote: The Impact of Felony Disenfranchisement Laws in the United States* (Washington, DC: Human Rights Watch, 1998) (http://www.hrw.org/reports98/vote/).
124. Randall Kennedy, *Race, Crime and the Law* (New York: Pantheon Books, 1997) p. 46.
125. Ibid., pp. 45–6.
126. Ibid., p. 48.
127. Ibid., p. 43.
128. Lerone Bennett, Jr., *Before the Mayflower: A History of Black America* (New York, Penguin, 1993) p. 262.
129. Ibid., pp. 497 and 503.
130. Quoted in 'Justice O'Connor on Executions,' *New York Times*, 5 July 2001.
131. Department of State, *Country Reports on Human Rights Practices for 1998–Volume II* (Washington: Government Printing Office, 1999) p. 1886.
132. See State Department, *Country Reports for 2000*, pp. 2212–63; State Department, *Country Reports for 2001*, pp. 2408–58.
133. See for instance, Yanshi, Ren, 'Human Rights Records in the United States' Beijing, 1 March 1999 [http://mprofaca.cronet.com/hr_in_usa.html].
134. Amnesty International, AI-Index: AMR 51/140/2002 dated 24 August 2002.
135. See for instance, Mark Steel, 'The Secret Plans of the World's Most Dangerous Rogue State,' Comments, 19 July 2001. American left-wing scholars have been using this term for some time. See Edward S. Herman, 'Global Rogue State', *Z Magazine*, February 1998. See also Noam Chomsky 'U.S. Policy: Rogue States,' *Z Magazine*, (*http://www.zmag.org/ZNET.html*). See also William Blum, *Rogue State: A Guide to the World's Only Superpower* (Monroe, ME: Common Courage Press, 2000).
136. *New York Times*, 'Dancing with Dictators' (Editorial), 1 September 2002.

7   China as a Security Threat

1. Quoted in Craig R. Whitney, 'With a "Don't Be Vexed" Air, Chirac Assesses US,' *New York Times* 17 December 1999.
2. Information Office of the State Council of People's Republic of China, *China's National Defense in 2000*, Section III (Beijing: Information Office of the State Council, 2000) (http://www.chinaguide.org/e-white/2000/index.html).
3. Department of Defense, *Annual Report on the Military Power of the People's Republic of China*, p. 38. (henceforth *Defense Report 2002*) (*http://www.defenselink.mil*) Much of the information in this section is based on this report unless otherwise stated.

4. Michel Oksenberg, Michael D. Swaine and Daniel C. Lynch, *The Chinese Future*, Pacific Council on International Policy Relations (Los Angeles, Rand Center for Asia Pacific Policy) p. 22 (*http://www.pacificcouncil.org/pdfs/china_today_book.pdf*).

5. Bates Gill, 'Chinese Defense Procurement Spending: Determining Intentions and Capabilities' in James R. Lilley and David Shambaugh (eds), *China's Military Faces the Future* (Armonk, NY: M. E. Sharpe, 1999) p. 197.

6. The Gaither report was not published but its conclusions became known. The Rockefeller report, published as *International Security – The Military aspect: Report of Panel II of the Special Studies Project* (New York: Doubleday, 1958) highlighted the weaknesses of the US armed forces to fight an all-out or a limited nuclear war. See G. Barraclough, *Survey of International Affairs, 1956–1958* (London: Oxford University Press: 1962) p. 354.

7. Some of the main disputes include the international boundary with India, with which it has a common border of over 3000 miles. Much of the border dispute with Russia was settled in 1997, but two small sections are yet to be settled. Two other land boundary disputes yet to be settled are with Tajikistan and North Korea. China has several disputes with neighboring countries in the East and the South China Sea. It has disputes over the Spratly Islands with Malaysia, Philippines, Taiwan, Vietnam, and possibly Brunei. There is also a maritime boundary dispute with Vietnam in the Gulf of Tonkin. The Paracel Islands currently occupied by China are also claimed by Vietnam and Taiwan. Senkaku-shoto (Senkaku Islands/Diaoyu Tai), currently under Japanese control, is claimed both by China and Taiwan. CIA, *World Factbook* (Washington, DC: Government Printing Office, 2000) p. 105.

8. US Department of Defense, *Annual Report on the Military Power of the People's Republic of China* (henceforth *Defense Report, 2000*) much of the information in this section comes from this report (*http://www.defenselink.mil/news/Jun2000/china06222000.html*).

9. Michael Pillsbury, *China Debates the Future Security Environment* (Washington, DC: National Defense University Press, 2000) p. 314.

10. *Defense Report 2002*, op. cit., p. 39.

11. *Defense Report 2000*, op. cit.

12. Ibid.

13. Chinese scholars readily acknowledge this weakness. For instance, Gao Heng, a research fellow at the Institute of World Economics and Politics, Academy of Social Sciences, Beijing, points out that 'China's high-tech military equipment is still in the embryonic stage and will not support military forces.' See Gao Heng, 'Future Military Trends,' in Michael Pillsbury (ed.), *Chinese Views of Future Warfare* (Washington, DC: National Defense University Press, 1998) p. 94.

14. Paul H. B. Godwin, 'The PLA Faces the Twenty-First Century: Reflections on Technology, Doctrine, Strategy, and Operations' in James R. Lilley and David Shambaugh (eds) (1999), op. cit., p. 42.

15. John Frankenstein, 'China's Defense Industries: A New Course' in James C. Mulvenon and Richard H. Yang (eds), *The People's Liberation Army in the Information Age* (Santa Monica, CA: Rand, National Security Research Division, Project Air Force, 1999) p. 201. See also Andrew N. D. Yang and Col. Milton WenChung Liao (ret.), 'PLA Rapid Reaction Forces: Concept, Training, and Preliminary Assessment,' pp. 48–57 in the same volume.

16. James Mulvenon, 'The PLA And Information Warfare,' in ibid. p. 185.

17. *Defense Report 2002*, op. cit., p. 16.

18. Ibid., pp. 16–17.
19. Ibid., p. 51.
20. Ibid., p. 51.
21. Ibid., p. 53.
22. Andrew J. Nathan, and Robert S. Ross, *The Great Wall and the Empty Fortress: China's Search for Security* (New York: W. W. Norton, 1997) p. 223.
23. Frank W. Moore, 'China's Military Capabilities' (Cambridge, MA: Institute for Defense and Disarmament Studies, June 2000) (*http://www.comw.org/cmp/fulltext/iddschina.html*). See also Michael D. Swaine, *Taiwan's National Security, Defense Policy, and Weapons Procurement Process* (Santa Monica, CA: Rand, National Defense Research Institute, 1999) p. 52.
24. Douglas T. Stuart, and William T. Tow, *A US Strategy for the Asia-Pacific*, Adelphi Paper, No. 299 (London: Oxford University Press, 1995) p. 37.
25. Moore (2000), op. cit.
26. Bates Gill, and Michael O'Hanlon, 'China's Hollow Military,' *The National Interest*, No. 56, Summer 1999.
27. Information Office of the State Council of the People's Republic of China, *China's National Defense* (Beijing: Information Office of the State Council, 1998) (*www.fas.org/nuke/guide/china/doctrine/cnd 9807/index.html*).
28. Wensi Xia, 'Zhu Rongji Opposed to Invading Taiwan,' in *Hong Kong Kai Fang* (Chinese), 3 September 1999, pp. 11–14.
29. *Defense Report 2000*, op. cit.
30. Richard L. Garwin, 'A Defense that Will Not Defend,' *The Washington Quarterly*, Vol. 23, no. 3, Summer 2000, p. 110.
31. Ibid., p. 111.
32. Andrew M. Sessler, John M. Cornwall, Bob Dietz, Steve Fetter, Sherman Frankel, Richard L. Garwin, Kurt Gottfried, Lisbeth Gronlund, George N. Lewis, Theodore A. Postol, and David C. Wright, *Countermeasures: A Technical Evaluation of the Operational Effectiveness of the Planned US National Missile Defense System* (henceforth UCS report), (Cambridge, MA: Union of Concerned Scientists, and MIT Security Studies Program 2000).
33. Ibid., p. 98.
34. GAO, *National Missile Defense; Even with Increased Funding Technical and Schedule Risks Are High*, GAO/NSIAD 98–153 (Washington, DC: Government Accounting Office, 1998) p. 19.
35. GAO, *Missile Defense: Status of the National Defense Program*, GAO/NSIAD 00–131 (Washington, DC: Government Accounting Office, 2000) p. 3.
36. Ibid., p. 4.
37. CBO, *Budgetary and Technical Implications of the Administration's Plan for National Missile Defense* (Washington, DC: Congressional Budget Office, 2000) Table 3, pp. 13–14. The CBO estimates for capability I is less than those given by the GAO for several reasons: CBO has assumed a deployment period ending in 2015, rather than 2026, which is the end of system's projected deployment. The CBO did not include the procurement costs and operation and support costs for ten years between 2016 and 2026. It also left out prior year costs. See GAO (2000), op. cit., p. 15.
38. Department of State. Office of the Spokesman, 'Text of Diplomatic Notes Sent to Russia, Belarus, Kazakhstan, and the Ukraine' 13 December 2001 (http://www.fas.org/nuke/control/abmt/news/diplomatic121401.htm).
39. Ralph Dannheisser, 'Senior Senate Democrats Criticize Bush ABM Treaty Withdrawal,' *Washington File*, 13 December 2001 (http://www.fas.org/nuke/control/abmt/news/dems121301.htm).

40. UCS Report (2000), op. cit., p. 112. See also Steven A. Hildreth and Amy F. Woolf, *Missile Defense: The Current Debate*, updated 18 October 2002, CRS Report for Congress, Library of Congress, Washington, DC, pp. 31–2.
41. Bruce G. Blair, Thomas B. Cochran, Tom Z. Collina, Jonathan Dean, Steve Fetter, Richard L. Garwin, Kurt Gottfried, Lisbeth Gronlund, Henry Kelly, Matthew G. McKinzie, Robert S. Norris, Adam Segal, Robert Sherman, Frank N. von Hippel, David Wright and Stephen Young, *Toward True Security: A US Nuclear Posture for the Next Decade* (Cambridge, Mass.: Union of Concerned Scientists, 2001) p. 26.
42. Mike Moore, 'Unintended Consequences,' *Bulletin of the Atomic Scientists*, Vol. 56, No. 1, Jan./Feb. 2000, p. 64.
43. Ibid.
44. Eric Schmidt, 'Bush Ordering Missile Shield at Sites in West,' *New York Times*, 18 December 2002.
45. *New York Times* (Editorial), 'The Rush to Build Missile Defense' 18 December 2002.
46. Ben Macintyre, 'Pentagon puts general in charge of space,' *The Times*, 9 May 2001.
47. Steve Boggan, 'Space – the Final Frontier in a New and Terrifying Arms Race,' *Independent*, 8 August 2001.
48. Peter Beaumont, 'Dr. Strangelove rides again,' *Observer*, 15 July 2001. See also Mark Steel, 'The secret plan of the world's most dangerous rogue state,' *Independent*, 19 July 2001.
49. Noam Chomsky, 'Hegemony or Survival,' 3 and 4 July 2001 (http://www.medialens.org/ articles/nc_hegemony_2.html).
50. Ji Guoxing, *SLOC Security in the Asia Pacific*, Occasional Paper of Asia-Pacific (Honolulu: Asia-Pacific Center For Security Studies, 2000) (http://www.apcss.org/Paper_SLOC_Occasional.html).
51. Richard Halloran, 'Now an Effort to Stop the Rot in U.S.–Japan Relations,' *International Herald Tribune*, 3 May 1999.
52. Russ Swinnerton, 'A Description of Regional Shipping Routes: Navigational and Operational Considerations,' *Maritime Studies*, No. 87, Mar./Apr. 1996, p. 16.
53. Ibid., p. 17.
54. Ibid.
55. Laura Jones-Kelley, 'Thai Project Brings Two Worlds to Port,' *Geofax* [Document no. 40180] (Conway Data, Inc., December 1990) p. 1.
56. United States Energy Information Administration, *Country Analysis Briefs: South China Sea Region*, March 2002, p. 5 (*http://www.eia.gov/emeu/cabs/schina.html*).
57. Ibid., pp. 5–6.
58. Scott Snyder, *The South China Sea Dispute: Prospects for Preventive Diplomacy*, Special Report (Washington, DC: US Institute of Peace, 1996) p. 4.
59. Sam Bateman, 'East Asia's Marine Resources and Regional Security,' *Maritime Studies*, No. 89, July/Aug., 1996, p. 19.
60. Quoted in the US Energy Information Administration (2002), op. cit., pp. 2–3.
61. Bateman (1996), op. cit., p. 14.
62. Hasjim Djalal, 'South China Sea Island Disputes' in *The Raffles Bulletin of Zoology*, Supplement No. 8, 2000, p. 12.
63. Brice M. Clagett, 'Competing Claims of Vietnam and China In The Vanguard Bank and Blue Dragon Areas of the South China Sea, Part I,' (Washington, DC: Covington & Burling 1995) (www.cov.com/publications/CLAGETT1.asp).
64. Quoted in Max Herriman, 'China's Territorial Sea Law and International Law of the Sea,' *Maritime Studies*, No. 92, Jan./Feb. 1997, p. 15.

65. Jing-dong Yuan, *Asia Pacific Security: China's Conditional Mutilateralism and Great Power Entente* (Carlisle, PA: Strategic Studies Institute, US Army War College 2000) pp. 20–1.
66. Clagett (1995), op. cit., Part I.
67. Brice M. Clagett, 'Competing Claims of Vietnam and China in the Vanguard Bank and Blue Dragon Areas of the South China Sea', Part II (Washington, DC: Covington & Burling 1995) (http://www.cov.com/publications/clagett2.asp).
68. Ibid.
69. Ibid., note 124.
70. Clagett (1995), op. cit, Part II.
71. For the details of the actions taken see Djalal (2000), op. cit., pp. 13–15.
72. Quoted in Herriman (1997), op. cit., p. 15.
73. Ibid., pp. 16–18.
74. John McBeth, 'Indonesia: Water strife: Washington opposes proposed sea-lane rules,' *Far Eastern Review*, 29 February 1996, p. 30.
75. Ji Guoxing, *SLOC Security in the Asia Pacific*, Occasional Paper, Asia Pacific Center for Security Studies, Honolulu, February 2000 (http://www.apcss.org/Publications/Paper_SLOC_Occasional.html).
76. IMO, 'Dramatic increase in Piracy and Armed Robbery,' Newsroom, 8 June 2001.
77. Jingxuan Lu, Hock Lim, Soo Chin Liew, Mingquan Bao and Leong Keong Kwoh, 'Oil pollution statistics in Southeast Asian waters compiled from ERS SAR Imagery,' *Earth Observation Quarterly*, No. 61, Feb. 1999, pp. 13, 16.
78. Daniel L. Byman and Roger Cliff, *China's Arms Sales: Motivations and Implications* (Santa Monica, CA: RAND Project Air Force, 1999) p. 7.
79. Ibid., pp. 8–10.
80. Shirley Kan, *Chinese Proliferation of Weapons of Mass Destruction: Current Policy Issues*, CRS Issue Brief, updated 10 July 2000, Congress Research Service, Library of Congress, Washington, DC, p. CRS-6.
81. CIA, Director of Central Intelligence (DCI), *Unclassified Report to the Congress on the Acquisition of Technology Relating to the Weapons of Mass Destruction and Advanced Conventional Munitions, 1 January through 30 June 2000* (http://www.fas.org/irp/threat/bian_jan_2002.html).
82. Bernd W. Kubbig, 'Regional Perspective: Europe' in Scott Parrish (ed.), *International Perspective on Missile Proliferation and Defenses*, Occasional Paper 5, Special Joint Series on Missile Issues (Monterey and Southampton: Monterey Institute of International Studies 2001) p. 49.
83. Kan (2000), op. cit., p. CRS-5.
84. Ibid., CRS-5. See also Kan, Shirley A., *China's Proliferation of Weapons of Mass Destruction and Missiles: Current Policy Issues*, CRS Issue Brief, Updated 12 March 2001, CRS, Library of Congress, p. CRS-5.
85. Gerald M. Steinberg, 'China's policies on Arms Control and Proliferation in the Middle East,' *China Report*, Special issue on China and the Middle East edited by R. Kumaraswamy, 1998, Vols 3–4, pp. 381–400.
86. Ibid.
87. Shai Feldman, *Nuclear Weapons and Arms Control in the Middle East* (Cambridge, Mass.: MIT Press, 1997) pp. 63–64.
88. Mingquan Zhu, 'The Evolution of China's Nuclear Nonproliferation Policy,' *The Nonproliferation Review*, Vol. 4, no. 2, Winter 1997, p. 40.
89. Ibid., p. 42.
90. George Bunn, Sydney D. Drell, Richard L. Garwin, Thomas Graham, Jr., Daryl G. Kimball, Damien J. LaVera, Jack Mendelsohn (Ed.), Paul G. Richards, Amy Sands,

White Paper on The Comprehensive Test Ban Treaty (Washington, DC: Lawyers' Alliance for World Security, 2000) p. 12.

91. Amy Sands and Jason Pate, 'CWC Compliance Issues' in Tucker, Jonathan B. (ed.), *The Chemical Weapon's Convention: Implementation Challenges and Solutions* (Monterey, CA: Monterey Institute of International Studies, 2001) pp. 20–1.

92. Information Office of the State Council (2000), op. cit., Section VI.

93. Byman (1999), op. cit., p. 43.

94. Damien J. LaVera, 'History and Summary of the CTBT' in *White Paper on The Comprehensive Test Ban Treaty* (2000), op. cit., pp. 9–12.

95. Alexander Kelley, 'Overview of the First Four Years' in Tucker (2001), op. cit., p. 12. See also Tucker, Jonathan B., 'Challenges to the Chemical Weapons Convention' in Michael Barletta and Amy Sands (eds), *Nonproliferation Regimes at Risk*, Occasional Paper 5 (Monterey, CA: Monterey Nonproliferation Strategy Group, Monterey Institute of International Studies, 1999) pp. 14–15.

96. Amy E. Smithson, 'U.S. Implementation of the CWC', in Tucker (2001), op. cit., p. 23.

97. Ibid., pp. 24–5; also Tucker (1999), op. cit., p. 15.

98. Ibid., p. 15.

99. Smithson (2001), op. cit., p. 26.

100. Seth Ackerman, 'Withholding the News: *The Washington Post* and the UNISCOM Spying Scandal,' *Extra*, Mar./Apr. 2000 (http://www.fair.org/extra/9903/unscom.html).

101. John Isaacs, 'Rejection of Biological Weapons Convention Protocol Latest Sign of U.S. Unilateralism,' Press release 22 May 2001 by the Council for a Livable World.

102. Secretary of Defense, *The United States Security Strategy for the East Asia–Pacific Region, 1998* (Washington: Government Printing Office, 1998), p. 26.

103. Daryl G. Kimball, 'The 1999 Senate Debate Over the CTBT,' *White Paper on The Comprehensive Test ban Treaty* (2000) p. 16.

104. Tariq Rauf, *'Towards NPT 2005: An Action Plan for The "13-STEPS" Toward Nuclear Disarmament Agreed At NPT 2000*, A report prepared for the Middle Powers Initiative (Monterey, CA: Center for Nonproliferation Studies, Monterey Institute for International Studies, 2001) p. 23.

105. During 1995–98 the US supplied 1284 Surface-to-Air missiles and 87 Anti-Ship missiles to its allies. During the same period Russia supplied only 140 surface-to-Air missiles to the region. China did not supply any surface-to-air missiles, and only 120 anti-ship missiles. See Richard F. Grimmett, *Conventional Arms Transfers to Developing Nations, 1991–1998*, CRS Report for Congress (Washington, DC: CRS, Library of Congress, 1999), p. CRS-71, Table 5.

106. Michael Barletta and Amin Tarzi, 'Challenges in the Middle East to Nonproliferation Regimes' in Michael Barletta and Amy Sands (eds), *Nonproliferation at Risk* (Monterey, CA: Nonproliferation Strategy Group, Monterey Institute of International Studies, 1999) p. 15.

107. Michael Ratner, 'International Law and war Crimes' in Ramsey Clark and Others, *War Crimes: A Report on United States War Crimes Against Iraq* (Washington Maisonneuve Press, 1992) p. 45.

8 Conclusion

1. President Eisenhower's Farewell to the Nation, 17 January 1961.
2. Gunnar Myrdal, at that time the head of the European Commission for Europe, felt that the 'possible direct influence [of the American loan that the Russians had asked for] on economic reconstruction and development in the Soviet Union should not be exaggerated, but as an element in building up a spirit of friendly cooperation and giving a momentum to trade it would have been of great importance.' See Gunnar Myrdal, *An International Economy: Problems and Prospects* (New York: Harpers, 1956) p. 138.
3. Some other countries, such as India had also benefitted from American food surplus disposal programs, as well as the foreign aid programs.
4. Radha Sinha, *Japan's Options for the 1980s* (Tokyo: Charles E. Tuttled Co, 1982) p. 245. For historical fears see H. A. L. Fisher, *A History of Europe*, Vol. II (Glasgow: Fontana/Collins, 1977) p. 1030.
5. Richard M. Freeland, *The Truman Doctrine and the Origins of McCarthyism: Foreign Policy, Domestic Politics, and Internal Security, 1946–1948* (New York, New York University Press, 1985) pp. 191–2.
6. Ibid., p. 241.
7. Eric Foner, *The Story of American Freedom* (New York: W. W. Norton 1998) p. 255.
8. Beale, Howard K. quoted in Foner (1998), op. cit., p. 255.
9. Freeland (1985), op. cit., p. 221.
10. Alonzo L. Hamby, *Man of the People: A Life of Harry S. Truman* (New York: Oxford University Press, 1995) p. 429.
11. Sinha (1982), op. cit., p. 245. See also Godfrey Jansen, 'Muslims and the Modern World,' *The Economist*, 3 January 1981, p. 34.
12. David Cole, 'National Security State,' *Nation*, 17 December, 2001.
13. The *Nation*, 'Secret Arrests are an Odious Concept,' (Editorial: Special Report), 5 August 2002. (Internet version).
14. Stanley Hoffmann, 'America Alone in the World,' *American Prospect*, Vol. 13, No. 17, 23 September 2002.
15. Josheph S. Nye Jr, *The Paradox of American Power: Why the World's Only Superpower Can't Go It Alone* (Oxford: Oxford University Press, 2002) p. 8.
16. H. W. Brands, *What America Owes the World: The Struggle for the Soul of Foreign Policy* (Cambridge: Cambridge University Press, 1998), pp. vii–viii.
17. Zbigniew Brzezinski, 'Confronting Anti-American Grievances,' *New York Times* (Editorial/Op-Ed.), 1 September 2002.
18. Pope John Paul II, 'Roots of Terror Need Scrutiny,' *Washington Post*, 7 September 2002.
19. Hassan Nafaa, 'Friends and Other Enemies,' *Al Ahram Weekly Online*, 18–24, October 2001, Issue No. 556.
20. Ali A. Mazrui, 'US 'act of war' has no global standards,' *Dawn*, 1 October, 2001.
21. Maqbool Ahmad Bhatty, 'Terrorism & the World Order,' *Dawn*, 26 September 2001.
22. Jihan Alaily, 'The search for vengeance,' *Al Ahram Weekly*, Online 20–26 September 2001, Issue No. 552.
23. Gamal Nkrumah, 'Stamping on a hornet nest,' *Al Ahram Weekly*, Online 20–26 September 2001, Issue No. 552.
24. Hosni Mubarak quoted in *Washington Post*, 'More in the War of Idea' (editorial), 28 December 2001.

25. Desmond Tutu, 'Apartheid in the Holy Land,' 30 April 2002 (http:www.counter-punch.org/tutu0430.html).
26. A CBS 60 Minutes interview between Leslie Stahl, co-editor of CBS News' award-winning Sunday evening news program '60 Minutes', and U.S. Secretary of State Madeleine Albright, on 12 May 1996.
27. Dina Ezzat, 'Time for Respect,' *Al Ahram Weekly, Online* 20–26 September 2001, Issue No. 552.
28. Jon Utley quoted in Mohamed Hakk, 'Shifting Fortunes,' *Al Ahram Weekly, Online* 8–14 November 2001, Issue No. 559.
29. Helmut Schmidt, *Men and Powers: A Political Retrospective* (translated from German by Ruth Hein), (New York: Random House, 1989 pp. 279–80.
30. Nafaa (2001), op.cit.

Select Bibliography

Aldridge, A. Owen, *The Dragon and the Eagle: The Presence of China in the American Enlightenment* (Detroit: Wayne State University Press, 1993).

Ambrose, Stephen E., *Ike's Spies: Eisenhower and the Espionage Establishment*, paperback (Jackson: University Press of Mississippi, 1999).

——, *Eisenhower: Soldier and President*, paperback (New York; Simon & Schuster, 1990).

——, *Rise to Globalism: American Foreign Policy since 1938*, paperback (New York: Penguin Books, 1985).

Amnesty International, *Amnesty International Report, 2001: China* (New York: Amnesty International, 2001).

——, *Broken Bodies, Shattered Minds: Torture and Ill-Treatment of Women* (New York: Amnesty International, 2001).

——, *Hidden Scandal, Secret Shame, Torture and Ill-Treatment of Children* (New York: Amnesty International, 2000).

——, *Stopping the Torture Trade* (New York: Amnesty International, 2001).

——, *United States of America Rights for All* (New York: Amnesty International, 1998).

Andrew, Christopher, *For the President's Eyes Only: Secret Intelligence and the American Presidency from Washington to Bush*, paperback (New York: Harper Perennial, 1996).

Ball, George W., *Diplomacy for a Crowded World: An American Foreign Policy* (London: The Bodley Head, 1976).

Barber, Benjamin R., *Jihad vs. McWorld: How Globalism and Tribalism Are Reshaping the World*, paperback (New York, Ballantine Books, 1996).

Bark, Dennis L. and David R. Gress, *A History of West Germany, 1, From Shadow to Substance, 1945–1963 and 2. Democracy and Its Discontents, 1963–1988* (Oxford: Basil Blackwell, 1989).

Barnet, Richard J., *The Alliance: America–Europe–Japan, Makers of the Postwar World* (New York: Simon and Schuster, 1983).

Barnett, A. Doak, *China and the Major Powers in East Asia*, paperback (Washington, DC: The Brookings Institution, 1977).

Beasley, W. G., *Japanese Imperialism, 1894–1945* (Oxford: Clarendon Press, 1991).

Beckmann, George M., *The Modernization of China and Japan* (New York: Harper and Row and John Weatherhill, Inc., Tokyo, 1965).

Bell and Daniel, *The End of Ideology*, paperback (Cambridge, MA: Harvard University Press, 1988).

Bennett Jr, Lerone, *Before the Mayflower: A History of Black America*, paperback (New York: Penguin Books, 1993).

Bernstein, Richard and Ross H. Munro, *The Coming Conflict With China* (New York: Alfred A. Knopf, 1997).

Birnbaum, Jeffrey H., *The Money Men: The Real Story of Fund-raising's Influence on Political Power in America* (New York: Crown Publishers, 2000).

Bloom, Allan, *The Closing of the American Mind: How Higher Education Has Failed Democracy and Impoverished the Souls of Today's Students* (New York: Simon and Schuster, 1987).

Blum, William, *Killing Hope: U.S. Military and CIA Interventions Since World War II*, paperback (Monroe, Maine: Common Courage Press, 1995).

Blunden, Caroline and Mark Elvin, *Cultural Atlas of China* (New York: Facts on File, Inc., 1983).

Bowie, Robert R. and Richard H. Immerman, *Waging Peace: How Eisenhower Shaped an Enduring Cold War Strategy* (New York: Oxford Universty Press, 1998).

Brandon, William, *Indians*, paperback (Boston: Houghton Mifflin, 1987).

Brands, H. W., *What America Owes the World: The Struggle for the Soul of Foreign Policy*, paperback (Cambridge, Cambridge University Press, 1998).

Braudel, Fernand, *A History of Civilizations* (translated from the French by Richard Mayne), paperback (New York: Penguin Books, 1995).

——, *The Mediterranean and the Mediterranean World in the Age of Phillip II*, (2 Vols), paperback (Translated from the French by Siân Reynolds), (London: Fontana Collins, 1976).

Brown, Dee, *Bury My Heart at Wounded Knee: An Indian History of the American West*, paperback (New York: Henry Holt, 1991).

Brown, Michael, E. Sean., M. Lynn-Jones and Steven E. Miller (eds),. *East Asian Security*, paperback (Cambridge, Mass.: The MIT Press, 1996).

Brugger, Bill (ed.), *China: The Impact of the Cultural Revolution* (London: Croom Helm, 1978).

Brundage, W. Fitzhugh (ed.), *Under Sentence of Death: Lynching in the South*, paperback (Chapel Hill: The University of North Carolina Press, 1997).

Brzezinski, Zbigniew, *The Grand Failure: The Birth and Death of Communism in the Twentieth Century*, paperback (New York: Macmillan – now Palgrave Macmillan, 1990)

Buck, John Lossing, *Land Utilization in China* (New York: Paragon Book Reprint Corp., 1968).

Buhite, Russell D., *Nelson T. Johnson and American Policy Toward China, 1925–1941* (East Lansing: Michigan State University Press, 1968).

Bundy, McGeorge, *Danger and Survival: Choices About the Bomb in the First Fifty Years* (New York: Random House, 1988).

Burr, William (ed.), *The Kissinger Transcripts: The Top Secret Talks with Beijing and Moscow* (New York: The New Press, 1999).

Byman, Daniel L. and Roger Cliff, *China's Arms Sales: Motivations and Implications*, paperback (Santa Monica, CA: Rand, Project Air Force, 1999).

Callio, David P., *Beyond American Hegemony: The Future of the Western Alliance*, paperback (New York: Basic Books Inc., 1987).

Chace, James and Caleb Carr, *America Invulnerable: The Quest for Absolute Security from 1812 to Star Wars* (New York: Summit Books, 1988).

Chanda, Nayan, *Brother Enemy: The War after the War* (San Diego: Harcourt Brace Jovanovich, 1986).

Chang, Iris, *The Rape of Nanking: The Forgotten Holocaust of World War II* (New York: Basic Books, 1997).

Chen, Jian, *China's Road to the Korean War: The Making of the Sino-American Confrontation*, paperback (New York: Columbia University Press, 1994).

——, *Mao's China and the Cold War*, paperback (Chapel Hill: The University of North Carolina Press, 2001).

Chomsky, Noam, *Necessary Illusions: Thought Control in Democratic Societies*, paperback (Boston, MA: South End Press, 1989).

——, *Deterring Democracy* (London: Verso, 1991).

——, *The New Military Humanism: Lessons from Kosovo*, paperback (Monroe, ME: Common Courage Press, 1999).

Chossudovsky, Michel, *Towards Capitalist Restoration?: Chinese Socialism after Mao* (Houndmills: Macmillan – now Palgrave Macmillan, 1986).

Churchill, Ward, *A Little Matter of Genocide: Holocaust and Denial in the Americas 1492 to the Present*, paperback (San Francisco: City Lights Books, 1997).

Clark, Ramsey and others, *War Crimes: A Report on United States War Crimes Against Iraq*, paperback (Washington, DC Maisonneuve Press, 1992).

Cliff, Roger, *The Military Potential of China's Commercial Technology*, paperback (Santa Monica, CA: Rand, Project Air Force, 2001).

Cohen, Warren I., *The Cambridge History of American Foreign Relations, Volume IV: America in the Age of Soviet Power, 1945–1991*, paperback, (Cambridge: Cambridge University Press, 1995).

Combs, Jerald A., *American Diplomatic History: Two Centuries of Changing Interpretations*, paperback (Berkeley, University of California Press, 1986).

Conant, Charles, *The United States in the Orient* (Port Washington: Kennikat Press, 1971, 1899).

Congressional Research Service, *The U.S. Government and the Vietnam War*, (three parts), (Washington: US Government Printing Office, 1984, 1985, 1988)

Currey, Cecil B., *Victory at Any Cost: The Genius of Viet Nam's Gen. Vo Nguyen Giap* (Washington, DC: Brassey's Inc., 1997).

Davidson, Basil, *The Story of Africa* (London: Mitchell Beazley, 1984).

Deng Xiaoping, *Selected Works* (Beijing: Foreign Language Press, 1984).

Dionne, Jr, E. J., *Why Americans Hate Politics* (New York: Simon & Schuster, 1991).

Dobrynin, Anatoly, *In Confidence: Moscow's Ambassador to Six Cold War Presidents (1962–1986)*, (New York: Times Books, Random House, 1995).

Domhoff, G. William, *Who Rules America?: Power and Politics in the Year 2000*, paperback (Mountain View, California: Mayfield Publishing Co., 1998).

Drew, Elizabeth. *The Corruption of American Politics: What Went Wrong and Why* (Secaucus, N.J.: Carol Publishing Group, 1999).

Dulles, Foster Rhea, *American Foreign Policy Toward Communist China 1949–1969*, paperback (New York: Thomas Y. Crowell Co., 1972).

EAAU, *China Embraces the Market: Achievements, Constraints and Opportunities*, paperback, (Canberra: Department of Foreign Affairs and Trade 1997).

Eberhard, Wolfram, *A History of China*, paperback, (Berkeley and Los Angeles: University of California Press, 1977).

Economy, Elizabeth and Michel Oksenberg, *China Joins the World: Progress and Prospects* (eds), paperback (New York: Council on Foreign Relations Press, 1999).

Edward S. Herman and Noam Chomsky, *Manufacturing Consent: The Political Economy of the Mass Media*, paperback (New York: Pantheon Books, 1988).

Elvin, Mark, *The Pattern of the Chinese Past* (London: Eyre Methuen, 1973).

Fairbank, John King, *The Great Chinese Revolution: 1800–1985* (London: Chatto & Windus, 1987).

——, *China Perceived: Images and Policies in Chinese–American Relations*, paperback (New York: Vintage Books, 1976).

Faulkner, Harold U., *The Decline of Laissez Faire 1897–1917*, Volume. VII, *The Economic History of the United States*, paperback (Armonk, New York: M.E. Sharpe Inc., 1951).

Fay, Peter Ward, *The Opium War, 1840–1842: Barbarians in the Celestial Empire in the Early Part of the Nineteenth Century and the War by Which They Forced Her Gates Ajar*, paperback (Chapel Hill: The University of North Carolina Press, 1997).

Fisher, H. A. L., *A History of Europe* (2 vols), paperback (Glasgow: Fontana/ Collins, 1977).

Foner, Eric, *The Story of American Freedom* (New York: W.W. Norton & Co., 1998).

Freeland, Richard M., *The Truman Doctrine and the Origins of McCarthyism: Foreign Policy, Domestic Politics, and Internal Security, 1946–1948*, paperback (New York: New York University Press, 1985).

Galbraith, John Kenneth, *The Culture of Contentment* (Boston: Houghton Mifflin, 1992).

Gardner, Paul F., *Shared Hopes: Separate Fears: Fifty Years of US–Indonesian Relations*, paperback (Boulder, Co.: Westview Press, 1997).

Gilpin, Robert, *The Political Economy of International Relations*, paperback (Princeton, NJ: Princeton University Press, 1987).

Gladney, Dru C., *Muslim Chinese: Ethnic Nationalism in the People's Republic*, paperback (Cambridge, Mass.: Council on East Asian Studies, 1996).

Gluckstein, Ygaei, *Mao's China: Economic and Political Survey* (London: George Allen & Unwin, 1957).

Goldman, Merle, *Sowing the Seeds of Democracy in China* (Cambridge, Mass.: Harvard University Press, 1994).

Goncharov, Sergei N., John W. Lewis and Xue Litai, *Uncertain Partners: Stalin, Mao, and the Korean War*, paperback (Stanford: Stanford University Press, 1993).

Grasso, June M., *Truman's Two-China Policy, 1948–1950* (Armonk, NY: M.E. Sharpe, Inc. 1987).

Glick, Brian, *War at Home: Covert Action Against U.S. Activists and What We Can Do About It*, paperback (Boston, MA: South End Press, 1989).

Gunther, John, *Inside U.S.A.* (New York: Harper & Brothers, 1947).

Hamby, Alonzo L., *Man of the People: A Life of Harry S. Truman* (New York: Oxford University Press, 1995).

Harding, Harry, *A Fragile Relationship: The United States and China Since 1972*, paperback (Washington, DC: The Brookings Institution, 1992).

——, *China's Second Revolution: Reform after Mao*, paperback (Washington, DC: The Brookings Institution, 1987).

Harding, Vincent, *There Is a River: The Black Struggle for Freedom in America*, paperback (San Diego: Harcourt Brace, 1981).

Harris, Sheldon H., *Factories of Death: Japanese Biological Warfare, 1932–45, and the American Cover-up*, paperback (London: Routledge, 1997).

Herman, Edward S. and Noam, Chomsky, *Manufacturing Consent: The Political Economy of the Mass Media* (New York: Pantheon Books, 1988).

Hill, Christopher, *Reformation to Industrial Revolution: British Economy and Society 1530–1780* (London: Weidenfeld & Nicolson, 1969).

Hobsbawm, E. J., *Industry and Empire: An Economic History of Britain Since 1750* (London: Weidenfeld & Nicolson, 1968).

Hofstadter, Richard, *The Paranoid Style in American Politics* (New York: Alfred Knopf, 1965).

Hoopes, Townsend and Douglas Brinkley, *FDR and the Creation of the U. N.* (New Haven: Yale University Press, 1997).

Human Rights Watch (HRW), *Fingers to the Bone: United States Failure to Protect Child Farmworkers* (New York: HRW, 2000).

——, *World Report, 2001* (New York: HRW, 2000).

——, *Losing the Vote: The Impact of Felony Disenfranchisement Laws in the United States* (Washington, DC: HRW, 1998).

——, *Unfair Advantage: Workers' Freedom of Association in the United States Under International Human Rights Standards* (New York: Human Rights Watch, 2000).

Huntington, Samuel P., *The Clash of Civilizations and the Remaking of World Order*, paperback (New York, Simon & Schuster, 1997).

Ienaga, Saburo, *The Pacific War, 1931–1945: A Critical Perspective on Japan's Role in World War II* (New York: Pantheon Books, 1978).

International Committee of Lawyers for Tibet, *A Generation in Peril: The Lives of Tibetan Children Under Chinese Rule, Paperback* (Berkeley: International Committee of Lawyers for Tibet, 2001).

Jespersen, T. Christopher, *American Images of China: 1931–1949* (Stanford: Stanford University Press, 1996).

Kahin, Audrey R. and George McT. Kahin, *Subversion as Foreign Policy: The Secret Eisenhower and Dulles Debacle in Indonesia*, paperback (Seattle: University of Washington Press, 1997).

Karnow, Stanley, *In Our Image: America's Empire in the Philippines*, paperback (New York: Ballantine Books, 1990).

Kennan, George F., *Memoirs 1950–1963*, paperback (New York: Pantheon Books, 1972).

Kennedy, Paul, *The Rise and Fall of the Great Powers: Economic Change and Military Conflict from 1500 to 2000* (London: Unwin Hyman, 1988).

Kennedy, Randall, *Race, Crime and the Law* (New York: Pantheon Books, 1997).

Kissinger, Henry, *Years of Upheaval* (Boston: Little, Brown and Co., 1982).

Korten, David C., *When Corporations Rule the World*, paperback (West Hartford, Conn. Kumarian Press, Inc. and San Francisco, Ca.: Berrett-Koehler Publishers, 1996).

Kueh, Y. Y. (with Brian Bridges) (ed.), *The Political Economy of Sino-American Relations: A Greater China Perspective*, paperback (Hong Kong: Hong Kong University Press, 1997).

Kwitny, Jonathan, *Endless Enemies: The Making of an Unfriendly World*, paperback (New York, Penguin Books, 1987).

LaFeber, Walter, *The Cambridge History of American Foreign Relations, Vol. II: The American Search for Opportunity, 1865–1913, paperback* (Cambridge: Cambridge University Press, 1995).

Lampton, David M., *The Making of Chinese Foreign and Security Policy in the Era of Reform*, paperback (Stanford: Stanford University Press, 2001).

Lardy, N., *China in the World Economy* (Washington, DC, Institute of International Economics, 1994).

Levathes, Louise, *When China Ruled the Seas: The Treasure Fleet of the Dragon Throne 1405–1433*, paperback (New York: Oxford University Press, 1996).

Lilley, James R. and David Shambaugh (eds), *China's Military Faces the Future*, paperback (Armonk, NY: M.E. Sharpe, 1999).

Lind, Michael, *The Next American Nation: The New Nationalism and the Fourth American Revolution*, paperback (New York: Free Press Paperbacks, Simon & Schuster 1996).

Lloyd, Henry Demarest, *Wealth Against Commonwealth* (New York: Greenwood Publishing Group Inc., 1976).

MAcarthur, John R., *Second Front: Censorship and Propaganda in the Gulf War*, paperback (Berkeley: University of California Press, 1993).

MacFarquhar, Roderick, *The Origins of the Cultural Revolution* (2 Vols), paperback (New York: Columbia University Press for Royal Institute of International Affairs and the Research Institute on Communist Affairs of Columbia University, 1974, 1983).

Mahan, Alfred Thayer, *Lessons of the War with Spain* (NY: Books for Libraries Press, 1970, 1899).

——, *The Problem of Asia* (Boston: Little Brown 1900).

Mann, Golo. *The History of Germany Since 1789*, (translated from the German by Marian Jackson), paperback (Harmondsworth: Penguin Books, 1990).

Mann, James, *About Face: A History of America's Curious Relationship with China, From Nixon to Clinton* (New York: Alfred A. Knopf, 1999).

Mathews, Christopher, *Kennedy & Nixon: The Rivalry that Shaped Postwar America*, paperback, (New York: Simon & Schuster, 1996).

McClelland, J. S., *A History of Western Political Thought* (London and New York: Routledge, 1996).

McGehee, Ralph, *Deadly Deceits: My 25 Years in the CIA* (Melbourne: NY Ocean Press, 1999).

McNamara, Robert S. (with Brian VanDeMark), *In Retrospect: The Tragedy and Lessons of Vietnam*, paperback (New York; Vintage Books, Random House, 1996).

Meisner, Maurice, *The Deng Xiaoping Era: An Inquiry into the Fate of Chinese Socialism 1978–1994* (New York: Hill and Wang, 1996).

Melman, Seymour, *The Permanent War Economy: American Capitalism in Decline*, paperback (New York: Simon and Schuster, 1974).

Mercer, Derrik (ed.), *Chronicle of the 20th Century* (London: Chronicle, 1988).

Miller, Stuart Creighton. *'Benevolent Assimilation': The American Conquest of the Philippines, 1899–1903*, paperback (New Haven: Yale University Press, 1982).

Mills, C. Wright, *The Power Elite*, paperback (New York, Oxford University Press, 2000).

Morison, Samuel Eliot, *The Oxford History of the American People, (3 Vols)*, Paperback (New York: Meridian, 1994).

Moynihan, Daniel Patrick, *Came the Revolution: Argument in the Reagan Era* (San Diego: Harcourt Brace Jovanovich, 1988).

——, *On the Law of Nations* (Cambridge, Mass.: Harvard University Press, 1990).

Mulvenon, James C. and Richard H. Yang, *The People's Liberation Army in the Information Age*, paperback (Santa Monica, CA: Rand, National Security Research Division, Project Air Force, 1999).

Muravchik, Joshua, *The Imperative of American Leadership: A Challenge to Neo-Isolationism* (Washington, DC, The AEI Press, 1996).

Myers, Ramon H, *The Chinese Peasant Economy: Agricultural Development in Hopei and Shantung, 1890–1949* (Cambridge, Mass.: Harvard University Press, 1970).

Myers, Ramon. Michel C. Oksenberg and David Shambaugh, *Making China Policy: Lessons from the Bush and Clinton Administrations*, paperback, (Lantham, MD: Rowman & Littlefield Publishers, Inc., 2001).

Nathan, Andrew J. and Robert S. Ross., *The Great Wall and the Empty Fortress: China's Search for Security*, paperback (New York: W.W. Norton, 1998).

Nathan, Andrew J., *China in Transition*, paperback (New York: Columbia University Press, 1997).

Neils, Patricia, *China Images: In the Life and Times of Henry Luce* (Savage, MD: Rowman & Littlefield, 1990).

Nish, Ian., *The Origins of The Russo-Japanese War*, paperback, (London: Longman, 1996).

Nye Jr, Joseph S., *Bound to Lead: The Changing Nature of American Power* (New York: Basic Books Inc., 1990).

——, *The Paradox of American Power: Why the World's Only Superpower Can't Go It Alone* (Oxford: Oxford University Press, 2002).

O'Brien, D. P., *The Classical Economists* (Oxford: Clarendon Press, 1975).

OECD, *China in the 21st Century: Long-term Global Implications*, paperback (Paris: OECD, 1996).

Palast, Greg, *The Best Democracy Money Can Buy: An Investigative Reporter Exposes the Truth About Globalization, Corporate Cons, and High Finance Fraudsters* (London: Pluto Press, 2002).

Parenti, Michael, *America Besieged*, paperback, (San Francisco, City Lights Books, 1998).

——, *Dirty Truths*, paperback, (San Francisco: City Lights Books, 1996).

Paterson, Thomas G., *Soviet–American Confrontation: Postwar Reconstruction and the Origins of the Cold War*, paperback (Baltimore: John Hopkins University Press, 1975).

Pearce, Jenny, *Under the Eagle: US Intervention in Central America and the Caribbean*, paperback (London: Latin American Bureau, 1982).

Perkins, Bradford, *The Cambridge History of American Foreign Relations, Volume I: The Creation of a Republican Empire, 1776–1865*, paperback (Cambridge: Cambridge University Press, 1995).

Pillsbury, Michael (ed.), *Chinese Views of Future Warfare*, paperback, rev. edn, (Washington, DC: National Defense University Press, 1998).

——, *China Debates the Future Security Environment*, paperback (Washington, DC: National Defense University Press, 2000).

Pollack, Jonathan D. and Richard H. Yang, *In China's Shadow: Regional Perspectives on Chinese Foreign Policy and Military Development*, paperback (Santa Monica: RAND, National Security Research Division, 1998).

Porter, Michael E., *The Competitive Advantage of Nations* (NY: The Free Press, 1990)

Prados, John, *Presidents' Secret Wars: CIA and Pentgon Covert Operations from World War II Through Iranscam*, paperback (New York: Quill William Morrow, 1986).

Rabe, Stephen G., *Eisenhower and Latin America: The Foreign Policy of Anticommunism*, paperback (Chapel Hill: The University of North Carolina Press, 1988).

Radtke, Kurt W. and Raymond Feddema (eds)., *Comprehensive Security in Asia: Views from Asia and the West on a Changing Security Environment* (Leiden: Brill, 2000).

Remer, C. F., *Foreign Investment in China* (New York: Macmillan – now Palgrave Macmillan, 1933).

Roberts, J. M., *The Pelican History of the World*, paperback (Harmondsworth: Penguin Books, 1981).

——, *The Triumph of The West* (London: British Broadcasting Corporation, 1985).

Robertson, Geoffrey, *Crimes Against Humanity: The Struggle for Global Justice* (London: Allen Lane, The Penguin Press, 1999).

Sabato, Larry J. and Glenn R. Simpson, *Dirty Little Secrets: The Persistence of Corruption in American Politics* (New York, Random House, 1996).

Said, Edward W., *Covering Islam: How The Media and the Experts Determine How We See the Rest of the World*, paperback (New York, Vintage Books, 1997).

Salinger, Pierre with Eric Laurent, *Secret Dossier: The Hidden Agenda Behind The Gulf War* (translated from the French by Howard Curtis), paperback (London: Penguin Books, 1991).

Schmidt, Helmut, *Men and Powers: A Political Retrospective* (translated from the German by Ruth Hein), 1st American edn (New York, Random House, 1989).

Schmitz, David F., *Thank God They're On Our Side: The United States & Right-Wing Dictatorships, 1921–1965*, paperback (Chapel Hill, North Carolina University Press, 1999).

——, *The United States and Fascist Italy, 1922–1940* (Chapel Hill, North Carolina University Press, 1988).

Scmitz, David F and Richard D. Challener (eds), *Appeasement in Europe: A Reassessment of U.S. Policies* (New York: Greenwood Press, 1990).

Schraeder, Peter Jay, *Interventions into the 1990s: U.S. Foreign Policy in the Third World*, paperback, (Boulder, Col.: Lynne Rienner Publishers, 1992).

Semmel, Bernard, *The Rise of Free Trade Imperialism: Classical Political Economy the Empire of Free Trade and Imperialism 1750–1850* (London: Cambridge University Press, 1970).

Shapiro, Herbert, *White Violence and Black Response: From Reconstruction to Montgomery*, paperback (Amherst, The University of Massachusetts Press, 1988).

Sinha, Radha, *Japan's Options for the 1980s*, paperback, (Tokyo: Charles E. Tuttle & Co., 1982).

Smith, Gaddis, *The Last Years of the Monroe Doctrine, 1945–1993*, paperback (New York: Hill and Wang, 1994).

——, *Morality, Reason & Power: American Diplomacy in the Carter Years*, paperback (New York: Hill and Wang, 1986).

Smith, Peter H., *Talons of the Eagle: Dynamics of U.S. – Latin American Relations* (New York: Oxford University Press, 1996).

Sorensen, Theodore C., *Kennedy* (New York: Konecky & Konecky, 1965).

Soros, George, *Open Society: Reforming Global Capitalism*, paperback (London, Little Brown, 2000).

Storry, Richard, *Japan and the Decline of the West in Asia 1894–1943* (London: Macmillan Press – now Palgrave Macmillan, 1979).

Su, Kaiming, *Modern China: A Topical History* (Beijing, New World Press, 1986).

Sulzberger, C. L., *The World and Richard Nixon* (New York: Prentice Hall Press, 1987).

Sutton, Antony C., *Wall Street and The Rise of Hitler* (Seal Beach, California, '76 Press, 1976).

Swaine, Michael D. and Ashley J. Tellis, *Interpreting China's Grand Strategy: Past, Present and Future*, paperback (Santa Monica, CA: RAND, Project Air Force, 2000).

Swaine, Michael D., *Taiwan's National Security, Defense Policy, and Weapons Procurement Processes*, paperback (Santa Monica, CA: RAND, National Defense Research Institute, 1999).

Tuchman, Barbara W., *Sand Against the Wind: Stilwell and the American Experience in China 1911–45*, paperback (London: Macdonald Futura Publishers, 1981).

Tyler, Patrick, *A Great Wall: Six Presidents and China, An Investigative History* (New York: Public Affairs, 1999).

US International Trade Commission (USITC), *Assessment of the Economic Effects on the United States of China's Accession to the WTO*, Investigation No. 332–403 (Washington, DC: USITC, 1999).

US National Advisory Commission on Civil Disorders, *The Report of the National Advisory Commission on Civil Disorders (Kerner Report)* (New York: New York Times Co., 1968).

US Congress, Joint Economic Committee, *China's Economic Future: Challenges to US Policy* (Washington: Government Printing Office, 1996).

US Department of State, Bureau of Democracy, Human Rights and Labor, *Country Report on Human Rights Practices-2000*, Washington, DC, February 2001. (Washington, DC: Government Printing Office, 2000). (Annual Publication.)

US GAO, *Export Controls: Statutory Reporting Requirements For Computers Not Fully Addressed* (Washington, DC: GAO, 1999).

US House of Representatives, *Report of the Select Committee on U.S. National Security and Military/Commercial Concerns with People's The Republic of China* (Cox Committee Report) (Washington: Government Printing Office, 1999).

US Trade Representative, *National Trade Estimate Report on Foreign Trade Barriers, 2000* (www.ustr.gov/reports/nte/2002/index.htm).

Valone, Stephen J., *'A Policy Calculated to Benefit China': The United States and the China Arms Embargo, 1919–1929* (New York: Greenwood Press, 1991).

Van Alstyne, Richard W., *The United States and East Asia*, paperback (London: Thames and Hudson, 1973).

Vogel, Ezra F. (ed.), *Living With China: U.S.–China Relations in the Twenty-first Century*, paperback (New York: W. W. Norton & Co., 1997).

Whitney, Griswold A., *Far Eastern Policy of The United States* (New York: Harcourt, Brace, 1938).

Williams, William Appleman, *The Tragedy of American Diplomacy*, paperback (New York: W. W. Norton & Co., 1972).

Wong, J. Y., *Deadly Dreams: Opium, Imperialism, and the Arrow War (1856–1860) in China* (Cambridge: Cambridge University Press, 1998).

Zhang, Shuguang, Zhang Yansheng and Wan Zhongxin, *Measuring the Costs of Protection in China* (Washington, DC: Institute for International Economics, 1998).

Index

Page references for tables are in *italics*; those for notes are followed by n.